# Economic Analysis of Law in European Legal Scholarship

Volume 11

The purpose of this book series is to publish high quality volumes in the growing field of law and economics research in Europe, from a comprehensive theoretical and practical vantage point. In particular, the series will place great emphasis on foundational and theoretical aspects of economic analysis of law and on interdisciplinary approaches in European Legal Scholarship. Following Nobel laureate Ronald Coase's famous essay "The Problem of Social Cost" (1960) fifty years ago law and economics has become the lingua franca of American jurisprudence. In recent decades, law and economics has also gained widespread popularity in Europe and its influence on Legal Scholarship is growing significantly.

Therefore, the economic analysis of law in European Legal Scholarship academic book series illustrates how law and economics is developing in Europe and what opportunities and problems – both in general and in specific legal fields – are associated with this approach within the legal traditions of European countries. Rather than further exploring economic analysis as such, the main focus of this series lies on the implementation of economic methods in legislation and legal adjudication from a European perspective. It takes into account the particular challenges the European legal systems face. Volumes will address law and economics research in Europe from a critical and comparative viewpoint. The studies in this series are strong and bold narratives of the development of economic analysis of law in European Legal Scholarship. Some are suitable for a very broad readership.

Contributions in this series primarily come from scholars in Europe. The purpose is to provide the next generation of European lawyers with the models and skills needed to understand and improve the economic analysis of law in their own legal field. The series includes monographs focusing on specific topics as well as collections of essays covering specific themes.

More information about this series at http://www.springer.com/series/11927

Klaus Mathis • Avishalom Tor
Editors

# Law and Economics of Regulation

Springer

*Editors*
Klaus Mathis
Faculty of Law
University of Lucerne
Lucerne, Switzerland

Avishalom Tor
School of Law
University of Notre Dame
Notre Dame, IN, USA

Economic Analysis of Law in European Legal Scholarship
ISBN 978-3-030-70529-9 ISBN 978-3-030-70530-5 (eBook)
https://doi.org/10.1007/978-3-030-70530-5



This Springer imprint is published by the registered company Springer Nature Switzerland AG.
The registered company address is: Gewerbestrasse 11, 6330 Cham, Switzerland

# Preface

This edited volume "Law and Economics of Regulation" is a collection of papers which were due to be presented at the 9th Law and Economics Conference in Lucerne on the 27th and 28th of March 2020, co-organised by the University of Lucerne, Institute for Economy and Regulation, and the Notre Dame Research Program on Law and Market Behavior (ND LAMB). Unfortunately, due to the global COVID-19 pandemic, the conference could not take place. Irrespective of these unfortunate circumstances, the editors and authors have created an edited volume on the current issues associated with economic analysis of regulation.

The main focus of this volume is on presenting European legal scholars' perspectives on the issues surrounding the Law and Economics of Regulation. These are complemented by insights from distinguished scholars from the USA, Israel, and New Zealand in order to foster the international dialogue among the different legal cultures. The thematic scope of this volume spans both the theoretical foundations and specific practical applications of the Law and Economics of Regulation.

We take this opportunity to thank all those who have contributed to the successful completion of this volume. Therefore, we would like to thank Lynn Gummow, MLaw, Lyanne Elsener, BLaw, Roger Moser, BLaw, Marc Schillig, BLaw, and Philipp Gisler for their reviewing and diligent proofreading. We are also grateful to Manuela Schwietzer at Springer Publishers for overseeing the publishing process.

Lucerne, Switzerland<br>Notre Dame, IN, USA<br>December 2020

Klaus Mathis<br>Avishalom Tor

# About This Book

Regulation today has grown into one of the main determinants of the modern economy. Nearly every sector—financial service providers, pharmaceutical companies, automotive manufacturers, food and beverage producers, travel agencies, social media platforms, and more—is subject to specific rules and standards in addition to general laws and regulations applicable across industries. The typical rationale for regulatory intervention is the promotion of the public interest. Fixing markets that lack competition, balancing information asymmetries, internalising externalities, mitigating systemic risk, or protecting consumers from irrational behaviour are frequently invoked both to substitute for and to complement the invisible hand of the market with the visible hand of the state.

Traditionally, law and economics literature has taken a mostly sceptical stance towards state interference and its justifications, from both normative and positive perspectives. In the late 1960s, Harold Demsetz criticised what he called the Nirvana approach to economics, i.e. the attempt to impose regulation whenever a difference between reality and a theoretical optimum is identified. Instead, he advocated a comparative institutional approach, according to which the institutional setting should only be amended if doing so actually yields preferable results. However, because regulation often yields unintended consequences, one should be hesitant to view regulation as the panacea that could turn an imperfect world into paradise. Not long thereafter, a second strand of economic thought championed by Stigler and others called into question the public interest rationale as the main driver of regulatory growth, suggesting instead that much regulation, in fact, serves the private interest of powerful interest groups rather than advancing social welfare.

Since the early contributions of Demsetz and Stigler, the debate over the law and economics of regulation has raised many questions whose implications span a variety of legal fields and almost every major economic sector: To what extent do different regulatory goals such as data privacy, environmental protection, or safety require different regulatory strategies? Which regulatory instruments should be implemented under different market conditions? What drives public agencies when they enact and enforce regulation? Is sectorial self-regulation a viable and legitimate alternative to regulation through government agencies? Which sanctions are most effective? This volume aims to explore theoretically and empirically these and related timely issues in the regulation of various economic sectors, from both the neoclassical and the behavioural economics approaches to regulation.

Part I of this volume, "Law and Economics of Regulation Theory", begins with the chapter "Public Services as a Strategy of Regulation" by Régis Lanneau. He analyses whether public services should be considered as a regulatory strategy instead of a service provided by the state. In doing so, he argues that public services and regulation cannot be regarded as two separate state interventions. The regulatory strategy employed reflects a command and control element coupled with some form of compensation. Subsequently, the author discusses the practical implications that such a reframing of public services would mean. Firstly, with regard to efficiency implications. Secondly, regarding the reach public services would have - if considered as a regulatory strategy.

The next chapter "Sectoral Self-Regulation as Viable Tool" by Rolf H. Weber analyses the strengths and weaknesses of self-regulation. Using distributed ledger technology as an example, he argues that a co-regulation approach relying on self-regulation together with a normative framework would provide the most efficient regulatory approach in technological fields. This is in part due to the flexibility such an approach offers to the fast-changing environment. What's more, he argues that the efficient involvement of all private and public actors affected by the rules is best invested in developing the regulatory framework while at the same time promoting innovation and competition in the given technological environment.

Yuval Feldman and Yotam Kaplan identify and discuss the existence of "ethical blind spots" in their chapter "Ethical Blind Spots & Regulatory Traps: On Distorted Regulatory Incentives, Behavioral Ethics & Legal Design". These are areas where, normally, law-abiding people fail to recognise their illegal and unethical conduct. While regulators should act to increase the ethical awareness to encourage compliance, they often have a greater incentive to protect the blind spots. The authors analyse this problem by looking to behavioural economics in order to identify why these blind spots exist and why regulators may not remedy this situation.

In "Law and Economics in Russian Law", Mikhail Antonov discusses the development of the Law and Economics movement in Russia. He begins his chapter by outlining the historical context of the Russian legal system and discussing the influences that Soviet Law had on the development of Russian Law, in particular the attitude towards the economic analysis of law. The early developments of post-Soviet law saw a rejection of economic analysis of law due to its association with Marxist based teachings. This distrust was further compounded by the actions of corrupt officials, who overruled the statutory law by using economic arguments as justification. With the introduction of the "Oligarch Policy" by Vladimir Putin in his first presidency, economic rhetoric was banned from courts and with it the economic analysis of law. Despite more recent interest among Russian Legal Scholars in the economic analysis of law, the use of it in courts is still treated with suspicion due to the historical connection to corruption.

Part II of this volume "Specific Applications of Law and Economics of Regulation" begins with Shmuel I. Becher's chapter "Key Lessons for the Design of Consumer Protection Legislation" that discusses the limitations of the legislative process. Starting from the standpoint that legislation can often fail to provide the desired result and sometimes achieve unintended consequences, he describes the key weaknesses of the legislative process. Using consumer law as an example, the unintended harms the consumers encounter are described. However, the author also identifies four principles, which he argues should improve the legislative process and prevent such failures. These four principles are: a more gradual and cautious approach, a multidisciplinary, evidence-based approach, a more humble decision-making process approach relying on temporary protection laws as opposed to more permanent legislation, and finally, he argues for a diffuse legislative approach delegating legislative and policy responsibility to administrative agencies or consumer organisations. The author draws on examples of different approaches to consumer law found in Europe, North America, Australia, New Zealand, and Israel.

"Regulation of Information About Unfolding Events in Securities Markets: A Behavioral Economics Perspective" by Ido Baum, Jaroslaw Beldowski, and Dov Solomon compares and contrasts the security market regulations in Europe and the USA. In particular, they focus on the regulations surrounding disclosures and analyse these from a behavioural economics perspective. The particular challenge posed is the disclosure of material unfolding events. The most significant differences between the two legal approaches rely on the definition of what information is considered to be material, and whether or not the disclosure of such information is mandatory or voluntary. The authors argue that cognitive biases, such as overconfidence, overoptimism, among others, influence the disclosure side, while conservatism, availability bias, or the ostrich effect influence the investor side. Against this background, the different legislative approaches pursued by the USA and Europe lead the authors to conclude that the disclosure architecture of both systems ought to pursue a more nuanced approach to take biases into account.

Mira Burri examines the data protection regulation in the context of global trade law in her chapter "Data Flows Versus Data Protection: Mapping Existing Reconciliation Models in Global Trade Law". The chapter begins by outlining various legal frameworks regarding data protection, as well as comparing and contrasting the EU regulation with the regulation in the USA. Subsequently, the author turns to the data protection rules that have emerged through free trade agreements as a result of the lacking regulatory framework from the World Trade Organisation. This analysis shows the tension between free data flows, which are considered essential in today's data-driven economy, and the states' duty and sovereign right to protect its citizens' privacy.

"The Concept of Regulatory Arbitrage" by Thomas Coendet discusses the practice of economic agents structuring their activities in such a manner as to optimise their gain by utilising the more favourable regulatory framework. In particular, the author discusses this practice within the finance background. The chapter provides a conceptual framework for the practice of regulatory arbitrage. He describes three of the most common regulatory arbitrage situations: choosing between different jurisdictions; choosing between different sets of regulation, and actively avoiding certain regulation. However, he argues that these are not simply cost–benefit analysis or regulatory avoidance decisions. Instead, the more complex economic and sociological background illuminated in this chapter shows that financial arbitrage is a more realistic concept than previously described.

Moran Ofir and Yevgeny Mugerman analyse the impacts that macroprudential tools have on the decision-makers in the mortgage market. Their chapter "(Un)-intended Consequences of Macroprudential Regulation" describes the changes in the housing market in Israel. The unprecedented increase of house prices and rent costs has resulted in various regulatory approaches to impose restrictions to ensure the stability of the financial system and avoid a housing market crash akin to the global financial crisis in 2008. They begin with a theoretical behavioural analysis of the mortgage decision-making process. Against this background, the authors then analyse the empirical data provided by the Israel Central Bank to understand how the macroprudential policy tools influence the mortgage market. In particular, they follow the borrowers' responses to the Loan-to-Value Limits, changes in the required capital adequacy of the banks, and the different provisions regarding payment-to-income, among others. They conclude that the regulatory provisions showed to have a lesser impact on the borrowers' decision than expected by the regulator.

In his chapter "Precautionary Antitrust: A Precautionary Tale in European Competition Policy", Aurelien Portuese argues that the new approach advocated by the European Commission for competition enforcement towards digital markets is an application of the precautionary principle. The Commission's approach, he argues, is neither a policy error nor a legal flaw—it is a regulatory preference for precaution over innovation and disruption. To substantiate this claim, the author begins by describing the precautionary principle and subsequently turns to a definition of precautionary antitrust. Against this background, he devises an explanatory framework as a guiding principle in the foreseeable trends in European and American antitrust enforcements.

The chapter "Regulation and Deregulation of Financial Markets from the Perspective of Law and Economics" by Mariusz J. Golecki discusses the traditional models used to regulate the financial market, namely: the transaction-oriented, institution-oriented, and market-oriented model. To best understand why the market-oriented model has become the more prevalent, the author illuminates the evolution of the law, particularly focusing on the changes in the USA and comparing that to the recent regulatory shifts in Europe. He concludes that the financial crisis proved that good regulation is essential in the financial market. Furthermore, good regulation requires a sound normative theory of both the derivatives and investors' behaviour. Subsequently, the role of judicial governance in this field is discussed, concluding that it does play a significant role as an alternative to market and political processes.

Ann-Sophie Vandenberghe discusses the impacts of the regulatory change regarding income security for disabled workers in the Netherlands. Her chapter "Privatizing Income Security for Disabled Workers: Unintended Consequences and Labour Market Imbalances" provides an in-depth analysis of the Dutch Government's move to privatise income security for disabled workers. She begins by outlining the challenges presented by the overuse of public schemes and the lack of support for reintegration into the workforce. Subsequently, the current regulations forcing private employers to continue to pay wages for sick employees for up to 2 years and the impact this regulation has had on the employment market are analysed. She concludes by making a clear case that while this regulatory change has achieved some improvements for employees, other aspects within the employment market have suffered from unintentional negative consequences.

The chapter "Regulating Innovation" by Markus Schreiber analyses the interplay of law and economics on innovation regulation. While innovation is one of the main drivers of economic growth, some of the regulatory attempts to encourage innovation have unintended consequences. A central question in this context is whether governments have a legitimate reason to interfere in the market by means of regulation, and if so, what is the economic rationale behind such regulation? The author elucidates and analyses in which instances governments have legitimate reasons to interfere in the market economy in order to promote innovation. In doing so, the impacts regulations have on innovation are examined before discussing the problems and economic consequences of legislators' attempts to promote innovation. The author concludes with a guideline for "best practices" for the furtherance of innovation through regulatory means.

The final chapter by James W. Coleman, "Matching Commitments: A New Approach to Regulation of the Commons" delves into the pitfalls faced by regulators with regard to protecting the climate while encouraging innovation. Climate change is a global problem that requires all countries to adopt a globally optimal level of climate regulation. A mere domestic approach will not achieve the required reduction in greenhouse gases nor provide sufficient incentives for other countries to tackle their emissions. To resolve this issue, the author proposes that the countries adopt a new strategy: climate matching commitments. Rather than relying on international treaties, prescribing unilateral reductions in greenhouse gas emissions, or cajoling other countries into taking the necessary measures, the author suggests climate regulations should automatically increase their response to regulations of other countries. So, instead of one country planning to cut its emissions by 40% by means of their domestic regulation, the regulator would commit to a lower emission with a promise to add to that specified reduction the same amount of reduction regulated by another key economy. This, the author argues, would encourage other countries to adopt more stringent regulations, as this would have a knock-on effect on others. This knock-on effect would ultimately benefit all. Such an approach would be more successful than continuing with the current international negotiation strategy, as each country is free to decide unilaterally what their baseline reduction would be.

# Contents

# Contributors

**Mikhail Antonov** Higher School of Economics, Saint Petersburg, Russia

**Ido Baum** Faculty of Law, Haim Striks School of Law, Tel Aviv, Israel

**Shmuel I. Becher** Faculty of Law, University of Wellington, Wellington, New Zealand

**Jaroslaw Beldowski** Economic Analysis College, International Comparative Studies Department, Warsaw School of Economics, Warsaw, Poland

**Mira Burri** Faculty of Law, University of Lucerne, Lucerne, Switzerland

**Thomas Coendet** KoGuan School of Law, Shanghai Jiao Tong University, Shanghai, China

**James W. Coleman** Southern Methodist University Dedman School of Law, Dallas, TX, USA

**Yuval Feldman** Bar-Ilan Law Faculty, Bar Ilan University, Ramat Gan, Israel

**Mariusz J. Golecki** University of Lodz, Łódź, Poland

**Yotam Kaplan** Bar-Ilan Law Faculty. Bar Ilan University, Ramat Gan, Israel

**Régis Lanneau** University of Paris Nanterre, Paris, France

**Yevgeny Mugerman** Bar-Ilan University, Ramat Gan, Israel

**Moran Ofir** Interdisciplinary Center (IDC) Herzliya, Herzliya, Israel

**Aurelien Portuese** Brussels School of Governance, Vrije Universiteit Brussels, Brussels, Belgium

**Markus Schreiber** Faculty of Law, University of Lucerne, Lucerne, Switzerland

**Dov Solomon** Commercial Law Department, College of Law and Business, Ramat Gan Law School, Ramat Gan, Israel

**Ann-Sophie Vandenberghe** Rotterdam Institute of Law and Economics (RILE), Erasmus School of Law, Rotterdam, The Netherlands

**Rolf H. Weber** Faculty of Law, University of Zurich, Zurich, Switzerland

# Part I
# Law and Economics of Regulation Theory

# Public Services as a Strategy of Regulation

**Régis Lanneau**

**Abstract** When legal regulations are considered, it is very unusual to analyze public services as a regulatory strategy. They are certainly a way for the "state" to intervene in the economy but most efforts by academics, lawyers and policy makers focus on the way to regulate them—from the condition of their creation to their reach and impact on competition—using orthodox (e.g. command and control or economic incentives) or heterodox (e.g. mandated disclosure or nudges) regulatory strategies. Under this traditional conceptualization, public services should be defined by the nature of the service they are providing, the nature having then an influence on the regulation of that service. The purpose of this paper is to reverse our perspective of public services regarding their relation vis-à-vis regulation. Public services are not mere services which need to be regulated keeping an eye on the influence of that regulation on distortion of competition, they are, essentially, a type of regulation. Not only is this approach more coherent with the use of this notion by European institutions and its practical legal relevance, it also forces us to reconsider the relevance of public services (as a type of regulation) compared to other regulatory strategies. As any other regulatory strategy, it should be used if and only if it is the efficient way to achieve what the regulation is aiming for. Such a conceptualization thus contributes to a limiting of blind spots when the efficiency of a public service (considered as a service) is considered.

## 1 Introduction

One of the main features of the modern welfare state is the provision of public services. From utilities (electricity, telecommunication, transportation, etc.) to healthcare, education and pension systems, from internal and external security to the development of a legal system, public services—used as a generic label to

R. Lanneau (✉)
University of Paris Nanterre, Paris, France
e-mail: regis.lanneau@sciencespo.fr

 
K. Mathis, A. Tor (eds.), *Law and Economics of Regulation*, Economic Analysis of Law in European Legal Scholarship 11,
https://doi.org/10.1007/978-3-030-70530-5_1

include services of general interest, service of general economic interest, services of general social interest, etc.—are everywhere. It is of course possible to criticize their reach, their quality or their costs, to consider that these, or part of these public services should, or should not, be delegated to private entities, or to advocate for some modification in their legal regime. But it is impossible to criticize the fact that one of the main functions of the state is to provide, directly or indirectly, public services.[1]

Such statement is even easier to make since it is, if not meaningless, largely empty. Indeed, when considered more carefully, it appears that no accepted and workable definition of public services[2] exists or of what makes the "publicness" of public services[3]... so that it would be possible to equate state intervention with public service—especially if redistribution is considered as a public service—making the statement a mere tautology.

It could be possible, at this stage, to clarify the concept a little more so that it would be more workable, to engage into a critical analysis of all the different definitions of public services (and related concepts) which could be found in the literature,[4] positive law or political statements. Such an analysis would certainly be enlightening. Indeed stressing that the "French" concept(s) of public services rests on the idea that the state pursues a superior end such that public services are inherently different from private services[5] is crucial to understand the regulation of public services in France or the difficulties that French academics have when dealing with European concepts of services of general interest, services of general economic interest or universal service obligations[6] since the "aura" which goes with the "public service" disappears. It would be equally relevant to stress that the idea of public service in the British or American tradition is largely replaced by the concept of "public interest", probably more economic in its nature since it is linked to the idea of public welfare.[7] But to identify and analyze a sufficient number of legal traditions while avoiding caricature is beyond the scope of this paper and largely irrelevant to the point it tries to make.

For the purpose of this paper, it suffices to state that the concept, is often defined through the nature of the services and, as such, it is legally open-ended: the definition of public services (or public interest) is too fuzzy to allow for a strict demarcation between what is and what is not a public service (positive definition) or what should or should not be a public service (normative definition). For example, the Commission's definition of service of general interest as service "that public authorities of the

[1]For example, see Mueller (2003) and Buchanan (1965).

[2]For example, see Sauter (2015), p. 10.

[3]Pesch (2008).

[4]For example, Prosser (2005).

[5]Finger and Finon (2011).

[6]Tourbe (2004).

[7]For example, Finger and Finon (2011).

member states classify as being of general interest"[8] is obviously open-ended and do not rest on a "feature" of the service but on the "will" of public authorities. Trying to break down public services between economic and non-economic public services is of no help. As the Commission explained in 2012:

> Since the distinction between economic and non-economic services depends on political and economic specificities in a given Member State, it is not possible to draw up an exhaustive list of activities that a priori would never be economic. Such a list would not provide genuine legal certainty and would thus be of little use.[9]

The fuzziness of the concept of public services and related concept is also recognized by the European Court of Justice:

> It must be made clear that in Community law and for the purposes of applying the EC Treaty competition rules, there is no clear and precise regulatory definition of the concept of an SGEI mission and no established legal concept definitively fixing the conditions that must be satisfied before a Member State can properly invoke the existence and protection of an SGEI mission.[10]

What is less open-ended (and thus more positive) is the fact that the legal qualification has an influence on the regulation. Article 106(2) of the TFEU states clearly that

> Undertakings entrusted with the operation of services of general economic interest or having the character of a revenue-producing monopoly shall be subject to the rules contained in this Treaty, in particular to the rules on competition, insofar as the application of such rules does not obstruct the performance, in law or in fact, of the particular tasks assigned to them.

For example, state aids are compatible with the Treaty if they are there to "compensate" some public service obligation (infra). It is also possible to grant some exclusive rights if these rights are required for the provision of the public service. In any case, being a "public service" does not automatically allow for a complete exemption of competition law. It is only insofar as the restriction of competition is necessary to ensure that the service can be provided under economically acceptable conditions that such restriction will be judged as compatible with the treaties. This provision of the TFEU should of course be interpreted in the context of economic liberalization which sets the default on market allocation of good and services and is more suspicious of state intervention. In this context, state provision of goods and services should be justified (from an economic point of view by market failures or social or territorial cohesion) and the question of the regulation of such provision becomes fundamental.

The purpose of this paper is not to offer new insights regarding the regulation of public services or to alleviate conceptual difficulties when public services are conceptualized through their nature. It is to reverse the perspective touched upon in the previous paragraph and explore the idea that "public service" is a strategy of

[8] Comm (2011), 900, p. 3.

[9] OJ 2012, C8/02 (2012); see also 2016/C 262/01 (2016), para. 14.

[10] Case T-289/03 (2008), para. 165.

regulation; that it is probably too artificial to consider regulation and public services as two different types of state intervention. This idea follows from the Commission's definition of service of general interest. Indeed, not only is the Commission stating that service of general interest (SGI) are services "that public authorities of the member states classify as being of general interest", it also adds "and, therefore, subject to specific public service obligation".[11] Wouldn't it then be possible to consider that what makes a public service is the presence of public service obligations, such that it is the legal regime—the concept of public service obligation remains fuzzy—and not the "publicness" of the service or of the obligations which determines what is considered as a public service? Surprisingly, this reconceptualization has not yet been offered in the literature on public services. In France, the opposition between the welfare state and the regulatory state still constitutes the mainstream approach.[12]

This new perspective certainly has a theoretical value. Indeed, if public service is a regulatory strategy, all state intervention could be analyzed through the same framework; there would not be any reason to "treat" public services in a different way than an environmental, safety or price regulation: their justification or relative efficiency could then be assessed in the same way. The "public service" is simply an option in a continuum of regulatory strategies; what should matter is only the efficiency of the regulation (at least from an economic point of view). Moreover, such a reconceptualization seems perfectly compatible with positive law and its evolution (since it is built on it). This conceptual exploration is also not without practical consequences: integrating "public services" within regulatory strategies will emphasize the possibility to use other strategies to achieve what public services try to achieve thus opening the box in which the conceptualization of public services through the "nature" of the service rendered confined legal reasoning. For example, this reconceptualization will have an influence on the "reach" of public services (infra, Sect. 3.2).

The purpose of this paper is to explore the characterization of public services as a type of regulation (Sect. 2) and some of its consequences regarding the assessment of the efficiency of this regulatory strategy (Sect. 3). As such, this paper does not seek exhaustivity on both topics, it merely tries to set the building blocks for a reconceptualization of public services as a regulatory strategy.

Before addressing these issues, for the sake of clarity the understanding of regulation which will be used in this paper and the legal framework on which this analysis is resting must first be specified.

In this paper regulation will not be understood[13] as broadly as to integrate legal and social mechanisms of social control. The traditional definition by Selznick ("sustained and focused control exercised by a public agency over activities that are valued by the community") will also not be used, not only because it is too

---

[11] Comm (2011), 900.

[12] For example, Chevallier (2004).

[13] Selznick (1985).

narrow since only public agencies are considered. But also because it is not concentrated on the means to achieve such a regulation. It also includes the "valued by the community" which makes the definition not fully operational. It will be defined in a more "positivistic" way as all the mechanisms used or established by the government (*lato sensu*) in order to (try to) control or harness the forces of supply and demand in a market. This definition, which draws on Stigler[14] is still broad and includes all control regarding the agents allowed to enter the market, the market price, the quality of the product, the selling condition, etc. but also regulation regarding health, safety and the environment.[15] It is, however, as axiologically neutral as possible and more characterized than a definition resting on the idea of social control.

The concept of public service will be analyzed in this paper by reference to European law and the related concept of service of general interest and services of general economic interest but also universal service obligation and public service obligation. I am convinced that the reconceptualization of public service as regulatory strategy could offer more clarity in the legal concepts used at the level of the European Union.

## 2 Public Service as a Type of Regulation

Like any other type of regulation, public services are concerned with the allocation of resources which would result from a situation of free market or, more precisely, a situation of non-intervention. Its purpose is obviously to influence the allocation of certain resources to make sure that they will not be allocated following a market logic, for example in order to ensure territorial or social cohesion (e.g. uniform price for electricity). Like any other regulation, public services are ways to harness the forces of supply and demand because it has an impact on the agents allowed to enter the market (e.g. legal protection could be offered to operators subjected to PSO), the market price (since public service is a type of price regulation, infra), the quality of the product (or its minimum quality; e.g. continuity), the selling condition (e.g. equal treatment or neutrality), etc.

It appears, through an analysis of positive law, that public services are a regulatory strategy which couples command and control regulation (or obligations backed by a sanction) (Sect. 2.1) with some compensatory mechanisms associated with the fulfillment of these obligations (Sect. 2.2). This latter feature is probably what characterizes the strategy "public service" compared to other types of command and control regulation.

This approach fully follows EU law since it merely translates the legal regime of public services. Indeed, SGI (be they service of general economic interest (SGEI) or social services of general interest (SSGI)) are defined by the existence of public

[14]Stigler (1971).

[15]Breyer (1982).

service obligations (PSO) and the existence of PSO is offering the possibility to compensate for the "charges of public service" without that compensation to be automatically qualified as a "state aid". It could even be possible to consider that PSO are defined by the possibility for these obligations to be compensated (for reason which will be explained in Sect. 2.2).

## 2.1 *Public Service as a Type of Command and Control Regulation*

Orthodox regulatory strategies are often divided between command and control strategies and economic incentives strategies.[16] The first ones rely on obligations backed by sanctions according to a classic Austinian understanding of the working of laws.[17] The second ones do not command anything; they merely incentivize through the creation of property rights or positive or negative taxation. Within this framework, public service strategy is a type of command and control regulation: it is a set of obligations backed by sanctions. Indeed, the operators submitted to PSO do not, in general, have the option to escape from their obligations. It does not mean that it would not be possible to conceptualize to structure PSO around an economic incentive strategy. Indeed, in Australia, but also in Finland and Belgium, the system of "pay or play" (pay a tax or assume public service missions) is closer to economic incentives strategies (see infra Sect. 3.1).

Like for any other command and control regulation, the purpose of "public service obligation" is to force (and not just to incentivize) operator(s) subject to the regulation to adopt a behavior they "would not assume if it were solely considering its commercial interest"[18] or assume to the same extent or under the same conditions. Defining a public service obligation in this way—which is often the way it is defined in the literature because of the definition adopted by the Council—is not sufficiently specific: any command and control regulation constraints operators in the way they provide goods and services and most command and control strategy are justified by some form of a public interest (otherwise, what would be the point of the regulation?).

Defining PSO by the content of the obligation it sets is also not satisfactory; it is sometimes unclear, when an obligation is considered, if that obligation is a PSO or not. In the energy sector, for example, it is possible to create a duty to supply on request. This obligation could be a regulation applicable to all distributors of energy or it could be considered as a PSO. When energy efficiency regulations are considered, it could also be a sectorial (simple) regulation or a PSO. When rules are trying to ensure security of supply, it could also be considered as a sectorial regulation or a

[16]For example, see Baldwin et al. (2012) and Breyer (1982).

[17]Austin (1832).

[18]Council Regulation (EEC) No. 2408/92.

PSO. Even when rules are set for ensuring equality of treatment over a geographical area (which could be the national geographic area) this could be considered as a mere price regulation or as a PSO. The same thing could apply for regulation regarding the environment (mandating that buses—or certain types of buses—should only be hybrid buses; mandating that farmers are farming more than one crops when the size of their farm is above a certain threshold), security of some infrastructure, or a certain fuel mix (producers of energy should produce at least 10% of energy from renewables could be a PSO or a mere sectorial regulation), etc. It could be possible to include considerations regarding efficiency to operate a distinction between when PSO and when mere regulations are "better", but this would then rely on other specificities of PSO and not only on the content of the obligation(s) (infra Sect. 3.1).

Sometimes, it seems, on the face of the obligation, that it is more likely to be a PSO. In the transportation sector, when there is an obligation to exploit a specific route including clauses regarding the frequency, timing of the service, or maximum permitted fare, this obligation is most probably a PSO. In other words, when the obligation is only targeting one operator in a market (except if it is a monopoly) or a small subset of operators, the presumption is that the obligation is a PSO. However, it is not because of the content of the PSO, it is because imposing a set of constraints on certain operators but not on other "similar" operators seems to be incompatible with the idea of free competition and maybe also the "rule of law" (since generality is a fundamental condition). It is certainly for that reason—as it will be explained below (infra Sect. 2.2)—that compensations are not only possible, but also probably required, to ensure the legality of the obligation.

In order to qualify a strategy as a "public service" strategy, it is possible to go one step further: PSO could be considered as a set of obligation plus a set or constraints on the pricing policy of operators; the combination of obligations could then help to identify when an obligation is a PSO or not. Indeed, quite often PSO and "public services" are linked with the idea of "affordability".[19] It is thus not sufficient to create obligations regarding the quality of a package of products or services; it is also required to constrain the pricing policy of the operators delivering these packages or part of these packages. Without such a constraint, the prices will simply evolve with the costs imposed by regulatory constraints. More constraints mean higher costs, and nothing would distinguish a classic obligation from a PSO. For example, forcing buses to use hybrid technology would only lead to an increase in price for consumers and the "affordability" of the service would then not necessarily be matched. When the cost of supplying the service is different depending on geographical characteristics (urban vs rural for example), without pricing constraints, prices charged will be different depending on consumers (rural consumers will pay more than urban ones to be connected to some infrastructures such as electricity). Moreover, affordability will not be ensured for some consumers (the cost could be "too" high and therefore out of the budget for rural consumers). Furthermore, the concept of affordability as a legal or as an economic concept is far from easy to define. If affordability is

[19] For example, COM (2003), 270 final, paras 49, 60.

imposed—as it seems to be the case for any public service—, it means, logically, that some—or all—consumers will benefit from the service or the good without paying (if we are only considering direct payment) for its "true" cost (prices will be below cost for these consumers). For example, supplying electricity in non-interconnected areas is extremely expensive. It is possible to impose a uniform pricing structure for electricity on a national territory, but this will imply that the consumers on non-interconnected islands will pay an electricity price well below the actual costs of serving their demand. Moreover, if affordability and universality regarding prices charged are imposed, obligations regarding the quality of the service are required since, otherwise, the quality will vary with the type of consumer! For example, it would be possible to limit the service offered in non-interconnected areas to the strict minimum (with a lenient concept of continuity) in order to lower the costs of serving this demand.

From that point of view, public services are mostly a type of price regulation which, to remain on topic, is combined with conditions regarding the quality of the good or the service delivered.

The approach discussed thus far seems to only target SGEI. Indeed, we assume that PSO concentrates on entities which already provide (and will continue to provide) goods and services subjected to PSO. The PSO will then only force them, or some of them, to provide goods or services with a different quality, to expand the range of goods and services offered, and to sell the good or the services to some consumers at a loss. Actually, the approach developed could also apply to "non-economic" SGI. Indeed, as the Commission said, "economic" and "non-economic" depends on political and economic specificities (supra), the relevance of the distinction should therefore not be overestimated. Of course, it would be possible to stress that in the case of a SGEI, competition law should apply and exceptions to competition law are possible; it is after all for that reason that the concept of PSO has been developed. However, applying this framework to "non-economic" SGI would not change things. Indeed, at an abstract level, it is not because a SGI is not a SGEI that no obligations are set regarding the quality of the service (e.g. right to trial within reasonable time) or the way it is delivered (e.g. principles of equality, continuity and neutrality in France). It is not because a SGI is not a SGEI that there are no constraints regarding the pricing of the services (e.g. the price of passport or of an ID card is the same all over France; appointment should not—officially—follow a supply and demand logic; the direct monetary price paid by consumers for an intervention by the police or fire service is the same and often equal to zero; the price for filling a complaint is also the same). Sure, from a technical point of view, calling these obligations PSO is not required: exception to competition law are linked with the "non-economic" nature such that there is no need to justify exception to competition law through PSO. However, it is also possible to consider that, in the realm of "non-economic" services, PSO always justify an exception to competition law. Moreover, in this paper, public service is considered as a regulatory strategy and from that point of view, SGI be they economic or not, could be conceptualized as a set of obligations regarding the quality of the service or the way to delivered it coupled with a set of constraints regarding the pricing policy of the operators delivering the service or the good.

For now, we characterized public service as a strategy of regulation without considering specific legal constraints on the type of obligations which could be imposed or the relative efficiency of that strategy. The latter problem will be addressed in the last section of this paper (infra, Sect. 3). The former is what justifies compensation mechanisms: to be "legal" (or simply to have a meaning) some obligations require a compensation scheme. The fact that the obligations set have to be compensated is certainly the defining feature of public service as a strategy of regulation. It is important to note, that the component of public services as a strategy of regulation (content, price constraint, compensation) should be considered not in a sequence but as a totality to use that strategy efficiently (infra Sect. 3).

## 2.2 *The Specificity of Public Service as a Type of Command and Control Regulation, the Existence of Compensation Mechanisms*

If there is a ban of non-hybrid buses in a certain area, it is, in general, not required to compensate buses operator(s) for that ban. However, if a mayor is including as a PSO the requirement that public transport in their town must be "hybrid", compensation is to be expected, especially if the pricing structure of public transports is not adjusted. The fact that the set of obligations imposed are compensated is probably the main feature of public services as a strategy of regulation. Without compensation, an obligation cannot really be a PSO.[20] This compensation could be a financial compensation (e.g. a sum money or a tax break) or a structural one (e.g. granting a monopoly or special rights like a reserved sector to facilitate cross-subsidization).

Traditionally, these compensations are considered as the main problem when the regulation of public services is addressed (and it is not definitive of a PSO). Indeed, there is a risk that the compensation will offer a competitive advantage (or disadvantage) to the operator in charge of the PSO. The question is then to identify and implement schemes which will be considered as legal following the conditions set in Altmark (Case C-280/00, para. 87–93):

1. the presence of clearly defined PSO,
2. objective,

[20] Surprisingly, the Commission considers that certain SGEI could be provided "without specific financial support" (Communication from the Commission on the application of the European Union State aid rules to compensation granted for the provision of services of general economic interest (2012/C, 8/02, para. 2)). The only way to make sense of such a statement is to consider that the compensation exists through an institutional structure like a "reserved sector" or some other structural benefits (like loans warranties, etc. . .).

3. transparent and established in advance parameters for calculating the compensation,
4. a compensation that is not exceeding what is necessary to cover all or parts of the costs incurred by the supply of a public service,
5. and a condition regarding the way to set the compensation in the absence of a public procurement procedure.

If public service is conceived as a type of regulatory strategy, the perspective changes. As it has been established previously, public service is a type of regulation which combines an obligation regarding the product or the way it is sold with some constraints regarding the pricing policy of the operator(s). This combination means that at least a small fraction of consumers are served at a price below costs (which is also a characteristic of a public service). In other words, a public service strategy, if we only consider its command and control side, imposes some "costs" which cannot be recovered (fully or in part) by the operator(s) in charge of that public service (because of the constraints on the pricing policy).

Without compensation(s), three regulatory risks exist:

1. The first risk is simple to understand: without compensation, the PSO could never be abided by or, and it is the same, the service could never be supplied.

   Let's assume that there is an operator offering transportation between city A and city B and that there is a regulatory constraint on the quality of vehicles that may be used. This will have an impact on its production costs. These costs could be recovered, in part, by increasing its prices. Such a price increase will have an influence on the demand which, logically, should then decrease. As long as the operator is making a zero or positive economic profit, it will remain on the market. If abiding by the obligations will lead to a negative economic profit, the operator will exit the market. This risk exists for any regulation and is not specific to PSO. Assume now that the operator, if it wants to offer a transportation between city A and B, has to abide by a set of obligations regarding not only the quality of the vehicle but also some specific obligations regarding the frequency of the service it is offering. Adding obligations will simply increase the production costs and lower the profitability of the activity and thus push the operator to exit the market. If, on top of that, a regulation imposes constraints on the pricing policy such that all customers would pay a price well below the costs of supplying the service, the operator will of course exit the market. Forcing it to remain on the market would lead to bankruptcy. Of course, the harsher the pricing constraints are, the higher the risk of exiting the market will be. Clearly, if a certain service can only be provided for free or at a price well below the costs of production, reasons for providing such a service are lacking.

   In the case in which no operators were previously supplying a certain service on the market, adding PSO without any form of compensation would not change the situation: the service will still not be provided and it would be impossible to find operators willing to subject themselves to these obligations.

   It is required to note that, regarding that risk, it is the combination of obligation and constraints on the pricing policy that will determine the number of suppliers.

By lowering obligations regarding the quality of the service or lowering the constraints on the pricing policy, an operator could find it relevant to provide the regulated service.

2. The second risk is that imposing PSO on certain operators but not on others could create a competitive disadvantage which could have an impact on the efficiency of the PSO, but also on the sustainability of the provision of the service (and ultimately on its legality, see, infra). Let's take the case of an electricity supplier. Assume that this supplier is obligated to supply on demand which includes the costs of building the necessary infrastructure required for doing so. This obligation is coupled with pricing constraints such that the operator cannot recover more than 50% of the costs incurred to supply a specific customer. It is clear, in such a situation, that this supplier will not enjoy building such infrastructure because whenever it is doing so, it is losing money. Furthermore, if the PSO is fully enforced, it will not have any choice but to comply (if it does not comply, then the quality offered will be lowered for high cost customers). Of course, it would be possible to consider that it could charge a higher electricity price in order to recover for the costs incurred by the PSO; such a model would be possible if there is only one supplier on the market. If, however, there are few electricity suppliers, the supplier subjected to PSO suffers a competitive disadvantage. Cross-subsidization will not be possible and, most probably, the profitability for the supplier subjected to PSO will be lower than the profitability of other suppliers. If we are assuming perfect competition in electricity supply, it is most likely that the supplier subjected to PSO will have an incentive to exit the market, especially if it is operating in more than one market. More importantly, the PSO will mess with price signals such that consumers will not necessarily be supplied by the most efficient supplier. If a compensation is set such that it is equal to the profitability cost of the PSO, price signals will not be distorted, and no supplier will suffer from an undue competitive disadvantage. In other words, compensation, in that situation, is a condition to ensure "fair" competition. It is not an "exception" to competition law. The need to compensate is not for the service to be provided, but more normatively, for the service to be provided efficiently (which could justify that only certain operators will be subjected to PSO).
3. The third risk, like the first one, is more positive than normative. Regulators and legislator face legal constraints whenever they regulate and imposing without compensating could be considered as unconstitutional, incompatible with European law or international law, or incompatible with some law if administrative regulations are considered.

If the PSO is only targeting one operator and is not compensated, it could be considered as incompatible with the principle of equal treatment.

> According to settled case-law, the general principle of equal treatment and non-discrimination requires that comparable situations are not treated differently unless differentiation is objectively justified.[21]

Imposing a burden (PSO) on certain operators but not on other is certainly incompatible with this principle. In such a situation, compensation is not only an option, but almost mandatory for saving the legality of the PSO! This point is clearly stated by the European Council:

> pursuant to Article 5 of the Council Decision of 13 May 1965 on the harmonisation of certain provisions affecting competition in transport by rail, road and inland waterway, any decision by the competent authorities to maintain any public service obligation defined in this Regulation entails an obligation to pay compensation in respect of any financial burdens which may thereby devolve on transport undertakings.[22]

In the third Postal Directive (2008/6/EC), the idea that "unfair financial burden" of universal service obligations (a type of PSO) should be subject to compensation. Nevertheless, what should be considered as "unfair" is not defined.

Even if equal treatment is respected, imposing PSOs on all operators might not necessarily be compatible with constitutional, European or international law if they are not compensated for. The PSO could be considered, for example, as incompatible with the freedom of enterprise or freedom of trade and industry. Especially since it includes constraints on the pricing policy of operators or forces them to supply services at a price below their costs. For example, if lawyers in Europe were required to provide free representation for the poor, it is not certain that such a provision will be considered as compatible with European or constitutional law. It would be the same if court ordered counsel could be chosen arbitrarily by a jurisdiction and then not paid for their services. If an obligation does not have to be compensated, this obligation, even if enacted for the public interest, is not really a PSO in the framework developed here. If the imposition of a price regulation does not lead to some compensation, this price regulation, even if associated with obligations regarding the quality of the service, is also not a PSO. It is at this level that the distinction between PSO and obligation gets more complex. Indeed, when the compensation is not a monetary compensation or the result of a financial regulation, but is associated with a reserved sector or some specific rights, some obligations could be considered as compensated by some legal feature of the market on which an operator operates. In France, the fact that lawyers benefit from a monopoly for part of their activities could be considered as already compensating some future new obligations associated with their services.

It thus appears that compensation(s) is just a way to mitigate these risks. It would appear that compensation(s) is often not optional considering the nature of PSO. In light of the economic and legal system in which the obligation is imposed, it is in fact a requirement. In other words, and under the framework developed in this section, the existence of compensation is definitional of what a PSO is. As such, a public

[21]Case T-58/05 (2007), para. 75.

[22]Regulation (EEC) No. 1191/69.

service is a strategy of regulation combining obligations regarding the quality of the service or the way it is supplied, some constraints regarding the pricing policy of the operator and a compensation. These three attributes are cumulative and should be addressed in a sequence when a regulation is designed. Indeed, the quality imposed, and the price constraints, will have an incidence on the compensation required. Not taking into account the links between these three elements is a sure path for inefficiencies.

## 3 Reconsidering the Efficiency of Public Service as a Type of Regulation

In the previous section, public service as a regulatory strategy was defined. In this framework, the distinction between a regulatory state and a welfare state is purely artificial; after all, and following a very positivistic approach, the only thing that a state can do is to enact and implement rules. The definition offered also has the advantage of not introducing any subjective consideration like "public interest", for which no legal definition can be found. This does not mean that such a consideration is not relevant. But it is not directly relevant for the purpose of defining the strategy (since a strategy only concentrates on the means and not the end). It is important to determine whether or not this strategy is a relevant one and also an efficient one. It also disregards the distinction between economic and non-economic services even if this distinction could also play a role in the reconceptualization (infra, Sect. 3.2) to concentrate on "public services" whatever their form or justification. Moreover, it offers a way to read positive law in a different way while still remaining compatible with it.

This exercise in conceptual exploration is not merely theoretical and abstract; It also has practical implications. Because it analyses regulation and public services under the same framework (since public services are a type of regulation), it forces us to reconsider the efficiency of that regulatory strategy (Sect. 3.1). Furthermore, it could also offer insights regarding the reach of public services (Sect. 3.2).

### *3.1 Inquiring Into the Relative Efficiency of Setting Obligation and Compensating for Them vs Other Modes of Regulation*

To assess the efficiency of a regulation, it is, in general, required to analyze it according to at least three criteria. The first, and probably one of the main criteria, is of course the cost-effectiveness of the strategy: Does the strategy attain the target at the lowest cost? This cost-effectiveness could then be broken down to consider information requirement—and their costs—for designing the regulation, designing costs, monitoring costs and enforcement costs. It is also possible to inquire into the costs of use under uncertainty: assuming that the information is not perfect, would it be better to use this or that strategy. The second criterion targets the flexibility of the regulation: is it possible to adapt it as conditions changes or as new information arises? The third considers the dynamic impact of the regulation: will it have an influence on innovation? Will it create incentive to improve the service or the production process of that service? To these three main criteria, it would be possible to add consideration regarding equity (the implication of the strategy regarding the distribution of income or wealth) and potential ancillary benefits (which are going beyond the purpose of the regulation). Of course, these criteria could be used to assess the relative efficiency of the strategy "public service" compared to other regulatory strategies.

Here the aim is to enquire into the practical consequence of the reconceptualization by offering a structured assessment of the relative efficiency of the public service strategy. Moreover, this reconceptualization makes it clear that the nature of the operator (or of the undertaking to follow EU law) subjected to PSO is irrelevant: the purpose of this regulatory strategy is merely to achieve something. In this paper, I will limit my development to few examples in order to show the relevance of analyzing public service and other types of regulation under the same framework.

Regarding the cost effectiveness of the strategy "public service", it is clear that this strategy is *a priori* costlier (from the point of view of public finances) than a strategy setting the same obligations but without compensation. Three consequences could be derived from that statement.

First, it is not required to use the "public service strategy" whenever a service is already provided "satisfactorily" on a market. Like any other regulation, it is useful if and only if the regulation "improves" things and, in this hypothetical situation, there is nothing that needs to be improved. This consequence follows the position of the Commission regarding PSO:

> it would not be appropriate to attach specific PSOs to an activity which is already provided [. . .] satisfactorily and under conditions, such as price, objective quality characteristics, continuity, and access to the service, consistent with the public interest, as defined by the state, by undertakings operating under normal market conditions[23]

Second, if it is possible to improve things, because, for example, the quality of the service (e.g. its safety) is not considered as sufficient, then, and since it is targeting all operators, it is probably not required to use a "public service" type of regulation. After all, and as the Commission states:

> it would not be appropriate to attach specific PSOs to an activity which [. . .] can be provided satisfactorily and under conditions, such as price, objective quality characteristics, continuity, and access to the service, consistent with the public interest, as defined by the state, by undertakings operating under normal market conditions.[24]

[23] Commission OJ 2012, C8/02 (2012), paras. 48–50.

[24] Commission OJ 2012, C8/02 (2012), paras. 48–50.

Third, it is only when the obligations regarding the quality of the service leads operators to increase their prices such that the service is no longer considered as "affordable" or no longer provided (because the price is so high that the demand is zero) that using the public service strategy could make sense.

Even in this third situation, it does not mean that public service strategy will automatically be the best strategy for at least two reasons. First, this strategy will consider only one side of the problem of affordability, the price charged by the operator. Indeed, the public service strategy, by definition, constraints the pricing policy of the operator and subsidizes the good or the service so that they are made affordable for the consumers. It does not consider the other side of the problem, the fact that affordability depends on resources. The same target could be achieved by simply using the tax system and redistributing income (COM (2003) 270: "once an affordable level has been set, the Member States should ensure that this level is effectively offered, by putting in place a price control mechanism (price cap, geographical averaging) and/or by distributing subsidies to the persons concerned"). The latter will have the advantage of avoiding the over-consumption that the provision of a service at a subsidized price naturally creates. For example, incentive to save energy is non-interconnected areas will be sub-optimal if an electricity operator is "forced" to sell its electricity at a regulated price and then compensated by subsidies. However, if redistribution is imperfect because of the information burden it requires (which will often be the case regarding health care or education), the public service strategy (subsidizing the service) could remain the second-best strategy. Second, the public service strategy is solving the affordability problem by constraining the pricing policy of the operator and subsidizing the provision of the service in exchange. However, since the affordability also depends on regulatory constraints, it could be the case that lowering these constraints would ensure affordability and increase welfare.

To assess the efficiency of the public service strategy, it is also required to consider the design of PSOs and of their compensation scheme. This will indeed have an impact on both the cost-effectiveness of the strategy but also on its dynamic efficiency.

Regarding the cost-effectiveness, it is obvious that over-compensating the PSOs would be inefficient. Indeed, it would be possible to achieve the same at a cheaper cost by lowering the compensation. This situation also explains the last condition of Altmark (para. 93):

> where the undertaking which is to discharge public service obligations, in a specific case, is not chosen pursuant to a public procurement procedure which would allow for the selection of the tenderer capable of providing those services at the least cost to the community, the level of compensation needed must be determined on the basis of an analysis of the costs which a typical undertaking, well run and adequately provided with means of transport so as to be able to meet the necessary public service requirements, would have incurred in discharging those obligations, taking into account the relevant receipts and a reasonable profit for discharging the obligations.

This provision targets overcompensation and only tries to lower the risk of overcompensation. Considering the information requirement and administrative costs associated with the design of an adequate compensation scheme, it is probably better to only set procedural conditions regarding this compensation scheme.

If compensation is ensured through a "reserved sector" (or a legal monopoly) which allows the operator to cross-subsidize, dynamic efficiency is not necessarily ensured. Indeed, because of the existence of a reserved sector, entry of more efficient operators will be jeopardized. This solution is thus probably inefficient when competition exists or is theoretically possible on at least part of the "reserved sector"; in such a situation financial compensation is probably preferable. If the circumstances are such that a natural monopoly exists, protecting the monopoly would not make sense: by definition, entry will not occur unless some technological changes transform the nature of the market. In which case a protection would lead to inefficiencies. Moreover, compensating through some "exclusive rights" raises the problem of evaluating the "value" of the compensation which of course has an impact on the assessment of a potential overcompensation. In Europe the tendency is, to operate a distinction (structural or accounting) between public service activities (activities subjected to PSOs) and non-public service activities so that the "costs" of the PSOs will be easier to identify. Offering special rights for compensating PSO does not appear as the privileged strategy of compensation.

The flexibility of PSOs will depend on the procedures required to modify them. The relative efficiency of PSOs compared to other regulation is difficult to assess on that matter. However, since PSOs are compensated, they are logically flexible. Increasing or decreasing the constraints will have impacts on the amount required for compensation. It is thus to be expected that modification of PSOs will be smoother than other command and control regulation which clearly have an influence on the relative competitivity of the undertakings subjected to them (except in the case in which all competitor are perfectly homogeneous). For that reason, it is also possible to wonder if PSOs will not engender less rent-seeking than other command and control strategies. This problem will not be addressed in here.

In the literature regarding the relative efficiency of command and control and economic incentives, economic incentives are often considered as more cost-effective. Following this logic, it would be possible to explore the possibility of an economic incentive approach of "public service" regulation. Under this logic, instead of mandating certain obligations and constraining prices in exchange of a compensation, it would be possible to impose a tax on operators and offer them the possibility to not pay that tax when they are following certain obligations. For example, assume a market comprising high-cost consumers and low-cost consumers, and some regulation mandating that all consumers have to be served at a reasonable price. In such a situation, serving high-cost consumers will be done at a loss for the operators. It would be possible, to solve the problem by allowing only one operator to operate on the market which will then have the possibility to charge higher cost for low cost consumers and lower cost for high cost consumers. It would even be possible to add subsidies to lower overall prices. It would also be possible to allow competition on that market and offer the option to operators: either you are serving high-cost consumers, or you are not. If you are, you will not have to contribute to a compensation fund. If you are not, you will have to contribute to the compensation fund. In general, those who opt to service high-cost consumers, will also be compensated through some subsidies. This system is the famous "pay or play" which can be found in Australia, but also in Finland (for postal service), in the UK (regarding basic telecommunication services) or in Belgium (for socially affordable tariffs). As long as the tax burden is lower than the cost of the universal service obligation or USO (subsidies included), an operator will choose to pay. If the tax burden is higher than the cost of the USO (subsidies included), it will choose the play option. That system has the benefit of introducing a form of competition to serve high cost consumers (if the subsidy is given according to the number of high cost consumers, operators might decide to lower their price or increase their quality—as long as it is a profitable strategy—to serve these consumers, which will in turn incentivize them to innovate). Such a system is nevertheless difficult to design and bears high administrative costs. Indeed, determining the tax rate(s) and the level of subsidies is far from being easy; if the tax rate is set at too high, entry will be jeopardized even if it would be efficient. If the subsidy is too high, inefficient operators will want to supply high-cost consumers. Of course, it would be possible through a series of trial and errors to find the right level of taxes and subsidies, but such a procedure will take time. Moreover, monitoring and enforcement costs in such a system are far from trivial: instead of having only one provider, many providers will exist on the market and the risk will be for them to choose a lower quality service level in order to increase the profitability of serving high-cost consumers. Of course, this system could be tailored at will with different tax level depending on the population served or different subsidies.

It is also possible to inquire into the possibility of incentivizing operator to achieve what a PSO tries to achieve through a system of property rights. In such a situation, each operator will have to obtain a certain number of certificates associated with the accomplishment of certain actions. Each operator will then have the possibility to "buy" or to "sell", on a dedicated market, these certificates. The system of tradable certificates for energy savings follows this logic. In such a system, operators will increase their prices to cover the costs of providing the tasks which will entitle them to receive certificates. The possibility to use this system and its relative efficiency to achieve the purpose of traditional PSOs would certainly deserve further inquiry. However, the purpose of this section is only to show that by conceptualizing public services as a regulatory strategy, new insights regarding the way to achieve the purpose of traditional PSOs will emerge.

## *3.2 Reconsidering the Reach of Public Services as a Regulatory Strategy*

In the previous section, only the cost dimension of PSOs was considered. Analyzing public service as a strategy of regulation will also help to identify the reach of public service compared to other types of regulation.

For a regulation to make sense (or to have a "public interest"), from an economic point of view, a market failure must be identified. This step is necessary, but it is not sufficient. Indeed, government failures should also be considered with regards to whether the result of the regulation will be worse than the absence of regulation (the welfare loss of the regulation will be higher than the welfare loss created by the market failure). An assessment of the relative costs of market and government failures is thus required to determine the need of intervention. Such an assessment is of course country and sector specific. In practice, however, if the market failure logic has an influence on the legality of a public service regulation, the influence of government failure is irrelevant.

According to the Commission, three types of market failures could justify the use of public services: externalities, merit and club goods, and solidarity. These words are not explicitly used by the Commission. The Commission only mentioned the situations in which

> the individual or the market fail to appropriately value all benefits occurring in the future or generated for society as a whole (e.g. in the case of education)", and the possibility that there is "a desire by society to encourage the provision and use of "merit goods" and "club goods" such as museums", or the existence of a "society's aspiration to ensure that all citizens, including the poorest can have access to certain services of an adequate quality.[25]

Nevertheless, it is difficult to believe that these notions are not molded around the neoclassical economic framework.

If the Commission excludes market or monopoly power and asymmetric information, it is because these market failures could be addressed efficiently using other regulatory strategies. It would indeed seem surprising that compensation would be required in these situations: what would be the point of compensating to make sure that an operator is not "abusing" their market power? Using standards or mandated disclosure could also be ways to address asymmetric information (even if these strategies are far from being perfect).

Regarding externalities, public service strategy would make sense only if there is a positive externality; a statement which is in line with the statement of the Commission. Indeed, the public service strategy combines obligations with compensation. For the compensation to make sense, the obligations set should generate some external benefits for the society, otherwise the compensation would not be required. Certainly, reducing a negative externality also generates benefits. However, the public service strategy also includes some pricing constraints among the obligation it sets and, because this pricing constraint generates some losses, the operator is compensated. In other words, the price paid by customers or certain customers is subsidized. Furthermore, subsidizing only makes sense in presence of positive externalities. Subsidizing in presence of negative externality would only increase the production of negative externalities.

Most public services strategies are used following this logic: education, providing meal for middle school students or high school student, music conservatory,

[25]COM (2001), 598, para. 3.

swimming pools, public parks, health care, public lightning, access to water, electricity, telecommunications, waste management, etc. generates positive externalities when they are available and available at an affordable price. Of course, since an externality is a concept more than a reality (especially when transaction costs are taken into account),[26] the justification for the existence of a positive externality is required and it is only through a judgment that this externality or its magnitude will be considered as justifying the use of the public service strategy and its design.

Among these positive externalities, network externalities are often used to justify some USOs. In the presence of network externalities, the benefits of using the network depends on the number of persons connected to that network. Since any individual is only considering their personal benefit of accessing the network, they are not considering the external benefit it is creation. Subsidizing their access to the network could then make sense. However, except regarding telecommunication, it is unclear that this phenomenon justifies many USO.

Solidarity, as it is conceptualized by the Commission, refers to some form of redistribution (for the ECJ, the conditions for finding solidarity were set out in the Poucet case, cases C-159/91 and C-160/91). The redistribution through PSOs and compensation should be more efficient than the redistribution through the tax system if a public service strategy is to be used efficiently. From an economic point of view, for redistribution to make sense it should increase the welfare of the society, which means that it should generate some positive externality. For example, it could be the case that social cohesion and the reduction of inequalities might increase the level of trust in the society which will have an influence on the growth rate (because coordination games will be easier to solve) or on transaction costs (because trust could be an alternative to contracts) and lower the level of social unrest. It could also be the case that redistribution from urban areas to rural areas will have a positive influence on urban pollution, on leisure opportunities for urban population, on biodiversity, etc. This could also justify actions in order to ensure territorial cohesion.

Of course, the risk is also to use the "public service" strategy and the narrative of solidarity when, actually, the redistribution generated by PSOs is the result of some form of rent-seeking; as has already been mentioned, government failures should not be disregarded. For example, rural population could lobby the government for more redistribution. In that situation, uniform pricing over the national territory would have the huge benefit of hiding the cost of redistribution which will make this procedure more likely to be accepted by the public.

The merit good logic is more political. Indeed, merit goods (or services) are goods for which the allocation is believed to be superior when it is done not on the basis of the ability or willingness to pay but on the basis of "needs", for example a basic healthcare insurance, contraception, libraries or good quality education.[27] Thus it is often considered that these "goods" will be "under-consumed" by consumers at

[26]See Dahlman (1979).

[27]Further development in Calabresi (2016).

market prices or under-supplied by producers since they are not ripping off all the social benefits that the provision of that good is generating (otherwise, no intervention would be required). In other words, merit goods are supposed to generate positive externalities. Since their allocation is better when it is based on a non-market allocation, offering them for free (for the consumers) could make sense. Nevertheless, other strategies could be considered from financial incentives, to education campaign or behavioral nudges. In practice, identifying these merit goods is far from easy.

Club goods are often used in relation to local public good. They are goods which are excludable, but which are not rivalrous in consumption (but congestion is still a possibility). The idea is that a group of individuals decide to create that good, since it derives mutual benefits from sharing the costs of provision. This could be the case for parks, libraries or public transport, but also for swimming pools, athletic facilities and other infrastructure. It is also possible to include social security at this level. As long as the service collectively provided is cheaper (for the quality desired) than buying the service from a purely private operator, collective provision of the good could make sense. Of course, and as Buchanan puts it,

> The central question in a theory of clubs is that of determining the membership margin, so to speak, the size of the most desirable costs and consumption sharing arrangement.[28]

The Commission did not mention the use of public services in presence of pure public goods. It is probably because these goods are rare: they must be non-excludable and the cost of providing the service to one more individual should be zero. In general, sovereign public services could enter into that category. However, from a legal point of view, the provision of these services does not raise many questions since state intervention in that domain is largely accepted.

## 4 Conclusion

Many more questions could have been addressed like the tradeoff between franchising and in-house production, the influence of the definition of freedom of trade on the reach of public services, etc. However, the purpose of this paper was simply to explore the relevance and some consequences of a reconceptualization of public services through their legal regime and not through the nature of the service provided. As such, it is possible to consider that public services are just one type of regulation among many others. They are not special regarding their justifications (market failures), and they are not special regarding the way they should be appreciated (efficiency). The reconceptualization offered also has the advantage of avoiding fuzzy notions like "public interest" or "general interest". Conceived as a

[28] Buchanan (1965).

strategy, what they try to achieve is not required for defining them and the question of the relative efficiency of this strategy compared to others is unescapable.

The exploration offered in this paper is not exhaustive of all issues intertwined with public services. It merely tries to set a framework for reconceptualizing a fundamental legal concept and a fundamental tool of state intervention.

## References


Austin J (1832) In: Rumble W (ed) The province of jurisprudence determined. Cambridge University Press, Cambridge

Baldwin R, Cave M, Lodge M (2012) Understanding regulation, theory, strategy and practice. Oxford University Press, Oxford

Breyer S (1982) Regulation and its reform. Harvard University Press, Cambridge

Buchanan J (1965) An economic theory of clubs. Economica 32(125):1–14

Calabresi G (2016) The future of law and economics. Yale University Press, New Haven

Case T-289/03 BUPA insurance Ltd and BUPA Ireland Ltd vs Commission, 2008, ECR II-81

Case T-58/05 Centeno Mediavilla and Others v Commission, 2007, EU:T:2007:218

Chevallier J (2004) L'état régulateur. Revue française d'administration publique 3(111):473–482

Commission Notice on the notion of State aid as referred to in Article 107(1) of the Treaty on the Functioning of the European Union 2016/C 262/01

Communication from the Commission on the application of the European Union state aid rules to compensation grated for the provision of services of general economic interest, 11/01/2012, OJ 2012, C 8/02

Communication from the Commission to the European Parliament, the Council, the European economic and social Committee and the Committee of the Regions, A quality framework for services of general interest in Europe, Comm (2011), 900

Dahlman C (1979) The problem of externality. J Law Econ 22(1):141–162

Directive 2008/6/EC of the European Parliament and of the Council of 20 February 2008 amending Directive 97/67/EC with regard to the full accomplishment of the internal market of Community postal services

European Commission, Report to the Laeken European Council, Service of General interest, 17/10/2001, COM (2001), 598

Finger M, Finon D (2011) From "service public" to universal service: the case of the European Union. In: Finger M, Künneke RW (eds) International handbook of network industries: the liberalization of infrastructures. Edward Elgar Publishing, Cheltenham

Green paper on services of general interest presented by the Commission COM (2003), 270 final

Mueller DC (2003) Public Choice III. Cambridge University Press, Cambridge

Pesch U (2008) The publicness of public administration. Adm Soc 40:170–193

Prosser T (2005) The limits of competition law: markets and public services. Oxford University Press, Oxford

Regulation (EEC) No. 1191/69 of the council of 26 June 1969 on action by Member States concerning the obligations inherent in the concept of a public service in transport by rail, road and inland waterway

Sauter W (2015) Public services in EU law. Cambridge University Press, Cambridge

Selznick P (1985) Focusing organizational research on regulation. In: Noll R (ed) Regulatory policy and the social sciences. University of California Press, Berkeley, pp 363–367

Stigler G (1971) The theory of economic regulation. Bell J Econ Manag Sci 2(1):3–21

Tourbe M (2004) Service public versus service universel: une controverse infondée ? Critique internationale 3(24):21–28

**Régis Lanneau** Paris. Professor of Public law, University of Paris Nanterre (200 avenue de la république, bureau F410, 92001 Nanterre Cedex). Lecturer at Sciences Po and the CNAM. regis.lanneau@sciencespo.fr. Fields of interest: regulation, law and economics, constitutional law, legal theory.

# Sectoral Self-Regulation as Viable Tool

**Rolf H. Weber**

**Abstract** Traditionally, regulatory theory analyses the strengths and weaknesses of the rule-making activities by governmental bodies. But during the last twenty years self-regulation has become a viable tool in many market sectors. This contribution shows that the self-regulation model could be further developed to an intertwined co-regulation approach; the merits are shown by using the example of developing a normative framework for the distributed ledger technology infrastructure.

## 1 Introduction

Law is supposed to have a stabilising function in society. Therefore, law is usually implemented based on formal proceedings by the competent authorities as "hard law".[1] Such sources of law constitute a robust system which is indeed stable. But hard law is confronted with the weakness that technological advances and social changes usually cannot be reflected within a short time since the legislative processes are mostly quite slow, particularly if sufficient negotiation flexibility is missing at the international level.[2]

In contrast, experience has shown, mainly in the technologically fast developing sectors of the economy, that "soft law" increasingly plays an important "substituting" role; such rules are usually issued by public or private bodies and do not comply with the procedural formalities applicable to give the rules a specific legal status.[3]

[1] Weber (2017a), p. 253.

[2] Weber (2012), pp. 10 et seq.

[3] Weber (2014), pp. 22 et seqq.

R. H. Weber (✉)
Faculty of Law, University of Zurich, Zurich, Switzerland
e-mail: rolf.weber@rwi.uzh.ch



K. Mathis, A. Tor (eds.), *Law and Economics of Regulation*, Economic Analysis of Law in European Legal Scholarship 11,
https://doi.org/10.1007/978-3-030-70530-5_2

Self-regulation is a prominent example for soft law and can be a viable source of the normative framework governing society.[4]

Furthermore, as Stigler pointed out 50 years ago, the typical rationale justifying regulation, namely the promotion of the public interest, is often not achieved by governmental regulation since powerful interest groups often profit to a greater degree than the civil society needing social welfare.[5] This contribution attempts to analyse how Stigler's approach can still have some merit today despite the changes in the circumstances of the market environment; in the respective analysis the regulation and governance of the new distributed ledger technology (DLT, mostly called Blockchain) will be used as practical example. For technical reasons (DLT as decentralised system) and for political reasons (lack of an appropriate multilateral organisation) a globally harmonised regulatory framework is unlikely to be implemented soon.

## 2 From Hard Law to Soft Law

### *2.1 Overcoming the Hard/Soft Law Dichotomy*

Social and ethical guidelines build an informal normative order, whereas hard law constitutes an institutional normative order.[6] However, the boundaries are blurring and the regulatory bodies are becoming intertwined, i.e. the hard/soft law dichotomy must be overcome.

The, often expressed, assumption that hard law is qualitatively better than soft law no longer holds in the present normative environment. As this contribution attempts to show, soft law can now provide several functions previously tied to hard law, for example the notion of coordinating the concerned actors and of improving the transactional efficiency.[7]

Developments in the financial markets, and even more so in information technology/Internet markets teach us the lesson that hard law is often not better positioned to regulate the social environment than soft law. The notion that legalisation entails a specific form of discourse, requiring justification and persuasion (as proposed by behavioural economics) as far as applicable rules and pertinent facts are concerned, is an element of self-regulation.[8]

---

[4]For specific examples and concerned markets segments see the descriptions given by Tambini et al. (2008), pp. 28 et seqq., 190 et seqq., 210 et seqq.

[5]Stigler (1971), pp. 3 et seqq.

[6]Weber (2014), pp. 42 et seq.; Weber (2017a), p. 258.

[7]Weber (2012), p. 11; Guzman and Meyer (2010), pp. 188 et seqq.

[8]Abott and Snidal (2000), p. 429.

## 2.2 *Historical Developments of Theoretical Approaches*

The argument that the dichotomy between hard law and soft law must be overcome is founded on a manifold of ideas developed in sociology and legal philosophy. Some of these include:

1. Hart described the process of formalisation and institutionalisation or codification of general standards as a way of building secondary norms.[9]
2. Linked to the increasing influence of civil society, Foucault called for an "art of government" in order to mirror the epistemic networks and the autonomous self-regulation initiatives.[10]
3. Slaughter developed principles for government networks, being set out as relatively loose, co-operative arrangements across borders.[11]
4. Teubner expressed the idea that the unity of regulatory regimes is significant for the perception of phenomena at the supra-, infra-, and trans-state levels in view of the law's new function as a system for the co-ordination of actions within and between semi-autonomous societal sub-systems.[12]
5. Berman pleaded for a "global legal pluralism" that encompasses more than one legal, or quasi-legal, regime in the same social field; since a single approach would not be appropriate in a hybrid reality with overlapping legal spheres, the creation of multiple parallel normative systems seems to be an alternative (as "jurisgenerative" model drawing on the variety of sources in ongoing political, economic, and legal iterations) if the concerned actors acquiesce to procedural mechanisms, institutions and practices.[13]
6. Weitzenboeck developed a network model composed of a variety of "hybrid" elements elucidating the networks' complexities.[14]

The manifold theoretical approaches show that different forms of legal sources can be relevant and appropriate; depending on the regulatory needs, the most suitable solution must be chosen.

## 2.3 *Reconciling Benefits and Risks of Soft Law*

Self-regulation encompasses various benefits. Amongst others, rules created by the participants of a specific community are usually efficient since they respond to real needs, mirror the technology, and provide the opportunity to flexibly adapt the legal

[9] Hart (2012).

[10] Foucault (2004).

[11] Slaughter (2004), pp. 12 et seq., 262 et seq.

[12] Teubner (1989), pp. 81 et seqq., 118 et seqq.

[13] Berman (2007), pp. 1158 et seqq.

[14] Weitzenboeck (2012), pp. 285 et seqq.

framework to the changing environment. Since self-regulation is negotiated by the involved community, the likelihood is high that such rules will enjoy broad acceptance.[15] Furthermore, the concerned persons/entities are incentivised to conduct permanent consultation processes for the development and the implementation of those private rules.[16] In short, the greater flexibility leads to better efficiency and cost-effectiveness, being basic objectives of the Law and Economics (hereinafter L&E) approach.

A further benefit of soft law consists in the fact that this regulatory model develops and establishes rules independently of the principle of territoriality; in other words, at least in principle self-regulation has a global reach. Furthermore, soft law is a normative order generated by the involved organisations that is responsive to changes in the concerned environment, and it is compliant with the principle of subsidiarity being a major structural pillar in democratic societies. The role of the governmental regulation is limited to situations in which the private actors do not find suitable solutions themselves.[17] Furthermore, a private or inter-agency process laying down a set of rules might also more easily realize new solutions than hard law.[18]

Obviously, self-regulation also carries some risks because the private rules are not always transparent and not every relevant group is necessarily involved. Furthermore, the active participants spending human and/or financial resources are confronted with a "free-rider problem".[19] In addition, self-regulation has a lower democratic legitimisation and, particularly, non-compliance with private rules might be confronted with enforcement problems and does not necessarily result in sanctions.[20]

Only if the risks of soft law can be reasonably overcome, it has a chance to play a role as a viable alternative regulatory tool. Nevertheless, the advantages of having efficient and flexible rules in an area where governmental regulations are hard to implement, should not be underestimated. Thereby, soft law should fit into the overall legal environment envisaged in order to realize a non-discriminatory and socially acceptable legal framework.[21]

---

[15]Weber (2014), p. 27.

[16]Guzman and Meyer (2010), pp. 179 et seqq.

[17]Weber (2012), p. 12; Gersen and Posner (2008), p. 589.

[18]Meyer (2008), p. 897.

[19]Weber (2014), p. 28.

[20]Tambini et al. (2008), pp. 282–284.

[21]Weber (2012), p. 13.

## 2.4 *Overlap of Regulatory Models*

Over time, by overcoming the traditional dichotomy hard law and soft law have moved closer to each other or even intermingled, as the following table shows:

| | | | | |
|---|---|---|---|---|
| **Hard Law** | Legitimized | ← | Partly legitimized | **Soft Law** |
| | Top-down bodies | ← | Bottom-up bodies | |
| | Stable/inflexible | ← | Adaptable/flexible | |

As expressed by the arrows, soft law is moving more and more towards hard law, i.e. notwithstanding the term "soft" the respective rules and guidelines have become or are becoming quite robust and are relatively narrow to the characteristics of the traditional hard law. It is to be expected that this development will continue over the next years.

# 3 From Self-regulation to Co-regulation

## 3.1 *Broadening Self-regulation*

As mentioned, rules considered by the "governed" persons as adequate guidelines appear to be legitimate since they are based on the fact that private incentives lead to a need-driven rule-setting process.[22] Insofar, soft law contributes to a more extensive building capacity and its enabling functionality serves to ease the co-ordination process while at the same time providing directionality to the establishment of cross-border standards. Soft law quality allows regulators to enter into arrangements by varying scope and specificity, and then to clarify (or change) the expectations of the involved actors.[23]

However, experience has shown that soft law in the form of self-regulation does not always cover the whole scope of a socially desirable legal framework. Under such circumstances, the self-regulation approach can be backed by a governmental "regime" particularly if a state is of the opinion that some basic rules should not be left to the private actors. In this case, legal doctrine calls the "legislative" approach as being a form of "co-regulation".

---

[22]See above part 2 of this article.

[23]Weber (2012), p. 12.

## 3.2 Increasing Importance of Co-regulation

In view of the rapid growth, the complex inter-relationships and the dynamic changes which have taken place in the new technological environment, it appears to be broadly accepted that a more flexible and innovation-friendly model of regulation is required.[24] However, irrespective of this need for flexibility, in various instances it makes sense to have self-regulation be approved by a public authority to become effective. This situation is called regulated self-regulation or co-regulation.[25]

Relatively widespread examples for such kinds of co-regulation already exist; the following regulatory ecosystems can be mentioned:[26]

- *Financial markets:* The supervision of compliance with anti-money laundering laws is mostly executed by self-regulatory bodies that in turn are regulated and supervised by the financial market authority.
- *Media markets:* Ethical guidelines for print and electronic media are often developed by private organisations and then accepted as part of the regulatory governmental framework.
- *Internet markets:* Domain names registries (such as Nominet and EURID) are usually privately organised but they operate under the control of governmental bodies.

The differentiated regulatory ecosystem having been developed over the last decade can be summarised in a pyramid as follows:[27]

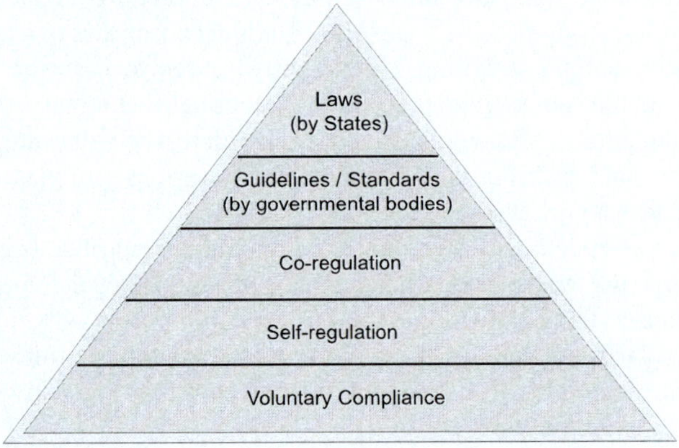


[24]This idea already goes back to Black (1995), pp. 32 et seqq.

[25]The term co-regulation was addressed for example by Hoffmann-Riem (2000) in relation to the media markets; for a detailed discussion see also Senn (2011), pp. 43, 139–148, 230.

[26]For a more detailed description see Marsden et al. (2020), pp. 9 et seq.

[27]Chart based on Marsden et al. (2020), p. 8.

Hereinafter, the described theoretical framework will be discussed with a special focus on the governance structures applying to the distributed ledger technology infrastructure; as a bridge to that, the aspect of regulatory quality will be addressed.

### 3.3 *Improving Regulatory Quality*

During the last two decades, regulatory theory has developed the following criteria which should be taken into account in order to improve the quality of regulation:[28]

- Is the regulatory action supported by legislative authority?
- Does the regulatory regime implement an appropriate scheme of accountability?
- Are procedures fair, accessible and open?
- Is the regulator acting with sufficient expertise? and
- Can the regulatory regime be qualified as an efficient system?

With the aim of improving the regulatory quality, the OECD Council has issued Guiding Principles for Regulatory Quality and Performance in 2005; these Guidelines encompass an extended scope of relevant aspects also reflecting the social developments:[29]

- Adoption of broad programs of regulatory reform that establish clear objectives and frameworks for implementation at the political level;
- Systematic assessment of impacts and review regulations in order to ensure that the intended objectives are efficiently and effectively reached in a changing and complex economic and social environment;
- Assurance of transparent and non-discriminatory regulations of independent regulatory institutions charged with their implementations, and of fair regulatory processes;
- Strengthening and review of scope, effectiveness and enforcement of competition policy;
- Design of economic regulation in all sectors with the objective of stimulating competition and of serving broad public interests;
- Elimination of unnecessary regulatory barriers to trade and investment by way of market openness throughout the regulatory processes;
- Identification of important linkages with other policy objectives and development of the respective policies.

In addition, an important element related to the improvement of regulatory quality is its continuous measuring, i.e. the ex post evaluations of regulatory tools and

[28]Basic economic research has been done by Baldwin et al. (2012), pp. 27 et seqq.

[29]OECD (2005); see also Weber (2017a), p. 255.

institutions.[30] The methods to be used for this measurement depend on the circumstances; relevant elements can consist in benchmarks and policy objectives.[31]

# 4 Distributed Ledger Technology as an Example

To ensure market confidence and consistency in its use, the distributed ledger technology needs international standards which are open, transparent and compatible with other technological systems. Even though many different distributed ledgers have been developed, standard ledger tools or respective interfaces are still missing.[32]

## *4.1 Regulatory Initiatives and Private Standardisation*

The distributed ledger technology (DLT) is by its very nature a cross-border infrastructure, lacking a central authority and waiving the existence of intermediaries. The fact that Blockchain as the most prominent distributed ledger technology is technologically designed by purpose in a way that intermediary functions are not needed anymore, causes regulatory challenges since governmental bodies cannot easily intervene into the data flow or the execution of transactions.[33] In the early stages, state regulators and in particular international organisations (such as the International Monetary Fund and the Financial Stability Board) concentrated on the normative treatment of virtual currencies (for example Bitcoin).[34]

At a later stage, the legal qualification of digital assets (so-called tokens) became important. Some countries have implemented so-called "Blockchain Laws"; amongst others, Liechtenstein, Malta and Gibraltar released such laws. Other countries (for example Switzerland, Singapore and Hong Kong) at least amended existing laws in order to cope with the new regulatory challenges of digital assets. However, legislative activities by public bodies usually only cover a limited scope of legal issues and do not envisage to implement a broad standardisation in the rule-making context.

An important aspect of the treatment of new technologies is the need for standardisation. In order to ensure market confidence and consistency in its use the distributed ledger technology must be compatible with regulations and surveillance functions within the general regulatory framework. Without establishing and

[30]OECD (2004).

[31]Weber (2017a), pp. 255 et seq.

[32]Weber (2017b), p. 3.

[33]Mougayar (2016), pp. 1 et seqq.

[34]For an overview see Weber (2017b), p. 2.

implementing open and transparent standards a broad adoption and application of the ledger technology will not be possible. Even though many different distributed ledgers have been developed by various organisations, standard distributed ledger tools or respective interfaces are still missing.[35]

As a first attempt at standardisation, the Linux Foundation's Hyperledger Project is noteworthy. Having been launched by some of the world's leading IT companies (and some global financial organisations), this collaborative open source project aims at advancing the blockchain technology's development by identifying and addressing major features for cross-industry open standards applicable to the distributed ledger technology. The Hyperledger Project is led by a diverse group of open source contributors.[36]

A particularly important player for discussing DLT standards is the International Organisation for Standardisation (ISO), the world's largest developer of voluntary international standards. In the DLT field, Standards Australia, a non-governmental and non-for-profit standards organisation recognised by the Australian government already submitted a proposal for international standards on blockchain technology and electronic distributed ledger technologies in spring 2016.[37] In the meantime, the so-called "ISO Blockchain Technology" group, led by Australia and consisting of 35 other ISO member countries, has developed a first set of blockchain standards.[38] Further efforts concern standardised terms of service for smart contracts.

In addition, sector-specific organisations, for example in the fields of maritime shipping, land transportation or digital customs handling, might also gain importance by way of implementing guidelines for cross-border transactions. The "Single Window" project in East Asia standardising electronic customs formalities is a good example.[39] The Organisation for Economic Cooperation and Development (OECD) as institution of the more developed countries, as well as the World Economic Forum (WEF) as private body equally support standardisation efforts, at least by preparing reports that show how different activities can be made interoperable ("Tokenisation of Assets and Potential Implications for Financial Markets",[40] "Building Value with Blockchain Technology"[41]).

---

[35] See the general discussion in Weber (2020), pp. 287 et seq.

[36] Information is available at: https://www.hyperledger.org/about.

[37] Standards Australia, Blockchain & Electronic Distributed Ledger Technologies: New Field of Technical Activity, http://www.standards.org.au/OurOrganisation/Events/Documents/Block-chain%20NFTA%20Information%20Sheet.pdf.

[38] ISO, Technical Committees, ISO/TC 307, Blockchain and Distributed Ledger Technologies, https://www.iso.org/committee/6266604.html.

[39] For further details see Weber (2011), pp. 1 et seqq.

[40] OECD (2020).

[41] World Economic Forum (2019).

## 4.2 Merits and Chances of the Applied Regulatory Approaches

Governmental regulators of all political levels (international, regional, national) started efforts to develop rules for the distributed ledger technology. However, experience has shown in the past that such an approach does not turn out to be very successful. On the one hand, governmental activities are regularly quite slow ("regulatory lag"), on the other hand, consensus on substantive issues is hard to achieve. Often, at least on the international level, a common understanding can only be realized on a relatively low level.

Therefore, the needed standardisation for the digital ledger technology being of utmost practical importance must be promoted by way of "private rule-making". Self-regulation is a viable approach and has its merits as shown in many industry sectors (banking, media, etc.). However, experience also conveys the lesson that rule-making exclusively vested in private bodies does not sufficiently take into account the public interests. Therefore, the models of "regulated self-regulation" or "co-regulation" appear to be more promising. Thereby, a top-down approach does not seem to be forward-looking since common visions of global norm-setting are difficult to evolve and global consensus-building is often quite cumbersome. Moreover, a bottom-up process based on a step-by-step approach looks more convincing since the possible forms of multi-stakeholderism allow the implementation of appropriate coordination and standardisation processes.

An efficient involvement of all potentially concerned private and public actors in the rule-making processes is desirable in order to establish a level playing field, which is suitable for the development of standards as well as for the promotion of innovation and competition in the given technological environment. The concerned market participants (i.e. private and also public actors, through existing or newly formed associations) would be best positioned to develop a regulatory framework which reflects the given technological realities as well as the societal expectations in a digital world.[42]

The inclusion of all stakeholders into the rule-making processes is a means for improving the regulatory quality since the manifold opinions and perceptions can be properly reflected: transparency and effectiveness of standard-developing will be high, and the assessment of impacts can be easily executed. These aspects are particularly important since standardisation encompasses organisational aspects and substantive elements. The first step consists in the identification and establishment of the most suitable standardisation bodies; the second step must be devoted to the discussions and negotiations of the appropriate contents of the standards.

A potential roadmap should start with the definition of the relevant issues, namely the requirements to be fulfilled by the distributed ledger technology in view of the societal needs and the realisable business models. Thereafter, the appropriate

[42]Weber (2020), pp. 285 et seqq.

organisations that are able to promote the standardisation of the terms and characteristics of the distributed ledger technology need to be identified. Finally, the development of the substantive standards becomes relevant: the individuals and organisations are to be appointed that are knowledgeable and experienced to develop the material principles by realizing a multistakeholder approach enshrining all relevant voices in the field.

## 5 Outlook

Normative frameworks are not static even if law usually cannot be adapted on short notice. The need for more flexibility in view of the fast-changing technological environment has broadened the path for alternative regulatory approaches. Self-regulation as a first step can be complemented by new forms such as co-regulation.

In the distributed ledger technology context, it appears to be unlikely for various reasons that a globally harmonised regulatory framework will be introduced in the next few years. A bottom-up approach, based on international standardisation organisations, being combined with general guidelines of regulators and embedded into modern decision-making concepts, might be more successful and improve regulatory quality. For this reason, private rule-making is and remains a viable tool in the modern world.

## References

Abott KW, Snidal D (2000) Hard and soft law in international governance. Int Organ 54:421–456

Baldwin R, Cave M, Lodge M (2012) Understanding regulation: theory, strategy and practice, 2nd edn. Oxford University Press, Oxford

Berman PS (2007) Global legal pluralism. South Calif Law Rev 80:1155–1237

Black J (1995) Constitutionalizing self-regulation. Mod Law Rev 59:24–55

Foucault M (2004) Naissance de la biopolitique. Cour au collège de France 1978/79. EHESS, Gallimard, Seuil, Paris

Gersen JE, Posner EA (2008) Soft law: lessons from congressional practice. Stanford Law Rev 61:573–627

Guzman AT, Meyer TL (2010) International soft law. J Leg Anal 2:171–225

Hart HLA (2012) The concept of law, 3rd edn. Clarendon, Oxford

Hoffmann-Riem W (2000) Regulierung der dualen Rundfunkordnung. Nomos, Baden-Baden

Marsden C, Meyer T, Brown I (2020) Platform values and democratic elections: how can the law regulate digital disinformation? Comput Law Secur Rev 36-105373:1–18

Meyer TL (2008) Soft law as delegation. Fordham Int Law J 32:888–942

Mougayar W (2016) The business blockchain. Wiley, Hoboken

OECD (2004) Regulatory performance: ex post evaluation of regulatory tools and institutions, Working Party on Regulatory Management and Reform. GOV/PCG/Reg(2004) 6, Paris

OECD (2005) Guiding principles for regulatory quality and performance. Paris

OECD (2020) The tokenisation of assets and potential implications for financial markets. Report of January 2020, http://www.oecd.org/finance/The-Tokenisation-of-Assets-and-Potential-Implications-for-Financial-Markets.html
Senn M (2011) Non-state regulatory regimes, understanding institutional transformation. Springer, Berlin
Slaughter A-M (2004) A new world order. Princeton University Press, Princeton/Oxford
Stigler GJ (1971) The theory of economic regulation. Bell J Econ Manag Sci 2:3–21
Tambini D, Leonardi D, Marsden C (2008) Codifying cyberspace: communications self-regulation in the age of Internet convergence. Routledge, London
Teubner G (1989) Recht als autopoietisches System. Suhrkamp, Frankfurt a.M.
Weber RH (2011) Legal framework for the single window concept in ASEAN: a successful movement towards trade facilitation in East Asian countries. Asian J Law Econ 2(4):1–24
Weber RH (2012) Overcoming the hard law/soft law dichotomy in times of (financial) crises. J Gov Regul 1(1):8–14
Weber RH (2014) Realizing a new global cyberspace framework. Normative foundations and guiding principles. Schulthess, Zürich
Weber RH (2017a) The role of law in constituting financial markets. J Int Bank Law Regul:253–260
Weber RH (2017b) Regulatory environment of the ledger technology. Comput Law Rev Int:1–6
Weber RH (2020) A new international trade framework for digital assets. In: Kolsky Lewis, Nakagama, Neuwirth, Picker, Stoll (eds). A post-WTO international legal order. Springer, Berlin, pp 277–291
Weitzenboeck EM (2012) A legal framework for emerging business models, dynamic networks as collaborative contracts. Edward Elgar, Cheltenham/Northampton
World Economic Forum (2019) Building value with blockchain technology: how to evaluate blockchain's benefits. Report of 16 July 2019. http://www3.weforum.org/docs/WEF_Building_Value_with_Blockchain.pdf

**Rolf H. Weber** Zurich. Professor emeritus of International Business Law at the University of Zurich and practicing attorney-at-law in Zurich. CH-8001 Zurich, Rämistr. 74/38, Tel. +41 (0)634 48 84. rolf.weber@rwi.uzh.ch. Fields of Interest: Information Technology and Internet Law, Competition Law, and International Finance and Trade Law.

# Ethical Blind Spots & Regulatory Traps: On Distorted Regulatory Incentives, Behavioral Ethics & Legal Design

**Yuval Feldman and Yotam Kaplan**

**Abstract** Illegal and unethical conduct often proliferates around ethical blind spots—scenarios and situations in which ordinary law-abiding people find it difficult to identify the harmfulness of their own actions. Ideally, regulators should act to diffuse ethical blind spots by trying to improve ethical awareness of potential perpetrators, in order to reduce wrongdoing. In practice, however, regulators might have a distorted incentive to conserve ethical blind spots rather than diffuse them. Regulators seek to bolster their perceived effectiveness by demonstrating intensive and rapid enforcement activity. To do so, regulators might prefer to ignore the underlying cognitive causes of unethicality, and instead constantly sanction those wrongdoers who repeatedly fall into the same trap of unintentional wrongdoing. We explore the origins of this problem in common regulatory incentive structures and in the standard design of legal norms.

## 1 Introduction

On a clear autumn night, one of the authors of this chapter was driving home after a long day at work. It was late at night, and the highway was empty and quiet. At one point, the highway crossed a residential area; this means the speed limit briefly dropped from 90 km/h to 80 km/h. The road in this particular point is straight and wide; also, a street camera is installed there. Not being fully mindful of all relevant facts, the driver was absentmindedly speeding and later fined $50. This incident suggests several points from a law enforcement perspective. First, the camera seems to be located in a spot where it is most likely to catch drivers speeding, but where its contribution to safety is minimal. Second, intentional wrongdoers would easily escape the camera by slowing down strategically (and momentarily), so the camera seems only useful to sanction non-deliberative violations. Third, the use of

Y. Feldman · Y. Kaplan (✉)
Bar-Ilan Law Faculty, Bar Ilan University, Ramat Gan, Israel
e-mail: Yuval.feldman@biu.ac.il; yotam.kaplan@biu.ac.il

 
K. Mathis, A. Tor (eds.), *Law and Economics of Regulation*, Economic Analysis of Law in European Legal Scholarship 11,
https://doi.org/10.1007/978-3-030-70530-5_3

technology seems to funnel regulators towards a specific type of enforcement activity, emphasizing the simplicity of sanctioning common and easy-to-identify violations. And finally, the driver is unlikely to challenge the relatively small fine; conversely, drivers who made grave traffic violation and are fined heavily are more likely to challenge sanctions in court.

More generally, this mundane midnight adventure can serve as a useful starting point for our discussion in this chapter. Violating the law can be immensely harmful, but is sometimes relatively harmless. When violations are harmless, ordinary people are highly likely to break the law through no malicious intention. Moreover, regulators might have a perverse incentive to focus their efforts on such situations in order to maximize the perceived efficiency of their regulatory activity. Thus, the scenario described above is a classic ethical blind spot, a situation in which ordinary, law-abiding people will find it easy to ignore or justify their own wrongdoing, and in which misconduct will therefore be extremely common. In other works, we argued that regulators ought to work to diffuse ethical blind spots in order to reduce unethicality;[1] in this chapter, we highlight regulators' disturbing tendency to conserve ethical blind spots, and to plant regulatory traps around them.

A rich literature in law, political science and economics studies the incentives of regulators.[2] The current chapter aims to connect this literature, mostly associated with public choice theory, with the study of behavioral ethics. We suggest this move helps explain some of the more curious patterns of regulatory behavior. Our analysis shows that some typical incentive structures that regulators face, especially when based on quotas and similar quantifiable measures, can lead them to focus their enforcement efforts on seemingly harmless behaviors instead of focusing on the true core of their regulatory mission.

Regulators typically seek to maximize the perceived effectiveness of their actions. That is, in order to accumulate prestige, appease their supervisors or appeal to the public, regulators will wish to show that they were able to effectively regulate, prevent wrongdoing and sanction violations.[3] To achieve this, regulators will wish to produce as many successful enforcement actions, at the lowest cost for themselves. Regulators will therefore have a natural incentive to focus their enforcement efforts on situations in which (1) wrongdoing is prevalent, and also (2) enforcement costs are low. In those situations, regulators will be able to identify and sanction the maximum number of violations, at minimal time and effort.

This framing of regulatory incentives suggests the importance of behavioral ethics research for regulatory incentives. The reason for this is that behavioral ethics research points out typical scenarios in which wrongdoing is common, and therefore

---

[1]Feldman and Kaplan (2020a).

[2]E.g. Self (1993); Latin (1991); Tengs et al. (1995); Breyer (1993) ; Tengs and Graham (1996), pp. 371–372; Hahn (1996), pp. 208, 235–238; Parker (2003); Hahn and Hird (1991); Hahn and Sunstein (2002); Richardson et al. (1982), pp. 34–35; Shavell (1980, 1984a, b); Glaeser and Shleifer (2003).

[3]Horn (1995).

also the scenarios on which regulators will wish to focus their efforts. More specifically, research in behavioral ethics points out two key categories of situations in which wrongdoing is expected to proliferate.[4] First, wrongdoing is predicted to be ubiquitous when legal norms are ambiguous and unclear;[5] second, wrongdoing would also be common when it does not produce a direct and observable harm.[6]

Out of these two choices, regulators will typically want to focus their efforts on the second (low harms) rather than the first (ambiguous norms). When legal norms are vague, wrongdoing will indeed be common, but the cost of enforcement will also be high. This is therefore not an ideal setting for regulators who wish to display maximal enforcement activity at minimal cost for themselves. Therefore, incentive-driven regulators might tend to focus their efforts on situations in which legal norms are clear, and harms resulting from violations are small or non-obvious. In those situations, wrongdoing can be extremely common, and enforcement costs would be low, which presents an ideal environment for self-promoting rational regulators.

We connect this insight with the literature contrasting clear-cut legal rules with vague legal standards,[7] to show that such scenarios, in which legal norms are clear but harms from their violations are small (or non-existent), are typical of the structure of any formal legal system. In particular, we show that regulators will tend to focus their enforcement efforts on violations that might not be actually harmful, but simply result from the over-inclusive nature of formal, bright-line legal norms. Importantly, while this will typically be the privately optimal strategy for a regulator who wishes to maximize perceived effectiveness, this will usually not represent a socially optimal enforcement policy. Below, we discuss the origins of this problem in more detail, and outline possible solutions.

The chapter proceeds as follows. Part I briefly describes three relevant literatures as foundation for our analysis. First, we present the findings of recent literature on behavioral ethics, highlighting the cognitive sources and situational antecedents of unethical and illegal behavior. Second, we briefly sketch a central insight from the literature on legal design, offering the distinction between clear-cut legal rules and more flexible legal standards. Third, we highlight one central point from existing literature on regulatory incentives, namely that regulators seek to maximize their prestige, promotion opportunities, and their reputation among colleagues, supervisors and the general public (especially voters when these are relevant). Part II is the core of the paper, bringing together the points surveyed in Part I to support our argument regarding the distorted incentives focusing regulatory activity. We show that regulators have a natural incentive to focus their enforcement activity in those situations in which legal norms are clear, but violations generate only minimal harm or risk. The reason for this is that in such cases the cost of enforcement is low (since legal norms are clearly defined) but violations are nevertheless common, since

[4] Feldman and Kaplan (2020a).

[5] Feldman and Teichman (2009) and Boussalis et al. (2018).

[6] Amir et al. (2016).

[7] Kaplow (1992), Kennedy (1976) and Gifford (1971).

ethical biases make it difficult for people to recognize their own violations when they appear to be harmless.[8] We also show that such categories of cases, when legal norms are clear but violations are not necessarily harmful, are a common and familiar structural feature of the formal legal system. We highlight the problematic nature of the resulting incentive structure for regulators, and its divergence from a socially desirable policy. Part III outlines possible solutions for the problem described in Part II, and explores the possibility of improving the incentives of regulators. This part also points out the possibility of further complications and distortions that can originate as a result of the basic problem described in Part II. A short conclusion follows.

## 2 Three Perspectives

This part briefly provides the scholarly background necessary for our analysis. We outline three main points: (1) wrongdoing is prevalent when legal norms are ambiguous or when legal violations appear to be harmless, (2) legal norms that are set to be clear-cut are, by definition, over-inclusive or under-inclusive, and (3) regulators have a natural incentive to focus their enforcement efforts on situations in which enforcement costs are low and wrongdoing is common. We later use these insights to show, in Part II that their accumulated effect leads to the distorted outcome in which regulators will tend to focus their efforts on enforcing mostly harmless violations of bright-line legal rules.

### *2.1 A Behavioral Ethics Approach to Wrongdoing*

Traditional accounts, especially in economic-oriented literature, provide a straightforward model of wrongdoing. According to this "homo-economics" model a potential perpetrator will choose to violate an ethical or legal norm if the benefit of doing so outweighs the prospective cost.[9] Under such a conception of calculated wrongdoing, the perpetrator will consider the possible gains from violating the law, compare those gains to the prospective cost of being sanctioned (by the law or by society) and decide accordingly whether to commit a wrong or comply with the law.

[8]See for example, Gino et al. (2010).

[9]Miceli (2004), "The economic approach to law assumes that rational individuals view legal sanctions [monetary damages, prison] as implicit prices for certain kinds of behavior, and that these prices can be set to guide these behaviors in a socially desirable direction"; Hirsch (1988), "Laws are authoritative directives that impose costs and benefits on participants in a transaction and in process after incentives"; Shavell (2002), "It is evident that both law and morality serve to channel our behavior. Law accomplishes this primarily through the threat of sanctions if we disobey legal rules".

The burgeoning literature on behavioral ethics challenges this received wisdom and suggests an alternative model of wrongdoing and decision-making in the context of ethical and legal dilemmas.[10] The starting point for the behavioral model of wrongdoing is that people generally prefer seeing themselves as "good people," meaning that they place a value on their self-perception as ethical people and law-abiding citizens.[11] Therefore, people will only rarely make a fully conscious decision to "act immorally." Instead, wrongdoing often occurs when self-perceived "good people" can commit a wrong while still convincing themselves they are acting morally.[12] In other words, the behavioral model of wrongdoing suggests that people will violate the law not when doing so is worthwhile in terms of the pertaining costs and benefits, but when they can do so while still maintaining the perception of an ethical self.

This general model closely relates to empirical findings regarding the multitude of cognitive biases and limitations that typically hinder people's ability to conduct an objective and candid ethical evaluation of their own conduct. This means that self-perceived "good people" can act illegally and immorally, while still maintaining an ethical self-image, even when a candid ethical evaluation would readily show that their behavior is in fact unethical.[13] In other words, people's ethical deliberations are often colored by their self-interest, making it easier for them to ignore or forgive their own wrongdoing. In other works, we suggest two main categories of such ethical biases: self-justified wrongdoing and self-blinded wrongdoing.[14] Under self-justified wrongdoing, perpetrators may be aware of the ethical dilemma, but simply conduct it in a distorted way, favoring their own self-interest. That is, biased ethical thinking, influenced by self-interest, will lead perpetrators to find excuses for their misconduct and believe their own morality even when a more candid analysis will reveal the immorality of their actions.[15] Conversely, under self-blinded wrongdoing, biased ethical thinking can lead perpetrators to completely ignore ethical dilemmas or fail to recognize them when they arise.[16] People have been shown to systematically fail to recognize facts that would make them feel uncomfortable; this means they will tend to ignore factors that will indicate that their own actions are immoral.[17]

Experimental works in behavioral ethics explores the situational antecedents of wrongdoing, or the "ethical blind spots" in which people can more easily excuse and ignore their own unethicality, and in which wrongdoing is ubiquitous.[18] Two main categories of such findings are relevant for the purposes of the current inquiry. First,

[10]For a review see Bazerman and Gino (2012).

[11]Feldman (2018).

[12]Mazar et al. (2008).

[13]Mazar et al. (2008).

[14]Feldman and Kaplan (2020b).

[15]Feldman and Kaplan (2020b).

[16]Feldman and Kaplan (2020b).

[17]Merritt et al. (2010), Balcetis and Dunning (2006), Shu et al. (2011) and Chugh et al. (2005).

[18]Bazerman and Tenbrunsel (2011).

people can more easily justify and ignore their own wrongdoing when the relevant legal or ethical norm is vague, ambiguous or poorly defined.[19] That is, when the ethical dilemma is not presented in clear terms, ethical biases become more active and dominant,[20] leading people to more easily ignore the dilemma completely, or justify their wrongdoing.[21] Second, people can more easily ignore and justify their own wrongdoing in cases where the harms from violating the legal norm are not immediately apparent. That is, when harms are low, caused to unidentified victims or when the harms are spread between many different victims,[22] it becomes easier for perpetrators to convince themselves that violating the legal norms is not ethically problematic, or even to ignore the ethical dilemma completely and act unethically without noticing they are doing so.[23]

## 2.2 Legal Design: Rules v. Standards

The classic literature on legal design offers a useful distinction between rules and standards.[24] Rules are legal norm that are clear-cut and offer a sharp distinction between two categories, usually "right" and "wrong" or "legal" and "illegal." For instance, a rule might set the speed limit on a specific road at 90 km/h: any higher speed violates the rule, while any lower speed is deemed legal.[25] Conversely, standards also typically attempt to distinguish between legal categories, but are vaguer or leave more room for discretion and interpretation.[26] For instance, a standard may establish that drivers must drive at an appropriate speed according to all relevant road conditions. Under such a standard, a specific behavior, or driving speed, will ultimately be deemed either legal or illegal, but it is not clear at the outset if a specific behavior will be considered to violate the standard or not.

This description of rules versus standards is used to explain the advantages and disadvantages of different legal arrangements.[27] Thus, legal arrangements that are more rule-like have an advantage in being easier to enforce and to adjudicate after the fact.[28] Rule-like arrangements also can help create legal certainty for citizens, provided that citizens are aware of the legal rule. Rules also have disadvantages, in

---

[19]Bazerman and Sezer (2016).

[20]Dana et al. (2007).

[21]Gino (2015).

[22]Amir et al. (2016).

[23]For a discussion of a more extensive list of causes of unethical behavior see Nicola and Cantarelli (2017).

[24]Kennedy (1976), p. 1685.

[25]Kennedy (1976), p. 1688.

[26]Kennedy (1976), p. 1688.

[27]Kaplow (1992), p. 557.

[28]Kennedy (1976), p. 1685.

being either over-inclusive or under-inclusive.[29] A rule, setting a bright-line distinction between what is allowed and what is not allowed, may be easy to understand, enforce and communicate, but will also often miss the mark. Since a rule does not consider all possible factors, but only predetermined and highly observable factors, it can easily misclassify a behavior as either forbidden or allowed, when a more full-scale consideration of all relevant factors would point to the opposite solution. For instance, a bright-line rule that sets the speed limit at 90 km/h will classify driving at 80 km/h as legal, even if, in a specific case, driving in this manner was clearly dangerous considering visibility and weather conditions. In such a case, the use of a vaguer standard will be necessary, in order to establish that any dangerous driving activity is forbidden. This means that standards, as compared to rules, can produce more accurate legal outcomes by being more flexible, but at a cost of being more difficult to adjudicate, communicate and predict.[30]

The distinction between clear rules and vague standards obviously relates closely to the antecedents on unethical behavior described above. Below, we make this connection more explicit after considering the incentive structure typically faced by regulators in charge of enforcing legal norms.

## 2.3 *The Incentives of Regulators*

Literature in law and in economics attributes a simple set of incentives to regulators. Regulators wish to maximize their prestige, their promotion opportunities, their reputation and so on, and all at a minimum cost for themselves.[31] This means that in steering regulatory efforts, regulators will wish to appear as effective as possible, while spending as little resources as possible. In order to accumulate prestige, promotions or rewards, regulators will want to identify and sanction as many legal violations as possible, using their limited resources as effectively as they can. Such incentive structure is especially pronounced when regulators operate under a quota-based incentive scheme.[32] This of course assumes that regulators indeed have an incentive at least to appear efficient. If regulators are left completely unsupervised, their sole incentive will be to lower their efforts, and the privately optimal behavior might be zero enforcement activity.[33] However, if regulators place a value on their reputation among colleagues, supervisors, or voters, they will have an incentive at least to produce what seems to be effective regulatory activity.

---

[29]Kennedy (1976), p. 1689.

[30]Kennedy (1976), p. 1689.

[31]Horn (1995).

[32]Justice Policy Institute (2012), p. 24; Bronstein (2014–2015); Rose (2015); Veto 309 (2004).

[33]Horn (1995); another important possibility widely discussed in the literature is that of regulatory capture; Dal Bó (2006) and Laffont and Tirole (1991).

This means that, when regulators have some discretion in directing their regulatory activity they will want to direct it in such a way as to present the maximum amount of regulatory results, or identification and sanction of violations, in as little time and effort as possible. Importantly, often regulators will have no discretion in exercising their authority, and in such cases their incentives might not make any difference. For instance, restaurant inspectors might be tied to a strict policy telling them which restaurant to inspect and when, and exactly what to check in each restaurant. When this is the case, and restaurant inspectors have no discretion in directing their regulatory efforts, their incentives should not matter to their activity and to the outcome of their efforts. But, to the extent that restaurant inspectors have some discretion in operating their authority, then their incentives might matter. Similarly, even if the inspectors themselves hold no discretionary power, whoever sets the policy according to which the individual inspectors operate surely did hold such discretion. The incentive of the regulator supervising the individual inspectors therefore might matter in such a case in terms of regulatory behaviors and regulatory outcomes.

# 3 The Distortion in Regulatory Incentives

We now turn to the core of our argument, and to inspect the way in which regulators will focus their enforcement efforts, when they have discretion to do so, in light of the findings of behavioral ethics and the literature on legal design described above. To maximize their perceived effectiveness, regulators will seek to focus their enforcement activities on situations in which (1) wrongdoing is common, and (2) the costs of enforcement are low. This combination of factors will assure that regulators can display the maximum number of successful regulatory enforcement actions in minimal time and effort.

As mentioned above, the findings of behavioral ethics research are highly relevant in this context, as they predict the situations in which wrongdoing will proliferate. Of course, regulators do not need to be aware of the results presented in behavioral ethics research in order to direct their activity in to these scenarios; instead, they can just be generally aware of situations and cases in which wrongdoing is more common, or in which they were more likely to identify and sanction wrongdoing in the past. We argue that this insight interacts in an important way with the legal design literature and with its distinction between rules and standards.

## *3.1 Enforcing Vague Standards*

Consider first regulators' incentives to enforce flexible and vague legal standards. Rationale regulators will not want to focus their efforts on enforcing standards, since under standards enforcement costs would be high. To be sure, behavioral ethics research suggests wrongdoing will proliferate under standards, since legal norms are not clearly defined and potential perpetrators will find it easier to ignore or justify their own wrongdoing. And, since wrongdoing is ubiquitous under standards, this should supposedly incentivize regulators to focus their enforcement efforts on standards, as under standards they would be more likely to find legal violations. However, this effect is negated by the fact that under standards the cost of enforcement will also be higher. In other words, standards do not present the ideal setting for regulators to maximize their perceived effectiveness, since regulators would naturally prefer settings in which (1) wrongdoing is common, and (2) enforcement costs are low.

For instance, assume a restaurant inspector can decide the amount of enforcement effort to dedicate to the enforcement of a relatively vague standard that declares that kitchens should be "clean enough as to not present health risks." Since this is a relatively imprecise threshold, we would expect it to be violated frequently, since restaurant owners' biased ethical thinking will make it easy for them to ignore or justify their divergence from it. For this reason, supposedly, it would make sense for inspectors to devout efforts to enforcing this norm, which is often violated. However, for exactly the same reason that the norm is likely to be violated frequently, it will also be costly for regulators to enforce it. That is, it would be relatively difficult for inspectors to prove that a specific kitchen is indeed not clean enough as to present a health risk; in comparison, it would be much easier for an inspector to prove that a more bright-line rule was violated, for instance to show that the height of the ceiling or the type of the sink used in the kitchen is in violation of a clear and specific rule-style requirement. More generally, rules would be easier for regulators to enforce, compared to standards, so there is little reason to expect that regulators will wish to focus their efforts on enforcing standards.

To give another example, if the vague standard provides that drivers should drive "according to road conditions," we should expect to find this standard frequently violated. The reason is that the standard, being vague, will create multiple opportunities for drivers to slide down the road of biased ethical estimations and justify their speeding as complacent with the relevant requirement. And, since wrongdoing is ubiquitous, regulators will supposedly have an incentive to direct their efforts to enforcing the standard in order to identify and sanction as many violations as possible. But, again, enforcing the vague norm will also be costly for the relevant regulators, police officers, since it is not easy to show (in a way later verifiable in a court of law), that specific driving behaviors violated the ambiguous norm of driving in accordance with all relevant conditions. Comparably, it would be much easier to show that a specific driver violated a bright-line rule, providing for instance a speed limit of 90 km/h.

This analysis, in itself, does not necessarily present a distortion in regulator's incentives, and is a direct result of the difference between rules and standards as described in existing literature. In this sense, this conclusion is just a natural extension of the legal design literature on rules and standards, and presents another aspect of the advantage of rules over standards. However, this analysis does leave us with the question of how regulators will choose to direct their efforts when they enforce bright-line rules, and the way this choice will interact with people's biased ethical thinking when harms resulting from legal violations are not immediately apparent.

## 3.2 Enforcing Clear-Cut Rules

To optimize their perceived effectiveness regulators will want to focus on enforcing rules rather than standards, in order to minimize the costs of enforcement. They will also want to identify situations under which the violations of rules are common, in order to maximize the number of successful regulatory sanctions. In other words, the ideal setting for regulators who wish to appear active and successful in their regulatory mission is a setting in which (1) perpetrators are operating under a clear-cut rule (and not a standard), and (2) misconduct proliferates. These cases are ideal for regulators since enforcement activity will be both relatively cheap, as well as capture many violations with relatively little regulatory investment.

Since regulators seeks to direct their activity towards scenarios in which enforcement costs are low and wrongdoing is common, they will wish to focus on scenarios in which perpetrators operate under a clear-cut rule, but harms from violating the rule are small or non-existing. As mentioned above, behavioral ethics research shows that wrongdoing can become extremely common when justifications are easy to come by, when violations are harmless, or when harms are not readily apparent to perpetrators. Behavioral ethics research shows that in such situations, ordinary, law-abiding citizens will often break the law, as biased ethical thinking will commonly lead them to fail to recognize their own wrongdoing, thus rendering violations of legal norms extremely common. Therefore, the ideal way for regulators to increase their perceived effectiveness would be to focus their activity towards situations where legal norms are clear (so enforcement is cheap), but justifiability is high since harms are not clearly present (so wrongdoing is common). In those cases, violations would be common, and enforcement costs minimal, which is ideal for regulators seeking to identify and sanction as many violations as possible.

This general prediction explains the example opening this chapter. Thus, the most effective regulatory policy, for a rationale regulator, would be to locate the road camera where speeding is essentially harmless, since those are the parts of the road in which drivers would be most likely to speed. Since road conditions indicate it is safe to speed, drivers will have difficulty recognizing their own offenses, and will tend to violate the law.

These conditions seem to be present under legal rules in rather typical scenarios, due to the over-inclusive and under-inclusive nature of clear-cut legal norms. As explained above, clear-cut legal rules have the advantage of being easy to communicate, adjudicate and enforce, at the cost of also being under-inclusive or over-inclusive. That is, in order to be clear and easy to operate, legal rules are willing to sacrifice accuracy and wrongly classify some cases. Thus, a clear rule that provides a speed limit of 90 km/h will mean that all drivers going over 90 km/h are violating the law, even if some of them, for instance those driving in hours in which the road is relatively empty, are actually generating no danger and causing no harm. This means that the basic structure of legal rules creates situations in which the law clearly declares some activities as forbidden or illegal, even when they are harmless or when the rationale for the prohibition is not in fact present. This, in itself, is a familiar result and an accepted cost of the use of bright-line legal rules. However, this result becomes somewhat more problematic when considered in conjunction with behavioral ethics insights regarding the cognitive origins of wrongdoing and with regulator's incentives to shape their enforcement activities.

Thus, when clear-cut rules are over-inclusive or under-inclusive, and set prohibitions that seem to go beyond what the underlying policy would seem to require, this would present a clear ethical blind spot. That is, in such situations, since the legal violations do not produce obvious and direct harms, biased ethical thinking will naturally become operative and lead people to violate the norm much more frequently. And, since in such cases wrongdoing is ubiquitous and legal norms are clear, this is the ideal setting for regulators to act if they seek to maximize the perceived effectiveness of their activity, or the number of times they can demonstrate that they identified and sanctioned a violation.

To illustrate this general claim, consider again the case of police officers engaged in the regulation of road traffic. For such police officers, it is very likely that the most rewarding course of action would be to focus on clear-cut rules, and on the cases in which those rules are over-inclusive. That is, police officers will seek out times and locations in which going over the speed limit seems to be effectively harmless, and then focus enforcement efforts on these times and locations. Other things being equal, this would be the best way for police officers to issue the maximum amount of tickets in the minimal amount of time. And, more important, although privately optimal for the police officers involved, this hardly seems to satisfy the requirements of a well-functioning regulatory system, which should ideally be guided in a very different way.

The literature on the effects of quotas on police work nicely illustrates this point more generally, demonstrating the distorting effects of quotas on regulatory incentives.[34] Thus, seeking to fill their quotas, police officers typically focus their

---

[34]Bronstein (2014–2015), p. 543, "But telling them that you want to arrest x number of people, you have to cite x number of people, it just encourages bad performance on the part of officers", "If citizens believe that tickets are being issued or arrests are being made for reasons other than the goal of law enforcement, which is about public safety," says Robinson, "then their trust in the legitimacy of the system is really eroded." "Police department activity quotas reduce police officer discretion and promote the use of enforcement activity for reasons outside of law enforcement's legitimate goals."; p. 572, "When enforcement activity is used as currency, it creates a danger that police officers will take enforcement action for their own personal benefit rather than for one of law enforcement's legitimate goals"; Veto 309 (2004), "When the summons procedure is utilized in questionable circumstances, suspicions are raised that revenue enhancement and not sound police methodology is the rational [sic]."; In Its Defense, Police Dept. cites Laziness of Its Officers (2013), "all in an effort to counter testimony from whistle-blower officers who say that commanders had created quotas that pressured them to make street stops without the proper grounds."

attention on smaller offences, which are easier to identify and sanction.[35] Enforcement in such cases becomes even easier if perpetrators, failing to recognize their own wrongdoing, also fail to conceal it.

This analysis demonstrates a troubling possibility, that also echoes true in many real-world contexts. That is, as a natural result of the structure of legal rules, the incentives of regulators, and the nature of the cognitive processes leading to wrongdoing, we might observe a distorted focus of regulatory enforcement efforts. When such distortion occurs, regulators will focus their efforts on instances where people violate formal legal rules precisely in these cases in which the rules are in fact unhelpful or unnecessary. This problematic tendency can be further exacerbated by the fact that when people violate norms while preserving an ethical self-image, they will not tend to act to conceal their actions since they are failing to admit their own unethicality. This will make enforcement in such cases even cheaper and easier for regulators, further strengthening their incentive to focus on violations that are in fact largely harmless.

It seems that recent trends in law enforcement, gearing towards heavier reliance on automatic enforcement, are exacerbating these problems. Thus, novel enforcement regulatory means (such as speed cameras) make it even cheaper to enforce bright-line rules, especially if they are expected to work with minimal human intervention. Automated enforcement is increasingly common in a multitude of regulatory contexts, such as traffic violation, environmental harms, and insider trading. Since automated enforcement is more easily designed to capture common violations of bright-line rules, it further distorts the regulatory incentive to focus on situations in which the over-inclusive nature of legal rules makes violation extremely common.

## 4 Possible Solutions and Additional Challenges

This part briefly outlines possible remedies for the problem of distorted regulatory incentives described above. We demonstrate that, although possible, such solutions are not trivial and might require some efforts and thinking on the part of policymakers. We also explore possible further complications that can originate from later responses to the basic problem described in Part II.

[35] Justice Policy Institute (2012), p. 24, "With an emphasis on number of arrests rather than type or quality of arrest, it may be easier for police and multi-jurisdictional task forces to increase their numbers by focusing on the low hanging fruit—the people in possession of a small amount of drugs. As Harry Levine determined in his study about marijuana arrests in New York City, some police agencies conduct performance reviews of individual officers based on the number of arrests. Regardless of whether this is a de facto quota, police officers clearly have an incentive to make as many arrests as possible. Drug offenses, particularly marijuana possession, are typically seen as "safe" with little risk of injury to officers."

### 4.1 Self-Correction & Displacement

One solution to the problem described above would be that potential wrongdoers would adjust their behavior according to the distorted incentives of regulators, which, in turn, might correct those distorted incentives. To see this possibility, consider again the case of the police officer who chooses to focus on common but harmless violations in order to maximize ticket output. As a response to this regulatory policy, it might be the case that drivers will learn to update their behavior and to avoid speeding especially in those cases in which speeding seems harmless. If drivers understand that speed limits are more likely to be enforced when speeding is actually harmless, they might correct their natural tendency and stop speeding in those instances. If indeed drivers will respond in this way, violations will cease being common in those instances, and regulators will accordingly stop directing their enforcement efforts towards them.

However, it seems doubtful to us that such self-correction is possible, or that it is common. This type of self-correction of the regulatory system seems to require a high level of sophistication and awareness by citizens. Thus, it critically depends on the assumption that drivers recognize regulatory enforcement patterns, and respond rationally to them. In reality, it would be surprising if citizens were that deeply aware of the focus on regulatory enforcement efforts, in a way that will allow them to alter their behavior accordingly, especially in the context of semi-deliberative or non-deliberative wrongdoing on which we focus here.

Similarly, and perhaps more important, even if citizens gradually become aware of the distorted focus of regulatory behavior, it is not necessary that self-correction of wrongdoing behavior will indeed occur. Instead, if the distorted focus of regulatory behavior becomes common knowledge, this may simply contribute to general distrust in regulatory agencies and in government intuitions more generally.

Even worse, if citizens indeed learn that regulators focus their efforts on easy-to-identify but relatively harmless violations, they may redirect their unlawful activity towards more severe types of violations. To illustrate this point, consider the example of tax authorities when designing their enforcement policies. If tax authorities are seeking to maximize the frequency of successful enforcement actions, they are most likely to focus their efforts findings mistakes or internal contradictions in tax form submitted by taxpayers. Those are easy-to-catch violations, that taxpayers are very likely to make. Yet, as a response to such enforcement policy, taxpayers' incentives to comply might be distorted, since it creates an incentive for them to refrain from submitting their tax forms in the first place. More generally, this means that an enforcement policy directed at easy-to-identify but relatively harmless violations can distort citizens' incentives to comply with the law, and funnel them towards more harmful illegal activity.

## 4.2 Goal-Based Incentives

The central type of solutions to the problem described in Part II seems to be to connect regulatory incentives more clearly to the underlying social goal the regulation is supposed to promote, and not to the frequency of successful regulatory enforcement actions. If regulators and enforcement agents are not measured according to perceived effectiveness of their regulatory efforts, that is, the number of successful enforcement incidents, but based on some measure more directly connected to the goals of their regulatory efforts, their incentives will be more naturally aligned with the socially desirable outcome. For instance, if police officers are rewarded for the actual safety of drivers and pedestrians in their precinct, and not evaluated based on the number of tickets they issued, this will circumvent their distorted incentive to maximize the number of tickets by focusing on harmless violations of clear norms.

Of course, tying the incentives of regulators directly to the social good their work is supposed to promote presents its own challenges. First, the social good each regulator is put in charge of is typically much more difficult to quantify, compared to the easier-to-measure frequency of regulatory enforcement actions.[36] Second, even if this social good is measured, it is more difficult to create a direct connection between this measure and the actions of the regulator or the enforcement agent. That is, if a specific police officer issued an exceptionally high number of tickets, this outcome is clearly traceable to the behavior and efforts of that specific police officer. This means that such outcomes will be, formally or informally, directly connected to that police officer's reputation, promotion opportunities, prestige or rewards. Conversely, if a police officer operated in a truly effective way, and found an optimal enforcement scheme that actually lowered the amount of accidents in a given area, it will be significantly more difficult (yet not impossible) to attribute this desirable outcome to the actions of the police officer.

In order to truly improve incentives for regulators and the outcomes of regulatory activity, policymakers must find ways to connect incentive structure of regulators more directly to the social goals their activity is meant to promote. This should be done, first, by measuring trends relating to those goals, and then offering reward to regulators that can effect these trends.

---

[36]Bronstein (2014–2015), pp. 543, 563; Rose (2015), "So why does numbers-based policing seem to persist in some departments? Maybe because it's an easy way to track officer productivity. Tim Dees, a retired Reno, Nev., police officer who has also taught criminal justice, says it's the quality of police work that counts, not the quantity. "That's a much more difficult metric to gauge," says Dees. "The satisfaction of the citizen, very difficult to put a value on that. And it's much easier for, frankly, lazy administrators to make it into a numbers game."; Numbers Game, "Mississippi's regional drug task force funding, contingent on the quantity of drug arrests, encourages the indiscriminate use of confidential informants to increase arrest numbers over the quality and public safety impact of the drug cases."

## 5 Conclusions

Regulation aims to enhance the welfare of citizens. However, it is not always easy to align the motivation of regulators with the long-term goal of protecting the public. For instance, a police officer may be evaluated based on the number of tickets they write; this is done to incentivize the police officer to enforce the law and promote the welfare of the general public. However, the outcome of this incentive scheme is not always easy to predict. It might be the case that the easiest way for the police officer to maximize the number of tickets they write is to find a specific time and place where drivers are systematically committing some minor violations, and then easily and repeatedly issue tickets with as little time invested as possible. And, although this might produce a very impressive tickets-an-hour ratio, it is not necessarily welfare-enhancing behavior by the police officer. To extrapolate on this example, the more general problem here is that regulators are often evaluated based on metrics that are easy to measure and verify, and not based on the true utility of their work. Since regulators work with limited resources, this can lead them to enforce the law in a selective and inefficient way. More specifically, regulators have a natural incentive to enforce the law on easy-to-catch routine offenders, and not on the most harmful offenders. This incentive interacts in important ways with the motivations of offenders.

Behavioral ethics research studies the multiple cognitive sources of unethical conduct. Thus, people tend to violate rules for many reasons: they might think they will not get caught, that the rule is misguided or unjust, that there is little or no harm in violating the rule, or that the rule is too vague. It is interesting to interact these tendencies of wrongdoers towards unethicality with regulators' incentives to demonstrate their effectiveness. When rules are vague or when enforcement is costly, people will tend to act unethically, but regulators will find it difficult to enforce the law and will therefore not tend to act. Conversely, when harms are low or rules seem to be misguided, people will tend to violate the law, and regulators will also tend to focus their efforts (because enforcement costs are low). Thus, the natural focus for regulator's activity seems to be on relatively harmless violations. In such cases, perpetrators often do not think they did anything wrong, so also do not bother to hide their violations, which in turn makes enforcement even cheaper.

In many cases it is important for regulators to focus on ordinary unethicality and on small routine violations, rather than on "smoking guns" and on extreme violations of the law. However, regulators' incentives push them to focus on the wrong type of ordinary unethicality: the type that people engage in because they think is harmless, not the type that is difficult to detect. This means that standard incentives schemes for regulators, as far as they are based on simple measures for "effective enforcement" might be lacking. This is mainly true when such incentive schemes do not include a direct observation of the underlying value the regulation is intended to promote (such as safety in the case of traffic regulation).

If indeed regulation is typically skewed towards easy-to-identify routine violations, this can have an adverse effect on citizen's beliefs and behavior. First, is people see that regulators systematically focus on relativity meaningless and harmless violations, this can slowly erode people's trust in the regulator and in the legitimacy of the regulatory framework. This, in turn, can also erode the power of social enforcement.[37] A misguided regulatory focus can easily appear to be overly formalistic, or even border-line corrupt. Second, if people see that regulators focus their activity on easy-to-identify violations, this can enhance their incentives to participate in wrongdoing that is more difficult to identify. In this sense, the natural incentive of regulators can turn relatively harmless unethicality into far more harmful conduct. For instance, tax authorities can choose to focus their efforts on those who lied in their forms, made innocent mistakes in their forms, or on those who did not submit forms at all. Obviously, all these groups violated the law, and in an ideal world all should receive the appropriate sanction. But, considering limited enforcement resources, regulators will often have to make a choice and will not be able to perfectly enforce the law. Given such limitations, regulators might choose to enforce the law on those who made innocent mistakes, and not on those who lied or did not submit forms at all. Mistakes will likely be easier to spot, as "offenders," almost by definition, are not trying to hide them, and, if regulators are evaluated by the number of violations they find, or by the overall unpaid tax they recover, focusing on mistakes will probably be the dominant strategy for a rationale regulator. And yet, this will also create a long-term incentive for taxpayers to avoid submitting their tax reports. In this sense, misguided regulatory incentive schemes can easily turn relatively "innocent" wrongdoing into much more harmful misconduct.

## References

Amir A, Kogut T, Bereby-Meyer Y (2016) Careful cheating: people cheat groups rather than individuals. Front Psychol 7:371

Balcetis EE, Dunning D (2006) See what you want to see: motivational influences on visual perception. J Pers Soc Psychol 91:612–625

Bazerman MH, Gino F (2012) Behavioral ethics: toward a deeper understanding of moral judgment and dishonesty. Annu Rev Law Soc Sci 8:85–104

Bazerman MH, Sezer O (2016) Bounded awareness: implications for ethical decision making. Organ Behav Hum Decis Process 136:95–105

Bazerman MH, Tenbrunsel AE (2011) Blind spots: why we fail to do what's right and what to do about it. Princeton University Press, New Jersey

Boussalis C, Feldman Y, Smith HE (2018) Experimental analysis of the effect of standards on compliance and performance. Regul Gov 12:277, 288

Breyer S (1993) Breaking the vicious circle: toward effective risk regulation

Bronstein N (2014–2015) Police management and quotas: governance in the CompStat era. Columbia J Law Soc Probl 48:543, 563, 572

Chugh D, Bazerman MH, Banaji MR (2005) Bounded ethicality as a psychological barrier to recognizing conflicts of interest. In: Moore DA, Cain DM, Loewenstein G, Bazerman MH (eds)

[37] Harel and Klement (2007).

Conflicts of interest: challenges and solutions in business, law, medicine, and public policy. Cambridge University Press, New York, pp 74–95
Dal Bó E (2006) Regulatory capture: a review. Oxf Rev Econ Policy 22:203–225
Dana J, Weber RA, Kuang JX (2007) Exploiting moral wiggle room: experiments demonstrating an illusory preference for fairness. Econ Theory 33:67–80
Feldman Y (2018) The law of good people: challenging states' ability to regulate human behavior. Cambridge University Press
Feldman Y, Kaplan Y (2020a) Big data & bonded ethicality. Cornell J Law Public Policy
Feldman Y, Kaplan Y (2020b) Behavioral ethics as compliance
Feldman Y, Teichman D (2009) Are all legal probabilities created equal? N Y Univ Law Rev 84:980
Gifford DJ (1971) Communication of legal standards, policy development, and effective conduct regulation. Cornell Law Rev 56:409
Gino F (2015) Understanding ordinary unethical behavior: why people who value morality act immorally. Curr Opin Behav Sci 3:107–111
Gino F, Shu LL, Bazerman MH (2010) Nameless+ harmless= blameless: when seemingly irrelevant factors influence judgment of (un)ethical behavior. Organ Behav Hum Decis Process 111:93–101
Glaeser E, Shleifer A (2003) The rise of the regulatory state. J Econ Lit 41:401–425
Hahn RW (1996) Regulatory reform: what do the government's numbers tell us? In: Hahn RW (ed) Risks, costs, and lives saved: getting better results from regulation. Oxford University Press, New York, p 208, 235–238
Hahn RW, Hird JA (1991) The costs and benefits of regulation: review and synthesis. Yale J Regul 8:233, 256
Hahn RW, Sunstein CR (2002) A new executive order for improving federal regulation? Deeper and wider cost-benefit analysis. Penn Law Rev 150:1489, 1519–1520
Harel A, Klement A (2007) The economics of stigma: why more detection of crime may result in less stigmatization. J Leg Stud 36(2):355–377
Hirsch WZ (1988) Law and economics: an introductory analysis 1
Horn MJ (1995) The political economy of public administration: institutional choice in the public sector. Cambridge University Press
In Its Defense, Police Dept (2013) Cites laziness of its officers. https://www.nytimes.com/2013/04/30/nyregion/to-defend-police-city-cites-officers-laziness.html
Justice Policy Institute (2012) Rethinking the blues: how we police in the U.S. and at what cost. p 24
Kaplow L (1992) Rules versus standards: an economic analysis. Duke Law J 42:557–629
Kennedy D (1976) Form and substance in private law adjudication. Harv Law Rev 89:1685
Laffont JJ, Tirole J (1991) The politics of government decision-making: a theory of regulatory capture. Q J Econ 106:1089–1127
Latin H (1991) Regulatory failure, administrative incentives, and the new Clean Air Act. Environ Law 21:1647
Mazar N, Amir O, Ariely D (2008) The dishonesty of honest people: a theory of self-concept maintenance. J Market Res 45:633–644
Merritt AC, Effron DA, Monin B (2010) Moral self-licensing: when being good frees us to be bad. Soc Pers Psychol Compass 4:344–357
Miceli TJ (2004) The economic approach to law 1
Nicola B, Cantarelli P (2017) What causes unethical behavior? A meta-analysis to set an agenda for public administration research. Public Adm Rev 77:327–339
Numbers Game, The Vicious Cycle of Incarceration in Mississippi's Criminal Justice System
Parker RW (2003) Grading the government. Univ Chic Law Rev 70:1345, 1356
Richardson G, Ogus A, Burrows P (1982) Policing pollution. A study of regulation and enforcement. Oxf Socio-Leg Stud:34–35
Rose J (2015) Despite laws and lawsuits, Quota-based policing lingers. NPR. https://www.npr.org/2015/04/04/395061810/despite-laws-and-lawsuits-quota-based-policing-lingers

Self P (1993) Government by the market? The politics of public choice. Macmillan International Higher Education
Shavell S (1980) Strict liability versus negligence. J Leg Stud 9:1–25
Shavell S (1984a) Liability for harm versus regulation of safety. J Leg Stud 13:357–374
Shavell S (1984b) A model of the optimal use of liability and safety regulation. Rand J Econ 15:271–280
Shavell S (2002) Law versus morality as regulators of conduct. Am Law Econ Rev 4:227
Shu LL, Gino F, Bazerman MH (2011) Dishonest deed, clear conscience: when cheating leads to moral disengagement and motivated forgetting. Pers Soc Psychol Bull 37:330–349
Tengs TO, Graham JD (1996) The opportunity costs of haphazard social investments in life-saving. In: Hahn RW (ed) Risks, costs, and lives saved: getting better results from regulation. Oxford University Press, New York, p 167, 177
Tengs TO, Adams ME, Pliskin JS et al (1995) Five-hundred life-saving interventions and their cost-effectiveness. Risk Anal 15:369, 371–372
Veto 309 (2004) N.Y. Bill & Veto Jacket, 2004 S.B. 6478

**Yuval Feldman** Mori Lazarof Professor of Legal Research, Bar-Ilan Law Faculty. Bar Ilan University, Ramat Gan, Israel 5290002. Yuval.feldman@biu.ac.il. Fields of Interest: Behavioural and Empirical Analysis of Regulation, Compliance and Enforcement.

**Yotam Kaplan** Assistant Professor, Bar-Ilan Law Faculty. Bar Ilan University, Ramat Gan, Israel 5290002. yotam.kaplan@biu.ac.il. Fields of Interest: Private Law Theory, Remedies, Economic Analysis of Law, Legal Theory.

# Law and Economics in Russian Law

**Mikhail Antonov**

**Abstract** This paper studies the development of economic analysis of law in Soviet and Russian law, and a number of factors influencing this development. In Soviet law, the influence of economics on law was theoretically conceived in terms of Marxist dialectics of basis and superstructure. When Russia left the USSR in 1991, judges had to evaluate whether application of Soviet legal rules would make sense or whether there were compelling economic reasons to decide cases otherwise. The privatization and other economic reforms of Yeltsin's Government were carried out with the help of rather inconclusive and inefficient legislation. In the 2000s, the economic analysis of law gained momentum in Russian law: an entire branch of the judiciary (commercial or arbitration courts) supported its application. After the Higher Commercial (Arbitrazh) Court was disbanded in 2014, Russian law is becoming formalistic again; references to economic analysis of law are rare both in case law and in legal scholarship. The author explains this development in the prism of the governmental centralization policies which imply that judges shall be guided only by the sovereign (state) will, without attempting to reinterpret or cast doubts on this will from the standpoint of economic rationality or from other standpoints.

## 1 Development in Soviet Law

Taken in a broader sense, "economic analysis of law" (EAL) had its counterparts in Soviet legal scholarship, albeit in forms different from those generally discussed in the West under this title. In "Capital" and in other writings Marx described law as epiphenomenon of economic relations, as one of elements of superstructure residing

M. Antonov (✉)
Higher School of Economics, Saint Petersburg, Russia
e-mail: mantonov@hse.ru

 
K. Mathis, A. Tor (eds.), *Law and Economics of Regulation*, Economic Analysis of Law in European Legal Scholarship 11,
https://doi.org/10.1007/978-3-030-70530-5_4

on the basis of production relations and sourced by production forces.[1] From this perspective, Marxists assumed that legal rules are based on the "objective" structure of society, which, in turn, reflects the economic background of social life. Predetermination of law by economic superstructure of society remained one of the main cornerstones of the Communist theory of law,[2] although, there has been a large diversity of opinions as to forms and modalities of this predetermination.[3] In any case, Soviet legal theory did not admit that judges may act as ultimate decision-makers in legal matters. This role was played by party officials who are empowered to express and implement the will of the ruling class or, in other words, the state.[4] This clearly differentiated Soviet theoreticians and their musing about impact of economics on legal system from the EAL and other post-realist conceptions of law and economics in the West.

In the first years of Soviet rule, the Marxist idea of predetermination of law by economic relations prompted Bolsheviks toward controversial social experiments. To a significant degree, these experiments were focused on interpretations of Marx's prophecy about withering away of the state and its law in the socialist society: in a classless society, law as the superstructure will be redundant as there will be no antagonism between social classes.[5] One of such experiments was carried out by the means of the 1917 First Decree on Courts which invalidated imperial laws and ordered that cases be decided at court pursuant to "revolutionary consciousness".[6] After this first attempt to cancel legal regulation failed, other theoretical and practical attempts to transform law have been undertaken in the 1920s. Some of them sought to replace legal normativity by economical pragmatism. Characteristically, Art.1 of the 1922 RSFSR Civil Code established that "Civil rights are protected by the law except in situations in which these rights are utilized contrary to their social and *economic purpose*" [emphasis author's own]. Different theoretical models were suggested to explain this transition from rulemaking to planning, e.g., the exchange theory of law by Eugeny Pashukanis.[7]

Another important development of Soviet law in this direction was the introduction of plan economy in the late 1920s. Professor Berman wrote:

---

[1]Marx and Engels (2007), p. 26, "Your jurisprudence is but the will of your class made into a law for all, a will whose essential character and direction are determined by the economic conditions of existence of your class."

[2]Kelsen (1955).

[3]See a successful critical comparison of Soviet legal theory with Marx's conception of law: Bodenheimer (1952).

[4]More on this decisionist side of Soviet law: Antonov (2018).

[5]Burbank (1995), Surely, within Marxism-Leninism one could have a rich panoply of different interpretations and approaches, e.g., comparing ideas of the young Marx with his later ideas of the period of Communist Manifesto, or critically juxtaposing ideas of Marx and Lenin, or analyzing the Soviet ideology against the background of Marx's and Lenin's writings (Sundberg 1987).

[6]The Decree "On Court" (22 November 1917) of the Council of People's Commissars of the Russian Soviet Federated Socialist Republic.

[7]Pashukanis (1980).

> Now, for the first time, positive content was given to the Marxist idea of the disappearance of State and Law under socialism. It was thought that Law, an instrument of the class-dominated State, would be replaced by Plan, the manifestation of the will of a class-less society [. . .] The Plan itself would differ from Law, since it would be an instrument neither of compulsion nor of formality but simply an expression of rational foresight on the part of the planners, with the whole people participating and assenting spontaneously. Society would be regulated, administered — much as traffic at an intersection is regulated by traffic lights and by rules of the road; but in a society without class conflict there would be few collisions and to deal with them it would be unnecessary to have a system of 'justice'. Social-economic expediency would be the ultimate criterion; disputes would be resolved on the spot.[8]

Nonetheless, law (both as a regulative system and as a system of thinking) continued to exist in Soviet society as a semi-autonomous field; it successfully resisted attempts to represent it only as a branch of economics or ethics, and gained the upper hand in the 1930s.[9] The new Communist theory of law was based on the approach by Stalin's General Prosecutor, Andrey Vyshinsky, who praised law as expression of political will of the state and of the Party. In this view, there was no place for economic determination in law—the will of political rulers (at that time—Stalin) could not be ideologically represented as programmed by production forces and relations: quite the contrary, it was Stalin who by his wisdom and will (presumably expressed in Soviet laws) changed the society and the economy. With this, legality (in the sense of unavoidable implementation of the state/party will expressed in legal texts) became one of the cornerstones of Soviet legal ideology from the 1930s on.[10] In the late 1930s, the idea that law is determined by economics—described in the Marxist-Leninist social philosophy in terms of basis and superstructure—was pushed on backburners, albeit was not directly rejected.[11] This ambivalent attitude to interconnection between law and economics continued in the following years, until Perestroika: on the one hand, this interconnection was formally recognized in Marxist-Leninist social philosophy, but on the other, it had no tangible support in Soviet legal theory.[12]

## 2 Early Development in Post-Soviet Law

The experience of lawlessness in the USSR saw the general distrust toward Marxist narratives about subjection of law to ideological and philosophical preconceptions in the Soviet population. The use of economic arguments in Soviet law (similar to the 1922 Civil Code cited above) was based on the Marxist basis-superstructure

[8]Berman (1950), pp. 30–31.

[9]Kamenka (1962).

[10]Smith (1982).

[11]Fuller (1949).

[12]Yavich (1985).

teaching and, therefore, also suffered from this general distrust. In the post-Soviet Russia, this distrust was only reinforced in the early 1990s when corrupted officials (including bribed judges) did not shy away from administering justice against the letter of the law, deploring bad quality of the laws and invoking economic reasonableness, efficiency, "laws of economics" and other reasons to justify their discretionary decisions, especially in privatization cases in which the statutory law was not unfrequently overruled.[13]

The underlying problem, along with that of corruption, was that the Russian judiciary in the 1990s was not prepared to alternative styles of legal thinking to the classic logic of subsumption and class will.[14] When the Communist Party ceased to be source of the state will, many judges just switched to other sources that informed them about the state will: such as commands from corrupted officials, *siloviki* (high officers of law-enforcement agencies) or superior judges. Unsurprisingly, the use of economic arguments to overrule the posited law brought dire results in this context and discredited the use of economic arguments in law for a while. For many Russians who lived through the privatization years, narratives about economic argumentation in court decisions are still associated with corruption and arbitrary power.

Another source for this distrust lies in negative connotations of the "shock therapy" (the set of economic reforms advised by the International Monetary Fund to Yeltsin's government) which led to the disastrous drop of Russian economy in the early 1990s. This "therapy" explicitly relied on the Smithian idea of the invisible hand of the market that would itself create necessary regulative mechanisms. The neoliberal idea that reforms should focus on the creation of spontaneous rules from which economic actors would benefit immediately, rather than of procedures and institutions which would be expensive and time-consuming, was devalued by the manner in which the judges acted.[15] The use of this neoliberal ideology was often connected to privatization cases with frauds and corruption when state officials and judges acted against the law pursuant the presumption of economic rationality: it was taken that any redistribution of ownership in favor of private business is useful and justified, no matter what the law said. In other words, everything goes if it supports economic growth. This rationality fitted the reform policy of Yeltsin well, who did not care much for legal frameworks: his Goverment pursued economic reforms first and introduced legal rules, if at all, only afterwards in order to legitimize the factual redistribution of state property among private actors.[16]

---

[13]Goldman (2003).

[14]A renown Russian expert with the long experience in various Western projects concerning the modernization of ex-USSR legal systems, points out at what he calls the "theoretical deformation of the legal framework" Golovko (2011), pp. 105–115, implying that obsolete legal knowledge is being reproduced at law schools in the ex-USSR.

[15]This idea being reflected in some writings of the founding fathers of EAL, e.g., Posner (1998).

[16]See about this strategy: Treisman (1999); "Konflikt zakona…" (1997).

## 3 Actual Development (from 2000 on)

The wind changed after Vladimir Putin decided to subject the market and its actors to the state will. Putin's "Oligarch Policy"—also known as the "Barbeque Agreement"[17]—during his first presidency (2000–2008) intended to subject economic life under state control and to exclude sources of legal normativity other than the state will. This development, to a certain extent, repeated the "Great Retreat" in the Soviet law in the 1930,[18] described above. The "Oligarch Policy" was designed to rein in those whose powers seemed, at times, virtually unchecked during Yeltsin's presidency (1991–1999), to restrict their access to politics, and to reprivatize some strategic Russian industries such as oil, gas, or media which were appropriated by oligarchs against the letter of the law. This development also swiftly banned economic rhetoric from court decisions: the regime of legality signifies that judges are bound by the law and cannot decide cases on other grounds as those contained in the law. Against this formalist background, the outcome of the privatization is usually considered by Russian lawyers as a paragon of illegality.[19]

A large amount of legal regulations was issued by the Russian State in these years, not all of these regulations were/are efficient and rational, and in many instances they were/are harmful. Characteristically, one of the contentious points of actual legal reforms in Russian law is still about so called "regulatory guillotine"—to significantly reduce the number of laws and by-laws in order to make legal regulation more comprehensive.[20] This idea persists in Russian law since the early 2000s. This deplorable quality of governmental regulatory activism in the 2000s motivate Russian lawyers who defended business (especially, in contract and corporate law) to think law in terms of EAL and this way to fight against the excessive formalism. Unsurprisingly (given their Soviet academic background), their thinking followed the old Marxist tradition of studying law as an expression of "objective" economic laws (regularities). EAL represented a good methodological foundation for building up such a defense: it was perfectly compatible with market economy,

---

[17]The agreement and the rule are reported inter alia by Professor Gelman: "In the summer of 2000, at a meeting with the oligarchs, Putin made Big Business an informal offer it couldn't refuse, which subsequently came to be called the 'barbecue agreement.' Essentially, the state would not revisit the question of property rights and would maintain an equal distance from the oligarchs, while Big Business would have to remain loyal to the authorities and not interfere in the most important political decisions. Those few oligarchs who didn't agree with the conditions of this informal agreement soon lost their assets and/or had to leave Russia" Gelman (2011).

[18]The return in the 1930s to the pre-revolutionary governance structure and methods, and to the positivist state-and-law theory in Soviet Russia, Timasheff (1946).

[19]E.g., the Russian authorities explained the famous YUKOS expropriation process by the fact that Khodorkovsky gained his wealth due to illegal decisions of judges and officials in the ways evidently incompatible with the law (ECtHR Judgment Yukos v. Russia (31 July, 2014) *Application No.14902/04;* RF Constitutional Court Ruling (19 January, 2017) No.1-P). The only defense of Khodorkovsky against this argument of legality was to argue that other, Putin-friendly oligarchs also acquired their wealth illegally.

[20]Medvedev (2019).

which stemmed from Anglo-American legal system which proved its economic efficiency; therefore, its introduction to Russian law was expected to stimulate investments and attract foreign capital—these ideas were voiced in 2010 by the Chief Justice of the former RF Higher Commercial (Arbitrazh) Court Anton Ivanov.[21]

In this context, the ideas of Richard Posner and other proponents of EAL quickly gained enormous interest among Russian lawyers in the mid-2000s;[22] leading American EAL authors are still among the most cited foreign legal scholars in Russia.[23] The 2004 Russian translation of Posner's key book gathered the momentum of EAL movement in Russia.[24] A number of important Russian legal scholars and several top judges argued in favor of widening of judicial rule-making power at the expenses of state administrative agencies, referring to EAL as to the most appropriate framework for adding "spontaneous legal order" to Russian law and for overcoming the "narrowness" of legal formalism.[25]

A significant number of Russian judges and other legal practitioners were fascinated with the seeming simplicity and practicality of EAL and of the realist approach behind it. The general perception of EAL in the mid-2000s in Russia connected it with discarding the relevance of legal texts for adjudication and underscoring the role of intuition along with stressing the importance of institutional constraints against political other biases that may predetermine judges' verdicts. To a great degree, this realist picture fits both internal and external points of view on Russian law (in the terms of H.L.A. Hart) and describes Russian legal practices more effectively than the deductivist vision of judicial decision-making as subsumption. Unsurprisingly, this perspective attracts those Russian lawyers who—while pessimistic about any immediate changes in the political governance and legislative policies of the ruling party—seek to improve the quality of judicial decision-making by granting more freedom to judges and enabling them, from time to time, to overrule inefficient regulations.

Following this development of the 2000s, a number of Russian economists and political scientists advocated a broader application of EAL in order to restrain the regulative ambitions of the government and to improve the deficient legal regulation.[26] They tried to cope with the problem stated above: on the one hand,

---

[21]Ivanov (2010).

[22]Oleinik (2014); It is another question whether these ideas were understood and utilized properly, Antonov (2011).

[23]According to the official Russian scientific database *RINZ* (a Russian analogue to Web of Science), Posner was cited in 375 Russian-language books and articles (and 2254 citations in all languages), as compared with, e.g., Ronald Dworkin (440 and 1548 citations, accordingly). See: http://elibrary.ru. Accessed on 30 April 2020.

[24]Posner (2004); This book is still the central reference point for Russian lawyers in matters of law and economics: this explains that the term "EAL" serves as the common denominator for this research, while "Law and Economics" and other coextensive terms are utilized rather rarely.

[25]The most representative work for this tendency is: Karapetov (2016).

[26]See critical analysis by one of the most influential Justices of the RF Supreme Court: Mamotov (2017).

comprehensive legislative regulation is unable to support economic growth, on the other hand, it is not possible to achieve such a growth without a well-established normative framework. This appearing contradiction can, as was hoped by the partisans of EAL in Russia, be solved if judges are allowed to rely on economic reasoning in cases when legislative texts leave gaps and loopholes.[27] In terms of Russian legal doctrine, economic arguments were expected to play the role which in Russian law is usually attributed to legal principles: to fill gaps in the legal regulation or to avoid evident injustice when applying legislative norms. The advantage of the use of EAL were evident to these scholars: economic arguments are less vague, more pragmatic and their application does not necessarily require a highly developed legal culture as it is the case with legal principles.[28]

Trying to strike a reasonable balance between its regulatory ambitions and the principal objective of economic growth, Russian government initially did not oppose further application of EAL at commercial (arbitrazh) courts. A pool of the high judiciary at the former RF Higher Arbitrazh Court under the leadership of Anton Ivanov argued for giving precedential value to decisions of their Court.[29] The respective changes have been brought into Russian law.[30] Unsurprisingly, the ideas inspired by legal realism and precedent law thrived in Russian law in these years, being in complete consonance with judicial activism defended by this part of the Russian judiciary.[31] Disappointed in the legislative power and in legal formalism, Russian lawyers hold high aspirations for EAL. Such way of thinking could not be easily reconciled with the authoritarian political regime in Russia; unsurprisingly, the Higher Arbitrazh Court was disbanded in 2014.[32]

## 4 Theoretical and Practical Problems with Application

The problem of combining of EAL with Russian reading of the principle of legality is that judges shall, first of all, apply posited rules and principles; when such rules or principles are missing or inadequate, judges make political and/or moral choices, introducing *ad hoc* rules. When making such choices, judges and other legal professionals may easily arrive at contradictory conclusions; not because they err but, simply, because they accept different axioms and frame their reasoning in different

[27] Volovik (2013).

[28] Karapetov (2016), pp. 12 et seqq.

[29] Henderson (2015).

[30] These landmark changes were implemented through Federal Law "On the Introduction of Changes to the Arbitration Procedure Code of the Russian Federation" (23 December 2010) No.379-FZ.

[31] Pomeranz and Gutbrod (2012).

[32] But commercial (arbitrazh) courts remained as a separate judicial branch, albeit now under the auspices of the RF Supreme Court.

narratives with regard to final ends, which are conventionally accepted in different systems of ethics. Technically, reference to EAL allows the courts to skip general principles of law and decide cases in the view of such final ends as economic efficiency or reduction of transactional costs.

Interestingly, Russian proponents of EAL sought to represent this theory as an antidote to the notorious nihilism of Russian legal culture. This nihilism is recognized by Russian government[33] and is usually explained by the fundamental problem of Russian legal development: laws do not express the balance of social interests but rather serve as tools of the government to administer and control the society.[34] The absence of a well-functioning civil society and of an efficient system of political representation is cited among the main reason of the detachment of Russian legislature from the social needs and from the interests which normally have to be reconciled at parliaments.[35] This detachment explains, among other reasons, why statutory rule-making usually lag behind economic development so that administrative and legislative regulation rather imposes unnecessary constrains on economic activities than promotes or supports them.[36]

From this perspective, giving more freedom to the judiciary to introduce economic rationality in interpretation and application of law sounded in the 2000s as a good idea to quite some Russian lawyers. In the words of the former Chief Justice Anton Ivanov:

> When considering court cases, judges shall first of all practice economic analysis of law in order to adequately evaluate legal norms and to interpret them correctly. When, in the context of a court dispute, one realizes the economic meaning of private-law norms and investigates the economic nature of business activities, one can verify their [norms] appropriateness as to the established economic relations under the conditions of market economy and, if necessary, *one revises these norms*.[37]

This noble dream was not supported by the real use made of economic methods by Russian judges: only few of them were capable of understanding economic nature of legal disputes, even at commercial (arbitrazh) courts.[38] Being unable to make sense of economic theory for decision-making at courts, Russian lawyers and judges are *de facto* nudged to continue the Soviet strategy of ideological use of economic arguments, relying on the basis-superstructure theory of Marx as a justification for deciding cases against the letter of the law. EAL is understood in Russian jurisprudence not in the perspective of philosophical pragmatism typical for US jurisprudence, but rather in terms of the Marxist-Leninist legal philosophy which stressed

[33] Buckley and Belton (2008).

[34] Kurkchiyan (2009).

[35] Hale (2002).

[36] Dahlke and Tissier (2012).

[37] Ivanov (2013); cited according to Kudriavtseva and Prokudina (2014), p. 32 [emphasis mine].

[38] Unfortunately, no research has been made in Russian law so far on this topic. In the absence of such a research, here I express only my own estimation based on around 20 years of practicing as a barrister at commercial (arbitrazh) courts.

that law is a merely reflection of economic situation (the dialectics of superstructure and basis), so that reference to "objectivity of laws of economy" justifies introduction of exceptions *ad hoc*.[39]

Generally, EAL is based on the presupposition that the identification of meanings of legal norms, inevitably, requires addressing extra-legal contexts and values. From this perspective, economic analysis can help judges to circumvent ineffective legislative norms through revealing their economic sense. As mentioned before, unlike their US counterparts, Russian proponents of EAL do not seek to establish standard of practical reasonableness, preferring to speak about "rationality of law" which, factually, refers to an exoteric knowledge about "ontological meanings of law". With this, EAL turns into the exoteric knowledge unchecked by public opinion or by the legal community.[40] In actual Russian case law, courts reasonably apply economic arguments only in anti-trust cases in which they reassess decisions of the Federal Anti-Monopoly Service: by their very nature, these decisions are based on economic criteria.[41] Anti-trust law remains, in my estimations, the only field in which EAL is effectively applied by Russian commercial courts, while in contract or corporate law results are suboptimal.

Along with this specific intellectual framework, there are other grounds which impeded adequate reception of EAL in Russian law. Despite the noble dream of the former Chief Justice Ivanov,[42] EAL is largely utilized in Russian legal scholarship not as an argumentation tool: historically it was perceived by judges as normative prescriptions imposed from above, from the former Higher Arbitrazh Court from the mid-2000s on.[43] These prescriptions were often unable to produce good results because their vagueness, as well as the inability of many judges to make sense of economic argumentation. "Law", as it is taught at Russian law schools, is only a set of commands from the sovereign. In this perspective, weighting economic consequences of a decision and thinking about the best economic outcome goes far beyond the legal sphere. Because of this, economic arguments can be seen as

---

[39]Gadzhiev (2012).

[40]I have tried to demonstrate the difference in legal reasoning between the US and the Russian traditions of use of EAL on the example of two prominent representatives of EAL, Antonov (2017).

[41]Shastitko (2014).

[42]Ivanov (2013).

[43]Notably, there has been almost no attempts in Russian legal scholarship to apply EAL to the legal issues (such as family law, housing law, criminal law, etc.) falling under the competence of another Russian court: the RF Supreme Court which, before the liquidation of the Higher Arbitrazh Court in 2014, heard all cases except commercial ones. The judiciary of the RF Supreme Court was always hostile to EAL and other Western theories undermining the established positivist doctrine inherited from Soviet law.

justification of arbitrary discretion in cases in which the judge is, for whatever reasons, reluctant to adjudicate the case according to the law.[44] The privatization case law is the typical example of this strategy.[45]

The prevalence of Austinian theory of law in Russian legal education means that the Russian judiciary is not taught to balance interests or to care about social welfare. Moreover, the judiciary does not consider it as its institutional task: according to the centuries-old tradition, the Russian Court System is seen as a mechanism of implementation of the sovereign will, its imposition onto the society.[46] This provides a completely different perspective for transplantation and utilization of EAL into Russian law. It is almost unthinkable, from the perspective of Russian legal theory, to discard statutory law that embodies the sovereign will and to apply an "economic sense" instead: drawing economic arguments to avoid application of a legal rule would contradict to the basic principle of legality (*dura lex sed lex*). If judges discard both formal law and its moral foundation, solving cases in terms of economic rationality, this can open up the way for decisionism, discretion and interests of the wealthier—such is the common point of concern made by Russian scholars against EAL. Therefore, replacing legal norms by economic arguments would normally be seen as a discretion and a challenge to the regime of legality and, indirectly, to the system of political and legal centralization.[47] It is on this positivist platform that adversaries of EAL resist its further incorporation into Russian law.

On the other side, EAL became attractive to many lawyers worldwide because the refutation of formalistic approach which identifies the law with legislative texts. For EAL, law is not about letters and paragraphs, but about human rationality which mandates the rules for reasonable settlement of disputes to the benefit of both litigants and the society. Those few Russian proponents of EAL who adopted this pragmatist perspective, argue that there is nothing wrong with judges who cannot find rational rules in statutory law and therefore turn toward extralegal reasoning, which also includes the reasons based on economic efficiency.[48]

This perspective recognizes the fact that judges sometimes decide against the letter of law: in some situations, a strictly formalistic decision really would make no economic sense. If laws base their legitimacy and, with it, their binding force on their purported reasonability and their implied acceptance by people as primary reasons for action, judges may legitimately enforce the common sense rule (an average social hallmark of reasonability) in spite of the resistance of individuals—and sometimes even in defiance of the "lawmaker's will". This scheme of legitimization may be

[44]Characterizing the judicial rulemaking in Russia, one of the contemporary Russian authors sums up that "the distinction between *judicial* lawmaking and *discretion* is somewhat blurred" Vereshchagin (2007), p. 63.

[45]Glinkina (1994).

[46]Nethercott (2007).

[47]Kashanin (2013).

[48]Shmakov (2011).

successfully justified in common-law systems and, with necessary caveats, in some civil-law systems.[49] But it does not fit the doctrine of state sovereignty to which Russian law largely adheres and which makes the state *legibus solutus* for any decisions in cases which the state deems to be "exceptional".[50]

As shown above, the pragmatism of EAL is hardly acceptable for Russian legal theory for a number of reasons. The main among them is that judges do not have the freedom to discard legislative texts or, at best, this freedom is recognized only in a very limited number of situations of extreme injustice. Against the backdrop of this ideology, the realist tenets of EAL sound as justification of *gouvernement des juges*. The idea of judicial freedom to decide cases basing on any other rationality than that which is mandated by legal texts is, for many civil-law scholars, irreconcilable with the very idea of legality.[51]

On the one hand, this theoretical position can be seen as a sign of Russian backwardness or underdevelopment of Russian culture;[52] on the other, one should appreciate also institutional and practical reasons for this Russian predisposition to legal positivism. Due to a number of historical and political reasons, Russian courts do not effectively prevent influences on judicial decision-making by those who have political and/or economic power, and moreover are generally reluctant to prevent these influences.[53] As a result, both transparence and independence of courts are far from being secured until now. Russia is notorious for political justice in its courts and, at the present moment, also for the relatively high level of corruption in courts.[54] In this context, and given the theoretical background of Russian legal culture, non-critical fusion of economic and legal rationalities into a single discourse can easily lead to offhandedness and discretion in adjudication. In the countries with weak legal culture and institutional framework, — and Russia is one of those countries, — this narrative can eventually foster corruption in courts, instead of curbing it and improving the court system.

## 5 Conclusion

One can ask whether further use of EAL by Russian judges can *de facto* justify their prerogative competences without judges being bridled with what Ronald Dworkin labelled as "integrity of law": coherent principles about justice, fairness and

[49] Kurochkin (2013).

[50] Antonov (2012).

[51] From this perspective, it is explicable why some Russian lawyers consider EAL as extremely pernicious to Russian law. E.g., Kurbatov (2012). The entire discussion in Kurbatov's blog is very representative to two polar attitudes toward EAL among Russian lawyers.

[52] *Wilson* (2008*)*.

[53] Pomeranz (2018).

[54] Popova (2012).

procedural due process, enforced by judges so to make each person's situation fair and just by the same standard.[55] This ethical element is largely absent from Russian publications on EAL. These publications mostly repeat the ontological argument of Marxist-Leninist theory of law about the dialectics of basis and superstructure, about objectivity in legal regulation, as well as the main practical thesis of Soviet legal theory: judges shall abide by the regime of legality but only insofar as it is not detrimental to political and, in our days also, wealthy commercial interests. Normally, Russian works on EAL are based on the postulation of a number of axiomatic "truths", underlying their esoteric economic concept of the law. These "truths" are represented as objective economic laws that govern human reasoning. That is why this new kind of "natural law" (laws dictated by human reason) is exempt from discussions about their final ends and moral justification: many Russian proponents of EAL reject such discussions in the same way one cannot discuss the ends and values of the universal law of gravitation or the regularities of economic cycles.[56]

When Russian scholars describe the economic sense, which, in their understanding, underlies a certain court battle or a type of such battles at Russian courts, this sense is neither the average person's worldly wisdom nor the expert knowledge of economists; rather, it is the insight of supreme judges into the correct ("economically justifiable") meaning of constitutional and statutory rules.[57] In Russian lawyer's experience, if there is a case decided at the court contrary to the letter of the law but with references to EAL, this hints at corruption schemes behind the curtains. There is no doubt that Russian judges can make use of EAL if they go beyond the Austinian legal theory and adopt other theoretical and methodological perspectives. But the question remains whether EAL can serve as an adequate tool for courts before Russian legal scholarship adjusts its methods accordingly.[58]

## References

Antonov M (2011) O nekotorykh teoreticheskikh problemakh primeneniia ekonomicheskogo analiza v Rossii [On some theoretical problems of application of economic analysis of law in Russia]. Pravo. Zhurnal VshE 3:10–25

Antonov M (2012) Theoretical issues of sovereignty in Russia. Rev Cent East Eur Law 37:95–113

Antonov M (2017) Law and economics, judicial pragmatism and their limits on both sides of the Atlantic. Rev Cent East Eur Law 42:73–94

Antonov M (2018) Legal realism in Soviet and Russian jurisprudence. Rev Cent East Eur Law 43:483–518

[55] Dworkin (1986), pp. 165 et seqq.

[56] Karapetov (2014).

[57] Gadzhiev (2017); The entire movement of "Constitutional Economics" is emblematic for this tendency. E.g. Gadzhiev (2010).

[58] This concern was voiced in 2014 by Chief Justice of the RF Constitutional Court, Valerii Zorkin (Zorkin 2014).

Berman HJ (1950) Justice in Russia: an interpretation of Soviet law. Harvard University Press, Cambridge, pp 30–31

Bodenheimer E (1952) Impasse of Soviet legal philosophy. Cornell Law Rev 38(1):51–72

Buckley N, Belton C (2008) Laying down the law: Medvedev vows war on Russia's legal nihilism. Financial Times. https://www.ft.com/content/e46ea1d8-c6c8-11dd-97a5-000077b07658

Burbank J (1995) Lenin and the law in revolutionary Russia. Slavic Rev 54(1):23–44

Dahlke S, Tissier M (2012) The practice of law and justice in Russia (eighteenth-twentieth centuries). Cahiers du monde russe 53(1):7–13

Dworkin R (1986) Law's empire. Harvard University Press, Cambridge

Fuller LL (1949) Pashukanis and Vyshinsky: a study in the development of Marxian legal theory. Mich Law Rev 47(8):1157–1166

Gadzhiev G (2010) Konstitutsionnaia ekonomika [Constitutional economics]. Iustitsinform, Moscow

Gadzhiev G (2012) Ontologiia prava [Ontology of law]. INFRA-M, Moscow

Gadzhiev G (2017) Rossiiskie issledovaniia v oblasti prava i ekonomiki: utochnenie iuridicheskoi kartiny mira [Russian research work in the field of law and economics: a clarification of the legal Weltanschauung]. http://ksrf.ru/ru/News/Documents/report_Гаджиев_2017.pdf

Gelman V (2011) Russia's crony capitalism: the swing of the pendulum. https://www.opendemocracy.net/od-russia/vladimir-gelman/russia%e2%80%99s-crony-capitalism-swing-of-pendulum

Glinkina S (1994) Privatizatsiya and kriminalizatsiya: how organized crime is hijacking privatization. Demokratizatsiya 2:385–391

Goldman M (2003) The piratization of Russia: Russian reform goes awry. Routledge, London

Golovko L (2011) The space for legal reform in Central Asia: between political limits and theoretical deformations. OSCE Yearbook 2010, Nomos, Baden-Baden

Hale HE (2002) Civil society from above? Statist and liberal models of state-building in Russia. Demokratizatsiia 10(3):306–321

Henderson J (2015) Precedent as a source of law in the Russian legal system. King's College London Law School Research Paper No. 2015-41. SSRN: https://ssrn.com/abstract=2661504

Ivanov A (2010) Rech' o pretsedente [A speech on precedent]. Pravo. Zhurnal VshE 2:3–11

Ivanov A (2013) Sud'by sudei [Destinies of judges]. RBK-Daily, 18 May 2013

Kamenka E (1962) The ethical foundations of Marxism. Routledge & Kegan Paul, London

Karapetov AG (2014) Modeli zashchity grazhdanskikh prav: ekonomicheskii vzgliad [Models of protection of civil rights: an economic perspective]. Vestnik ekonomicheskogo pravosudiia 11:24–80

Karapetov AG (2016) Ekonomicheskii analiz prava [Economic analysis of law]. Statut, Moscow

Kashanin A (2013) Neopredelennost' prava i usmotrenie pravoprimenitelia kak ogranichiteli ispol'zovaniia tsentralizovannykh metodov regulirovaniia [Legal indeterminacy and judicial discretion as limitations on the centralized methods of regulation]. Voprosy gosudarstvennogo i munitsipalnogo upravleniia 4:19–36

Kelsen H (1955) The Communist theory of law. Praeger, New York

Konflikt zakona i pravovaia reforma (1997) (iz vystuplenii uchastnikov kruglogo stola v IGP RAN) [The Conflict between the law and legal reforms (from Presentations Made at the Round Table at the Institute of State and Law of the RF Academy of Sciences)]. Gosudarstvo i pravo 12

Kudriavtseva E, Prokudina L (2014) Kak napisat' sudebnoe reshenie [How to write a court decision]. Iurait, Moscow

Kurbatov A (2012) Amerikanizatsiia rossiiskogo prava. Ekonomicheskii analis prava kak sredstvo unichtozheniia ego doktriny [Americanization of Russian law: economic analysis of law as a tool for destruction of the doctrine]. Zakon.ru. https://zakon.ru/blog/2012/02/06/amerikanizaciya_rossijskogo_prava_ekonomicheskij_analiz_prava_kak_sredstvo_unichtozheniya_ego_doktri

Kurkchiyan M (2009) Russian legal culture: an analysis of adaptive response to an institutional transplant. Law Soc Inq 34(2):337–364

Kurochkin S (2013) Ekonomicheskii analiz prava kak perspektivnyi metod poiska reshenii aktual'nykh problem iurisprudentsii (na primere grazhdanskogo sudoproizvodstva) [Economic analysis of law as a perspective method in searching solutions to current problems of jurisprudence (on the Example of Civil Court Process)]. Rossiiskii iuridicheskii zhurnal 2(89):166–175

Mamotov V (2017) Ekonomicheskii analiz prava v sisteme iuridicheskoi metodologii: poniatie, sushchost', kritika [Economic analysis of law in the system of legal methodology: concept, nature and critics]. Vestnik MGU. Pravo 5:83–94

Marx K, Engels F (2007) Manifesto of the Communist Party. International Publishers, New York

Medvedev D (2019) Reguliatornaia gil'otina uluchshit usloviia dlia biznesa s 2020 goda [Regulatory guillotine will improve business conditions from 2020]. Kommersant (21 October 2019). https://www.kommersant.ru/doc/4133241

Nethercott F (2007) Russian legal culture before and after Communism: criminal justice, politics, and the public sphere. Routledge

Oleinik O (2014) Ekonomicheskii analiz prava v rossiiskoi nauke i praktike [Economic analysis of law in Russian scholarship and practice]. Zakon 12:44–53

Pashukanis E (1980) The general theory of law and Marxism. In: Beirne P, Sharlett R (eds) Pashukanis: Selected writings on Marxism and law. Academic Press, New York, pp 40–131

Pomeranz W (2018) Law and the Russian State: Russia's legal evolution from Peter the Great to Vladimir Putin. Bloomsbury, London

Pomeranz W, Gutbrod M (2012) The push for precedent in Russia's judicial system. Rev Cent East Eur Law 37(1):1–30

Popova M (2012) Politicized justice in emerging democracies: a study of courts in Russia and Ukraine. Cambridge University Press, Cambridge

Posner R (1998) Creating a legal framework for economic development. World Bank Res Obs 13 (1):1–11

Posner R (2004) Ekonomicheskii analiz prava [Economic analysis of law]. Ekonomicheskaia shkola, 2 vol., Saint Petersburg

Shastitko A (2014) Empiricheskaia otsenka roli ekonomicheskogo analisa v rossiiskom antitraste [Empirical evaluation of the role of economic analysis of law in Russian anti-trust law]. Vestnik MGU. Ekonomika 2:22–43

Shmakov A (2011) Ekonomicheskii analiz prava [Economic analysis of law]. Infra-M, Moscow

Smith GB (1982) The development of "socialist legality" in the Soviet Union. In: Maggs PB, Smith GB, Ginsburg G (eds) Law and economic development in the Soviet Union. Westview Press, Boulder, pp 77–97

Sundberg JWF (1987) On Marxism as a legal practice. Wash Univ Law Q 65:823–838

Timasheff NS (1946) The great retreat: the growth and decline of Communism in Russia. Dutton Amp Company, New York

Treisman D (1999) After Yeltsin Comes... Yeltsin. Foreign Policy 117:74–86

Vereshchagin A (2007) Judicial law-making in Post-Soviet Russia. Routledge, Abingdon

Volovik O (2013) Ekonomicheskii analiz prava kak sredstvo preodoleniia sudebnogo formalisma [Economic analysis of law as a tool to overcome formalism of judges]. Voprosy ekonomiki i prava 4:35–39

Wilson JC (2008) Russia's cultural aversion to the rule of law. Columbia J East Eur Law 2 (2):195–232

Yavich LS (1985) Sushchnost' prava. Sotsial'no-filosofskoe ponimanie genezisa, razvitiia i funktsionirovaniia iuridicheskoi formy obshchestvennykh ontoshenii [The nature of law: a social-philosophical understanding of genesis, development and function of legal form of social relations]. Izdatel'stvo LGU, Leningrad

Zorkin V (2014) Ekonomika i pravo: novyi kontekst [Law and economics: the new context]. Rossiiskaia gazeta. https://www.eg-online.ru/article/251651/

**Mikhail Antonov** Saint Petersburg. Professor of Legal Theory at Higher School of Economics. 198099 Saint Petersburg, Promyshlennaya ulitsa 17. +7 812 980 00 30. mantonov@hse.ru. Fields of Interest: Comparative Law, History of Legal Ideas, Economic Analysis of Law, Legal Philosophy and Legal Theory.

# Part II
# Specific Applications of Law and Economics of Regulation

# Key Lessons for the Design of Consumer Protection Legislation

**Shmuel I. Becher**

**Abstract** Legislation, even when well-intended, sometimes fails to provide the desired results. By design, the legislative process suffers from "noise" and is typically driven by diverse motives. Inevitably, then, the legislative process generates some mistakes. In spite of these mistakes, the legal discussion of the mechanics of the legislative process is partial and underdeveloped. Focusing on consumer protection legislation, this chapter aims to fill some of this gap. It makes two complementary arguments. Descriptively, the chapter succinctly points to some predominant weaknesses in the legislative process. It illustrates how consumer protection laws may not only fail to achieve their desired results but can also backfire and harm consumers. Normatively and prescriptively, the chapter calls for a nuanced and holistic attitude to consumer protection legislation. It argues for more cautious and tailored consumer protection legislation, which benefits from healthy skepticism. The chapter identifies four principles for improving the process of consumer law-making. First is a more careful approach to legislation, where legislatures progress in a gradual and moderate way. The second proposed principle is to approach the legislative process from a multi-disciplinary, evidence-based, empirical perspective. The third principle suggests adopting a humble decision-making process, which employs temporary consumer protection laws. Finally, the fourth principle offers diffusing and delegating some, or perhaps more, legislative and policy responsibility to administrative agencies and consumer organisations. The chapter draws on consumer protection examples from Europe, North America, Australia, New Zealand and Israel. However, it is largely general in nature. If proven successful, the proposed design principles may be scaled up and implemented in additional jurisdictions and other domains.

S. I. Becher (✉)
School of Accounting and Commercial Law, Victoria University of Wellington, Wellington, New Zealand
e-mail: Samuel.becher@vuw.ac.nz

 
K. Mathis, A. Tor (eds.), *Law and Economics of Regulation*, Economic Analysis of Law in European Legal Scholarship 11,
https://doi.org/10.1007/978-3-030-70530-5_5

# 1 Introduction

Legislation, even when well-intended, sometimes fails to provide the desired results. The legislative process suffers from "noise" and is not an exact science. By design, it is typically influenced by various players and driven by diverse motives. Inevitably, then, the legislative process generates some mistakes.

In spite of these detrimental mistakes, the legal discussion of the mechanics of the legislative process is partial and underdeveloped. The legal literature does not sufficiently address means to improve the design issues that often lead to legislative mistakes. Focusing on consumer protection legislation, this chapter aims to fill some of this gap.

This chapter makes two complementary arguments. First, it shows how the process of legislating consumer protection laws is flawed and sometimes produces troublesome outcomes. Descriptively, Part 2 succinctly points to some predominant weaknesses in the legislative process. Thereafter, Part 3 illustrates how consumer protection laws may not only fail to achieve their desired results but can also backfire and harm consumers. This is dubbed the problem of unintended consequences.

Next, the chapter makes its second argument, calling for a nuanced and holistic attitude to consumer protection legislation. Normatively and prescriptively, this chapter argues for more cautious and tailored consumer protection legislation, which benefits from healthy skepticism. In particular, Part 4 identifies four principles for improving the process of consumer law-making. First, it suggests a more careful approach to legislation, where legislatures progress in a gradual and moderate way. Second, it recommends approaching the legislative process from a multi-disciplinary, evidence-based, empirical perspective. Third, it suggests adopting a humble decision-making process, which employs temporary consumer protection laws. Fourth, it recommends diffusing and delegating some, or perhaps more, legislative and policy responsibility to administrative agencies and consumer organisations.

This chapter draws on consumer protection related examples from Europe, North America, Australia, New Zealand and Israel. However, it is largely general in nature. If proven successful, the proposed approach may be scaled up and implemented in other domains and additional jurisdictions.

# 2 Consumer Protection Legislation

Various reasons can lead to sub-optimal consumer protection legislation. To begin, consumer protection legislation tackles numerous markets, failures and complex challenges. Policymakers and legislatures cannot be expected to possess the expertise required for tackling all these challenges efficiently.[1] Simply put, it is unrealistic

[1] Hayek (1945).

to assume that legislatures will have the relevant knowledge required to make optimal decisions.[2] Thus, institutional limitations and lack of expertise render the legislative process prone to mistakes.[3]

The body of knowledge that humans possess is enormous and dynamic. Products, services, ideas and markets are developing at a pace we have never experienced before. Our understanding of consumers and their interests is also changing. We now better understand that consumers are heterogeneous and have different preferences and responses—which makes consumer protection policy even more challenging.[4]

No doubt, it is hard for legislation to track all these developments and respond timely to economic, scientific and technological developments. Oftentimes, these developments were unforeseen at the time the policy or legislation was formulated.[5] Indeed, legislatures will typically be too slow-moving and too rigid in their procedures,[6] and firms will outsmart legislative efforts.[7] Furthermore, policymakers may discard good ideas if such ideas are likely to be perceived as "extreme."[8]

At the same time, legislatures—like other decisionmakers—tend to be overly confident.[9] They are likely to be swayed by cognitive biases.[10] Among other things, they do not always admit complexity and are likely to overestimate their knowledge and capacity to make good choices.

Additionally, the legislative process is often influenced by interest groups, lobbying, and short-term political considerations. In this regard, public choice (PC) theory provides an appealing lens through which to take account of these influences. This is especially true in the context of consumer protection legislation.

According to the PC framework, the legislative process can be viewed through a market lens. Legislation is mainly determined by demand patterns,[11] which are assumed to be dominated by interest groups who may form coalitions.[12] In our context, traders and firms can often cooperate and create well-organised and powerful interest groups.[13] Business organisations represent strong and usually affluent interest groups, which can tentatively coordinate and achieve a great deal of influence on legislatures.[14]

---

[2]Schuck (2014).

[3]Baxter (1994), p. 128.

[4]Cf. Ben-Shahar and Bar Gill (2013), p. 114.

[5]Becher (2008), p. 759; Romano (2014), p. 27.

[6]See generally Calabresi (1982).

[7]Willis (2015), p. 1327.

[8]Bregman (2014).

[9]Chabris and Simons (2010).

[10]Schuck (2014), pp. 154–160.

[11]Eskridge et al. (2007) and Stancil (2008).

[12]Stancil (2008), p. 1277.

[13]Eskridge et al. (2007), pp. 48–53.

[14]Eskridge et al. (2007), pp. 50–51.

Consumers, however, might suffer from "collective action" and the classic free-rider problem.[15] They will find it complicated and time-consuming to coordinate their moves. Consumers, as individuals, are diffused and insufficiently incentivised to influence legislation.[16] They might as well have heterogeneous and conflicting interests.[17] This undermines consumers' ability to pressure legislatures.[18] Finally, consumers might not have adequate resources for effective participation in the legislative process.[19] Thus, consumers will not be properly represented in the legislative process and will find it difficult to counter the pressure that well-organised industry groups generate.[20]

With respect to the supply side of this market, PC theory predicts that legislatures will be motivated by their desire to be (re)elected.[21] Given this structure, PC theory posits that legislatures are prone to enact statutes that concentrate benefits on specific interest groups.[22] At the same time, the costs associated with these statutes are likely to be distributed amongst the general public.[23]

Legislative initiatives aimed at empowering consumers are likely to reduce businesses' superiority over consumers. Businesses, thus, are likely to encounter such initiatives. At the same time, those policies that distribute benefits broadly on consumers are unlikely to be properly supported and advanced by interest groups.[24] Therefore, PC theory predicts that legislatures will supply too few consumer protection statutes that are publicly-inclined.[25]

As an illustration, consider the initiative to implement user-friendly front-of-package food health labelling. Such initiatives call for simplified and intuitive labelling schemes. Typically, the schemes employ colour-coded labels that provide consumers with a quick and easy way to assess the overall healthiness of foods. Examples include the UK traffic lights and the French Nutri-Score.

These, and other similar initiatives, have the potential to better consumers' food choices and thus, improve their health. Yet they have been failing miserably on the legislative front. As Goyens points out:

> [. . .] compulsory front-of-pack nutrition labelling with colour coding was discussed in the context of the adoption of the Food Information to Consumers Regulation, but was eventually dropped due to heavy industry lobbying. Despite consumer praise for the clarity and usefulness of colour-coded schemes, industry has long fiercely opposed having a red mark

---

[15] O'Connor (2001), p. 370; Gillette (2005), p. 1008.

[16] Gillette (2005), p. 1007, n. 122; Gillette (1996), p. 196.

[17] Letsou (1995).

[18] Kripke (1982), p. 583.

[19] Baxter (1994), p. 125; Boss (1994), p. 94; Rubin (1993), p. 761.

[20] Rubin (1993), p. 787.

[21] Eskridge et al. (2007), p. 57.

[22] Eskridge et al. (2007), p. 57.

[23] Eskridge et al. (2007), p. 58.

[24] Eskridge et al. (2007), p. 59.

[25] Eskridge et al. (2007), p. 59.

on their products (due to the behavioural connotations connected with red as a symbol for danger).[26]

One may argue that consumers can nevertheless be well-represented by consumer organisations. Indeed, some consumer agencies and organisations successfully represent, advocate, and support consumers' interests. Nonetheless, consumer organisations are frequently less active and less effective when it comes to influencing consumer protection legislation. First, ex-ante legislation is often a way to prevent problems or minimise them. However, people often undervalue ex-ante prevention and overvalue ex-post treatment and intervention.[27] Prevention is future-oriented, does not have a clear and immediate manifestation, and is therefore an unappreciated job. Second, consumer organisations will typically have highly limited resources and are likely to find it too challenging to compete against traders.[28] While industries can attract many of the brightest and sharpest minds with generous payments, high status and lavish working conditions, consumer organisations may find it harder to attract such minds.[29]

## 3 The Problem of Unintended Consequences

Consumer protection legislation is sometimes not only biased or ineffective but may also prove quite harmful. For starters, protective legislation may inflict greater costs on consumers than benefits.[30] Ex-ante regulatory protection often entails additional expenses to traders, who then pass these costs on to consumers.[31]

The problem of rolling costs on to consumers is a well-known concern. But there are other, more nuanced and less obvious, concerns that stem from the ways firms and consumers respond to legislation. Simply put, legal interventions—even well-intended—sometimes do not turn out as planned. A few examples of unintended consequences resulting from consumer protection legislation are briefly discussed next.

### *3.1 Lending, Credit Regulation, and Price Caps*

Perhaps one of the most classic, yet debated, examples of unintended consequences is interest rate caps. At first sight, rate caps are a sensible response to unscrupulous

[26]Goyens (2018), p. 16.
[27]Sullivan et al. (2010).
[28]Braucher (1988), p. 403; Silber (1997), p. 235.
[29]Schuck (2014), p. 204
[30]Letsou (1995), p. 620.
[31]Ben-Shahar and Bar Gill (2013), p. 110.

traders who take advantage of vulnerable consumers by charging them excessive interest rates. Interest rates are often part of a manipulative, well-crafted scheme that capitalises on consumers' bounded rationality.[32] Excessive interest rates may offend our sense of fairness.

However, capping interest rates may not be the optimal solution as doing so can make credit less available to borrowers. From an economic perspective, interest rates reflect risk. Poor consumers are risky borrowers, which is mirrored in their interest rates. According to this line of reasoning, by limiting interest rates, legislatures can trigger a market response that will actually drive poor consumers out of the market by limiting their access to safe credit.[33]

Another problem with price caps may arise when firms operate in multi-dimensional markets.[34] Legislatures often focus on specific, salient problems. Policymakers are drawn to visible initiatives, especially those intended to solve pressing problems that receive public attention.[35] At the same time, unobserved yet rather important initiatives are under-produced.[36]

For instance, annual fees charged by banks are often a relatively salient attribute, so legislatures may seek to impose price caps to reduce these fees.[37] However, addressing complex problems in isolation may yield misguided inferences. In this context, banks have a strong profit incentive to offset the loss in revenues, preferably by increasing other, non-salient fees.[38] Thus, banks may respond to annual fee caps by increasing revenues from other dimensions, such as currency conversion fees and rates. Legislatures often fail to effectively address these unintended consequences.

## 3.2 *Information Disclosures*

The previous example discussed some unintended consequences with respect to the regulation of financial markets. Throughout the analysis, it focused on *traders'* behaviour. However, policymakers may find it hard to tailor legal interventions to *consumers'* behaviour as well.

Consider, for instance, information disclosures. Consumers are assumed to base their decisions on available information. Mandated disclosures can inform consumers and contribute to an efficient market equilibrium. Put simply, information disclosures are assumed to help consumers by bridging informational gaps.

[32] Bar-Gill (2012) and Becher et al. (2021).

[33] Pinheiro and Ronen (2016), pp. 95–96.

[34] Bar-Gill (2015).

[35] Romano (2014), p. 27.

[36] Romano (2014), pp. 27–28.

[37] Bar-Gill (2015), pp. 469–470..

[38] Bar-Gill (2015), pp. 469–470..

Following this logic, legislatures in many countries have been continuously content to propose and enact consumer protection mandated disclosures.

However, mandating information disclosures is a contested strategy. First, it is doubtful that legislative bodies can tailor disclosure duties to consumers' individual capabilities and true needs. Often, information disclosures are misaligned with the way consumers absorb and analyse information.[39] This makes such disclosures unlikely to be read. Moreover, mandating too many disclosures may cause information overload.[40] Where consumers face large amounts of information, they are unlikely to make good use of it. For these and other reasons, many academics question the wisdom of imposing information disclosure duties.[41]

To use a specific example, let us return to food labelling. Some consumers do read such labels, but many others find them hard to read.[42] Of those consumers who read food labels, many do not understand the information revealed and do not know how to make use of it. Furthermore, the information is not usually presented in an intuitive and user-friendly way.[43] On top of that, the information is typically presented to consumers when they are in a hurry and beset by other tasks or decisions.

Aside from being costly and perhaps inefficient, food labelling may have another unintended consequence. Retailers realise that packaging is a potential source of information for consumers. Thus, they often transform packaging into another source of enticing marketing—one that attracts consumers' limited attention.[44] This may worsen the problems associated with information disclosure. More generally, it reflects firms' ability and incentive to meet the formal legal requirements, rather than its spirit.[45]

In addition, legislatures may find it hard to predict consumers' responses to disclosed information due to other contextual reasons. For instance, consumers' belief as to the legislature's motivation may play a crucial role in the former's behaviour.[46] With disclosures regarding genetically modified food (GMOs), consumers may attribute various motivations to legislatures, such as public health or an ideological belief in consumers' right to know.[47] The perceived motivation,

---

39 Becher (2007), pp. 167–177; Davis and Davis (1996), p. 279.

40 Ben-Shahar and Schneider (2014), pp. 105–106.

41 Hillman (2006), pp. 849–850.

42 Black and Rayner (1992), pp. 3–9; Jones and Richardson (2007); Grunert et al. (2010); Prepared Foods (2016), https://www.preparedfoods.com/articles/118201-do-consumers-read-the-nutrition-facts-label [accessed 5 March 2020]; Hennessy (2014), https://www.foodnavigator-usa.com/Article/2014/03/03/How-much-do-consumers-use-and-understand-nutrition-labels. Accessed 5 March 2020.

43 Jones and Richardson (2007), p. 238.

44 Jones and Richardson (2007), p. 243.

45 Cf. Willis (2015), p. 1327.

46 Bar-Gill et al. (2019).

47 Bar-Gill et al. (2019), p. 213.

however, plays a crucial role in the way consumers *respond* to said disclosures.[48] As the authors of a recent study explain:

> Consumers who misperceive the regulator's true motive, or mix of motives, will draw false inferences from the mandated disclosure. If consumers think that the disclosure is motivated by evidence of harm, when in fact it is motivated by a belief in a right-to-know or by interest-group pressure, then they will be inefficiently deterred from purchasing the product.[49]

Research also suggests that trying to warn consumers via disclosures can, in fact, increase the very kind of behaviours they attempt to prevent. Thus, warning labels can increase drinking and driving,[50] intensify the craving to smoke and inhale more deeply,[51] or enhance the desire to eat unhealthy food.[52] Such backfiring effects may be explained using Brehm's theory of psychological reactance.[53] According to this theory, threatening consumers' choice may lead consumers to become more attracted to the threatened attitude or behaviour.[54]

Moreover, disclosures can also backfire by silencing consumers and impacting their "moral calculus of transactional harm".[55] Experimental research suggests that while disclosures may not influence consumers' behaviour ex-ante, it may nevertheless make consumers less likely to challenge harsh policies.[56] Put simply, disclosures may lead consumers to view the relevant policies and practices as more legitimate and binding than they are. In consumers' minds, disclosures shift more of the responsibility and blame to themselves.

## 3.3 *Unhealthy Foods and Addictive Substances*

The discussion of food and GMO labelling leads us next to consider the unintended consequences of regulating unhealthy foods and addictive substances more generally. One major problem with regulating unhealthy products relates to firms' incentives. If a product is banned, or otherwise regulated, firms may come up with new products to substitute the old.

In a way, this is happening now with the regulation of tobacco products. The U.S. Food and Drug Administration (FDA) initiated a plan that comprehensively regulates tobacco and nicotine products.[57] In response, firms started selling synthetic

---

[48] Bar-Gill et al. (2019), p. 220.

[49] Bar-Gill et al. (2019), p. 209.

[50] Ringold (2002), pp. 51–52.

[51] Lindstrom (2008) and Siegel (2011).

[52] Bushman (1998), pp. 99–100.

[53] Brehm (1966).

[54] Clee and Wicklund (1980), p. 389.

[55] Wilkinson-Ryan (2014).

[56] Wilkinson-Ryan (2017).

[57] Zettler et al. (2018), pp. 1947–1951.

nicotine, which "currently fall[s] into a regulatory gap."[58] This is so because synthetic nicotine products are not considered a "tobacco product" under the relevant legislation.[59] This, of course, severely undermines the FDA's initiative to combat tobacco products.

Interestingly, the FDA recently launched an anti-vaping campaign titled "The Real Cost".[60] One problem with this campaign was its dilution in a sea of pro-vaping messages. A study that examined pro- and anti-vaping posts on Instagram found that promotional vaping posts outnumbered the anti-vaping ones in a 10,000 to 1 ratio.[61] Additionally, the study found that contrary to the FDA's intentions, vaping posts received almost three times more "likes" after the campaign started.[62] The study also found that the number of vaping posts that had more than 100 likes grew six-fold.[63] Study participants suggested that while the anti-vaping campaign promoted scare tactics, offering guidance on how to quit vaping would be more effective.[64]

Of course, firms have the incentive to identify loopholes in any regulatory regime that governs their business. Another interesting example that relates to our context is the Health Star Rating (HSR) system, adopted in Australia and New Zealand. The system allows food producers to display a star rating—on a 1 to 5 scale—on their food packaging. Roughly speaking, the HSR is calculated by factoring both healthy and unhealthy ingredients.[65]

Breakfast cereals, for instance, generally contain large quantities of sugar. As such, they could not display an attractive HSR rating. In order to overcome this problem, cereal producers added fiber—a "good" ingredient—to offset the large quantities of sugar in their products.[66] Producers were also able to display a high HSR rating by calculating the healthiness of products on an "as prepared" basis. This allowed a firm to present chocolate milk powder as a healthy product under the assumption that its consumers would mix the powder with skim milk.[67] Overall, unbeknownst to consumers, this may increase consumption of unhealthy foods.

A tax increase on beer further illustrates the importance of considering the response of both firms and consumers to legislation. From an economic perspective, increasing the price of beer is likely to reduce its demand and consumption. This is especially true for consumers who are price-sensitive—frequently, teenagers. However, research has shown that while taxing beer indeed reduced consumption by

---

58 Zettler et al. (2018), p. 1935.

59 Federal Food, Drug, and Cosmetic Act, 21 U.S.C. § 321 (2012) (defining a tobacco product).

60 Food and Drug Administration (2020).

61 Vassey et al. (2020).

62 Vassey et al. (2020).

63 Vassey et al. (2020).

64 Vassey et al. (2020).

65 Health Star Rating (2020).

66 Becher et al. (2021, 2019).

67 Becher et al. (2021, 2019).

teenagers, these consumers then moved on to consume more cannabis.[68] Generally speaking, reducing the demand for one unhealthy product may increase demand for another.

Lastly, regulation that is effective in reducing the consumption of an unhealthy food or substance can simultaneously trigger other health-related problems. For example, reducing the consumption of cigarettes may increase obesity rates.[69] Crafting a sensible policy must consider and weigh such effects.

## 3.4 *Small Claims Courts*

Consumers face various problems which may limit their access to justice.[70] They are often unaware of their rights, may not notice the harm they suffer,[71] and may lack the necessary motivation or resources to complain and insist on their rights.[72] Consumers may likewise be intimidated by legal procedures, let alone fighting large and powerful corporations in court.[73] Some consumers may not trust the legal system, and others may experience language and cultural barriers. These and other reasons led many legal systems to introduce small claims courts (or tribunals).

Small claims courts are an important component of the consumer protection landscape. Usually, these courts are less formal and more procedurally flexible. Such courts also allow consumers to bring their cases without paying hefty fees. Moreover, in many small claims courts, representation is not allowed. In short, these courts are believed to be quicker, cheaper, more level, and more convenient for consumers as laypeople.[74]

Firms apparently do not like the idea of appearing in courts without proper legal representation. As it turns out, in some cases, businesses try to outsmart the system, looking for creative solutions. A prominent approach taken by firms is to employ "semi-professionals", such as law students and legal interns, as their legal representatives.[75] In some countries, this seems to be the prevalent norm.[76]

In an empirical study, we examined the legal outcomes of this practice in relation to litigation over car accident damages.[77] One sample of cases included individual plaintiffs who sued other individuals. According to the rules that govern small claims

[68]DiNardo and Lemieux (2001), p. 994.

[69]Tokely (2014), p. 30, n. 135.

[70]Palmer (2014), pp. 496–499.

[71]Felstiner et al. (1980–81).

[72]Ramsay (1981).

[73]Galanter (1974), p. 103.

[74]Conley and O'Barr (1990), pp. 26–27.

[75]Becher and Klein (2010), p. 349.

[76]Becher and Klein (2010), p. 349.

[77]Becher and Klein (2010), pp. 354–366.

disputes, both plaintiffs and defendants were unrepresented. The other sample included cases where individual plaintiffs sued insurance companies, which were represented by said "semi-professionals." All cases were of the same type and nature—minor damages to cars involved in collisions.

Unexpectedly, individual plaintiffs were *more successful* when suing represented insurance companies than when suing other individuals.[78] Limiting firms' ability to be legally represented in small claims courts is perceived to be a move that protects consumers and levels the litigation field. However, such a protective measure can actually lower consumers' likelihood to win legal cases.

Other, apparently well-intended, moves in the context of small claims courts may backfire as well. In Ontario, Canada, the legislatures attempted to increase consumers' access to justice by raising the maximum amount allowed in small claims lawsuits.[79] Unfortunately, this resulted in crowding out smaller disputes, which seemingly need small claims courts as a litigating platform most of all.[80]

## *3.5 Cooling-off Periods & the Right to Exit*

Consumer protection laws also provide consumers with autonomous remedies. An important measure frequently employed by legislatures is cooling-off periods. Such periods enable consumers to cancel or exit transactions, after the fact, at no (or nominal) cost. Some regimes, such as New Zealand and the United States, allow "open doors" in rather specific and sometimes narrow circumstances.[81] Other jurisdictions, such as Israel and the EU, grant consumers more general cooling-off periods.[82]

Providing consumers with cooling-off periods and the right to exit may seem like a sensible approach. Cooling-off periods present consumers with more time to reflect on the transaction they have entered.[83] This extra time also allows examination of other, competing options. A cooling-off period may grant consumers the opportunity to experience the good or service, thereby learning more about it.[84] Consumers can thus be sure that the transaction at stake is in line with their preferences.

---

[78] Becher and Klein (2010), p. 359.

[79] Niblett and Yoon (2017), p. 6.

[80] Niblett and Yoon (2017), pp. 34–35.

[81] 15 U.S.C. § 1635 (2012); Truth in Lending Act, 15 U.S.C. §§ 1601–1667 (2012); 16 C.F.R. § 429.1 (2018); Fair Trading Act 1986 pt 4A s 36M (NZ).

[82] Becher and Zarsky (2010), pp. 129–150; Borges and Irlenbusch (2007), pp. 85–86.

[83] Ben-Shahar and Posner (2011), pp. 141–144.

[84] Becher and Zarsky (2011).

In addition, where consumers are allowed to exit, sellers have a stronger incentive to provide goods of reasonable quality. Knowing that consumers can cancel the transaction at will, firms are more likely to satisfy consumers' expectations. These rights are also beneficial in terms of consumer choice and competition, since cooling-off periods reduce switching costs. Finally, the very option to cancel a transaction, that is—knowing that one's actions and decisions are reversible, may be psychologically reassuring.

Nevertheless, despite these potential advantages, open doors are often more of a trap than protection. Only a few consumers exercise their cooling-off period rights.[85] Yet, consumers are likely to overestimate and overvalue open doors.[86] In short, consumers over-rely on cooling-off periods, while overlooking their limitations and costs.[87]

Moreover, consumers fail to predict the likelihood that they will want to exploit open doors owing to cognitive biases.[88] After purchasing a good, consumers are prone to overvalue the goods they possess due to the endowment effect and the sunk cost effect. These effects prevent consumers from deviating from previous lines of action. Thus, they diminish consumers' tendencies to cancel or exit transactions.

On top of that, consumers who can reverse their decisions are more preoccupied with them. These consumers are more likely to contemplate possible alternatives and be indecisive with respect to their purchases.[89] Thus, consumers who are granted open doors may experience less contentment and more anxiety over their purchasing decisions.

Lastly, in markets with no mandatory right to exit, sellers can grant consumers cooling-off periods to signal quality and reliability. But if open doors are mandatory and imposed across the board, they stop serving as a positive signal. This further undermines consumers' ability to choose wisely among the various products that are being offered in the market. Unfortunately, policymakers overlook the ways open doors undermine, rather than enhance, consumers' welfare.

## 4 An Alternative Model of Legislation

In an attempt to level the playing field, legislatures often introduce well-intended means. But regulating consumer markets is a thorny and complex task. Prominent consumer protection measures—from credit regulation to information disclosures, food labelling, or the mechanics of small claims courts—can backfire and yield unintended negative consequences.

[85]Sovern (2014).

[86]Becher and Zarsky (2011), p. 80.

[87]Becher and Zarsky (2011), p. 80.

[88]Becher and Zarsky (2011), p. 80.

[89]Becher and Zarsky (2011), p. 82.

This Part proposes a roadmap for better consumer protection legislation, focusing on four main ideas. The first suggests that regulation should be gradual and moderate. The second recommends engaging in an interdisciplinary cost-benefit analysis, based on empirical evidence and data. The third explores the idea of temporary consumer protection laws. The fourth recommends that administrative agencies and consumer organisations assume a greater role in consumer protection policy and legislation.

## 4.1 *Gradual and Moderate Legislative Steps*

Revolutions have always sparked human imagination and attention. Our mind is attracted to the unique and the exceptional. Conspicuous occurrences are salient and receive disproportionate attention.

This can impact legislatures in three different ways. First, it may entice legislatures to focus on vivid and remarkable events or problems. This may happen even if such events and problems do not objectively justify the correlating investment of public resources. Second, it can push or incentivise policymakers into proposing grand schemes and "magic bullets" that could appear elegant and clever, and attract public and media attention. Third, it may encourage legislatures to adopt and implement initiatives before sufficient evidence about the initiatives has been gathered.

Big bangs and overnight solutions are rare. Implementing seemingly bright ideas in the messy, real-world is rarely as easy as it may initially seem. Instead of overnight solutions, much may be said in favour of doing things gradually.[90]

Indeed, significant progress in history has been made incrementally.[91] For a major change, innumerable minute steps are usually required.[92] Progress gradually (*festina lente*) is wise advice, relevant to long-term saving, slimming, meeting sporting challenges, writing projects, and many other spheres.[93]

While some commentators urge judges to adopt an incremental approach, relatively little has been said in favour of incrementalism in legislation.[94] Interestingly, however, a gradual approach to legislation has been adopted by the Finnish government.[95] Its legislative design is to enact new laws in stages, meanwhile considering feedback. The idea is to start "small" and "simple"; thereafter, progressing gradually as feedback, data and experiences are gathered.

---

[90]Hocking (2011).

[91]This is true in math, art, physics, human rights, and many other disciplines. It is also reflected in the idea of "standing on the shoulders of giants."

[92]Hirshman (2012).

[93]Cf. Kay (2011), pp. 187–195.

[94]Levmore (2010), pp. 816–817.

[95]See Trufelman (2017).

Consider, for instance, the Finnish approach to the idea of Universal Basic Income. Here, it has been observed that:

> The experiment itself is fascinating, not just because of *what* Finland is testing but also *how* they are testing it. Finland is trying out a unique, design-oriented way of thinking about government. Rather than rolling out laws on a massive scale, they are trying to craft legislation in stages, with user feedback, just as one would create a piece of design.[96]

To facilitate reaching that end, the Finnish government established an "experimentation unit," which proposes "prototypes of laws."[97] Before applying these more broadly, the legislature seeks to empirically assess the effectiveness of said prototypes.[98] Thus, the Finnish government decided that it should not begin by revolutionising the welfare system.[99] Rather, it started by implementing the idea of Universal Basic Income with a random sample of people.[100]

Academics have acknowledged the value of such experiments and trials.[101] In our context, adopting an incremental approach allows policymakers to focus their attention more effectively. Approaching an issue incrementally reduces the amount and variety of information that needs to be considered. This enhances the prospects of analysing the issue at hand in a more manageable way.

Moreover, many of the problems associated with unintended consequences can be mitigated by an incremental approach to legislation. For instance, legislatures can examine the effects of information disclosures in stages, looking first into the ways consumers and retailers respond to them in a specific market. Only after empirical data and feedback have been gathered should legislatures move on to consider disclosures more generally. The same can be said for enacting cooling-off periods gradually. Overall, such an approach minimises the loss that failures entail, and may generally make the use and implementation of empirical and scientific data more credible.[102]

## 4.2 *Interdisciplinary, Empirical Approach*

The idea of empirically examining the effects of legislation brings us to our next proposal: incorporating an interdisciplinary, empirical approach to regulation. By using the term "interdisciplinary", we imply engaging people with diverse

96 See Trufelman (2017); see also Klein (2016), p. 8.

97 See Trufelman (2017).

98 Trufelman (2017).

99 Trufelman (2017).

100 At the first stage the legislature attempts to examine how Basic Income affects those who receive it. See Trufelman (2017).

101 Abramowicz et al. (2011), p. 1005; Romano (2014), p. 28.

102 Dubner (2016).

backgrounds, expertise, and interests. Involving people with different expertise and backgrounds can help meet the need to respond to a constantly changing world.

For example, in regulating the consumption of unhealthy foods, a prudent policy approach might require insights from economists, tax experts, behavioural specialists, nutritionists, health practitioners, historians, food engineers, educators and lawyers. At the same time, policymakers may wish to consider various distinct voices, including groups such as consumers or consumer organisations, producers, importers, traders, and marketers.

Addressing consumer law issues from an interdisciplinary perspective may assist in mitigating some of the hurdles identified above.[103] First, by engaging people from a range of disciplines and viewpoints, one minimises the likelihood of examining things in isolation. This, in turn, reduces the risk of experiencing unintended consequences. Second, there is a significant body of knowledge that deals with consumer law from various perspectives. An interdisciplinary approach that employs this knowledge decreases the problems associated with lack of institutional expertise. It supplements the legislature and aids its efforts. Third, an interdisciplinary discourse allows more arguments to be balanced and considered, thereby lessening the potential effect of interest groups and lobbyists.

Regulation should also strive to be evidence-based, making good use of empirical data and findings. It is tempting and relatively easy to use intuition and common sense. It is also rather enticing to listen to the views of the public or media. But empirical data can correct for individual and public biases, and incorrect assumptions.

Evidence-based decision-making is a vast topic in various disciplines, such as management[104] and medicine.[105] Similarly, evidence should inform policy.[106] Within an evidence-based framework, legislatures are advised to integrate critical thinking and evidence-based information into the legislative process. This can help regulators to think clearly and comprehensively about the challenge they wish to tackle. Next are a few illustrations of how empirical data can impact consumer law policy.

Considering the potential role of empirical findings in relation to GMOs, empirical data can enrich the discussion in at least three ways. First, it can shed light on whether GMOs are dangerous; and if they are, to what degree. Contrary to common beliefs, scientific evidence does not indicate that GMOs are unhealthy.[107] If legislators ban or discourage the consumption of GMOs due to inaccurate information provided by interested parties, scientific findings may be imperative.

Second, empirical evidence may also shed further light on the possible consequences of not banning or discouraging the consumption of GMOs. For instance,

[103]See discussion supra Part II.

[104]CEBMa (2018).

[105]CEBM (2018).

[106]Lunn and Frances (2013).

[107]World Health Organization (2014).

markets that lack GMOs may be more expensive and offer consumers less choice. Alternatively, banning GMOs may result in an overuse of land, an environmental aspect worth considering.

Third, empirical evidence may help policymakers understand how consumers interpret and respond to GMO labelling. Remarkably, one such study found that consumers do not regard GMO labels as warnings.[108] As noted, another study found that consumers' understanding may depend on what is perceived to be the legislature's intent.[109] Assuming that policymakers aspire to use GMO labelling to warn consumers, these findings may be invaluable.

Experimental data can also assist regulators in identifying counterintuitive outcomes of seemingly straightforward protective measures. The idea of disclosing actual use patterns provides a specific illustration. Many consumers find mail-in rebates attractive. Yet, most consumers overestimate the probability that they will redeem these rebates, while not utilising them in practice. Thus, it has been suggested that traders should be required to disclose actual redemption rates. The assumption behind this requirement is that equipped with the correct information of low redemption rates, consumers will make smarter decisions.[110]

A controlled experiment in the U.S. sought to examine this hypothesis.[111] Surprisingly, the authors found that such disclosures had a backfiring, reverse effect. That is, rather than reducing consumers' willingness to purchase products that offer a rebate, these disclosures made such products more attractive to consumers. The culprit, again, is a behavioural bias in the form of overoptimism. The authors opine that while the disclosures inform people about the behaviour and the failure of the average consumer, the majority of people erroneously believe they will perform better than average.[112]

Moving from the US to the EU, the Court of Justice of the European Union has recently considered what information businesses should provide to consumers in relation to the products' country of origin. According to EU law, food producers must indicate the country of origin of foods if a failure to do so might mislead the consumer as to the true country of origin of the food.[113] The case in hand focused on whether consumers had a right to know if the products they consumed came from occupied territories that are held by the state of Israel.[114]

As the discussion around GMO labelling reveals, policymakers (and courts) must realise that such information, which appears to be objective and factual, might not be so. Consumers' perceptions vis-à-vis labelling that informs consumers that the

---

[108] Reidel (2015).

[109] Bar-Gill et al. (2019), p. 209.

[110] Bar-Gill and Ferrari (2010), p. 109; Sovern (2006), p. 1703.

[111] Taha and Mercer (2015).

[112] Taha and Mercer (2015).

[113] Art 26(2)(a) read in conjunction with art. 9(1)(1) FIR.

[114] C-363/18 Organisation juive européenne, Vignoble Psagot Ltd v Ministre de l'Économie et des Finances [2019] ECL 954.

product originates from the occupied territories might be more nuanced. Regardless of a product's desirability, consumers may interpret the label as signalling a moral disapproval. If policymakers believe that such a label merely provides factual information that consumers may find important for political or ethical reasons, this belief may be unfounded. In fact, such a label may impact consumers' moral perspectives.

When it comes to using evidence for law-making, the relatively new field of neuroscience is an exciting venue. Scanning people's minds, reading, and comprehending their responses bears great potential for the law. Indeed, this may have a profound impact on the fundamentals of consumer law.

To understand why, recall that policymakers and courts need to determine the scope of protection under consumer law. In forming the boundaries of consumer law, many legislatures employ concepts such as "the average consumer," "the reasonable consumer," "reasonable expectations," and "common sense". In the EU, for example, it is assumed that "the average consumer" is able to protect her interests when provided with accurate information.[115] This imaginary "average consumer" is believed to be "reasonably well informed, observant[,] and circumspect" when making decisions.[116] Accordingly, legislatures need to determine what would be a reasonable level of protection for the ordinary, average consumer.

The EU is not alone in envisaging "reasonable consumers" and numerous other doctrines illustrate the use of general, imprecise standards in the realm of consumer law. One additional example is the New Zealand doctrine of unsubstantiated representations.[117] According to this doctrine, traders should have "reasonable grounds" to support the representation they make before disseminating them to the public. Yet one general exception to this rule is where the nature of the representation is such "that a reasonable person would not expect [it] to be substantiated."[118]

Much ink has been spilled on the use of vague legal norms. Commonly, these norms are called "standards" rather than "rules." Rules are specific, relatively clear, and accurate. While legal rules provide good guidance, they are also rigid. Prime examples are deadlines (e.g., for submitting a tax return or making an appeal), age requirements (e.g. for voting, drinking alcohol or driving), minimum wages, and speed limits.

At the same time, standards are open and dynamic norms which allow discretion, flexibility, and adaptations. Yet they do not serve as a good guide of behaviour ex-ante. Terms such as "reasonable," "average," and "common-sense" are legal standards. As such, they facilitate the development of consumer law. Nonetheless, at times they may be too vague, easily manipulated, or ill-fitted.[119] Standards accord

[115]European Financial Services Round Table (2004), p. 31.

[116]European Financial Services Round Table (2004), p. 31; see European Commission (2020).

[117]Fair Trading Act 1986, pt 1 s 12A (NZ).

[118]Fair Trading Act 1986, pt 1 s 12A (NZ).

[119]Willis (2015), pp. 1349–1350.

courts much discretion, while judging individuals, occurrences and behaviours only in hindsight.

Strikingly, neuroscience may provide policymakers and judges with empirical data that might render the use of many standards unnecessary.[120] Brain scans can help determine what consumers think and believe or when they are confused or misled. Neuroscience can demonstrate what exactly the "average" or "reasonable" consumer thinks and believes. Such data is evidently superior to expecting legislatures and judges to intuit consumers' thoughts and minds. Instead of assuming how consumers use their common-sense, fMRIs can provide accurate assessments of consumers' attitudes and responses.[121] If brain scans reveal exactly what goes on in consumers' minds, legislatures and courts can use this evidence to better align consumer law with the actual protection that consumers need. Under these circumstances, policy guesswork clearly becomes inferior, if not inappropriate.

From a different perspective, consider the General Data Protection Regulation (GDPR), which requires privacy policies to be drafted and communicated using transparent, clear and plain language.[122] Lawyers typically understand the term "plain language" to be a standard; a general and not well-defined requirement. Indeed, the GDPR, despite being a comprehensive piece of legislation, does not further define its plain language requirement.

However, a variety of linguistic tools can assist in empirically determining whether a text is written in plain language. In a recent study, we examined the readability of EU privacy policies post GDPR employing two of these tools—the Flesch Reading Ease test and the Flesch-Kincaid test.[123] Reviewing a sample of more than 200 privacy policies of highly popular EU websites, we found that almost all are not readable for the average consumer. This further illustrates how adopting an interdisciplinary and empirical attitude towards what might seem vague legal standards can shed important light on consumer protection legislation and its effectiveness.

A final example demonstrating the importance of an evidence-based consumer protection policy is found in another aspect of the GDPR: consumers' right to protect their privacy by opting-out from data collection. A recent study that examined consumers' actual behaviour found that a non-negligible number of consumers indeed exercised their right.[124] However, the reality is more nuanced, and consumers are heterogenous. Thus, the study also found that the remaining consumers are more persistently trackable. The data also indicated that "the average value of the remaining consumers to advertisers has increased, offsetting most of the losses from consumers that opt-out". Thus, the GDPR assisted sophisticated consumers

---

[120] Bartholomew (2018).

[121] Bartholomew (2018), p. 526.

[122] GDPR, Article 7, 12.1; Recital 39, 42, 58.

[123] Becher and Benoliel (2020).

[124] Aridor et al. (2020).

but failed to protect the less privacy-conscious consumers, who probably need such protection the most.

## *4.3 Temporary Consumer Protection Laws*

An evidence-based consumer law regime, however advantageous, is not a panacea. For starters, much of what we believe today to be true knowledge and correct facts will turn out to be untrue within a few years. This is sometimes dubbed "the half-life of facts" or "the half-life of knowledge."[125] In line with the need for a modest regulatory strategy, we next recommend a legislation regime where temporary legislation is favoured. In essence, temporary laws are automatically terminated unless re-affirmed.[126]

The idea of temporary laws has not gone unnoticed.[127] Temporary legislation has some advantages as it affords a better opportunity for policymakers "to incorporate a greater quantity and quality of information into legislative judgments."[128] Temporary legislation may be a way to acknowledge the inherent limits of legislation, as it better facilitates the need to test and experiment. Furthermore, it may well counter and minimise the negative outcomes of the legislative desire and incentive to respond to acute, "hot," topics. But although experienced and discussed in some other domains, the idea of temporary laws has generally been overlooked in the realm of consumer protection.

From yet another related perspective, one of the troubling aspects of misguided legislation and unintended consequences may result from the status quo bias. Once legislatures enact a (consumer protection) law, it is unlikely to be revoked. As manifested in other walks of life, people have a strong bias toward the status quo and a tendency to maintain established courses.[129]

This is also known as the power of inertia. Given the status quo bias, it is easy to see why, once a law is enacted, it is not likely to be revisited and/or revoked.[130] Revisiting a law consumes energy and requires attention. Not questioning the chosen path is easy and tempting. It economises on our scarce resources and limited mental abilities.[131]

But revisiting laws can prove quite beneficial. Our knowledge of the world, as well as our societal values and beliefs, are constantly changing.[132] With the

[125]Arbesman (2012).

[126]Cf. Gersen (2007).

[127]Listokin (2008), pp. 522–533; Ginsburg et al. (2014), p. 294; Romano (2014), p. 28.

[128]Gersen (2007), p. 248.

[129]Kahneman (2011), pp. 304–305; Thaler and Sunstein (2008), pp. 34–35.

[130]Schuck (2014), pp. 172–182.

[131]Ritov and Baron (1992).

[132]Arbesman (2012), p. 30.

exponential growth in knowledge and research techniques, this reality is only likely to become more and more prevalent.[133] This provides another justification for enacting consumer protection laws in a cautious, gradual and tentative manner.

To be sure, temporary laws come with a price. People are drawn to surety and feel uncomfortable with uncertainty. Temporary legislation might cause some confusion and reduce players' ability to rely on it. It entails intertemporal legislative dynamics and increased legislative transaction costs.[134] Yet, enacting and periodically revisiting tentative laws has some promising potential gains.[135] A series of recurring decisions has significant benefits. It can help legislatures correct mistakes, overcome inertia, and examine new data and unpredicted developments.

## 4.4 *Diffusing and Delegating Legislative Responsibilities*

We have repeatedly seen that legislatures operate within institutional limitations, exposed to noise and pressure. To minimise the problems that this reality generates, diffusing and delegating legislative responsibilities to more isolated policymakers may be an interesting path to consider. Slightly restated, it may well be that administrative bodies and agencies can participate more forcefully in the legislative process.

Administrative organisations are assumed to be much more isolated from political pressure, lobbying, and interest groups. Of course, such organisations can also fall prey to regulatory capture. However, in the context of consumer organisations, personnel who serve in these bodies are not usually elected by the public. Often, they have relevant expertise and professional backgrounds. Many choose to serve in these organisations to better their society, viewing their roles and efforts as a call and duty. Therefore, these individuals may have a better ability to focus on the important matters that are not necessarily at the forefront of public attention.

In the context of consumer markets, enforcement agencies and public organisations may enjoy a higher degree of expertise. Consumer agencies are constantly exposed to the challenges that consumer markets pose. They often deal with, analyse and aggregate numerous consumers' complaints. Presumably, such bodies also have better access to, and dialogue with, experts. Therefore, they are positioned at a superior starting point, equipped with better expertise and a more balanced and holistic position.

The idea of according administrative agencies and public organisations with more legislative power well-suits the framework sketched in this chapter. For example, it goes hand-in-hand with the call to advance an impartial, evidence-based consumer

---

[133] Gersen (2007), p. 298.

[134] Gersen (2007), pp. 262–266.

[135] To realize these gains, legislation design should also account for the omission bias, which may cause legislatures not to revisit laws even when enacted temporarily.

law policy. Consider, for instance, the phenomenon of group psychology. Humans are social creatures, and the sense of belonging is an important component of being social. While groups have a lot of value, the pressures they create can be quite significant and lead to remarkable results.[136]

When it comes to political and ideological groups, things can go quite astray in many ways.[137] Here, the desire to be a loyal member of one's political group can, at times, trump rational thinking and distort one's judgement. In other words, when political issues are at stake, many would prefer to adhere to the group's expectations and viewpoint, rather than "getting it right."[138]

It is easy to view consumer law policy as a political debate. Key issues relating to regulating markets, adopting paternalistic measures to protect consumers, levelling the consumer-firm playing field, or the degree to which society should hold individuals responsible for their actions and decisions in the marketplace are all influenced by political ideology. Virtually every evidence-based issue in the realm of consumer law policy can become politicised.

At the same time, political attitudes often remain unchanged, even when new facts and information is at hand. Motivated reasoning leads people in general, and politicians in particular, to interpret new information and evidence in ways that support their pre-existing beliefs.[139] The literature repeatedly demonstrates that people will manipulate the data they encounter so that it will conform to their already existing beliefs.[140]

Legislatures, pressured by their political group, are likely to exhibit cultural cognition, which is defined as "the tendency of individuals to conform their beliefs about disputed matters of fact [...] to values that define their cultural identities".[141] Rather than examining data impartially, legislatures are prone to base their perceptions and opinions on group beliefs and values. Legislatures are generally not equipped with scientific knowledge and are not trained to pursue precision and accuracy. If the debates over consumer law policy are mainly framed as political, crafting the right legal rules becomes increasingly difficult, if not impossible.

Administrative bodies, however, are more likely to refrain from transferring evidence-based issues into political ones. Consumer organisations, then again, can produce a better environment, where evidence is not easily polluted by political views and values. Such organisations are more professional. They have a better chance to advance an institutional climate where trained people examine data in a more objective and scientific way, outside of political context and group pressure. They are also less likely to experience an institutional gridlock. Moreover, professional bodies are also more likely to overcome the tendency to oversimplify complex

[136]Asch (1951), p. 177.

[137]Fein (2012).

[138]Haidt (2012).

[139]Kunda (1990), p. 488; Westen et al. (2006).

[140]Cultural Cognition (2020).

[141]Cultural Cognition (2020).

issues and "fit them into our preconceived models."[142] Presumably, they are better positioned to implement and scale-up scientific, empirical and evidence-based findings and interventions in policymaking.

Assuming more of the legislative work should be allocated to administrative bodies, an important preliminary point is the institutions' governance structure. Clearly, the chosen composition, which should have an open and adaptable design, can influence an institution's ability to fulfil its purpose. It may also affect the public's confidence. Of course, determining the optimal composition is a complex task. As a starting point, the analysis above suggests that its members should ideally include those with expertise in law, economics, psychology, brain studies, wellbeing, consumer behaviour, and marketing.

In this context, it is also worth noting that studies illuminate how to increase group intelligence.[143] First, the research suggests that collective group intelligence does not seem to be related to factors such as individuals' IQs or the presence of natural leaders.[144] Instead, the literature identifies three key components that may enhance group intelligence.[145] The first is equal distribution of contributions. When all group members make roughly the same contribution, overall group intelligence is maximised.[146] The second is the quality of conversation within the group. If individuals exhibit empathy and ability to read others' moods and feelings, group intelligence will benefit.[147] In other words, social intelligence or social sensitivity augment group intelligence.[148] The third vital factor for group intelligence is the inclusion of more women in the group. Generally speaking, the more women in a group, the better its collective intelligence.[149] Administrative bodies and expert organisations seem to be better positioned than legislatures to utilise these insights.

Last but not least, administrative bodies and consumer organisations are better positioned for crafting innovative regulatory solutions. Overall, they have a more positive approach to change. They have a higher degree of expertise, possess a lot of knowledge, and are less committed to formal, procedural aspects. They may as well be willing to take more risks and test new concepts and ideas.

[142]Woolley et al. (2010).

[143]Woolley et al. (2010).

[144]Woolley et al. (2010).

[145]Woolley et al. (2010), p. 688.

[146]Woolley et al. (2010), pp. 686, 688.

[147]Woolley et al. (2010), p. 688.

[148]Woolley et al. (2010), pp. 686, 688.

[149]Woolley et al. (2010), p. 688.

## 5 Conclusion

Consumer law has had many achievements in advancing better efficiency and fairness in the marketplace. Consumer laws protect consumers from various types of manipulation. It provides consumers with important information. It removes, at least in part, dangerous and risky products from the market.

Along these lines, it has been concluded that:

> one of the principal reasons consumer protection regulation has predominantly been a success is that, when such regulation is effectively articulated and enforced, everyone wins: consumers, because of the protection of quality and safety of products and services, and businesses, because of increased consumer trust.[150]

While not ignoring these accomplishments, there is much room for improvement. After surveying some difficulties and pointing to the phenomenon of unintended consequences, this chapter proposed four major changes to the process of consumer law legislation. However concisely presented, together these suggestions may serve as a starting point for facilitating significant improvements.

The general sentiment reflected in the proposals delineated in this chapter is one of caution and modesty. Carefulness and humbleness, however, should not be confused with despair, inaction, or pessimism. The need for consumer protection is not likely to decrease any time soon. Traders—armed with knowledge, experience, data, power, new technologies, and expertise—are likely to pursue any possible opportunity to maximise their bottom line. Consumer protection proponents should, therefore, stay vigilant.

This chapter focused on design principles of consumer legislation. Of course, this is merely part of the puzzle, which should not be viewed in isolation. As markets change, norms evolve, and technologies develop, we may need to re-think our regulatory framework. For starters, online information flows, market reputation mechanisms and public education may all play vital roles in the consumer protection landscape. This may result in a need to redefine the balance between regulating consumer markets and relying on meta-legal mechanisms.

To be sure, none of the recommendations made in this chapter, or their combination, should be viewed as a silver bullet. Implementing these recommendations requires a significant shift in the way regulators and legislators approach consumer law. Activating these changes will also necessitate a re-thinking of the allocation of public resources.

As in many other areas, clear thinking about regulation demands awareness and practice. It requires thinking about thinking. It necessitates open-mindedness, patience, courage and vision. There are many tricky challenges to consider. But these challenges should not prevent us from advancing the design of consumer law regulation.

---

[150] Wood (2017).

**Acknowledgements** I thank William Britton and Alana Harrison for excellent research assistance.

## References

Abramowicz M, Ayres I, Listokin Y (2011) Randomizing law. Univ Pa Law Rev 159(4):929–1005

Arbesman S (2012) The half-life of facts: why everything we know has an expiration date. Current, Maine

Aridor G, Che Y, Nelson W et al (2020) The economic consequences of data privacy regulation: empirical evidence from GDPR. Available at https://papers.ssrn.com/sol3/papers.cfm?abstract_id=3522845&dgcid=ejournal_htmlemail_consumer:law:ejournal_abstractlink. Accessed 6 Mar 2020

Asch S (1951) Effects of group pressure upon the modification and distortion of judgments. In: Guetzkow H (ed) Groups, leadership and men. Carnegie Press, Pittsburgh

Bar-Gill O (2012) Seduction by contract: law, economics, and phycology in consumer markets. Oxford University Press, Oxford

Bar-Gill O (2015) Price caps in multiprice markets. J Leg Stud 44:453–476

Bar-Gill O, Ferrari F (2010) Informing consumers about themselves. Erasmus Law Rev 3 (2):93–119

Bar-Gill O, Schkade D, Sunstein C (2019) Drawing false inferences from mandated disclosures. Behav Pub Policy 3(2):209–227

Bartholomew M (2018) Neuromarks. Minn Law Rev 103:521–585

Baxter T (1994) The UCC thrives in the law of commercial payment. Loy L A Law Rev 28:113–130

Becher S (2007) Behavioural science and consumer standard form contracts. La Law Rev 68:117–180

Becher S (2008) Asymmetric information in consumer contracts: the challenge that is yet to be met. Am Bus Law J 45(4):723–774

Becher S, Benoliel U (2020) Law in book and law in action: readability of privacy agreements and the GDPR. In: Mathis K, Avishalom T (eds) Consumer law and economics. Springer, New York

Becher S, Klein A (2010) The paradox of power and representation in small claims court? Insurance claims, power gaps and the judge's foot. Hapraklit Law Rev 50:327–401

Becher S, Zarsky T (2010) Consumers' right of withdrawal: a well-reasoned right or a pyrrhic victory? Tel Aviv Univ Law Rev 32:127–203

Becher S, Zarsky T (2011) Open doors, trap doors, and the law. Law Contemp Probl 74:63–94

Becher S, Feldman Y, Lobel O (2021) In: Gersen J, Steckel J (eds) Poor consumer(s) law: the case of high-cost credit and payday loans. Cambridge University Press, Cambridge

Becher S, Lai J, Gao H, Harrison A (2019) Hungry for change: the law and policy of food health labelling. Wake Forest Law Rev 54:1305–1360

Ben-Shahar O, Bar Gill O (2013) Regulatory techniques in consumer protection: a critique of European consumer contract law. Common Mark Law Rev 50:109–126

Ben-Shahar O, Posner E (2011) The right to withdraw in contract law. J Leg Stud 40(1):115–148

Ben-Shahar O, Schneider C (2014) More than you wanted to know: the failure of mandated disclosure. Univ Pa Law Rev 159:647–749

Black A, Rayner M (1992) Just read the label: understanding nutrition information in numeric, verbal and graphic forms. HMSO, London

Borges G, Irlenbusch B (2007) Fairness crowded out by law: an experimental study on withdrawal rights. J Inst Theor Econ 163(1):84–101

Boss A (1994) Foreword: "Is the UCC dead, or alive and well? An introduction to the practitioners' perspectives". Loy L A Law Rev 28(4):89–100

Braucher J (1988) Defining unfairness: empathy and economic analysis at the Federal Trade Commission. Boston Univ Law Rev 68:349–430

Bregman R (2014) Utopia for realists: the case for a universal basic income, open borders, and a 15-hour workweek. The Correspondent, Amsterdam

Brehm J (1966) A theory of psychological reactance. Academic Press, New York

Bushman B (1998) Effects of warning and information labels on consumption of full-fat, reduced-fat, and no-fat products. J Appl Psychol 83(1):97–101

Calabresi G (1982) A common law for the age of statutes. Harvard University Press, Cambridge

CEBM (2018) Centre for evidence-based medicine. CEBM. http://www.cebm.net. Accessed 5 Mar 2020

CEBMa (2018) Welcome to the center for evidence-based management. CEBMa. https://www.cebma.org. Accessed 5 Mar 2020

Chabris C, Simons D (2010) The Invisible Gorilla: how our intuitions deceive us. Harmony, Pennsylvania

Clee M, Wicklund R (1980) Consumer behavior and psychological reactance. J Consum Res 6 (4):389–405

Conley J, O'Barr W (1990) Rules versus relationships: the ethnography of legal discourse. University of Chicago Press, Chicago

Cultural Cognition (2020) The Cultural Cognition Project at Yale Law School, Cultural Cognition. http://www.culturalcognition.net. Accessed 6 Mar 2020

Davis C, Davis E (1996) Information load and consistency of decisions. Psychol Rep 79:279–288

DiNardo J, Lemieux T (2001) Alcohol, Marijuana, and American youth: the unintended consequences of government regulation. J Health Econ 20(6):991–1010

Dubner S (2016) In praise of incrementalism. Freakonomics. http://freakonomics.com/podcast/in-praise-of-incrementalism/. Accessed 5 Mar 2020

Eskridge W, Frickey P, Garrett E (2007) Cases and materials on legislation, statutes and the creation of public policy, 4th edn. West Academic Publishing, Minnesota

European Commission (2020) Consumers. http://ec.europa.eu/justice/consumer-marketing/unfair-trade/unfair-practices/is-it-fair/is-it-unfair/index_en.htm. Accessed 6 Mar 2020

European Financial Services Round Table (2004) Consumer protection and consumer choice, European Financial Services Round Table. http://www.efr.be/documents/publication/09.2004.02%20Consumer%20Protection%20-%20Breaking%20the%20deadlock%201Feb2004.pdf. Accessed 6 Mar 2020

Fein J (2012) You are a tribal person. Psychology Today. https://www.psychologytoday.com/us/blog/life-is-trip/201208/you-are-tribal-person. Accessed 6 Mar 2020

Felstiner W, Abel R, Sarat A (1980–81) The emergence and transformation of disputes: naming, blaming, claiming .... Law Soc Rev 15(3):631–654

Food and Drug Administration (2020) The real cost campaign. https://www.fda.gov/tobacco-products/public-health-education/real-cost-campaign. Accessed 5 Mar 2020

Galanter M (1974) Why the "haves" come out ahead: speculations on the limits of legal change. Law Soc Rev 9(1):95–160

Gersen J (2007) Temporary legislation. Univ Chic Law Rev 74:247–298

Gillette C (1996) Rules, standards, and precautions in payment systems. Va Law Rev 82 (2):181–251

Gillette C (2005) Pre-approved contracts for internet commerce. Houst Law Rev 42(4):975–1013

Ginsburg T, Masur J, McAdams R (2014) Libertarian paternalism, path dependence, and temporary law. Univ Chic Law Rev 81:291–359

Goyens M (2018) Using behavioural economics for rather than against consumers – a practitioner's perspective. Intereconomics 53:12–17

Grunert K, Wills J, Fernández-Celemín L (2010) Nutrition knowledge, and use and understanding of nutrition information on food labels among consumers in the UK. Appetite 55(2):177–189

Haidt J (2012) The righteous mind: why good people are divided by politics and religion. Vintage, Visalia

Hayek F (1945) The use of knowledge in society. Am Econ Rev 35(4):519–530
Health Star Rating (2020) Health Star Rating. http://www.healthstarrating.gov.au/internet/healthstarrating/publishing.nsf/content/home. Accessed 5 Mar 2020
Hennessy M (2014) How much do consumers use (and understand) nutrition labels? Food Navigator-USA. https://www.foodnavigator-usa.com/Article/2014/03/03/How-much-do-consumers-use-and-understand-nutrition-labels. Accessed 5 Mar 2020
Hillman R (2006) Online boilerplate: would mandatory website disclosure of E-standard terms backfire? Mich Law Rev 104(5):837–856
Hirshman L (2012) Victory: The Triumphant Gay Revolution. Harper Perennial, New York
Hocking W (2011) In praise of incremental steps and modest ideas. Phys Canada 67(3):177–181
Jones G, Richardson M (2007) An objective examination of consumer perception of nutrition information based on healthiness ratings and eye movements. Public Health Nutr 10(3):238–244
Kay J (2011) Obliquity: why our goals are best achieved indirectly. Penguin Books, London
Kahneman D (2011) Thinking, Fast and Slow
Klein E (2016) Universal basic income. Arena Mag 142:6–8
Kripke H (1982) Reflections of a drafter. Ohio State Law J 43:577–584
Kunda Z (1990) The case for motivated reasoning. Psychol Bull 108(3):480–498
Letsou P (1995) The political economy of consumer credit regulation. Emory Law J 44:587–678
Levmore S (2010) Interest groups and the problem with incrementalism. Univ Pa Law Rev 158:815–858
Lindstrom M (2008) Inhaling fear. New York Times
Listokin Y (2008) Learning through policy variation. Yale Law J 118(3):480–553
Lunn P, Frances R (2013) Using evidence to inform policy. Gill & Macmillan Ltd, Dublin
Niblett A, Yoon A (2017) Unintended consequences: the regressive effects of increased access to courts. J Empir Leg Stud 14(1):5–30
O'Connor G (2001) Rendering to Caesar: a response to Professor O'Reilly. Admin Law Rev 53:343–393
Palmer J (2014) Access to justice for consumers. In: Tokeley K (ed) Consumer law in New Zealand, 2nd edn. LexisNexis, Wellington
Pinheiro T, Ronen J (2016) Unintended consequences of the Credit Card Act. J Law Finance Account 1:93–138
Prepared Foods (2016) Do consumers read the nutrition facts label? Prepared Foods. https://www.preparedfoods.com/articles/118201-do-consumers-read-the-nutrition-facts-label. Accessed 5 Mar 2020
Thaler RH, Susntein CR (2008) Nudge: Improving Decisions about Health, Wealth and Happiness
Ramsay I (1981) Consumer redress mechanisms for poor-quality and defective products. Univ Toronto Law J 31:117–152
Reidel J (2015) New study: consumers don't view GMO labels as negative 'warnings'. UVM Today. https://www.uvm.edu/uvmnews/news/new-study-consumers-dont-view-gmo-labels-negative-warnings. Accessed 5 Mar 2020
Ringold D (2002) Boomerang effect: in response to public interventions: some unintended consequences in the alcoholic beverage market. J Consum Policy 25(1):27–63
Ritov I, Baron J (1992) Status-Quo and omission biases. J Risk Uncertain 5:49–61
Romano R (2014) Regulating in the dark and a postscript assessment of the iron law of financial regulation. Hofstra Law Rev 43(1):25–93
Rubin E (1993) Thinking like a lawyer, acting like a lobbyist: some notes on the process of revising UCC Articles 3 and 4. Loy L A Law Rev 26:743–789
Schuck P (2014) Why the government fails so often: and how it can do better. Princeton University Press, Princeton
Siegel M (2011) Gruesome cigarette-pack warnings say too much. Bloomberg
Silber N (1997) Substance abuse at UCC drafting sessions. Wash Univ Law Q 75:225–242
Sovern J (2006) Toward a new model of consumer protection: the problem of inflated transaction costs. William Mary Law Rev 47(5):1635–1709

Sovern J (2014) Written notice of cooling-off periods: a forty-year natural experiment in illusory consumer protection and the relative effectiveness of oral and written disclosures. Univ Pitt Law Rev 75:333–386

Stancil P (2008) Assessing interest groups: a playing field approach. Cardozo Law Rev 29:1273–1318

Sullivan R, Behncke I, Purushotham A (2010) Why do we love medicines so much? EMBO Rep 11 (8):572–578

Taha A, Mercer M (2015) Unintended consequences: an experimental investigation of the (in)-effectiveness of mandatory disclosures. Santa Clara Law Rev 55(2):405–441

Tokely K (2014) In: Tokeley K (ed) Consumer law in New Zealand, 2nd edn. Wellington, LexisNexis

Trufelman A (2017) The Finnish Experiment. 99% Invisible. https://99percentinvisible.org/episode/the-finnish-experiment/. Accessed 5 Mar 2020

Vassey J, Metayer C, Kennedy C et al (2020) #Vape: measuring E-cigarette influence on instagram with deep learning and text analysis. Front Commun 4:1–75

Westen D, Blagov P, Harenski K et al (2006) Neural bases of motivated reasoning: an fMRI study of emotional constraints on Partisan political judgment in the 2004 U.S. presidential election. J Cogn Neurosci 18(11):1947–1958

Wilkinson-Ryan T (2014) A psychological account of consent to fine print. Iowa Law Rev 99:1745–1784

Wilkinson-Ryan T (2017) The perverse consequences of disclosing standard terms. Cornell Law Rev 103(1):117–175

Willis L (2015) Performance-based consumer law. Univ Chic Law Rev 82:1309–1409

Wood J (2017) Consumer protection: a case of successful regulation. In: Drahos P (ed) Regulatory theory: foundations and applications. Australian National University Press, Canberra

Woolley A, Chabris C, Pentland A et al (2010) Evidence for a collective intelligence factor in the performance of human groups. SCI 330:686–688

World Health Organization (2014) Frequently asked questions on genetically modified foods. Available at http://www.who.int/foodsafety/areas_work/food-technology/faq-genetically-modified-food/en/. Accessed 5 Mar 2020

Zettler P, Hemmerich N, Berman M (2018) Closing the regulatory gap for synthetic nicotine products. Boston Coll Law Rev 59(6):1933–1982

**Shmuel I. Becher** Professor of Law at Victoria University of Wellington. Samuel.becher@vuw.ac.nz. Fields of Interest: Contract Law, Consumer Law, Economic Analysis of Law, Behavioural Analysis of Law, Law and Wellbeing, Empirical Legal Studies, Legal Education, Negotiation and Conflict Resolution.

# Regulation of Information About Unfolding Events in Securities Markets: A Behavioral Economics Perspective

**Ido Baum, Jaroslaw Beldowski, and Dov Solomon**

**Abstract** In this chapter we focus on disclosure—the foundation of securities regulation—of uncertain future events. We note two major differences in the United States and European disclosure regimes: the definition of materiality of information about unfolding events and whether disclosure of material unfolding events is voluntary or mandatory. We analyze both regimes through the lens of behavioral law and economics, identifying a variety of cognitive biases influencing corporate decision makers on the disclosing side (overconfidence, overoptimism, status quo bias, and Fechner's law) and investors on the receiving end (conservatism, the ostrich effect, availability bias, and difficulty in assessing probabilities). We find that the U.S. regime is likely to produce excessively optimistic disclosures. We also show that the European regime imposes impossible market prediction requirements on corporate insiders. Our analysis suggests that disclosure architecture in both jurisdictions would benefit from a more nuanced approach that takes into account these cognitive biases.

I. Baum (✉)
Faculty of Law, Haim Striks School of Law, Rishon Le Zion, Israel
e-mail: baumi@colman.ac.il

J. Beldowski
Economic Analysis College, International Comparative Studies Department, Warsaw School of Economics, Warsaw, Poland
e-mail: jbeldo@sgh.waw.pl

D. Solomon
Commercial Law Department, College of Law and Business, Ramat Gan Law School, Ramat Gan, Israel
e-mail: solomon@clb.ac.il

 
K. Mathis, A. Tor (eds.), *Law and Economics of Regulation*, Economic Analysis of Law in European Legal Scholarship 11,
https://doi.org/10.1007/978-3-030-70530-5_6

# 1 Introduction

Disclosure is the foundation of securities regulation.[1] The classic law and economics approach to securities regulation argues that a rich information environment for investors in the market and low information asymmetry between market participants and corporate insiders facilitate the efficient allocation of resources and contribute to market liquidity and capital market development.[2]

U.S. and E.U. disclosure regimes both compel companies to generate comprehensive timely disclosures that will inform their current and potential investors, thereby creating an efficient market. According to the efficient market hypothesis (EMH)—the prevailing hypothesis underlying securities regulation—stock prices fully reflect all available information.[3] The semi-strong form of the EMH claims that stock prices instantly change to reflect new public information.[4] Therefore, without trading on the basis of inside information it is impossible to "beat the market" and consistently produce excess returns because market prices continually reflect the "fair value" of the corporation and should react only to new public information.

With respect to the timing and content of material current disclosures, the regulatory regimes in the United States and European Union strive to generate the same functional outcome.[5] Consequently, most disclosures in both regimes focus on financial or factual information about past events. For example, a corporation's annual financial reports document its activities during the previous year and their impact on the corporation's financial parameters. Although investors may have different opinions and sentiments about this information, such opinions are based on a common set of facts. However, investors are particularly interested in information about events that are likely to happen in the future. The uncertainty of future events means that an investor's superior ability to predict how uncertain processes are likely to unfold presents an opportunity to extract an above-average return in the stock market. At the same time, this information is extremely valuable to corporate insiders. When material information is not disclosed, corporate insiders who are privy to nonpublic information and outsiders who come into possession of inside information may illegally use this information to trade in corporate securities, thereby gaining an unfair advantage over uninformed market participants.[6]

Both the U.S. and Europe have legal regimes that govern the disclosure of information about unfolding events that have not yet fully materialized and at the same time prohibit insider trading when material information is nonpublic. There are some strict differences in the regulatory architecture of these two regimes. In

[1] Bainbridge (2000), p. 1023; Pritchard (2018), p. 1064.

[2] Pritchard (2018), p. 1075.

[3] Fama (1970); Zamir and Teichman (2018).

[4] Zamir and Teichman (2018), pp. 404–409.

[5] Baum and Solomon (2019).

[6] On the importance of information to securities markets see Goshen and Parchomovsky (2006); Klöhn (2015).

particular, they differ in two important elements: the definition of "materiality" and the existence of an obligation to disclose material information.

Materiality is a common and important legal principle in the law broadly and in securities regulation in particular. In a seminal case, the United States Supreme Court explained that information is material "if there is a substantial likelihood that a reasonable shareholder would consider it important in deciding how to vote."[7] The concept of materiality is important to both disclosure obligations and insider trading prohibitions. Securities regulation regimes generally require corporations to make current and periodic disclosures about material information.[8] Insiders are required to abstain from trading in the corporation's securities for as long as the information remains nonpublic. This disclose-or-abstain rule[9] is designed to prohibit corporate insiders who possess nonpublic material information from having an unfair advantage in the market.

Determining whether information is or is not material is a routine task for corporate officers and securities lawyers.[10] The determination can be based on precise numerical thresholds, such as the effect of a certain transaction on the annual revenue of the corporation, the value of its asset portfolio, or its obligations. Some information, though, is not immediately measurable but is material. Examples include regulatory changes that may influence the future value of the corporation, the risk of death or incompetence of the corporation's founder,[11] and the unforeseeable spread of a virus that hampers international trade.

Determining informational materiality becomes complicated when events are unfolding. The United States and Europe have different methods of determining the materiality of information regarding such events. In the United States, materiality is determined by balancing the magnitude of an event and its probability.[12] The E.U., on the other hand, has a bright-line materiality test.[13] These different approaches yield different outcomes. Information about future events of great magnitude will be considered material under the U.S. test at a relatively early stage of their development, whereas information about future events of smaller magnitude will become material earlier in Europe.[14]

---

[7]TSC Industries Inc. v. Northway, Inc., 426 U.S. 438, 449 (1976). See also Georgiev (2017), p. 606.

[8]This chapter focuses on current and continuous disclosures, but the issue discussed here applies also to periodic disclosures that need to be made when events are still in the process of materializing.

[9]See, e.g., Chiarella v. United States, 445 U.S. 222, 227 (1980).

[10]Soderquist and Gabaldon (2014); Choi and Pritchard (2015), p. 48. For a comparative analysis of materiality tests using Bayes Rule see Schulzke and Berger-Walliser (2017).

[11]See Lin (2009), p. 413. For an example, see the disclosure by Google (now Alphabet) co-founder Sergey Brin about his potential Parkinson's disease risk. Miguel Helft Google Co-founder Has Genetic Code Linked to Parkinson's, N.Y. Times (Sept. 19, 2008), http://www.nytimes.com/2008/09/19/technology/19google.html.

[12]See infra Sect. 2.

[13]See infra Sect. 3.

[14]See infra Sect. 4.

The other major difference between the U.S. and E.U. disclosure regimes is in the obligation to disclose material information regarding uncertain future events. It has long been debated whether corporations should be *required* to disclose information or left free to decide whether to do so voluntarily. The classic perception of law and economics scholars is that the corporate setting provides ample "natural" incentives for corporate officers to disclose information candidly and timely in order to create long-term trust.[15] Nevertheless, the debate has been generally settled in favor of mandatory disclosure on the grounds that it creates a standardized baseline that enables investors to compare corporations in the market.[16] The resonating exception to the mandatory disclosure rule in the United States is information about material uncertain events.[17] The U.S. regime relies on market-based incentives to prompt disclosure of such events.[18] In contrast, the E.U. mandates disclosure of intermediate stages of unfolding events whenever they become material, while also allowing delaying disclosure when there are justifications for doing so.[19]

There are two significant consequences of these interjurisdictional differences. First, the difference in the materiality thresholds for high-magnitude future events suggests that restrictions on insider trading apply in the United States before they do in the European Union. The interplay between the application of insider trading prohibitions and disclosure incentivizes U.S. insiders to voluntarily disclose information about high-magnitude events at a relatively early stage. Since insiders are inclined to voluntarily disclose information when they intend to trade on the basis of that information, they have an incentive to disclose only information that they subjectively believe will move the market price.

Second, voluntary disclosure declutters the information space provided to investors, reduces the overload problem, and enables investors to focus on the information that decision makers in the corporation perceive to be the most important.[20] The difference in the regimes implies that the information provided to investors about this very important event category is significantly different in the two jurisdictions. To put it simply, compared with the United States, the information provided to investors under the European disclosure regime is overloaded with less important events and harder for unsophisticated investors to evaluate.[21]

---

[15] Easterbrook and Fischel (1984), pp. 673–677. For a behavioral critique of this position see Langevoort (1997), p. 112.

[16] Georgiev (2017), p. 613.

[17] The SEC rarely addresses disclosures regarding events that are in the process of materializing. The only exception, when the SEC does deal with future events, is the SEC's position on projections. See Disclosure of Projections of Future Economic Performance, S.E.C. Release No. 5362, 1973 WL 149257 (Feb. 2, 1973). Park (2018), p. 1143 n. 43, observes a shift to encouraging projections.

[18] See infra Sect. 2.

[19] See infra Sect. 3.

[20] Ben-Shahar and Schneider (2014), p. 95.

[21] Baum and Solomon (2020).

No analysis of securities regulation that is intended to examine the practicalities of the market is complete nowadays unless it integrates insights from behavioral economics and behavioral finance. This is especially true with respect to the regulation of disclosure duties.[22] Economic analysis of law is based on the initial assumption that people are rational wealth maximizers and on the efficiency criterion.[23] The classic assumption is that efficient markets create incentives for market participants to engage in accurate and efficient disclosures. Zamir and Teichamn wrote in response that "behavioral analysis suggests that the effectiveness of such market mechanisms may be limited."[24]

Behavioral law and economics documents the systematic divergence of human behavior from the strict models of law and economics. By now, there is an ocean of literature describing the effects of cognitive biases on human decisions in general and in the financial investment arena in particular.[25]

Some scholars went so far as to say that "after perusing the growing behavioral finance literature, we wonder how investors are able to make any positive return from the market."[26] That is an exaggeration, as those critics themselves admitted. Not all humans have the same biases at the same time in the same situations.[27] But there seems to be a consensus that humans cannot be educated to entirely overcome cognitive biases.[28] Hence, it is important to take known, well-documented systematic cognitive biases into consideration in structuring regulatory regimes. Surprisingly, there is very little literature on the behavioral aspects of the current European securities regulation. Furthermore, to the best of our knowledge, application of behavioral law and economics research to the study of comparative regulation in this field is nonexistent. This is troubling because securities regulation is a field in which developed countries try to advance a higher level of functional homogeneity in an effort to globalize financial markets. Behavioral law and economics can direct the attention of policy makers to crucial concerns not addressed by classic law and economics literature. Take trust, for example. Trust is extremely important in financial investments. Trust is also strongly influenced by cognitive biases. One manifestation of how biased trust in markets can influence financial globalization is "home bias." This cognitive bias causes investors to under-diversify their investments on a global level and overinvest in stock of corporations located in their own countries.[29] This phenomenon, which is discussed in a body of literature that reveals the tendency of investors to engage in naïve diversification,[30] can be mitigated by

[22]Zamir and Teichman (2018), p. 172.

[23]Posner (1998), p. 12; Posner (1973), p. 761.

[24]Zamir and Teichman (2018), p. 172.

[25]For a general survey see, e.g. Zamir and Teichman (2018); Choi and Pritchard (2003), pp. 7–14.

[26]Choi and Pritchard (2003), p. 14.

[27]Choi and Pritchard (2003), p. 14.

[28]Choi and Pritchard (2003), p. 5.

[29]Barberis and Thaler (2002), p. 40.

[30]Zamir and Teichman (2018), p. 379.

finding ways to increase the accessibility of foreign securities, which depends on, among other things, harmonizing disclosure regimes and guaranteeing an internationally comparable level of market integrity with respect to insider trading prohibitions.

Insights from behavioral economics and behavioral finance are particularly valuable in analyzing the issue discussed in this chapter: making decisions under conditions of uncertainty. Our objective in this chapter is to outline key insights from behavioral law and economics that should be considered in regulating information about unfolding events and to assess the implication of these insights on the current regulatory regimes as part of a comparative assessment of U.S. and E.U. regulation.

This chapter proceeds along the following path. Section 2 describes the regulatory architecture in the United States. Section 3 attends to the regulatory architecture in the European Union, and Sect. 4 compares the two regimes through the lens of classic economic analysis. Section 5 discusses the applicable cognitive biases. In Sect. 6, we conclude our discussion.

## 2 The Regulatory Architecture in the United States

This section outlines the U.S. regime governing the disclosure of material unfolding events. The United States should be credited with most innovations in securities regulation,[31] and dealing with information about uncertain future events is no exception.

### *2.1 Definition of Materiality*

The first question that needs to be addressed in the design of a regime that governs information in securities markets is what information is important to investors. The term used globally for this purpose is "materiality." However, with regard to unfolding future events, different jurisdictions have different definitions of "materiality." In the United States, probability/magnitude is the prevailing test for determining the materiality of uncertain future events. The test is judge-made law.

The most important decision of a U.S. court on determining the materiality of future events using the probability/magnitude test was *Texas Gulf Sulphur* in 1968.[32] The case concerned insider trading allegations, and the court had to determine whether information about a potential initial discovery of iron ore was material. The court formulated the test as follows:

[31] E.g. Ventoruzzo (2017), p. 13.

[32] SEC v. Texas Gulf Sulphur, 401 F.2d 833 (2d Cir. 1968).

> Whether facts are material [ . . .] will depend at any given time upon a balancing of both the indicated probability that the event will occur and the anticipated magnitude of the event in light of the totality of the company activity.[33]

A few years later, the United States Court of Appeals for the Third Circuit adopted another test in a case about disclosure of negotiations in anticipation of a transaction. According to the holding of *Greenfield v. Heublein*, information about an anticipated transaction becomes material only when an agreement in principle is reached, generally in the form of an initial agreement on the structure of the deal and the price.[34] The agreement-in-principle test is a bright-line test—a rule as opposed to a standard. Although this test applies to disclosure of negotiations leading to a merger or acquisition, it can be applied to any material transaction of the corporation. The bright-line rule is simpler to apply because it focuses on a particular set of circumstances that can be observed and verified.

In 1988, the Supreme Court of the United States weighed in and, in one of the most important precedents in securities regulation, *Basic Inc. v. Levinson*, expressly rejected the bright-line rule. The Court ruled that the probability/magnitude test should be applied in determining the materiality of information about negotiations in furtherance of an anticipated merger and should in fact be an overarching test for materiality.[35]

## 2.2 Voluntary Disclosure

The underlying principle of federal securities regulation in the United States is standardized periodic mandatory disclosure of corporate quantitative and qualitative information. However, information about unfolding future events, which is particularly important for investors, is the major exception to the rule.[36] Events that are not governed by mandatory disclosure obligations in the United States are governed by

---

[33]SEC v. Texas Gulf Sulphur, 401 F.2d 833 (2d Cir. 1968) p. 849.

[34]Greenfield v. Heublein, 742 F.2d 751, 756–57 (3rd Cir. 1984).

[35]Basic Inc. v. Levinson, 485 U.S. 224, 234–36 (1988). The Delaware court also adopted the probability/magnitude test in Alessi v. Beracha, 849 A.2d 939, 944–50 (Del. Ch. 2004), overturning an earlier ruling in Bershad v. Curtiss-Wright Corp., 535 A.2d 840 (Del. 1987), that favored the bright-line rule.

[36]A company listed on a U.S. stock exchange does have some obligations to make prompt public disclosure of material information. See, e.g., New York Stock Exchange Listed Company Manual § 202.05 (2019), http://wallstreet.cch.com/LCMTools/PlatformViewer.asp?selectednode=chp_1_1&manual=%2Flcm%2Fsections%2Flcm-sections%2F (last visited Apr. 30, 2019); NASDAQ Stock Market Rules § 5250(b)(1) (2019), http://nasdaq.cchwallstreet.com/NASDAQTools/PlatformViewer.asp?searched=1&selectednode=chp_1_1_4_3_10_7&CiRestriction=delist&manual=/nasdaq/main/nasdaq-equityrules/ (last visited Apr. 30, 2019). However, a breach of stock exchange requirements is not enforceable by the SEC or by an investor seeking damages. See Horwich (2016), pp. 1128–1129. Also, Stock exchanges have rarely imposed sanctions for violations of their prompt disclosure rules. Hazen (2009), p. 511.

Securities Exchange Commission (SEC) Rule 10b-5,[37] the focus of which is preventing fraudulent representations—the so-called fraud on the market.

The U.S. Supreme Court clearly stated in *Matrixx Initiatives, Inc. v. Siracusano* that Rule 10b–5(b) "does not create an affirmative duty to disclose any and all material information."[38] This means that corporations are not obligated to disclose information about unfolding material events. However, if a corporation is asked a question regarding such events, it must respond truthfully[39] or avoid the question by responding with the admittedly somewhat revealing "no comment."[40] Once information about an uncertain future event has been voluntarily made public, there is an obligation to update it when material developments occur.[41]

The fact that the United States lacks a general duty to disclose material nonpublic information about uncertain future events is a major difference between the United States and the European Union in the arena of securities regulation. Arguably, this information gap has been narrowed in recent years. For example, the list of events that require immediate disclosure in the United States according to Form 8-K of the SEC was expanded. However, the gap between mandated disclosure in the United States and the European Union remains wide.[42]

## 3 The Regulatory Architecture in the European Union

The Market Abuse Regulation (MAR) governs the regulation of both insider trading prohibitions and issuer disclosure duties in the European Union.[43] The MAR has replaced the Market Abuse Directive (MAD)[44] in order to harmonize the European market through a direct application of its regulatory architecture in E.U. member states. The E.U. regime governing the disclosure of material unfolding events is the outcome of a long legislative process driven by a desire to increase investor protection and investors' faith in the integrity of markets and at the same time ensure

[37]C.F.R. § 240.10b-5 (2017).

[38]Matrixx Initiatives, Inc. v. Siracusano, 563 U.S. 27, 44 (2011).

[39]According to the language of Rule 10b-5(b), it is unlawful to make false or untrue statements, a rule that is enforceable by the SEC or through civil actions.

[40]Basic, 485 U.S. at 239; Gow et al. (2019).

[41]See, e.g., In re Int'l Bus. Machs. Corp. Sec. Litig., 163 F.3d 102, 110 (2d Cir. 2010).

[42]See generally Hazen (2009), p. 551.

[43]The Market Abuse Regulation (EU) No. 596/2014 (MAR) and the Directive on Criminal Sanctions for Market Abuse 2014/57/EU (known as MAD II) entered into force on 3 July, 2016. MAD II required transposition into national law of member states of the European Union by that date. The MAR and MAD II replace the previous Market Abuse Directive 2003/6/EC (MAD I).

[44]Directive 2003/6 of the European Parliament and of the Council of 28 January 2003 on Insider Dealing and Market Manipulation (Market Abuse), 2003 O.J. (L 96) 6 (EU), http://www.esma.europa.eu/system/files/Dir_03_6.pdf.

a single rulebook and a level playing field.[45] The European regulatory regime emphasizes a continuous disclosure obligation and a particular obligation to make *ad hoc* disclosures regarding ongoing events. The continuous disclosure obligation is a "cornerstone" of this regulatory architecture and is described as serving the "greater purpose of market efficiency and not simply the prevention of insider trading."[46] At the same time, the MAR introduced what is probably the most complex set of rules anywhere for handling inside information. A non-exhaustive list contains Article 7 of the MAR, which defines "inside information;" Article 8, which focuses on the prohibition of insider trading ("dealing" in the preferred terminology of the MAR); Article 9, which lists exceptions to the prohibition; Article 10, which clarifies that disclosure of material information to third parties in itself constitutes a violation of the MAR; and Article 18, which requires corporations to keep lists of insiders in order to keep track of those who possess inside information.[47]

## 3.1 Definition of Materiality

Closing the gap with the United States, the MAR unifies the definitions of "materiality" that apply to insider trading restrictions and issuer disclosure duties. This is consistent with one of the MAR's tenets, which strives to increase uniformity. At the same time, the MAR also significantly increases the amount of information available to investors.[48]

The European definition of "material events" puts an emphasis on corporate securities' price-sensitivity to the relevant information. The notion of "inside information" is a key element of the MAR. This is the term used by the MAR to define the concept of material information. Article 7(1)(a) of the MAR uses the previous definition (from the MAD) and holds that inside information is

> information of a precise nature, which has not been made public, relating, directly or indirectly, to one or more issuers or to one or more financial instruments, and which, if it were made public, would be likely to have a significant effect on the prices of those financial instruments or on the price of related derivative financial instruments.

This definition can be broken down into several components that together constitute "inside information." First, the information must be of a "precise nature." Second, the information must not be public. Third, the information has to relate to the corporation or the financial instruments that relate to the corporation. Fourth, the information must be likely to have an effect on the price of the relevant financial instrument. Fifth, the likely effect on the price must be "significant."

---

[45] Mock (2017), p. 3.

[46] Pietrancosta (2017), pp. 47, 51–52.

[47] See also generally Ventoruzzo (2014), p. 3.

[48] Pietrancosta (2017), pp. 51–52.

Some of the vague terminology in this provision, in particular with respect to the meaning of "precise nature," is clarified in Article 7(2) of the MAR, which explains that information will be deemed to be of a precise nature if it indicates

> a set of circumstances which exists or which may reasonably be expected to come into existence, or an event which has occurred or which may reasonably be expected to occur, where it is specific enough to enable a conclusion to be drawn as to the possible effect of that set of circumstances or event on the prices of the financial instruments [. . . ]. In this respect in the case of a protracted process that is intended to bring about, or that results in, particular circumstances or a particular event, those future circumstances or that future event, and also the intermediate steps of that process which are connected with bringing about or resulting in those future circumstances or that future event, may be deemed to be precise information.[49]

This complicated definition is meant to recognize that unfolding events can be material and that even intermediate steps leading to a future event may be sufficiently precise to be considered material. Article 7(2) of the MAR thus codified the meaning of "precise" as adjudicated by the *Geltl v. Daimler* decision of the European Court of Justice (ECJ).[50] In that case, the ECJ affirmed a question referred from a German court regarding whether intermediate steps leading to a final event, in this case the resignation of Daimler's Chairman, should be regarded as precise information.

More importantly, *Geltl v. Daimler* touched on the issue of the probability threshold beyond which uncertain future events should be considered inside information. The ECJ held that a future event should be expected to occur if there is a realistic prospect that it will come to pass.[51] It is now commonly understood that the ECJ's language, and the use in Article 7(2) of the MAR of the expression "reasonably [. . .] expected to occur," reflect a requirement that the likelihood of the uncertain event should be slightly higher than 50 percent for it to be considered inside information.[52]

The MAR also tries to clarify the meaning of the wording "significant effect on the prices of [. . .] financial instruments." Article 7(4) of the MAR explains that information having a significant effect is "information [that] a reasonable investor would be likely to use as part of the basis of his or her investment decisions." It remains unclear whether deciding that the information is or is not material rests entirely on the perception of the investor or the sensitivity of the price to the information needs to be accounted for.

The condition that the information must have a "significant" effect on the price is obviously designed to reduce the disclosure of unimportant information. If the

[49]Article 7(3) of the MAR clarifies that "an intermediate step in a protracted process shall be deemed to be inside information if, by itself, it satisfies the criteria of inside information as referred to in this Article."

[50]Case C-19/11, Markus Geltl v. Daimler AG, ECLI:EU:C:2012:397 (2012). For a discussion of the case, see Krause and Brellochs (2013). See also Kersting (2014), pp. 16–17.

[51]Geltl, ECLI:EU:C:2012:397 at para. 56.

[52]Kersting (2014), p. 17; Case C-628/13 Lafonta v. Autorite des marches Financieres (11 March 2015). See also Hansen (2016), pp. 18–19.

information concerns a relatively unimportant event, then it should have little to no significant effect on the price—*ergo*, no materiality. However, it is difficult to speculate in advance about what would be perceived by investors or by courts as a significant change. Even relatively small expected changes in the price may be considered significant in some cases, particularly in hindsight.[53] To be on the safe side, European corporations may disclose information even when the likelihood of the potential significant effect on the price of the corporations' financial instruments seems low or obscure.

## *3.2 Mandatory Disclosure and the Option of Delayed Disclosure*

E.U. securities regulation is characterized by a broad mandatory continuous disclosure regime.[54] As noted above, the MAR ties the mandatory disclosure obligation to the concept of inside information. Article 17(1) of the MAR requires issuers to disclose to the public "as soon as possible" any information that falls within the ambit of "inside information." The MAR prohibits trading by insiders in possession of inside information.[55]

Mandatory disclosure increases the wealth of information available to investors but creates a potential negative cost in the form of beneficial transactions or activities that will fail to materialize due to premature disclosure. The drafters of the MAR had to address the potential downsides of premature disclosures and did so by adding the possibility of delaying *ad hoc* disclosures.[56] Delays are permitted only when three conditions are met: an immediate disclosure is likely to prejudice a legitimate interest of the issuer; the delay is not likely to mislead the public; and the issuer can ensure the confidentiality of the information before it is disclosed.[57] The MAR requires issuers that have decided to delay a disclosure to notify "competent authorities" of the delay after the disclosure is finally effected and explain how they met the

---

[53]See Case C-45/08 Spector Photo Group NV v. CBFA [2009], paras. 66-69. Ventoruzzo and Picciau (2017), p. 204.

[54]For a broad critique of mandated disclosure in consumer regulation, see Ben-Shahar and Schneider (2014), pp. 3–4.

[55]MAR, Art. 14. This Article also precludes attempted insider trading and the unlawful disclosure of inside information.

[56]MAR, Art. 17(4). Art. 17(5) of the MAR adds specialized conditions regarding delayed disclosure of material inside information by credit institutions and banks.

[57]See generally European Securities and Markets Authority (ESMA), Final Report: Guidelines on the Market Abuse Regulation—Market Soundings and Delay of Disclosure of Inside Information (13 July 2016); See generally Lombardo and Mucciarelli (2017). Articles 17(7) and 17(8) of the MAR impose the obligation to disclose information as soon as possible if confidentiality has been breached, or even if a sufficiently accurate rumor undermines the secrecy of the information.

conditions associated with the delay.[58] However, the general approach to delays is *de facto* very lenient.[59]

## 4 A Comparative Economic Analysis of the Different Regimes

In this section, we explain the consequences of the complex interplay between disclosure obligations, the definition of "materiality," and insider trading prohibitions in the U.S. and E.U. We start by comparing the different materiality tests.

In both jurisdictions considered here, a piece of information is material if a reasonable investor would be likely to use it in making an investment decision.[60] Consider the situation when the future event is a transaction that the corporation is aiming to conclude. The process often starts with initial negotiations and then proceeds to a letter of intent, a memorandum of understanding (MoU), a due diligence process followed by the signing of an agreement, and, finally, closing the deal. Because a deal might go sour at any of these stages, only when it is fully consummated can one say with absolute certainty that it is final.

The European test focuses on the likelihood of the foreseen transaction being consummated. Hence, the European test can be treated as a bright-line rule because when the likelihood threshold of the future transaction is crossed, the information regarding it becomes material. This is not a conventional bright-line rule, though. The European rule is somewhat complicated in that it requires a subjective assessment of whether a particular set of "precise" facts or circumstances indicates that the transaction is more likely than not to occur.[61] One can refer to it as a "probabilistic bright-line test." The European bright-line test can be applied to any developing event that can be broken down into intermediate steps.[62]

---

[58]The MAR leaves to member states the possibility of deciding whether they require the issuer to report the delay decision immediately, as in Austria, or ex post, as in Germany. Hoessl-Neumann and Baumgartner (2018), pp. 20–21. Regulators are allowed to opt out of or waive the compulsory post-delayed-disclosure report. See Article 17(4) of the MAR.

[59]Hoessl-Neumann and Baumgartner (2018), p. 31.

[60]Ventoruzzo and Picciau (2017), pp. 175, 200.

[61]Ventoruzzo and Picciau (2017), pp. 180–81.

[62]ESMA guidelines on delayed disclosure include various examples of uncertain situations that would require disclosure but also may justify a delayed disclosure, including "ongoing negotiations . . . where the outcome or normal pattern of those negotiations would be likely to be affected by public disclosure" or negotiations to prevent an event in which "the financial viability of the issuer is in grave and imminent danger, although not within the scope of the applicable insolvency law." European Securities and Markets Authority, *Final Report:* Guidelines on the Market Abuse Regulation—Market Soundings and Delay of Disclosure of Inside Information (13 July 2016). According to the ESMA, the announcement of a merger that is subject to regulatory approval cannot be delayed and must include foreseen regulatory hurdles. However, a delayed disclosure would be legitimate with regard to the announcement of additional regulatory conditions imposed by the

The E.U. bright-line test differs from the U.S. probability/magnitude test in that the former always requires an *ex ante* assessment of probability based on a clear set of circumstances. Determining the probability of a future event is difficult, and the European rule emphasizes that the probability of the event needs to be substantial. The probabilistic outlook must be clearly "positive."[63] This is in stark contrast with the U.S. test, which has no lower probability boundary below which future events are never considered material.

The European regulation tries to incorporate the magnitude of the forecasted event in Article 7 of the MAR, which provides that the expected price movement of the corporation's financial instruments must be "significant."[64] Unlike in the United States, significance is measured in the European Union by the expected price movement as a result of the disclosure and not by an estimation of the effect of the event on the corporation.[65] This is an important characteristic of the European regulation because it relies heavily but implicitly on the assumption that securities markets function according to the EMH. Even without insights from behavioral economics, this regulation is not easily digested. Indeed, price movements are dependent on the subjective evaluations of investors and traders in the market and thus may not reflect what corporate insiders know about the potential impact of an event on the corporation. Furthermore, the efficiency of the market also influences price movements pursuant to disclosure of new information, so less efficient markets may respond to disclosure in unexpected ways.

The U.S. test focuses on both the probability that the event will take place and the expected magnitude of its final effect on the corporation. Unlike the European test, the U.S. test does not require that the information be "precise."[66] Accordingly, the

---

authority after a merger such as the sale of a corporate unit or a corporate activity in a particular geographic region or a prudential requirement to increase capitalization. Id. at 17–18.

[63] Ventoruzzo and Picciau (2017), pp. 175, 192.

[64] The direction of the effect on the price is irrelevant. Ventoruzzo and Picciau (2017), p. 193.

[65] Share price is considered the best proxy for shareholder wealth and the reflection of overall corporate performance. Ferrarini and Ungureanu (2018), p. 340. However, it is unclear why the E.U. regulation prefers to estimate the effect of an event on a proxy of the corporate performance when the issuer disclosing the information is usually an insider well positioned to assess the impact of the information on the corporation itself. See also the discussion in JOMO FOMO, basic v. levinson assumption on share price.

[66] The definition of inside information in the MAR includes a particular clarification regarding protracted processes like mergers, making it clear that intermediate steps can and should be addressed as material information if the conditions of Article 7 of the MAR are met. The wording of Article 7(3) of the MAR is interpreted in the literature as meaning that for an intermediate step to be considered material it must be "precise" and have in and of itself a significant effect on the price of the corporation's financial instruments. See Ventoruzzo and Picciau (2017), p. 204. This is different from the U.S. probability/magnitude test, first because the latter test does not require precision or specificity of circumstances, and second because the U.S. rule looks at any given time at the final effect of the event on the corporation, whereas the E.U. intermediate step requires an evaluation of the potential effect that disclosure of the intermediate step will have on the price of the financial instrument. Some European scholars argue that the ECJ has relaxed the precision

U.S. test will regard as material future events that are large in magnitude but low in probability due to their vague and factually imprecise initial state.

The difference between the tests means that the same uncertain event will become material at different points in time in Europe and the United States. Consider two identical corporations subject to different materiality regimes that are facing the same major future event. Under the U.S. test, information about a future event of great magnitude may become material at a relatively early stage, even if the probability of the event taking place is lower than the standard bright-line likelihood. Thus, the U.S. test triggers earlier application of insider trading restrictions regarding future events of great magnitude, but without mandatory disclosure the U.S. corporation has no obligation to make this information public. For the European corporation, the information is not considered material and therefore neither disclosure nor insider trading prohibitions apply.

Future events of smaller magnitude may not be considered material information in the United States until a relatively advanced stage, when their likelihood of occurring is high. Under the European regime, information about a future event of smaller magnitude must be disclosed—unless the corporation explicitly decides to delay the disclosure[67]—when the bright-line likelihood threshold is crossed if informing the market about the intermediate step is expected to generate a significant effect on the price of the corporation's financial instruments. This means that unless the corporation explicitly decides to delay the disclosure, it will have to be revealed at this point.[68]

In other words, events of smaller magnitude are generally considered material earlier under the European regime than under the U.S. regime. Now combine this understanding with the mandatory/voluntary disclosure divide.

Let us assume that the *frequency* of events of smaller magnitude in the life of corporations is much higher than the frequency of dramatic high-magnitude events. It is reasonable to expect that the distribution of events in the life of a corporation is a normal one with a maximum value centered at zero. This is so because corporations experience a huge number of daily small events that are generally insignificant for investors. Only a small number of events have a high potential to be of significant magnitude (positive or negative), and events of high-magnitude are probabilistically quite rare.

If this is the case, the E.U. mandatory disclosure regime clutters the information landscape for investors with relatively unimportant information and suppresses important information. In contrast, the U.S. voluntary disclosure regime with regard to unfolding events declutters the informational landscape but imposes insider trading prohibitions in regard to material and important information such that if decision makers want to trade on this information, they must disclose it first. In the

---

requirement in its decision in Lafonta but the probability threshold remains higher than in the United States. See Hoessl-Neumann and Baumgartner (2018), p. 18.

[67]See also Ventoruzzo and Picciau (2017), pp. 372–375.

[68]The pressure to disclose in the MAR is very strong. Ventoruzzo (2017), p. 14.

United States, such a disclosure explodes into a barren information landscape like a water fountain in a desert.

# 5 Insights from Behavioral Law and Economics

In this section, we use insights from behavioral law and economics to evaluate how the different regulatory regimes, both designed to produce an optimal information space for investors and other market participants, change as a result of cognitive biases of corporate insiders and investors.

A plethora of cognitive biases have been documented in the behavioral economics and behavioral finance literature. We do not claim to cover all of them. This part focuses on some of the major relevant cognitive biases in the literature, with particular attention to the biases that were documented in the context of securities regulation architecture and that may apply to disclosure and insider trading prohibitions regarding information about anticipated events.

## *5.1 Corporate Decision Makers*

In applying insights from behavioral economics to the U.S. and E.U. regulatory architectures, it makes sense to start by looking at the decision to disclose information. After all, in spite of the fact that the regulatory architectures are designed to supply investors with information, they are directed at the corporate insiders who make disclosure decisions. After evaluating the consequences of behavioral biases on managerial decision-making, one can better assess the information that is provided to retail investors, institutional investors, and the public at large.

### 5.1.1 Optimism Bias and Overconfidence

Individuals tend to be optimistic about themselves and their own futures as well as about their own abilities and capabilities. That means that with regard to themselves, individuals tend to overestimate the probability of positive events and underestimate the probability of negative events.[69] For example, individuals tend to be optimistic about their health. Furthermore, individuals tend to maintain their optimism even after they are supplied with information that, given their life experience, should alter

[69] Sharot (2011), p. 941.

their perception of the future event.[70] Sharot found that optimism bias has biological underpinnings.[71]

The optimism bias is a human phenomenon and as such it applies to U.S. and E.U. decision makers alike. In our context, it means that individuals tend to overestimate the probability of an event that will have a "good" impact on their business and underestimate the probability of an event that is likely to have "bad" repercussions.

A corollary to overoptimism is overconfidence. Overconfidence explains the high rate of business failures among entrepreneurs that enter the market.[72] It breeds excessive risk taking and insufficient recognition of negative signals.[73] That managers tend to be overoptimistic and overconfident is empirically indicated by the rate at which managers miss their corporate projections and the rate at which corporate takeover moves end in failure.[74]

It is important to note that even in organizations that supposedly include internal checks and balances designed to reduce cognitive biases of individuals, these biases are likely to persist. Benabou found that people in organizations with anticipatory preferences choose how to interpret and recall public signals about future prospects. Wishful thinking (denial of bad news) was shown to be contagious when it is harmful to others and self-limiting when it is beneficial. Similarly, willful blindness (information avoidance) spreads when it increases the risks borne by others. Groupthink can be explained by the fact that when information flows upward from the lower echelons of the corporation to the decision makers, subordinates may filter the information according to their self-interest.[75] This general phenomenon in hierarchies implies that not only realism but also delusion will trickle down from top leadership to the entire firm.[76] Indeed, unrealistic optimism is often associated with catastrophic consequences driven by group overoptimism. An often-cited example is the 2008 financial crisis—investors and managers believed that markets are unlikely to fail.[77] This insight suggests that in many cases what seems to be fraudulent concealment of bad news is *de facto* the result of cognitive biases. Zamir and Teichman observed:

> The key point in this regard is that corporate fraud often does not spring from a deliberate decision to cheat investors, but rather from several features of the company's decision-making process. [. . .] [C]ognitive forces such as the confirmation bias, escalation of commitment, and overconfidence may cause management to discount any looming negative information that suggests that the plan is misconceived. This individual behavior can be

[70]Sharot (2011), pp. 942–943.

[71]Sharot (2011), p. 944.

[72]See Camerer and Lovallo (1999), p. 306; Zamir and Teichman (2018), p. 363.

[73]Gervais and Odean (2001).

[74]Barberis and Thaler (2002), p. 58.

[75]Langevoort (1997), pp. 120–122.

[76]Benabou (2013), pp. 429–462.

[77]Benabou (2013), pp. 429–462.

magnified in a group setting, when the silence of other group members in the face of bad information strengthens the perception that there is no cause for alarm.[78]

A common incarnation of the overconfidence bias is overprecision. "Overprecision" is defined as excessive belief in the accuracy of one's estimation. It has been found that when people are asked to estimate whether they are 90% or more certain of their precise estimate, they tend to be more than 90% confident about the precision of their estimation but wrong more than 50% of the time.[79] In other words, when corporate decision makers are required to estimate the probability of a future event, they are likely to be overoptimistic, overconfident, and quite certain that their biased estimation is accurate.

The implications of the optimism bias both in the U.S. and E.U. are that "good" information will be deemed material sooner than is optimal and "bad" information will be deemed material later than it should be. The information provided to investors will necessarily be influenced by this deviation from the classic law and economics model. In Europe, given that disclosure is mandatory, the total mix of information will be overoptimistic. Furthermore, because of the unique European bright-line test, if low-magnitude "good" events tend to occur more frequently than high-magnitude events and their probability of occurring is overestimated, then the total mix in the European market will be even more cluttered by information about relatively unimportant (yet overestimated) events.

In the U.S., where disclosure is voluntary, the total mix will also be slanted towards overoptimism. In this setting, the optimism bias can be expected to create an additional effect: a more cluttered information space that is a bit closer to the cluttered European total mix of information. This is a result of the probability/magnitude test being applied overoptimistically. Because the probability of "good" events is overestimated, smaller-magnitude events will be perceived to be material sooner than they really are because the subjective increase in their probability means that their expected value will be higher than their true value is. This implies that some of these events will be considered "material" sooner than they really are and often they will be voluntarily disclosed—inaccurately and prematurely.

Finally, the overconfidence bias can also enrich our analysis in the context of insider trading prohibitions. Behavioral traits of senior managers may have implications for the possibility of their using nonpublic information for their own benefit. Managers have more opportunities to use inside information.[80] They are also people with a greater tendency to take risks.[81] Consequently, managers are more likely to use inside information if they believe they can benefit from doing so. Although they may not always profit from the use of inside information because they are overconfident and overoptimistic and therefore may be victims of their own hubris, this behavior can undermine the integrity of the market. The U.S. approach to insider

[78]Zamir and Teichman (2018), p. 372.

[79]See generally Moore and Healy (2008).

[80]Haft (1982), pp. 1056–1057.

[81]Langevoort (1997), p. 112; Zamir and Teichman (2018), p. 362.

trading prohibitions, by which prohibitions are triggered sooner than in the E.U. and more strictly enforced, is compatible with the need to dampen the effects of managerial hubris.

### 5.1.2 Status Quo Bias

The fundamental difference between the U.S. and European disclosure regime regarding anticipated events, the voluntary/mandatory divide, can be analyzed through the lens of the status quo bias framework. The literature about the effect of the status quo bias on individual decision makers is well developed. It supports the premise that people tend to prefer and stick with the status quo even when a pure cost-benefit analysis prescribes a different choice.[82]

Both the United States and European Union adhere to the famous overarching abstain-or-disclose rule. However, in the European architecture, once a decision that information is material is reached, the status quo is "disclose." In other words, the European routine default is to "opt in," and delaying requires active "opting out" by corporate decision makers. A decision to delay disclosure is a change that requires attending to the implications of delay, explaining the reasons for the delay within the corporate decision hierarchy, documenting the reasons for the delay, and where applicable reporting the reasons to the relevant authorities. Disclosure is thus not only the mandatory norm but also the preferred and easy action in terms of the status quo bias. This observation implies that disclosure of some information that should have been delayed will not be delayed. It follows that the under-application of the option to delay may occasionally have detrimental effects on corporations' activities.

The voluntary U.S. disclosure regime with regard to anticipated events means that the U.S. status quo default is "opt out" and that disclosing requires active "opting in" by management, which in turn often requires investing in convincing all decision makers that disclosure is beneficial, drafting an accurate announcement, and monitoring the impact of the disclosed information to assess whether updates are required. This design is likely to deter some optimal disclosures. Hence, the total mix in the U.S. may be suboptimal because the disclosure of some information will be inappropriately delayed.

Counterintuitively, this should have a positive impact on corporate performance in the United States. The U.S. compensation culture is significantly based on linking pay to performance through executive stock options plans.[83] Europe generally lags behind the United States with regard to stock option compensation plans.[84] Elsewhere, we have argued that the lack of private managerial interest in stock price

[82]Samuelson and Zeckhauser (1988), pp. 57–59.

[83]See generally Mathieu (2013).

[84]Ryan Browne, European Start-ups Call for Stock Option Reform to Help Them Compete with Silicon Valley, CNBC.com (Nov. 28, 2018), https://www.cnbc.com/2018/11/28/30-european-startup-ceos-call-for-stock-option-reform.html.

diminishes decision makers' interest in decluttering the information space of the European market. In contrast, the typical U.S. manager is motivated to disclose material price-sensitive information to bolster the value of their stock option compensation package.[85] An important incentive for voluntary disclosure of unfolding events in the U.S. is therefore the desire of managers to "cash out" by trading on their stock options or other equity-based compensation. However, cashing out reduces managerial performance incentives because it reduces the number of stock options in the managerial compensation package and thus weakens the correlation between performance and compensation levels. If voluntary disclosure is restrained by the status quo bias, cashing out will be delayed because of the abstain-or-disclose condition. The upshot of this delay is that managers remain incentivized by their equity-based remuneration schemes for longer periods of time. Ironically, if equity-based compensation is, as it is perceived to be, one of the reasons for managerial short-termism, then voluntary disclosure combined with the existence of the status quo bias should dampen this undesired managerial behavior.

### 5.1.3 Fechner's Law

The so-called "Fechner's Law" suggests that individuals are less able to discern (and also that they pay less attention to) small changes in the probability of large-magnitude events as compared to big changes in the probability of small-magnitude events.[86] This phenomenon means that U.S. managers may not optimally discern that the probability of a large-magnitude event that was disclosed at an early stage has changed (positively or negatively) when the probabilistic change is relatively small, in spite of the fact that the small change has a higher value than a big probability change with regard to a small-magnitude event does.

For example, when the probability of an anticipated but uncertain transaction that is worth U.S. $250 million in revenue to the corporation decreases from 6 to 5%, the change for investors is U.S. $2.5 million. When a smaller transaction worth U.S.$5 million drops from 80% likely to 40% likely, the impact on investors is only U.S. $2 million. However, Fechner's law implies that the former change will not be disclosed due to the human difficulty in discerning small probabilistic changes and that the latter development will be disclosed because of the more easily observable change in probability.

This phenomenon narrows the information gap between the U.S. and the E.U., but not in an efficient way. As we noted, in the E.U., the information space about future events is likely to be cluttered with relatively small and less important facts. Fechner's law suggests that with respect to voluntarily disclosed information, updates in the U.S. regime are likely to clutter the information space with information that is probabilistically more observable but nominally less important.

---

[85] Baum and Solomon (2020).

[86] See Moyer and Landauer (1967), pp. 1519–1520; Longo and Lourenco (2007), pp. 1400–1407.

## 5.2 *Investors*

Securities disclosure regimes tend to overload investors with information. This is by now common wisdom. It is also widely accepted that investors cannot digest the flood of information in the market even if this information is supplied in the most easily digestible way. When discloses face endless amounts of information, they simply stop reading.[87] The overload problem characterizes every securities regime known to us. It concerns, and is affected by, all disclosure duties, not just those pertaining to information about uncertain future events. It is unclear whether the general disclosure regime in the United States is more or less burdensome than the European disclosure regime in this respect. We therefore assume that they are equally burdensome with respect to overloading the investors with data. We focus on the marginal effect of disclosures regarding uncertain future events. By "marginal" we do not mean that this information is less important. On the contrary, because the semi-strong EMH assumes that all disclosed information is already captured in the market price of the security, the differences in the regimes that govern the timing and probabilistic character of future events is crucial.

There are several well-documented cognitive biases that reinforce the concern that investors may misjudge forward-looking information about uncertain events. Furthermore, a combination of cognitive biases raises the concern that sharing information about uncertain future events at a very early stage will cause investors to believe that these events are more likely than not to occur. In other words, when voluntary disclosure takes place under the U.S. materiality test, behavioral economics raises concerns about the ability of investors to respond to these disclosures accurately. Moreover, although there is no empirical research to confirm the hypothesis, the structure of the disclosure regime in the E.U. supports the presumption that the information space in the European setting will be cluttered by more information about less important unfolding events.[88] Clearly, disclosure rules need to take into account the fact that sometimes less is more from the point of view of investors.[89]

In this section we describe pertinent investor biases and analyze their respective impact in the U.S. and European settings.

### 5.2.1 Conservatism Bias

"Conservatism bias" means that people are not likely to update their perceptions sufficiently even when they are presented with new information.[90] Zamir and Teichman explain that "the effect of well-designed disclosures might erode over

[87]Zamir and Teichman (2018), p. 173.

[88]See supra Sect. 3.

[89]Baum and Solomon discuss this in greater detail in Baum and Solomon (2020).

[90]See generally: Hilbert (2012), pp. 211–237.

time, unless special effort is put into constantly altering the disclosure in a bid to stave off habituation."[91]

This bias is likely to affect investors in the U.S. regime more than investors in the European regime. If information about an anticipated event is revealed relatively early and with a comparatively small probability of occurring when it is voluntarily disclosed in the U.S., then its rate of change is higher. In other words, there is a higher likelihood that the magnitude of the event or its probability will change over time. For example, if a merger of high magnitude is revealed when the probability of its consummation is 10%, then the corporation will be updating on its probability when it increases to 50% but will also update if later for some reason the probability drops to 20% or the magnitude of the merger falls by half. In the latter cases, conservatism bias means that investors will not be able to internalize the new information accurately. Consequently, the response of investors with respect to a buy-or-sell decision will be distorted.

Because investors under the U.S. regime are exposed to information at a much earlier stage than are investors under the E.U. regime, the former are likely to be more influenced by this effect.

### 5.2.2 Overoptimism, the Ostrich Effect, and the Ability to Assess Probabilities

Several identified biases support the presumption that individual investors may not be able to judge probabilities adequately. The neglect-of-probability bias suggests that when they make decisions, people neglect probability altogether even when events are uncertain. Choi and Pritchard argued that in general, "investors are often simply poor judges of probabilities."[92]

People are also affected by the optimism bias discussed earlier.[93] At the same time, both corporate decision makers and investors may be affected by the so-called ostrich effect, which suggests that with regard to major negative events, people tend to ignore or at least underestimate probabilistic information. For example, people avoid collecting additional information about the future if doing so is likely to bring bad news to their attention. People monitor and attend to information more actively when they are given preliminary good news, but when they are given adverse news they put their heads in the sand to avoid receiving additional information. The ostrich effect has been documented in a finance context in a study examining the account-monitoring behavior of Scandinavian and American investors in two datasets. In both datasets, investors monitored their portfolios more frequently in rising markets than when markets were flat or falling.[94]

---

[91] Zamir and Teichman (2018), p. 174.

[92] Choi and Pritchard (2003), p. 12.

[93] See discussion on optimism bias in Sharot (2011).

[94] Karlsson et al. (2009), pp. 95–115.

Behavioral economics teaches us that investors overlook or misunderstand risk.[95] Benartzi and Thaler found that employees who invested the majority of their pensions in their employer's stock failed to understand the risk of not diversifying and evaluated the risk profile of the company more optimistically than they did the risk profile of an index fund. Interestingly, that study was done after Enron's and WorldCom's collapses.[96]

This combination of biases is likely to have a stronger impact on U.S. investors rather than on European investors. In both the European and U.S. regimes, this combination of biases means that information disclosed to the public will be slanted toward positive news and that the likelihood that future events will be bad will be underestimated by investors. The bias for good versus bad news is likely to be higher in the U.S. setting where the decision to disclose is voluntary, which means managers may delay the disclosure of negative information because of their misguided belief that given more time the uncertain negative event will not occur. Consequently, when information about negative events will eventually hit the market, U.S. investors suffering from the same optimism bias and ostrich effect may not be able to fully internalize the implications of the bad news about the corporation.

In other words, given the higher attention to voluntary disclosure in the U.S. disclosure architecture, this group of biases suggests that U.S. securities markets will tend to be more biased toward optimistic evaluations of uncertain future events. At the same time, the U.S. market should also suffer from more volatility as a result of a higher frequency of negative events that were not fully anticipated and attended to by the market.

### 5.2.3 Availability Cascades

The availability bias means that investors are likely to overestimate the probability of an event if a similar event recently materialized.[97] For example, if pharmaceutical company A announced that it successfully tested a medication that will cure COVID-19, an announcement by company B that it is also on the verge of finding a cure and starting tests will cause investors to estimate that company B's success is probable although there is no reason to do so.

Availability cascades create a self-reinforcing process in which a collective belief gains more and more plausibility in the eyes of individual members of the general population because of repetition in public discourse.[98]

This cognitive bias may be used, intentionally or unintentionally, to manipulate investors into overestimating the probability of uncertain future events in a setting of

[95] Zamir and Teichman (2018), p. 373.

[96] Benartzi and Thaler (2007) p. 91.

[97] Choi and Pritchard (2003), p. 14.

[98] See Kuran and Sunstein (1998), pp. 683–768.

voluntary disclosure. By voluntarily disclosing positive information that has high magnitude but low probability and then updating constantly on the status of the event, insiders can manipulate investors into overestimating the likelihood of the event.[99] This effect is likely to occur even without manipulative intentions. It can also happen in relation to negative future events: once an event has been voluntarily disclosed, an obligation arises to update the market with any further material development. For example, when a dominant CEO is diagnosed with an illness that may affect performance of his or her managerial duties and the information is shared with the public, ongoing disclosure of developments in the CEO's condition is required.[100] When investors are provided with a stream of information about the development of the illness, they may underestimate the possibility of recovery or overestimate the speed with which the illness is likely to worsen to the point that it incapacitates the CEO.

Although availability cascades also exist in the European setting, the European regime dampens their effect. First, the bright-line materiality threshold means that the larger-magnitude, more eye-catching news will be subject to mandatory disclosure at a relatively later stage in Europe than in the United States. Consequently, overall, there will be less time for repetition. Second, even if a corporation chooses to voluntarily disclose an event in the European market before disclosure is required by the European bright-line test, because the mandatory disclosure regime in Europe produces more information the salience of particular news and its repetition is watered down.

Counterintuitively, information technology that is supposed to help investors cope with excessive information may introduce availability cascades. Websites or applications that are designed to filter undesired information and help investors focus on news about a particular corporation or about particular developments[101] potentially increase the likelihood that their users will be influenced by intentional or unintentional availability cascades.

## *5.3 The Impossibility of Forecasting Price Movements*

The E.U. regime requires that decision makers determine the materiality of information about future events by estimating its impact on the price of the relevant securities. Indeed, this is the premise of the EMH.[102] However, there is ample

---

[99] In fact, it has been shown that investors are likely to see and be influenced by patterns even if these patterns do not exist in reality. Then they tend to use these patterns as heuristics for financial investment decisions. For examples, if investors perceive a series of optimistic reports as a pattern leading to some positive corporate outcome they will generally overestimate the positive outcome and invest in the corporate's stock. See Durham et al. (2003).

[100] Lin (2009), p. 413.

[101] An example is the website Finviz.com, at: https://finviz.com/screener.ashx?v=111&ft=4.

[102] Langevoort (1996), p. 669.

evidence that investors do not respond to new information rationally. Empirical observations support the conclusion that markets do not behave according to the EMH.[103] It follows that rational expectations about the movement of prices are going to be—to use mild terminology—inaccurate.

First of all, bounded rationality suggests that investors, even experts, cannot optimally digest all available information. The cluttered information space in the E.U. implies that investors fail to use all available information in making their investment decisions. The work of Benartzi & Thaler showed that even sophisticated economists use heuristics to make complicated investment decisions in situations that require solving an optimization problem and evaluating a future desired return.[104]

Rabin and Schrag argued that even with an infinite amount of information, a decision maker suffering from confirmatory bias will not update his or her beliefs in the correct direction but rather may end up believing a wrong hypothesis with almost absolute certainty. For example, if investors believe that company A is better than company B, new information will be taken in a way that confirms this perception and reinforces it "too strongly."[105] This will be the case even if the initial belief is wrong. With respect to investors, then, over-informing investors through mandatory disclosure is not likely to change incorrect or inaccurate beliefs; rather, it will reinforce them. This means that mandatory disclosure is not only costly, but it also could generate an unexpected opposite reaction in the market price of the securities.

According to the "disposition effect," when an individual investor sells a stock in their portfolio, they have a propensity to sell a stock that has gone up in value since purchase rather one than one whose value has decreased.[106] This is largely explained by Tversky and Kahneman's prospect theory, which says that individuals evaluate gambles by thinking about gains and losses, not final wealth levels, and that they process gains and losses using a value function that is concave for gains and convex for losses.[107] In the same vein, Odean found that under the "disposition effect" investors realize their profitable stocks investments at a much higher rate than their unprofitable ones except in December.[108] The extent to which this behavior affects market prices depends on the trading activities of other market participants, such as professional traders and institutional investors.[109]

---

[103]Zamir and Teichman (2018), p. 371. For example, according to the so-called "Momentum Effect" stock that rose for 6 consecutive months continue to rise in the seventh month 10% more on average than stock that had no such consecutive performance. For literature on other examples see Barberis and Thaler (2002), p. 33.

[104]Benartzi and Thaler (2007), p. 86.

[105]Rabin and Schrag (1999).

[106]Barberis and Xiong (2009), p. 751.

[107]This is first illustrated in the seminal paper of Kahneman and Tversky (1979), later extended in Tversk and Kahneman (1992).

[108]Odean (1998).

[109]Odean (1998) and Shefrin and Statman (1985).

In the aggregate, these behavioral biases undermine the European regulation's expectation that corporate decision makers will base their materiality assessment on price sensitivity. This is because the reaction of the market to information is extremely hard to foresee. As a result, whether a piece of information will have a "significant effect" on the price is unforeseeable and attempting to make that assessment is useless.

## 6 Conclusion

While pure economic analysis suggests that the U.S. regime is superior to the European regime in how it addresses disclosure of material unfolding events, insights from behavioral economics allow a more nuanced evaluation of the two regimes. We found that the status quo bias suggests that decision makers in U.S. markets may be less inclined to voluntarily disclose information. Hence, such disclosures may arrive later rather than sooner. Fechner's law implies that the U.S. disclosure regime underperforms with regard to updating the market on developing information, which is particularly important with regard to unfolding events. These deficiencies are exacerbated by overoptimism and overconfidence.

According to the classic analysis of law and economics, the U.S. materiality test triggers insider trading prohibitions earlier than the E.U. regime does. Behavioral insights suggest that in both jurisdictions, "good" information will be deemed material sooner than optimal and "bad" information will be deemed material later than it should be. In that respect, the U.S. insider trading architecture is better suited to dampening the effects of managerial overconfidence.

On the receiving side, disclosure regimes tend to overload investors with information. We find that the combination of overoptimism, the ostrich effect, and investors' inability to accurately assess probabilities is likely to have a stronger effect on U.S. investors than on European investors. U.S. securities markets will tend to be more biased toward optimistic evaluations of uncertain future events.

Because the U.S. regime forces earlier disclosure of information about unfolding events more often than the European regime does, conservatism bias means that U.S. investors will not be able to internalize updated information accurately. Consequently, investor response to updated information may be distorted.

Finally, the European regime assumes that corporate decision makers can assess securities' price-sensitivity to the relevant information. However, behavioral economics suggests that the Europeans' reliance on this assumption is misplaced.

While this chapter sheds light on the effects of cognitive biases on securities markets, we do not argue that securities regulation should eliminate all cognitive biases from the market. This is not feasible, nor is such an approach desirable as long as these cognitive biases are not systematically slanted in one direction or abused by one particular party in the market (e.g., corporate insiders) in a way that expropriates the rights or assets of another (e.g., public investors).

**Acknowledgements** The authors would like to thank Lior Alona Goldman for excellent research assistance.

## References

Bainbridge SM (2000) Mandatory disclosure: a behavioral analysis. Univ Cincinnati Law Rev 68:1023–1060

Barberis N, Thaler RN (2002) A Survey of Behavioral Finance. http://papers.ssrn.com/sol3/papers.cfm?abstract_id=327880

Barberis N, Xiong W (2009) What drives the disposition effect? An analysis of a long-standing preference-based explanation. J Financ 64(2):751–784

Baum I, Solomon D (2019) When should you abstain? A call for a global rule of insider trading. University of Cincinnati Law Review 88:67–100

Baum I, Solomon D (2020) More JoMo Less FoMo: the case for voluntary disclosure of uncertain information in securities regulation. Va Law Bus Rev 14

Benabou R (2013) Groupthink: collective delusions in organizations and markets. Rev Econ Stud 80:429–462

Benartzi S, Thaler R (2007) Heuristics and biases in retirement savings behavior. J Econ Perspect 21(3):81–104

Ben-Shahar O, Schneider CE (2014) More than you wanted to know: the failure of mandated disclosure. Princeton University Press, Princeton, Woodstock Oxfordshire and Beijing

Camerer CF, Lovallo D (1999) Overconfidence and excess entry: an experimental approach. Am Econ Rev 89:306–318

Choi SJ, Pritchard AC (2003) Behavioral economics and the SEC. Stanford Law Rev 56:1–74

Choi SJ, Pritchard AC (2015) Securities regulation: cases and analysis. Foundation Press

Durham G, Hertzel MG, Martin JS (2003) The Market Impact of Trends and Sequences in Performance: New Evidence. http://ssrn.com/abstract=411021

Easterbrook FH, Fischel DR (1984) Mandatory disclosure and the protection of investors. Va Law Rev 70:669–716

Fama EF (1970) Efficient capital markets: a review of theory and empirical work. J Financ 25 (2):383–417

Ferrarini G, Ungureanu MC (2018) Executive remuneration. In: Gordon JN, Ringe W (eds) The Oxford handbook of corporate law and governance. Oxford University Press, Oxford, pp 334–363

Georgiev GS (2017) Too big to disclose: firm size and materiality blindspots in securities regulation. Univ Calif Los Angeles Law Rev 64:602–683

Gervais S, Odean T (2001) Learning to be overconfident. Rev Financ Stud 14:1–27

Goshen Z, Parchomovsky G (2006) The essential role of securities regulation. Duke Law J 55:711–782

Gow ID, Larcker DF, Zakolyukina AA (2019) Non-answers During Conference Calls (Chicago Booth Research Paper No. 19-01; Fama-Miller Working Paper; Rock Center for Corporate Governance at Stanford University Working Paper No. 237, 2019). https://ssrn.com/abstract=3310360

Haft RJ (1982) The effect of insider trading rules on the internal efficiency of the large corporations. Mich Law Rev 80:1051–1071

Hansen JL (2016) Say when: when must an issuer disclose inside information? Nordic & European Company Law LSN Research Paper Series No. 16-03 (2016)

Hazen TL (2009) The law of securities regulation. West Publishing Company, Eagan

Hilbert M (2012) Toward a synthesis of cognitive biases: how noisy information processing can bias human decision making. Psychol Bull 138(2):211–237

Hoessl-Neumann M, Baumgartner A (2018) Dealing with Corporate Scandal Under European Market Abuse Law: The Case of VW, Stanford-Vienna European Union Law Working Paper No. 37. https://ssrn.com/abstract=3281009

Horwich A (2016) The legality of opportunistically timing public company disclosures in the context of rule 10b5-1. Bus Lawyer 71:1113–1150

Kahneman D, Tversky A (1979) Prospect theory: an analysis of decision under risk Econometrica 47:263–291, later extended in Tversk A, Kahneman D (1992) Advances in prospect theory: Cumulative representation of uncertainty. J Risk Uncertain 5: 297–323

Karlsson N, Loewenstein G, Seppi D (2009) The ostrich effect: selective attention to information. J Risk Uncertain 38:95–115

Kersting C (2014) Insider dealing and Ad Hoc disclosure requirements in the new E.U. market abuse regulation. Bank Financ Serv Policy Rep 3(1):15–23

Klöhn L (2015) Inside information without an incentive to trade? What's at stake in 'Lafonta v. AMF'. Capital Mark Law J 10:162–180

Krause H, Brellochs M (2013) Insider trading and the disclosure of inside information after Geltl—a comparative analysis of the ECJ decision in the Geltl vs Daimler case with a view to the European market abuse regulation. Capital Markets Law J 8:283–299

Kuran T, Sunstein CR (1998) Availability cascades and risk regulation. Stanford Law Rev 51 (4):683–768

Langevoort DC (1996) Selling hope, selling risk: some lessons for law from behavioral economics about stockbrokers and sophisticated customers. California Law Rev 84:627–702

Langevoort DC (1997) Organized illusions: a behavioral theory of why corporations mislead stock market investors (and cause other social harms). Univ Pa Law Rev 146:101–172

Lin TCW (2009) Undressing the CEO: disclosing private, material matters of public company executives. Univ Pa J Bus Law 11:383–426

Lombardo S, Mucciarelli FM (2017) Market soundings: the interaction between securities regulation and company law in the United Kingdom and Italy. ECGI Working Paper 362/2017. http://ssrn.com/abstract_id=3012183

Longo MR, Lourenco SF (2007) Spatial attention and the mental number line: evidence for characteristic biases and compression. Neuropsychologia 45(7):1400–1407

Mathieu E (2013) Beyond Wall Street: Germany, The United States and executive compensation. Brooklyn J Int Law 38:579–654

Mock S (2017) History, application, interpretation, and legal sources of the market abuse regulation. In: Ventoruzzo M, Mock S (eds) Market abuse regulation commentary and annotated guide. Oxford University Press, Oxford, pp 3–12

Moore DA, Healy PJ (2008) The trouble with overconfidence. Psychol Rev 115(2):502–517

Moyer RS, Landauer TK (1967) Time required for judgements of numerical inequality. Nature 215 (5109):1519–1520

Odean T (1998) Are investors reluctant to realize their losses? J Financ 53(5):1775–1798

Park JJ (2018) Insider trading and the integrity of mandatory disclosure. Wis Law Rev 2018:1133

Pietrancosta A (2017) Public disclosure of inside information and market abuse. In: Ventoruzzo M, Mock S (eds) Market abuse regulation commentary and annotated guide. Oxford University Press, Oxford, pp 343–384

Posner RA (1973) The economic approach to law. Texas Law Rev 53:757–782

Posner RA (1998) Economic analysis of law. Wolters Kluwer Law & Business, New York

Pritchard AC (2018) Corporate governance, capital markets and securities law. In: Gordon JN, Ringe W (eds) The Oxford handbook of corporate law and governance. Oxford University Press, Oxford, pp 1063–1081

Rabin M, Schrag JL (1999) First impressions matter: a model of confirmatory bias. Q J Econ 114 (1):37–82

Samuelson W, Zeckhauser R (1988) Status Quo Bias in decision making. J Risk Uncertain 1:7–59

Schulzke KS, Berger-Walliser G (2017) Toward a unified theory of materiality in securities law. Columbia J Transnational Law 56:6–70

Sharot T (2011) The optimism bias. Curr Biol 21:941–945
Shefrin H, Statman M (1985) The disposition to sell winners too early and ride losers too long: theory and evidence. J Financ 40:777–790
Soderquist LD, Gabaldon TA (2014) Securities law. Foundation Press
Ventoruzzo M (2014) Comparing Insider Trading in the United States and in the European Union: History and Recent Developments. ECGI Working Paper No. 257/2014. http://ssrn.com/abstract=2442049
Ventoruzzo M (2017) The concept of insider dealing. In: Ventoruzzo M, Mock S (eds) Market abuse regulation commentary and annotated guide. Oxford University Press, Oxford, pp 13–31
Ventoruzzo M, Picciau C (2017) Inside information. In: Ventoruzzo M, Mock S (eds) Market abuse regulation commentary and annotated guide. Oxford University Press, Oxford, pp 175–207
Zamir E, Teichman D (2018) Behavioral law and economics. Oxford University Press, Oxford

**Ido Baum** Tel Aviv. Associate Professor of Law at the Haim Striks School of Law, College of Management-Academic Studies (COLMAN) and Co-Director of the Heth Center for the Research of Competition and Regulation. baumi@colman.ac.il. Fields of Interest: Corporate Law, Securities Regulation, Economic Analysis of Law, Insolvency, Civil Procedure and Media Law.

**Jaroslaw Beldowski** Warsaw. Associate Professor at Warsaw School of Economics, Economic Analysis College, International Comparative Studies Department. jbeldo@sgh.waw.pl. Fields of Interest: Law and Economics/ Economic Analysis of Law, Courts, Contract Law and Economics, International Financial Markets, Economics of Regulation.

**Dov Solomon** Petah Tikva. Associate Professor of Law and head of the Commercial Law Department and the LL.M. program at the College of Law and Business, Ramat Gan Law School. solomon@clb.ac.il. Fields of Interest: Corporate Law, Securities Regulation, Securitization, Commercial Law, Secured Transactions and Economic Analysis of Law.

# Data Flows versus Data Protection: Mapping Existing Reconciliation Models in Global Trade Law

**Mira Burri**

**Abstract** With the increased role of data in societies, the interfaces between trade and privacy protection have become multiple and intensified, and raise important questions as to adequate regulatory design that can reconcile economic and non-economic concerns, national and international interests. This chapter is set against this complex backdrop and seeks to provide a better understanding and contextualization of the theme of data protection and its interfaces with global trade law. It addresses this task by looking first at the existing international, transnational, and selected national frameworks for privacy protection and briefly sketches their evolution over time. In a second step, the chapter explores the application of the rules of the World Trade Organization, which are still in a pre-internet state, to situations where privacy concerns are affected. The chapter then looks at the data-relevant rules that have emerged in free trade agreements with a focus on the reconciliation mechanisms that these treaties provide. The chapter concludes with an appraisal of the current state of affairs and some thoughts on the pros and cons of the available legal solutions for reconciling trade and privacy protection.

---

M. Burri (✉)
Faculty of Law, University of Lucerne, Lucerne, Switzerland
e-mail: mira.burri@unilu.ch

 
K. Mathis, A. Tor (eds.), *Law and Economics of Regulation*, Economic Analysis of Law in European Legal Scholarship 11,
https://doi.org/10.1007/978-3-030-70530-5_7

## 1 Introduction: Trade and Privacy Protection in the Data-Driven Economy

Privacy protection is not necessarily a theme of direct relevance for international trade law. Trade treaties,[1] as well as classic trade law treatises, do not cover the topic of privacy.[2] The interface between trade and data protection became only relevant due to technological advances, which permitted the easy flow of information across borders and exposed the tensions between economic and non-economic interests.[3] During the late 1970s and the 1980s, as satellites, computers, and software significantly changed the dynamics of communications, the trade-offs between allowing data to flow freely and asserting national jurisdiction became readily apparent. Some states, echoing the concerns of large multinational companies, started to worry that barriers to information flows may seriously hinder economic activities and looked for mechanisms that can prevent the erection of such barriers. It was clear that some sort of a balancing mechanism was needed. Such a mechanism was found, in a soft legal form, in the principles elaborated under the auspices of the Organisation for Economic Co-operation and Development (OECD).[4] Yet, as the OECD itself points out, while this privacy framework endured and will be briefly discussed later in this chapter, the situation then is profoundly different from the challenges in the realm of data governance we face today.[5] Ubiquitous digitization and powerful hardware, coupled with the society's increased reliance on the internet, have changed the volume, the intensity, and indeed, the nature of data flows.[6]

The value of data and Big Data,[7] as well as the risks associated with data collection, data processing, its use and re-use, by both companies and governments, have dramatically changed. On the one hand, data has become so essential to economic processes that it is said to be the "new oil".[8] Although this is a flawed statement, since data is not exhaustible and may lose its value over time,[9] it shows well the high value associated with it. Like other factors of production, such as

---

[1]The General Agreement on Tariffs and Trade (GATT) 1947 makes no reference to privacy and most of the free trade agreements up to very recently make no mention of it.

[2]See e.g. Jackson (1989); Jackson et al. (1995); Jackson (1998); Wolfrum et al. (2011), pp. 1–24.

[3]See e.g. Kuner (2011); Aaronson (2015), pp. 672, 680–685.

[4]OECD (1980).

[5]OECD (2013).

[6]See Manyika et al. (2011); Mayer-Schönberger and Cukier (2013); Cohen (2013); Richards and King (2014).

[7]There are no clear definitions of small versus Big Data. Definitions vary and scholars seem to agree that the term of Big Data is generalized and slightly imprecise. One common identification of Big Data is through its characteristics of volume, velocity, and variety, also referred to as the "3-Vs". Increasingly, experts add a fourth "V" that relates to the veracity or reliability of the underlying data. See Mayer-Schönberger and Cukier (2013), p. 13. For a brief introduction on Big Data applications and review of the literature, see Burri (2019).

[8]The Economist (2017).

[9]Among other arguments, see Burri (2019); for a full analysis, see Scholz (2019).

natural resources and human capital, it is increasingly the case that much of modern economic activity, innovation, and growth cannot occur without data.[10] Studies have revealed the vast potential of data as a trigger for more efficient business operations and highly innovative solutions in all areas of societal life.[11] Emerging technologies, like Artificial Intelligence (AI), are highly dependent on data inputs as well, so the future of the data-driven economy is in many aspects at stake.[12] Companies, as well as governments, are therefore encouraged to use the potential of data and to mobilize their resources aptly, so as to make the data-driven economy real.[13]

On the other hand, the increased dependence on data has brought about a new set of concerns. The impact of data collection and use upon privacy has been particularly widely acknowledged by scholars and policy-makers alike, as well as felt by regular users of digital products and services.[14] The risks have only been augmented in the era of Big Data and AI, which presents specific distinct challenges to the protection of personal data and, by extension, to the protection of personal and family life. For starters, Big Data puts into question the very distinction between personal and non-personal data. On the one hand, it appears that one of the basic tools of data protection—that of anonymization, i.e. the process of removing identifiers to create anonymized datasets—is only of limited utility in a data-driven world, as in reality, it is now rare for data generated by user activity to be entirely and irreversibly anonymized.

On the other hand, Big Data analytics enable the re-identification of data subjects by using and combining datasets of non-personal data, especially as data is persistent and can be retained indefinitely.[15] Big Data also puts into question the fundamental elements of existing privacy protection laws, which often operate upon requirements of transparency and user consent.[16] Equally, data minimization as another core idea of privacy protection is challenged, as firms are "hungry" to get hold of more data, and the sources of data from smart devices, sensors, and social networks interactions multiply.[17] These challenges have not been left unnoticed and have triggered the reform of data protection laws around the world, best exemplified by the European Union's General Data Protection Regulation (GDPR). The reform initiatives are, however, not coherent and are culturally and socially embedded, reflecting societies' deep understandings of constitutional values, relationships between citizens and the state, and the role of the market, as is illustrated by the discussion of the differences

[10] Manyika et al. (2011).

[11] See e.g. Manyika et al. (2011); Mayer-Schönberger and Cukier (2013); Henke et al. (2016).

[12] Irion and Williams (2019); The Royal Society (2017).

[13] See e.g. Manyika et al. (2011); Henke et al. (2016); Bughin et al. (2016).

[14] Ohm (2010); Schwartz and Solove (2011); Tene and Polonetsky (2013); The White House (2014); Gasser (2016); Bennett and Bayley (2016); Pan (2016); Council of Europe (2017).

[15] The White House (2014), pp. 14–15; also Ohm (2010); Rubinstein (2013), p. 77.

[16] Rubinstein (2013), p. 78.

[17] Tene and Polonetsky (2013).

between the US and the EU approaches to data protection that follows later in the chapter.

With the increased value of data and the associated risks, governments have also sought new ways to assert control over it—in particular by prescribing various measures that "localize" the data, its storage or suppliers, so as to keep it within the state's sovereign space.[18] This kind of erecting barriers to data flows impinges directly on trade and may endanger the realization of an innovative data economy.[19] The provision of any digital products and services, cloud computing applications, or the development of the Internet of Things (IoT) and AI are impossible under restrictions on cross-border flows of data.[20] Data protectionism may also be associated with certain costs for the economy that endorses it.[21]

Overall, with the increased role of data in societies, the interfaces between trade and privacy protection have become multiple and intensified, and raise important questions as to adequate regulatory design that can reconcile economic and non-economic concerns, national and international interests. This chapter is set against this complex backdrop and seeks to provide a better understanding and contextualization of the theme of data protection and its interfaces with global trade law. It addresses this task by looking first at the existing international, transnational, and selected national frameworks for privacy protection and briefly sketches their evolution over time. In a second step, the chapter explores the application of the rules of the World Trade Organization (WTO), which admittedly are in a pre-internet state, to situations where privacy concerns are affected. The chapter then looks at the data-relevant and data protection rules that have emerged in preferential trade venues with a focus on the reconciliation mechanisms that these treaties provide. The chapter concludes with an appraisal of the current state of affairs and some thoughts on the pros and cons of the available legal solutions for reconciling trade and privacy protection.

## 2 Legal Frameworks for the Protection of Privacy

### *2.1 International Rules for the Protection of Privacy*

The right to privacy is established in international law and is now commonly referred to as one of the fundamental human rights to which every human being is entitled to. The core privacy principle can be found in Art. 12 of the Universal Declaration of

---

[18]See Chander (2016), p. 2; also Chander and Lê (2015).

[19]USITC (2013, 2014); For a country survey, see Chander and Lê (2015).

[20]See Chander (2016), p. 2.

[21]See e.g. Ferracane (2020); Taylor (2020).

Human Rights (UDHR),[22] and the right to privacy was given formal legal protection in Art. 17 of the International Covenant on Civil and Political Rights (ICCPR), which guaranteed individuals protection of their personal sphere as broadly conceived.[23] But the protection has not been robust, and some scholars have shown by looking at the negotiation histories of the UDHR and the ICCPR that the right to privacy as an umbrella term almost accidentally found its way into the treaties and was only later enshrined in national constitutions.[24] Over the years, the international framework for privacy has expanded, in particular, due to the effects of new technologies and the new perils they may bring to data protection. Even though the Human Rights Committee has not yet developed a specific set of obligations in the domain of privacy law, it did recognize some of its core aspects, such as that personal information ought to be protected against both public authorities and private entities, the need for data security, the right of data subjects to be informed about the processing of their data and the right to rectification or elimination of unlawfully obtained or inaccurate data.[25] In 1990, the UN General Assembly also adopted Guidelines for the Regulation of Computerized Personal Data Files[26] that stipulate minimum guarantees and include certain key principles of data protection, such as lawfulness, fairness, accuracy, purpose-specification, relevance and adequacy of data collection and processing, and data security. However, the Guidelines are non-binding, and states may depart from the mentioned principles for reasons of national security, public order, public health or morality, and the rights of others.[27]

The Council of Europe (CoE) has played an important role in the evolution of the international regime by endorsing stronger and enforceable standards of human rights' protection in its forty-seven members through the 1950 European Convention on Human Rights (ECHR), and in particular, through the body of case-law developed by the European Court of Human Rights (ECtHR) on Art. 8.[28] This jurisprudence not only stressed the obligations of states to protect individual's privacy but also importantly clarified the limitations of the right to privacy imposed either by key

---

[22]"No one shall be subjected to arbitrary interference with his privacy, family, home or correspondence, nor to attacks upon his honour and reputation. Everyone has the right to the protection of the law against such interference or attacks".

[23]The text of Art. 17 is identical with Art. 12 UDHR but the two sentences are framed as separate paragraphs.

[24]Diggelmann and Cleis (2014).

[25]UN Office of the High Commissioner for Human Rights (1988), para. 10.

[26]UN General Assembly (1990).

[27]UN General Assembly (1990), para. 6.

[28]Art. 8 "Right to respect for private and family life" reads: 1. Everyone has the right to respect for his private and family life, his home and his correspondence. 2. There shall be no interference by a public authority with the exercise of this right except such as is in accordance with the law and is necessary in a democratic society in the interests of national security, public safety or the economic well-being of the country, for the prevention of disorder or crime, for the protection of health or morals, or for the protection of the rights and freedoms of others.

public interests or by the rights of others.[29] Different aspects of data protection were further endorsed through a number of CoE resolutions and ultimately through Convention 108 for the Protection of Individuals with Regard to Automatic Processing of Personal Data, which opened for signature in 1981 and was last amended in 2018. The CoE is the first international instrument that established minimum standards for personal data protection in a legally binding manner.[30]

## 2.2 *Transnational Rules for the Protection of Privacy: The OECD and the APEC Frameworks*

As earlier mentioned, the OECD was the first organization to endorse principles of privacy protection in recognizing both the need to facilitate trans-border data flows as a basis for economic and social development and the related risks.[31] The 1980 OECD Guidelines on the Protection of Privacy and Transborder Flows of Personal Data[32] sought to achieve this balance by agreeing upon certain basic principles of national and international application. These maintained free data flow, permitted legitimate restrictions, and offered a basis for national implementation and international cooperation.[33] The OECD Guidelines endorse in particular eight principles, applicable in both the public and the private sector, along which countries should develop their own privacy protection frameworks. These principles are: (1) collection limitation; (2) data quality; (3) purpose specification; (4) use limitation; (5) security safeguards Principle; (6) openness; (7) individual participation; (8) accountability, and have become an essential part of all national data protection regimes that were developed later on, including the EU framework, which is discussed in more detail in the next section. In trying to keep pace with newer technological advances, the OECD Guidelines were revised in 2013,[34] but these core principles remained unaltered. Several new concepts were added, including: national privacy strategies; privacy management programmes; and data security breach notification, which again permit for flexibility in implementation but recognize the newer demands from governments to approach data protection as an ever more important topic. Two features remain critical to the OECD Guidelines, and these are the focus on the practical implementation of privacy protection through an approach grounded in risk

[29]For a comprehensive guide to the jurisprudence, see European Court of Human Rights (2019).

[30]See e.g. European Union Agency for Fundamental Rights and Council of Europe (2018), pp. 15–16.

[31]OECD (2011), p. 7.

[32]OECD (1980).

[33]OECD (1980).

[34]OECD (2013).

management and the need to address the global dimension of privacy through improved interoperability.[35]

The 2005 APEC Privacy Framework[36] is in many ways similar to the OECD Privacy Guidelines[37] and contains a set of principles and implementation guidelines that were created in order to establish effective privacy protection that avoids barriers to information flows in the Asia Pacific Economic Cooperation (APEC) region of 21 countries. Building upon the Privacy Framework, APEC has developed the Cross-Border Privacy Rules (CBPR) system, which has now been formally joined by Australia, Chinese Taipei, Canada, Japan, South Korea, Mexico, Singapore, and the United States.[38] The CBPR system does not displace a country's domestic law, nor does it demand specific changes in it, but provides a minimum level of protection through certain compliance and certification mechanisms. It requires that participating businesses develop and implement data privacy policies that are consistent with the APEC Privacy Framework and the APEC Accountability Agents can assess this consistency. The CBPR system is in this sense analogous to the EU–US Privacy Shield, which we discuss later, in that they both provide means for self-assessment, compliance review, recognition, dispute resolution, and enforcement.[39] Both the OECD and APEC privacy frameworks are non-binding[40] but do illustrate the need for international cooperation in the field of data protection, as well as the importance of cross-border data flows as a fundament of contemporary economies.

## 2.3 *National Approaches for Data Protection: The European Union versus the United States*

### 2.3.1 Data Protection in the EU

The EU subscribes to a rights-based, omnibus data protection. The right to privacy is a key concept in EU law and has been given significant weight that reflects deep cultural values and understandings. Building upon the Council of Europe's ECHR, which protects the right to private and family life,[41] the Charter of Fundamental

[35]OECD (2013).

[36]APEC (2005).

[37]The APEC framework endorses similar to the OECD Privacy Guidelienes principles: (1) preventing harm; (2) notice; (3) collection limitations; (4) use of personal information; (5) choice; (6) intergrity of personal information; (7) security safeguards; (8) access and correction; and (9) accountability. Greenleaf (2004), pp. 16–18.

[38]http://cbprs.org.

[39]Waters (2009), pp. 74–89.

[40]Some scholars have argued that such soft law frameworks are nonetheless far-reaching, as their implemnetation depends on the power of reputational constraints as treaties do. See e.g. Brummer (2011), pp. 263–272.

[41]Art. 8 ECHR.

Rights of the European Union (CFREU) distinguishes between the right of respect for private and family life in Art. 7 and the right to protection of personal data, which is explicitly enshrined in Art. 8.[42] This distinction is no coincidence but reflects the heightened concern of the EU and translates into a positive duty[43] to implement effective protection of personal data and to regulate the transmission of such data. The 1995 Data Protection Directive formed an important part of this ongoing project of the EU. As the regulatory environment profoundly changed, in particular, the use and role of data in the economy but also in broader societal contexts, as sketched earlier, the Directive urgently demanded an update so as to ensure the needed high level of protection of privacy. The more active involvement of the EU as a supranational unity was also prompted by the changes brought about by the Treaty of Lisbon, which entered into force in 2009.[44] Next to this broad underlying need to modernize existing rules and make them fit for the new digital space, there were several more concrete decisions and events that triggered the change, as well as made it politically feasible. An important, albeit not directly related, development were the revelations made in 2013 by Edward Snowden. These exposed the depth and breadth of surveillance by the US National Security Agency (NSA), which incidentally also involved access to data of millions of private users, including from the systems of Google, Facebook, Apple, and other big (US-based) internet players.[45] Other triggers of reform were a series of crucial decisions by the Court of Justice of the European Union (CJEU), which brought about important changes in existing legal practice, as well as in the overall understanding of individual's rights protection on the internet in Europe. The *Google Spain* case[46] is perhaps the best known in this context, as it coined the so-called "right to be forgotten", which gave priority to privacy over free speech rights and the economic rights of the information intermediaries, such as Google search. Another notable case was the *Schrems I* judgment of 6 October 2015,[47] which rendered the Safe Harbor Agreement between the EU and the US invalid and illuminated the importance of cross-border data flows, as well as the difficulties in reconciling it with the fundamental right to privacy.

The new EU data protection act, the GDPR, serves the same purpose as the 1995 Data Protection Directive and seeks to harmonize the protection of fundamental

---

[42] Art. 8 "Protection of personal data" reads: 1. Everyone has the right to the protection of personal data concerning him or her; 2. Such data must be processed fairly for specified purposes and on the basis of the consent of the person concerned or some other legitimate basis laid down by law. Everyone has the right of access to data which has been collected concerning him or her, and the right to have it rectified; 3. Compliance with these rules shall be subject to control by an independent authority.

[43] European Court of Human Rights (2003) Refah Partisi (The Welfare Party) and Others v. Turkey. App Nos. 41340/98, 41342/98, 41343/98 and 41344/98. Grand Chamber Judgment of 13 February 2003.

[44] See Kuner (2012); also Lynskey (2015).

[45] See e.g. Brown and Korff (2014).

[46] Court of Justice of the European Union (2014) C-131/12.

[47] Court of Justice of the European Union (2015) C-362/14, [hereinafter Schrems I].

rights and freedoms of natural persons in respect of processing activities and to ensure the free flow of personal data between the EU Member States. The GDPR endorses a clear set of principles[48] and particularly high standards of protection, including enhanced user rights (such as the aforementioned right to be forgotten,[49] but also the right to transparent information,[50] the right of access to personal data;[51] the right to data portability,[52] the right to object[53] and the right not to be subject to automated decision-making, including profiling[54]). The GDPR accordingly foresees also heightened responsibilities of entities controlling and processing data, including data protection by design and by default,[55] and higher penalties for non-compliance.[56]

Noteworthy is also the firmer grasp of the GDPR in terms of its territorial reach. Art. 3(1) specifies the territorial scope as covering the processing of personal data in the context of the activities of an establishment of a controller or a processor in the EU, regardless of whether the processing takes place in the Union or not. However, the GDPR may also apply to a controller or processor not established in the EU, where the processing activities are related to: (a) the offering of goods or services, irrespective of whether a payment of the data subject is required, to such data subjects in the EU; or (b) the monitoring of their behaviour as far as their behaviour takes place within the EU.[57] This is, in effect, a substantial extension of the scope of EU data protection law and bound to have a significant impact in its implementation, potentially becoming applicable to many US and other foreign companies targeting the EU market.[58]

---

[48] Art. 5 GDPR specifies that personal data shall be processed lawfully, fairly and in a transparent manner in relation to the data subject (principle of lawfulness, fairness and transparency); collected for specified, explicit and legitimate purposes (principle of purpose limitation); processing must also be adequate, relevant and limited to what is necessary (principle of data minimization); as well as accurate and, where necessary, kept up to date (principle of accuracy); data is to be kept in a form which permits identification of data subjects for no longer than is necessary for the purposes for which the personal data are processed (principle of storage limitation); data processing must be secure (principle of integrity and confidentiality); and the data controller is to be held responsible (principle of accountability).

[49] Art. 17 GDPR.

[50] Art. 12 GDPR.

[51] Arts 13, 14, 15 and 19 GDPR.

[52] Art. 20 GDPR.

[53] Arts 21 GDPR.

[54] Art. 22 GDPR.

[55] Art. 25 GDPR.

[56] Depending on the infringement, data protection authorities can impose fines up to 20'000'000 EUR, or in the case of an undertaking, up to 4% of its total worldwide annual turnover of the preceding financial year, whichever is higher. See Art. 83(5) and (6) GDPR.

[57] Art. 3(2) GDPR. Guidance to determine whether a controller or a processor is offering goods or services to EU data subjects is provided in Recital 23 GDPR, as well as in more detail by the EU data protection authority (see European Data Protection Board 2019).

[58] See e.g. Schwartz (2013a); Tene and Wolf (2013); Burri and Schär (2016); Kuner (2016).

In the context of the extraterritorial application of the GDPR and what has been particularly controversial, as exemplified by the *Schrems I* judgment, is the possibility that the European Commission finds that a third country offers "an adequate level of data protection".[59] This would mean that the EU unilaterally evaluates the standards of protection in partner countries. The effect of such a decision is that personal data can flow from the EU (and Norway, Liechtenstein, and Iceland, as members of the European Economic Area) to that third country without any further safeguards being necessary.[60] In other words, transfers to the third country become assimilated to intra-EU transmissions of data. The European Commission has so far recognized Andorra, Argentina, Canada (commercial organizations), Faroe Islands, Guernsey, Israel, Isle of Man, Japan, Jersey, New Zealand, Switzerland, and Uruguay as having an adequate level of data protection.

The adequacy test is somewhat strengthened post-*Schrems I*, and the Commission should "take into account how a particular third country respects the rule of law, access to justice as well as international human rights norms and standards and its general and sectoral law, including legislation concerning public security, defence and national security as well as public order and criminal law".[61] The first country subject to an adequacy decision after the adoption of the GDPR is Japan.[62] In a 58-page decision,[63] the Commission found by looking at both the levels of protection provided by Japanese general and sectoral data protection regulations, as well as the redress and oversight mechanisms, that the adequacy standard of Art. 45 GDPR, "interpreted in light of the Charter of Fundamental Rights of the European Union, in particular in the *Schrems* judgment, is met".[64]

In the absence of an "adequacy decision", a controller or processor may transfer personal data to a third country only if they provide appropriate safeguards, and on condition that enforceable data subject rights and effective legal remedies for data subjects are available.[65] Such appropriate safeguards may be provided for, by: (a) a legally binding and enforceable instrument between public authorities or bodies; (b) binding corporate rules; (c) standard data protection clauses adopted by the Commission; (d) standard data protection clauses adopted by a supervisory authority and approved by the Commission; (e) an approved code of conduct with binding and

---

[59]The adoption of an adequacy decision involves a proposal from the European Commission; an opinion of the European Data Protection Board; an approval from representatives of EU countries; and the adoption of the decision by the European Commission. At any time, the European Parliament and the Council may request the European Commission to maintain, amend or withdraw the adequacy decision on the grounds that its act exceeds the implementing powers provided for in the regulation.

[60]Art. 45(1); Recital 103 GDPR.

[61]Art. 45(2); Recital 104 GDPR.

[62]Negotiations are ongoing with South Korea and many of the existing adequacy decisions are up to renewal.

[63]European Commission (2019).

[64]European Commission (2019), para. 175.

[65]Art. 46(1) GDPR.

enforceable commitments; or (f) an approved certification together with binding and enforceable commitments. While the GDPR brings more clarity and certainty with regards to these clauses, they are still related to higher costs and provide only a second-best option.[66] Overall, under the EU data protection regime, there is a priority given to the protection of privacy over economic rights, and the EU seeks to "export" these higher standards either by binding individual countries through the adequacy decision or by applying EU law to foreign businesses that use EU citizens' data under the GDPR.

### 2.3.2 Data Protection in the US

The United States shares a fundamentally different idea of privacy protection, which is deeply rooted in its history and understood as the protection of liberty.[67] In this sense, it "focuses more on restrictions, such as the Fourth Amendment, that protect citizens from information collection and use by government rather than private actors. In fact, private actors are often protected from such restrictions by the First Amendment".[68] In addition, policies around internet freedom in the United States have continuously sought "to preserve and expand the internet as an open, global space for free expression, for organizing and interaction, and for commerce",[69] and this has been recently confirmed by the White House strategy on AI.[70]

While under the First Amendment, free speech has been given robust protection in the US, data protection is regulated in a fragmented manner in some federal privacy laws and a great number of state laws.[71] These laws either concern the public sector only or they are information-specific or medium-specific, as they regulate, for instance, health information, video privacy, or electronic communications. While the Federal Trade Commission (FTC) can use its competence to adjudicate on unfair or deceptive trade practices to discipline companies that fail to implement minimal data security measures or fail to meet its privacy policies, the US does not have an official data protection authority.[72] As a consequence of this fragmentation, there is no coherent definition of personal data, nor is there one of sensitive personal data. There are no restrictions on the transfer of personal data by private entities, and self-regulation and best practices are the common models of privacy protection. Data is also seen as a transaction commodity, and data exports to other countries are not

[66] Drake (2017).

[67] See e.g. Whitman (2004); Schwartz (2013b); Schwartz and Solove (2014).

[68] Downes (2016).

[69] Clarke et al. (2014), p. 158.

[70] The White House (2019).

[71] See e.g. Tourkochoriti (2016).

[72] For a great overview of US privacy laws, see Deckelboim (2017).

limited. Overall, there is a clear tendency towards liberal, market-based governance in contrast to the socially protective, rights-based governance in Europe.[73]

### 2.3.3 Bridging the EU–US Differences: From Safe Harbor to the Privacy Shield

Reconciling these different understandings of privacy between the two major players in the area of data governance has had many implications, including for trade law, as the chapter shows below. Transatlantic data flows are of economic significance for both partners[74] and have so far been enabled through an ingenious set of legal mechanisms. First, under the so-called "Safe Harbor" scheme,[75] which contained, in essence, a series of principles concerning the protection of personal data to which US undertakings subscribe voluntarily.[76] The CJEU found, however, in the above-mentioned *Schrems I* judgment that the Safe Harbor did not provide a level of protection of fundamental rights that is essentially equivalent to that guaranteed within the EU.[77] The Court observed in particular that the Safe Harbor scheme applies solely to US undertakings that adhere to it but does not bind US public authorities. It was also apparent that US national security, public interest, and law enforcement requirements prevail over the Safe Harbor Agreement so that in effect, US undertakings can disregard, without limitation, the rules laid down by that scheme where they conflict with such requirements,[78] thereby affecting the fundamental rights of EU citizens. The Court also found that US legislation is not limited to what is strictly necessary, as it permits, in general terms, the storage of all the personal data of all the persons whose data is transferred from the EU to the US with no differentiation, limitations, or exceptions based on the objective pursued. Furthermore, there is no objective criterion laid down that limits the access of the public authorities to the data and its subsequent use. This, together with the lack of legal remedies,[79] led the Court to ultimately declare the Safe Harbor Decision invalid.[80]

The Safe Harbor agreement was subsequently and after intense negotiations, replaced by the so-called EU–US Privacy Shield[81] The Privacy Shield is much more stringent and detailed than the Safe Harbor. While US companies (both data controllers and processors) still self-certify on an annual basis, the new arrangement provides more substantial obligations upon US companies to protect the personal

[73]Reidenberg (2000).

[74]See e.g. Weiss and Archick (2016).

[75]European Commission (2000).

[76]See Farrell (2003); Schwartz and Solove (2014).

[77]Schrems I, para. 97.

[78]Schrems I, para. 86.

[79]Schrems I, paras. 93–95.

[80]Schrems I paras. 105–106.

[81]European Commission (2016a). For an overview, see European Commission (2016b).

data of European citizens according to a set of clearly defined principles.[82] In addition, there are much stronger monitoring and enforcement mechanisms. Organizations may choose independent recourse mechanisms in either the EU or in the United States, including the possibility to voluntarily cooperate with the EU data protection authorities (DPAs). Where organizations process human resources data, the cooperation with the DPAs is mandatory. Other alternatives include independent Alternative Dispute Resolution or private-sector developed privacy programmes that commit to the Privacy Principles.[83] It is, in this sense, the purpose of the Privacy Shield framework to provide data subjects with a number of possibilities to enforce their rights, lodge complaints regarding non-compliance by US companies, and ultimately, to have their complaints resolved.[84] Next to the enhanced individual safeguard mechanisms and for the first time, there is an explicit assurance from the US that any access of public authorities to personal data will be subject to clear limitations, safeguards, and oversight mechanisms. US authorities have affirmed the absence of indiscriminate or mass surveillance.[85] There is, in addition, a new redress possibility through the EU–US Privacy Shield Ombudsperson, who is to be independent of the US Intelligence Community and can address individual complaints.[86] In the European Commission's assessment, all this conforms with the standards set out in the *Schrems I* judgment, according to which legislation involving interference with the fundamental rights guaranteed by Articles 7 and 8 CFREU must impose "minimum safeguards", cannot include "on a generalized basis, storage of all the personal data of all the persons whose data has been transferred from the European Union to the United States", and must provide sufficient legal remedies.[87] Despite these additional safeguards, in a recent judgment,[88] the CJEU invalidated yet again the EU–US Privacy Shield, as it found serious risks for the rights of EU citizens due to the still persisting primacy of US law enforcement requirements over those of the Privacy Shield;[89] the lack of necessary limitations on the power of the US

---

[82] European Commission (2016a), paras. 19–29 refer to the Notice Principle, Data Integrity and Purpose Limitation Principle, Choice Principle, Security Principle, Access Principle, Recourse, Enforcement and Liability Principle, and Accountability for Onward Transfer Principle. The principles are additionally detailed in Annex II attached to the Commission's implementing decision.

[83] European Commission (2016a), para. 40.

[84] European Commission (2016a), paras. 43–63.

[85] European Commission (2016a), paras. 64–90.

[86] European Commission (2016a), paras. 119–122. For a great analysis of the EU-US Privacy Shield, see Deckelboim (2017).

[87] European Commission (2016a), at paras. 90 and 124 citing the Schrems I judgment.

[88] Court of Justice of the European Union (2020) C-311/18.

[89] Court of Justice of the European Union (2020) C-311/18, para. 164.

authorities, particularly in light of proportionality requirements;[90] and the lack of remedies for EU data subjects,[91] including deficiencies in the ombudsman mechanism.[92]

## 3 Privacy under the WTO Framework

As noted at the outset, privacy and data protection have not been a negotiation topic during the Uruguay Round (1986–1994), and WTO law has not so far undergone any changes that reflect their growing importance or digital transformation in general.[93] Yet, despite this and although WTO law represents a "hard" form of international law, it does include specific mechanisms meant to reconcile economic and non-economic interests, international commitments, and domestic values and sensitivities. Key amongst these mechanisms are the "general exceptions" formulated under Art. XX GATT 1994 and Art. XIV GATS. They permit WTO Members to adopt measures, which would otherwise violate their obligations and undertaken commitments, under the condition that these measures are not disguised restrictions on trade. Particularly interesting for this chapter's discussion are the possibilities that Art. XIV GATS may open for maintaining existing and adopting new data restrictions based on grounds of privacy protection.

While Art. XIV GATS enumerates different grounds as possible justifications, such as the protection of human, animal or plant life or health,[94] especially pertinent for us are two categories: (a) those relating to public order or public morals[95] and (b) those that are necessary to secure compliance with laws or regulations.[96] In the latter context, it is stated that this may be the case in particular when necessary to secure compliance with laws or regulations relating to "the protection of the privacy of individuals in relation to the processing and dissemination of personal data and the protection of confidentiality of individual records and accounts".[97] The focus here is on this provision, and for the sake of revealing how it is relevant for data flows, it is assumed that the rules of the EU GDPR are tested under it because they were found to either violate the market access or the national treatment obligations of the EU under the GATS.[98]

[90] Court of Justice of the European Union (2020) C-311/18, paras. 168–185.

[91] Court of Justice of the European Union (2020) C-311/18, paras. 191–192.

[92] Court of Justice of the European Union (2020) C-311/18, paras. 193–197.

[93] Burri (2015); WTO (2018).

[94] Art. XIV(b) GATS.

[95] Art. XIV(a) GATS. See Wu (2008); Delimatsis (2010).

[96] Art. XIV(c) GATS. For a commentary of Art. XIV GATS, see Cottier et al. (2008).

[97] Art. XIV(c)(ii) GATS.

[98] For a fully-fledged analysis of how this may be occur, see Weber (2012); Irion et al. (2016), pp. 27−33.

Art. XIV GATS, similarly to Art. XX GATT involves several legal tests, as established by the WTO jurisprudence: (i) first, the panels and the Appellate Body consider whether the measure falls within the scope of one of the listed objectives in the exception; (ii) second, the measure must address the relevant public interest at issue, with a sufficient nexus between the measure and the objective pursued;[99] (iii) the thirdly, the measure is examined under the chapeau (the introductory paragraph) of Art. XIV GATS. With regard to (i), there has been a wide margin of appreciation given to WTO Member in their choice of objectives they seek to protect. The second step is much more complex and triggers the so-called "necessity" test. The Appellate Body has noted that there are different degrees of necessity. At one end of this continuum lies "necessary" understood as "indispensable", which at the opposite side, "necessary" is taken to mean as "making a contribution to". The Appellate Body noted that a "necessary" measure is located significantly closer to the pole of "indispensable" than to simply "making a contribution to".[100] The more important the interest that the measure is designed to protect and the greater the contribution to the objective, the easier it is to accept the measure as "necessary".[101] However, the Appellate Body has also stated that the requirement for measures "relating to" a goal (as is the case with the GATS privacy exception), is "more flexible textually" than a strict "necessity" requirement and may simply require a "substantial" or "reasonable" relationship of the measure to the objective pursued.[102]

Ultimately, it has also been clarified that this "weighing and balancing"[103] of factors should also include a comparison of the challenged measure and its possible alternatives.[104] In order to show that the measure does not meet the necessity test, a claimant can demonstrate that a less trade-restrictive alternative to the measure has been "reasonably available". The alternative measure cannot pose prohibitive costs or substantial technical difficulties to implement.[105] A measure that has been provisionally justified under the above material requirements of Art. XIV(c)(ii) must also meet the chapeau test, which says that a measure should not be applied in a manner that would constitute a means of arbitrary or unjustifiable discrimination between countries where like conditions prevail, or as a disguised restriction on trade in services. The chapeau has been interpreted as directed at preventing abuses or

---

[99]WTO Appellate Body (2005) [hereinafter US – Gambling], at para. 292; see also WTO Appellate Body (2007), paras. 119–124.

[100]WTO Appellate Body (2000) [hereinafter Korea – Beef], para. 161.

[101]US – Gambling, para. 6.536; see also WTO Appellate Body (2015); WTO Panel (2015) [hereinafter Argentina – Financial Services], paras 7.655, 7.685, 7.727, referring to Korea – Beef, paras. 162, 163.

[102]Korea – Beef, para. 49 (citing WTO Appellate Body (1996), para. 19 and WTO Appellate Body (1998), para. 141).

[103]See US – Gambling, para. 78; WTO Appellate Body (2009) [hereinafter *China* – Publications and Audiovisual Products], para. 239.

[104]US – Gambling, para. 306; Argentina – Financial Services, para. 7.684.

[105]Argentina – Financial Services, para. 7.729 referring to US – Gambling, para. 308.

misuses of the right to invoke the exception[106] and by evaluating the "consistency of enforcement" of the challenged measure.[107]

Admittedly, these tests set a high hurdle for WTO Members, and the "success rate" for passing through them has been rather low.[108] Scholars have argued that if the EU would be challenged before a WTO panel, its GDPR may fail to satisfy the test—on several particular grounds. Irion et al. have argued that the EU may face a problem with finding appropriate evidence on the performance of its data protection law.[109] For instance, the EU–US Safe Harbor agreement,[110] which has now been invalidated, was not particularly stringent as shown by the *Schrems I* judgment, and one can argue that this undermines the strength of a challenged measure's contribution to securing compliance with EU data protection law. Second and this is a critical argument, it can be well maintained that there are less trade-restrictive measures that are reasonably available for the attainment of the EU's desired level of data protection. The GDPR is indeed in many senses excessively burdensome with sizeable extraterritorial effects, as noted earlier. Especially if compared with other data protection rules around the world, it may be difficult to prove that privacy cannot be otherwise protected.[111] Even if the provisions on the transfer of personal data to third countries were to be deemed necessary to secure compliance with the GDPR, there is an argument to be made that these provisions have not been consistently implemented and would ultimately fail the chapeau test. If the EU has denied a third country's application for adequacy assessment or a request to negotiate a sectoral scheme similar to that of the US–EU Safe Harbor, or its newer version of the Privacy Shield, it seems that the chapeau test requirements are hard to meet. The EU may be effectively discriminating between different countries in finding adequate levels of protection there and in engaging in cooperation with them so that these are secured in terms of substance and procedure.[112]

The general exception clause under Art. XIV GATS is a good example of both the flexibility of WTO law, as well as of its potential to intervene in domestic matters in an attempt to discipline WTO Members and draw a line between licit and illicit protectionism. Despite the current deadlock at the WTO and the crisis of its dispute resolution system, the interpretation of Articles XX GATT and XIV GATS remains

---

[106]Argentina – Financial Services, para. 7.743.

[107]US – Gambling, para. 351. In US – Gambling, the Appellate Body confirmed that the US ban on online gambling did not meet the requirement of the chapeau of Art. XIV GATS due to ambiguity in relation to the scope of one US statute, which appeared to permit domestic suppliers to have remote betting services for horse racing.

[108]Only one case has so far passed all the tests. See WTO Appellate Body (2001); also Howse (2002).

[109]Irion et al. (2016), pp. 36–39; also MacDonald and Streatfeild (2014), pp. 640–650.

[110]European Commission (2000).

[111]Bygrave (2014); Rotenberg (2016).

[112]Irion et al. (2016), pp. 36–39.

of critical importance, as many free trade agreements (FTAs) stimulate their application *mutatis mutandis*.[113]

# 4 Developments in Free Trade Agreements

As legal adaptation under the umbrella of the WTO has stalled, many issues of digital trade and data governance have been addressed in free trade agreements (FTAs), either of bilateral or regional nature. Indeed, from the 347 FTAs agreed upon between 2000 and 2019, some 184 FTAs have provisions on digital trade. The United States has been a legal entrepreneur and played a key role by endorsing liberal rules in the implementation of its "Digital Agenda".[114] The agreements reached since 2002 with Australia, Bahrain, Chile, Morocco, Oman, Peru, Singapore, the Central American countries,[115] Panama, Colombia, South Korea, and Japan, as well the updated North American Free Trade Agreement (NAFTA) with Canada and Mexico, all contain critical WTO-plus (going above the WTO commitments) and WTO-extra (addressing issues not covered by the WTO) provisions in the broader field of digital trade. The emergent regulatory template on digital issues is not, however, limited to US agreements but has diffused and can be found in other FTAs as well. Singapore, Australia, Japan, and Colombia have been among the primary drivers of this diffusion. In this section, we map the emerging regulatory landscape in particular with regard to data-relevant norms.[116]

## *4.1 Overview of Data-Related Rules in FTAs*

One can, in general, speak of the relevance for trade rules for data and data flows, as they matter for data at least in three ways: (i) because they regulate the cross-border flow of data by regulating trade in goods and services as well as the protection of intellectual property; (ii) because they may install certain beyond the border rules that demand changes in domestic regulation - for example, with regard intermediaries' liability; and (iii) finally, because trade law can limit the policy space that regulators have at home.[117] In addition to this generic trade law framework, the last

[113]For instance, the recent Digital Economy Partnership Agreement (DEPA) between Chile, Singapore and New Zealand.

[114]Wunsch-Vincent (2003).

[115]The DR-CAFTA includes Costa Rica, El Salvador, Guatemala, Honduras, Nicaragua and the Dominican Republic.

[116]This analysis is based on a dataset of all data-relevant norms in trade agreements (TAPED). See Burri and Polanco (2020) and http://unilu.ch/taped.

[117]See in this sense Burri (2017); Casalini and López González (2019).

decade has also witnessed the emergence of entirely new rules that explicitly regulate data flows. This section focuses on these rules in particular. It needs to be mentioned at the outset that there is no common agreement on a definition of data flows in FTAs, despite the wide-spread rhetoric around the term and its frequent use in reports and studies.[118] Important to note in this regard is that despite the different terms used in treaty language, there seems to be a tendency for a broad and encompassing definition of data flows, (1) where there are bits of information (data) as part of the provision of a service or a product and (2) where this data crosses borders, although the data flows do not neatly coincide with one commercial transaction and the provision of certain service may relate to multiple flows of data.[119] In addition, it may be noted that there has not been a distinction between different types of data so far—for instance, between personal and non-personal data, personal or company data, or machine-to-machine data.[120] Yet, personal information is commonly included explicitly in the data-related provisions in FTAs, where the potential clashes with domestic data protection regimes become evident.

Overall, specific data-related provisions are a relatively new phenomenon and can be found primarily in dedicated e-commerce chapters of FTAs but only in a handful of agreements. These are rules referring to the cross-border flow of data and rules banning or limiting data localization requirements. Provisions on data flows can also found in chapters dealing with discrete services sectors, where data is inherent to the very definition of those services - such as in the telecommunications and financial services sectors.[121]

---

[118]See e.g. Casalini and López González (2019); OECD (2019a).

[119]As the OECD (OECD (2019a), p. 1) further clarifies: "the actual flow of data reflects individual firm choices: accessing the OECD library from Paris, for instance, actually means contacting a server in the United States (the OECD uses a US-based company for its web services). Moreover, with the cloud, data can live in many places at once, with files and copies residing in servers around the world".

[120]For instance, Sen classifies data into personal data referring to data related to individuals; company data referring to data flowing between corporations; business data referring to digitised content such as software and audiovisual content; and social data referring to behavioural patterns determined using personal data (see Sen (2018), pp. 343–346). Aaronson and Leblond categorize data into personal data, public data, confidential business data, machine-to-machine data and metadata, although they do not specifically define each of these terms (see Aaronson and Leblond (2018)). The OECD has also tried to break data into different categories. See OECD (2019b).

[121]This chapter does not cover specific services sectors. For a more detailed analysis, see e.g. Burri (2020a).

## 4.2 Rules on Data Flows and Data Localization

Non-binding provisions on data flows appeared early and can already be found in the 2000 Jordan-US FTA.[122] Yet, it is only in recent years that these rules have been made binding and more comprehensive. Particularly important in this context were the negotiations of the Transpacific Partnership Agreement (TPP),[123] between the US and eleven countries in the Pacific Rim,[124] as the TPP sought to be a bold twenty-first century trade deal and move away from the brick-and-mortar WTO Agreements.[125] While the TPP did not eventually materialize because the Trump administration withdrew from it, it gave the basis for two important treaties—(1) the Comprehensive and Progressive Agreement for Transpacific Partnership (CPTPP)[126] between the remainder of the TPP parties; and (2) the renegotiated NAFTA, which is now referred to as "United States Mexico Canada Agreement" (USMCA). The CPTPP and the USMCA electronic commerce chapters build upon the TPP and, in this sense, reflect the US agenda on the relevant issues; they create a comprehensive template for digital trade with strong rules on data flows. We look in turn at these treaties.[127]

The CPTPP seeks for the first time to explicitly restrict the use of data localization measures. Art. 14.13(2) prohibits the parties from requiring a "covered person to use or locate computing facilities in that Party's territory as a condition for conducting business in that territory". The soft language from the US-South Korea FTA on free data flows is now also framed as a hard rule: "[e]ach Party shall allow the cross-border transfer of information by electronic means, including personal information, when this activity is for the conduct of the business of a covered person".[128] The rule has a broad scope, and most data that is transferred over the internet is likely to be covered, although the word "for" may suggest the need for some causality between the flow of data and the business of the covered person.

Measures restricting digital flows or localization requirements under Art. 14.13 CPTPP are permitted only if they do not amount to "arbitrary or unjustifiable

[122] A similar wording is used in the 2008 Canada-Peru FTA, 2010 Hong-Kong-New Zealand FTA, the 2011 Korea-Peru FTA, the 2011 Central America-Mexico FTA, the 2013 Colombia-Costa Rica FTA, the 2013 Canada-Honduras FTA, the 2014 Canada-Korea FTA, and the 2015 Japan-Mongolia FTA. The 2007 South Korea-US FTA was the first agreement with more concrete language on data flows, albeit in a soft law form (Korea-US FTA, Art. 15.8).

[123] The Trans-Pacific Partnership Agreement, full text available at: https://ustr.gov/trade-agreements/free-trade-agreements/trans-pacific-partnership/tpp-full-text [hereinafter TPP].

[124] Australia, Brunei, Canada, Chile, Japan, Malaysia, Mexico, New Zealand, Peru, Singapore and Vietnam.

[125] See e.g. Ravenhill (2017).

[126] The Comprehensive and Progressive Agreement for Transpacific Partnership, full text available at: http://international.gc.ca/trade-commerce/trade-agreements-accords-commerciaux/agr-acc/cptpp-ptpgp/text-texte/index.aspx?lang=eng.

[127] For a fully fledged analysis, see Burri (2017); also Burri (2020b).

[128] Art. 14.11(2) CPTPP.

discrimination or a disguised restriction on trade" and do not "impose restrictions on transfers of information greater than are required to achieve the objective".[129] These non-discriminatory conditions are similar to the test formulated by Art. XIV GATS and Art. XX GATT 1994, which, as earlier noted, is meant to balance trade and non-trade interests. The CPTPP test differs from the WTO norms in one significant element: while there is a list of public policy objectives in the GATT and the GATS (such as public morals or public order), the CPTPP provides no such enumeration and simply speaks of a "legitimate public policy objective".[130] This permits more regulatory autonomy for the CPTPP signatories. However, it also may lead to abuses and overall legal uncertainty. Further, it should be noted that the ban on localization measures is somewhat softened with regard to financial services and institutions.[131] An annex to the Financial Services chapter has a separate data transfer requirement, whereby certain restrictions on data flows may apply for the protection of privacy or confidentiality of individual records, or for prudential reasons.[132] Government procurement is also excluded.[133]

After the withdrawal by the United States from the TPP, there was some uncertainty as to the direction the United States will follow in its trade deals in general and on matters of digital trade in particular. The USMCA casts the doubts aside. The USMCA has a comprehensive electronic commerce chapter, which is now also appropriately titled "Digital Trade" and follows all critical lines of the CPTPP in ensuring the free flow of data through: a clear ban on data localization (Art. 19.12), providing a non-discrimination regime for digital products (Art. 19.4), and a hard rule on free information flows (Art. 19.11). The USMCA keeps the clause on exceptions that permits the pursuit of certain non-economic objectives. Art. 19.11 specifies, very much in the sense of the CPTPP, that Parties can adopt or maintain a measure inconsistent with the free flow of data provision if this is necessary to achieve a legitimate public policy objective, provided that the measure: (a) is not applied in a manner which would constitute a means of arbitrary or unjustifiable discrimination or a disguised restriction on trade; and (b) does not impose restrictions on transfers of information greater than are necessary to achieve the objective.[134] The USMCA clarified further that "a measure does not meet the conditions of this paragraph if it accords different treatment to data transfers solely on the basis that they are cross-border in a manner that modifies the conditions of competition to

[129] Art. 14.11(3) CPTPP.

[130] Art. 14.11(3) CPTPP.

[131] See the definition of "a covered person" in Art. 14.1, which is said to exclude a "financial institution" and a "cross-border financial service supplier".

[132] The provision reads: "Each Party shall allow a financial institution of another Party to transfer information in electronic or other form, into and out of its territory, for data processing if such processing is required in the institution's ordinary course of business".

[133] Art. 14.8(3) CPTPP.

[134] Art. 19.11(2) CPTPP.

the detriment of service suppliers of another Party",[135] which effectively makes a link to the necessity test under WTO law and practice.

Subsequent treaties, such as the 2016 Chile-Uruguay FTA and the 2016 Updated Singapore-Australia FTA, and the 2019 US-Japan Digital Trade Agreement closely follow the CPTPP template and enhance the diffusion of the rules on data flows and data localization. In contrast, the European Union has been cautious in inserting rules on data in its free trade deals, and presently none of its treaties has such rules of binding nature. It is only recently that the EU has made a step towards such rules, whereby Parties have agreed to consider in future negotiations commitments related to the cross-border flow of information. Such a clause is found in the 2018 EU-Japan EPA[136] and in the modernization of the trade part of the EU-Mexico Global Agreement. In the latter two agreements, the Parties commit to "reassess" within three years of the entry into force of the agreement, the need for inclusion of provisions on the free flow of data into the treaty. This signals a repositioning of the EU on the issue of data flows, as well as EU's wish to link this commitment in due time with the high data protection standards of the GDPR.[137]

## 4.3 Rules on Data Protection

83 FTAs so far include provisions on data protection. Yet, the nature of the awarded protection varies considerably and can include a mixed bag of binding and non-binding provisions, which is symptomatic of the very different positions of the major actors and the inherent tensions between the regulatory goals of data innovation and data protection. Earlier agreements, such as the 2000 Jordan-US FTA Joint Statement on Electronic Commerce, address privacy issues in hortorary provisions.[138] Later agreements remain still in the domain of soft law but include a variety of cooperation activities to improve the level of protection of privacy and curb obstacles to trade that requires transfers of personal data. These activities include sharing information and experiences on regulations, laws, and programmes on data protection,[139] or the overall domestic regime for the protection of personal information;[140] technical assistance in the form of exchange of

[135] Art. 19.11(2) CPTPP, footnote 5.

[136] Art. 8.81 EU-Japan EPA.

[137] See European Commission (2018).

[138] Art. II Jordan-US Joint Statement on Electronic Commerce.

[139] See e.g., Art. 10.8.5 and Art. 10.15(b) Brazil-Chile FTA; Art. 13.7(b) Canada-Korea FTA; Art. 13.10.2 Australia-Japan FTA; Art. 12.5(b) Chile-Colombia FTA; Art. 14.05(b) Nicaragua-Taiwan FTA; Art. 13.4(b) Panama-Singapore FTA; Art. 14.5(b) CAFTA-DR-US; Art. 15.5(b) Chile-US FTA.

[140] Art. 13.3.1(b)(i) Australia-Indonesia FTA; Art. 19.14.1(a)(i) USMCA; Art. 13.14(b)(i) Australia-Peru FTA; Art. 9.12(c)(i) Singapore-Sri Lanka FTA; Art. 9.9(c) Singapore-Turkey

information and experts,[141] research and training activities;[142] or the establishment of joint programmes and projects.[143]

FTAs have also dealt with personal data protection regarding the adoption of domestic standards. While some merely recognize the importance or the benefits of protecting personal information online,[144] in several treaties, parties specifically commit to adopt or maintain legislation or regulations that protect the personal data or privacy of users. Representative of this group are again the CPTPP and the USMCA. Art. 14.8(2) requires every CPTPP party to "adopt or maintain a legal framework that provides for the protection of the personal information of the users of electronic commerce". Yet, no standards or benchmarks for the legal framework have been specified, except for a general requirement that CPTPP parties "take into account principles or guidelines of relevant international bodies".[145] A footnote provides some clarification in saying that: "[f]or greater certainty, a Party may comply with the obligation in this paragraph by adopting or maintaining measures such as a comprehensive privacy, personal information or personal data protection laws, sector-specific laws covering privacy, or laws that provide for the enforcement of voluntary undertakings by enterprises relating to privacy".[146] Parties are also invited to promote compatibility between their data protection regimes, by essentially treating lower standards as equivalent.[147] Overall, the goal seems to be to prioritize trade over privacy rights.

The USMCA is unusual in two aspects when compared to the CPTPP and the usual US position on data protection issues: while Art. 19.8 remains soft on prescribing domestic regimes on personal data protection; it recognizes principles and guidelines of relevant international bodies. Art. 19.8 states in particular that *"[i]n the development of its legal framework for the protection of personal information, each Party should take into account principles and guidelines of relevant international bodies, such as the APEC Privacy Framework and the OECD Recommendation of the Council concerning Guidelines governing the Protection of Privacy and Transborder Flows of Personal Data (2013)"*.[148] The USMCA Parties also recognize key principles of data protection, which include: limitation on collection; choice; data quality; purpose specification; use limitation; security safeguards;

FTA; Art. 13.5 China-Korea FTA; Art. 16.6.2 Colombia-Costa Rica FTA; Art. 1506.2 Canada-Colombia FTA.

[141] Art. 30 Chile-EC AA.

[142] Art. 10.8.1(b) Korea-Vietnam FTA.

[143] Art. 30 Chile-EC AA.

[144] Art. 13.7.1 Australia-Indonesia FTA; Art. 10.2.5(f) and Art. 10.8.1 Brazil-Chile FTA; Art. 8.78.3 EU-Japan EPA; Art. 14.5.1 Central America-Korea FTA; Art. 16.2.2(e) Canada-Honduras FTA.

[145] Art. 14.8(2) CPTPP.

[146] Art. 14.8(2) CPTPP, footnote 6.

[147] Art. 14.8(5) CPTPP.

[148] Art. 19.8(2) USMCA.

transparency; individual participation; and accountability,[149] and aim to provide remedies for any violations.[150] This is interesting because it goes beyond what the US may have in its national laws on data protection and also because it reflects some of the principles the European Union has advocated in the domain of the protection of privacy. One can, of course, wonder whether this is a development caused by the "Brussels effect", whereby the EU "exports" its own domestic standards and they become global,[151] or whether we are seeing a shift in US privacy protection regimes as well.[152]

As signalled earlier, the EU has sought more commitments for privacy protection in its FTAs. Many of the EU's agreements have special chapters on the protection of personal data, including the principles of purpose limitation, data quality and proportionality, transparency, security, right to access, rectification and opposition, restrictions on onward transfers, and protection of sensitive data, as well as provisions on enforcement mechanisms, coherence with international commitments and cooperation between the Parties in order to ensure an adequate level of protection of personal data.[153] The EU has also pushed for more safeguards, so that its partners adopt appropriate measures to ensure the privacy protection while allowing the free movement of data, establishing a criterion of "equivalence". Parties also commit to inform each other of their applicable rules and negotiate reciprocal, general, or specific agreements,[154] as exemplified by the additional adequacy decisions of the European Commission, most recently with Japan. As noted above, the EU wishes to permit data flows only if coupled with the high data protection standards of the GDPR. In its currently negotiated trade deals with Australia, Indonesia, New Zealand, and Tunisia, as well as in the EU proposal for WTO rules on electronic commerce,[155] the EU follows a distinct model of endorsing and protecting privacy as a fundamental right.[156] Also, there is broad carve-out, in the sense that: *"Each Party may adopt and maintain the safeguards it deems appropriate to ensure the protection of personal data and privacy, including through the adoption and*

---

[149] Art. 19.8(3) USMCA.

[150] Art.19.8(4) and (5) USMCA.

[151] See Bradford (2020a); Bradford (2020b).

[152] For a great analysis, see Chander et al. (2019).

[153] Chapter 6, Arts 61-65 Cameroon-EC Interim EPA; Chapter 6, Arts 197-201 CARIFORUM-EC EPA. Other agreements merely recognize principles for the collection, processing and storage of personal data such as: prior consent, legitimacy, purpose, proportionality, quality, safety, responsibility and information, but without developing this in detail: Art. 11.2.5(f) Argentina-Chile FTA, footnote 1; Art. 8.2.5(f) Chile-Uruguay FTA, footnote 3.

[154] Art. 8.54.2 EC-Singapore FTA; Understanding 3 Additional Customs-Related Provisions, Arts 9.2 and 11.1; Art. 10 of Protocol on Mutual Administrative Assistance on Custom Matters EC-Ghana EPA; Art. 10.2 of Protocol 5 on Mutual Administrative Assistance on Custom Matters Bosnia and Herzegovina-EC SAA; Art. 45 and Protocol No 7 Algeria EC Euro-Med Association Agreement.

[155] WTO (2019).

[156] See European Commission (2018).

*application of rules for the cross-border transfer of personal data. Nothing in this agreement shall affect the protection of personal data and privacy afforded by the Parties' respective safeguards"*.[157] The EU thus reserves ample regulatory leeway for its current and future data protection measures. The exception is also fundamentally different than the objective necessity test under the CPTPP and the USMCA because it is subjective in nature and safeguards the EU's right to regulate.[158]

## 5 Pros and Cons of the Different Reconciliation Models

The above sections revealed not only the intensified contestation between free data flows as an essential element of the data-driven economy and the protection of privacy as a sovereign right of states to safeguard their citizens, but also the very different regulatory approaches that have been sought to reconcile these interests. In the face of failing international cooperation and the diverging positions of the major stakeholders of the EU and the US, trade venues, and perhaps oddly or even wrongly so,[159] have become platforms for rule-creation that try to interface data flows and privacy protection. We are far from an optimal model, however, and states are still grappling to find viable mechanisms, which not only provide a level of certainty and market access for businesses but also reflect the state's societal values.

Each of the existing models does come with specific pros and cons. The international framework is not fully developed with regard to privacy protection; it is not binding, nor does it have mechanisms that can effectively reconcile the clash of rights. The transnational regimes under the OECD and APEC, whereas still not binding and of club nature, have provided agreement on some basic regulatory principles that shape domestic frameworks, while at the same time ensuring the free flow of information. As the underlying principles of these frameworks become increasingly integrated into trade law, which enhances their regulatory strength and diffusion across countries, they may provide a good way to tackle the tensions. Oversight and enforceability in case of violations, remain however important questions without an adequate answer. For countries, like the EU Member States, that demand appropriate checks and balances for the protection of individual rights, they may not be enough. In the area of international trade law, we have the generic exception clauses under Art. XX GATT and Art. XIV GATS, which have also been replicated in a number of FTAs *mutatis mutandis*. They provide for a stringent test that seeks to constrain protectionism when states pursue non-economic objectives. Since we have no jurisprudence, it is unclear how they will be applied in practice, and whether, for instance, the EU's GDPR will not be found in violation of the EU's commitments under the GATS. It is also questionable whether an *ex post*, timewise

[157]European Commission (2018) (emphases added).

[158]Yakovleva (2020) p. 496.

[159]Yakovleva (2020).

protracted, case-by-case examination of alleged infringements can match the fluidity of the digital economy and the high stakes at hand. The CPTPP and the USMCA templates are modelled along the WTO norms but are linked to an even higher degree of uncertainty, as the legitimate objectives are not clearly spelled out.

Coupled with the low privacy protection guarantees that these treaties provide, there seems to be a priority given to economic rights. Such a stance, although it may make certain economic sense and boost growth and innovation, may be unacceptable for some actors, such as notably the European Union, which place a high value on fundamental rights and seek to ensure their effective protection. The EU has accordingly sought to export its high standards of protection through an extension of the territorial application of the GDPR and unilateral adequacy decisions that short of international harmonization provide for an adequate level of protection of EU citizens' data. This unilateral approach, while justified on the side of the EU, may be linked to higher costs of compliance for foreign firms and countries and may have negative implications even for the EU's economy and innovation capabilities in the era of Big Data and AI. One innovative solution discussed above is the EU–US Privacy Shield as a flexible mechanism that reconciles the high standards of protection in the EU and the relatively low levels of personal data protection in the US. The EU–US Privacy Shield is by no means perfect, as it fails to satisfy high demands of bindingness and enforceability, even post-*Schrems I* and as revealed by the latest CJEU judgment of *Schrems II*. It may still be worthwhile contemplating to what extent such or similar mechanisms may be improved and possibly made viable in plurilateral or multilateral contexts.[160] While the current negotiations on electronic commerce under the auspices of the WTO reveal little agreement and willingness to move forward at this stage,[161] preferential trade venues can serve as governance laboratories and pave the way towards regulatory cooperation and possible implementation of the Privacy Shield model.

Summing up, one can underscore that privacy protection has clearly become a key topic on the trade negotiation tables, and there is new rule-making evolving that seeks to interface the demands of the digital economy to permit free-flowing data and the sovereign wish to safeguard the rights and values embedded in individual societies adequately. Trade policy has the capacity to promote trade and innovation despite varying standards for privacy protection, but there is an apparent demand for enhanced regulatory cooperation.[162] As the complexity of the data-driven society rises, such regulatory cooperation seems indispensable for moving forward, as there is a distinct need for effective reconciliation mechanisms and oversight.

[160]Mattoo and Meltzer (2018).

[161]See e.g. Willemyns (2020); Burri (2021).

[162]Bollyky and Mavroidis (2017), pp. 11–13 (Bollyky and Mavroidis discuss the need for regulatory competition in the context of global value chains; their argument is only strengthened in the domain of digital trade); also Ahmed (2019), pp. 99–120.

## References


Aaronson SA (2015) Why Trade Agreements are not setting information free: the lost history and reinvigorated debate over cross-border data flows, human rights and national security. World Trade Rev 14(4):671–700

Aaronson SA, Leblond P (2018) Another digital divide: the rise of data realms and its implications for the WTO. J Int Econ Law 21(2):245–272

Ahmed U (2019) The importance of cross-border regulatory cooperation in the Era of Digital Trade. World Trade Rev 18(S1):99–120

APEC (2005) APEC privacy framework. APEC Secretariat, Singapore

Bennett CJ, Bayley RM (2016) Privacy protection in the era of "big data": regulatory challenges and social assessments. In: van der Sloot B, Broeders D, Schrijvers E (eds) Exploring the boundaries of big data. University of Amsterdam Press, Amsterdam, pp 205–227

Bollyky TJ, Mavroidis PC (2017) Trade, social preferences, and regulatory cooperation: the new WTO-think. J Int Econ Law 20(1):1–30

Bradford A (2020a) The Brussels effect. Northwest Univ Law Rev 107(1):1–68

Bradford A (2020b) The Brussels effect: how the European Union rules the world. Oxford University Press, Oxford

Brown I, Korff D (2014) Foreign surveillance: law and practice in a global digital environment. Eur Human Rights Law Rev 3:243–251

Brummer C (2011) How international financial law works (and how it doesn't). Georgetown Law J 99(2):257–327

Bughin J et al (2016) Digital Europe: pushing the frontier, capturing the benefits. McKinsey Global Institute, Washington, DC

Burri M (2015) The international economic law framework for digital trade. Zeitschrift für Schweizerisches Recht 135(5):10–72

Burri M (2017) The governance of data and data flows in trade agreements: the pitfalls of legal adaptation. UC Davies Law Rev 51:65–132

Burri M (2019) Understanding the implications of big data and big data analytics for competition law: an attempt for a primer. In: Mathis K, Tor A (eds) New developments in competition behavioural law and economics. Springer, Berlin, pp 241–263

Burri M (2020a) Data flows and global trade law. In: Burri M (ed) Big data and global trade law. Cambridge University Press, Cambridge

Burri M (2020b) Telecommunications and media services in preferential trade agreements: path dependences still matter. In: Krajewski M, Hoffmann R (eds) European yearbook of international economic law: coherence and divergence in agreements on trade in services. Springer, Berlin

Burri M (2021) Towards a new treaty on digital trade. J World Trade 55(1)

Burri M, Polanco R (2020) Digital trade provisions in preferential trade agreements: introducing a new dataset. J Int Econ Law 23(1):187–220

Burri M, Schär R (2016) The reform of the EU data protection framework: outlining key changes and assessing their fitness for a data-driven economy. J Inf Policy 6:479–511

Bygrave LA (2014) Data privacy law: an international perspective. Oxford University Press, Oxford

Casalini F, López González J (2019) Trade and Cross-Border Data Flows. OECD Trade Policy Papers No. 220

Chander A (2016) National Data Governance in a Global Economy. UC Davis Legal Studies Research Paper: 495

Chander A, Lê UP (2015) Data nationalism. Emory Law J 64(3):677–739

Chander A, Kaminski ME, McGeveran W (2019) Catalyzing privacy law. University of Colorado Law Legal Studies Research Paper, pp 19–25

Clarke RA et al (2014) The NSA report: liberty and security in a changing world. Princeton University Press, Princeton, NJ

Cohen JE (2013) What privacy is for. Harv Law Rev 126:1904–1933

Cottier T, Delimatsis P, Diebold N (2008) Article XIV GATS: general exceptions. In: Wolfrum R et al (eds) Max Planck commentaries on World Trade law: trade in services, vol 6. Martinus Nijhoff Publishers, Leiden, pp 287–328

Council of Europe (2017) Guidelines on the Protection of Individuals with Regard to the Processing of Personal Data in a World of Big Data. Strasbourg. T-PD(2017)01. 23 January 2017

Deckelboim SJ (2017) Consumer privacy on an international scale: conflicting viewpoints underlying the EU-U.S. Privacy shield framework and how the framework will impact privacy advocates, national security, and businesses. Georgetown J Int Law 48:263–296

Delimatsis P (2010) The puzzling interaction of trade and public morals in the digital Era. In: Burri M, Cottier T (eds) Trade governance in the digital age. Cambridge University Press, Cambridge, pp 276–296

Diggelmann O, Cleis MN (2014) How the right to privacy became a human right. Hum Rights Law Rev 14(3):441–458

Downes L (2016) The Business Implications of the EU-U.S. "Privacy Shield". Harv Bus Rev. 10 February 2016. https://hbr.org/2016/02/the-business-implications-of-the-eu-u-s-privacy-shield

Drake G (2017) Navigating the Atlantic: understanding EU data privacy compliance Amidst A sea of uncertainty. South Calif Law Rev 91(1):163–194

European Commission (2000) Commission Decision 2000/520/EC of 26 July 2000 Pursuant to Directive 95/46/EC of the European Parliament and of the Council on the Adequacy of the Protection Provided by the Safe Harbour Privacy Principles and Related Frequently Asked Questions Issued by the US Department of Commerce. OJ [2000] L 215/7

European Commission (2016a) Commission Implementing Decision of 12 July 2016 Pursuant to Directive 95/46/EC of the European Parliament and of the Council on the Adequacy of Protection Provided by the EU-US Privacy Shield. C(2016) 4176 final. 12 July 2016

European Commission (2016b) EU-US Privacy Shield: Frequently Asked Questions. MEMO/16/434. Brussels. 29 February 2016

European Commission (2018) Horizontal Provisions for Cross-Border Data Flows and for Personal Data Protection in EU Trade and Investment Agreements. https://trade.ec.europa.eu/doclib/docs/2018/may/tradoc_156884.pdf

European Commission (2019) Commission Implementing Decision 2019/419 of 23 January 2019 Pursuant to Regulation (EU) 2016/679 of the European Parliament and of the Council on the Adequate Protection of Personal Data by Japan under the Act on the Protection of Personal Information. OJ L [2019] 76

European Court of Human Rights (2019) Guide on Article 8 of the European Convention on Human Rights: Right to Respect for Private and Family Life, Home and Correspondence. Council of Europe, Strasbourg

European Data Protection Board (2019) Guidelines 3/2018 on the Territorial Scope of the GDPR. Version 2.0. 12 November 2019

European Union Agency for Fundamental Rights and Council of Europe (2018) Handbook on European Data Protection Law. Publications Office of the European Union, Luxembourg

Farrell H (2003) Constructing the international foundations of E-Commerce – the EU-US Safe Harbor Arrangement. Int Organ 57(2):277–306

Ferracane MF (2020) The costs of data protectionism. In: Burri M (ed) Big data and global trade law. Cambridge University Press, Cambridge

Gasser U (2016) Recoding privacy law: reflections on the future relationship among law, technology, and privacy. Harv Law Rev 130(2):61–70

Greenleaf G (2004) The APEC privacy initiative: "OECD Lite" for the Asia-Pacific? Privacy Laws Bus Int Newslett 71

Henke N et al (2016) The age of analytics: competing in a data-driven world. McKinsey Global Institute, Washington, DC

Howse R (2002) The appellate body rulings in the shrimp/turtle case: a new legal baseline for the trade and environment debate. Columbia J Environ Law 27(2):491–521
Irion K, Williams J (2019) Prospective policy study on artificial intelligence and EU Trade Policy. The Institute for Information Law, Amsterdam
Irion K, Yakovleva S, Bartl M (2016) Trade and privacy: complicated bedfellows? How to achieve data protection-proof Free Trade Agreements. Institute for Information Law, Amsterdam
Jackson JH (1989) The world trading system: law and policy of international economic relations. MIT Press, Cambridge
Jackson JH (1998) The World Trade Organization: constitution and jurisprudence. Royal Institute of International Affairs, London
Jackson JH, Davey WJ, Sykes AO (1995) Legal problems of international economic relations. West Group, St. Paul, MN
Kuner C (2011) Regulation of transborder data flows under data protection and privacy law: past, present and future. OECD Digital Economy Paper: 187
Kuner C (2012) The European Commission's Proposed Data Protection Regulation: A Copernican Revolution in European Data Protection Law. Bloomberg BNA Privacy and Security Law Report
Kuner C (2016) Reality and illusion in EU data transfer regulation post schrems. German Law J 18 (4):881–918
Lynskey O (2015) The foundations of EU data protection law. Oxford University Press, Oxford
MacDonald DA, Streatfeild CM (2014) Personal data privacy and the WTO. Houston J Int Law 36 (3):625–652
Manyika J et al (2011) Big data: the next frontier for innovation, competition, and productivity. McKinsey Global Institute, Washington, DC
Mattoo A, Meltzer JP (2018) International data flows and privacy: the conflict and its resolution. J Int Econ Law 21(4):760–789
Mayer-Schönberger V, Cukier K (2013) Big data: a revolution that will transform how we live, work, and think. Eamon Dolan/Houghton Mifflin Harcourt, New York
OECD (1980) Guidelines for the protection of personal information and transborder data flows. OECD Publishing, Paris
OECD (2011) The evolving privacy landscape: 30 years after the OECD privacy guidelines. OECD Digital Economy Papers No. 176
OECD (2013) The OECD privacy framework: supplementary explanatory memorandum to the revised OECD privacy guidelines. OECD Publishing, Paris
OECD (2019a) Trade and Cross-Border Data Flows. Trade Policy Papers: 220
OECD (2019b) Data in the digital age. OECD Going Digital Policy Note. OECD Publishing, Paris. www.oecd.org/going-digital/data-in-the-digital-age.pdf. Accessed 4 August 2020
Ohm P (2010) Broken promises of privacy: responding to the surprising failure of anonymization. UCLA Law Rev 57(6):1701–1778
Pan SB (2016) Get to know me: protecting privacy and autonomy under big data's penetrating gaze. Harv J Law Technol 30(1):239–261
Ravenhill J (2017) The political economy of the trans-pacific partnership: a "21st Century" trade agreement? New Polit Econ 22(5):573–594
Reidenberg JR (2000) Resolving conflicting international data privacy rules in cyberspace. Stanf Law Rev 52(5):1315–1371
Richards NM, King JH (2014) Big data ethics. Wake Forest Law Rev 49(2):393–432
Rotenberg M (2016) Privacy law sourcebook 2016: United States Law, international law, and recent developments. Electronic Privacy Information Center, Washington, DC
Rubinstein IS (2013) Big data: the end of privacy or a new beginning? Int Data Privacy Law 3 (2):74–87
Scholz LH (2019) Big data is not big oil: the role of analogy in the law of new technologies. Tennessee Law Rev 86:863–893
Schwartz PM (2013a) Information privacy in the cloud. Univ Pa Law Rev 161(6):1623–1662

Schwartz PM (2013b) The EU-US privacy collision: a turn to institutions and procedures. Harv Law Rev 126:1966–2009

Schwartz PM, Solove DJ (2011) The PII problem: privacy and a new concept of personally identifiable information. New York Univ Law Rev 86(6):1814–1894

Schwartz PM, Solove DJ (2014) Reconciling personal information in the United States and European Union. California Law Rev 102(4):877–916

Sen N (2018) Understanding the role of the WTO in international data flows: taking the liberalization or the regulatory autonomy path? J Int Econ Law 21(2):323–348

Taylor RD (2020) "Data localization": the internet in the balance. Telecommun Policy 44 (8):102003

Tene O, Polonetsky J (2013) Big data for all: privacy and user control in the age of analytics. Northwest J Technol Intellect Prop 11(5):239–273

Tene O, Wolf C (2013) Overextended: Jurisdiction and Applicable Law under the EU General Data Protection Regulation. Future of Privacy Forum White Paper

The Economist (2017) The World's Most Valuable Resource Is No Longer Oil, but Data. Print Edition. 6 May 2017

The Royal Society (2017) Machine learning: the power and promise of computers that learn by example. The Royal Institute, London

The White House (2014) Big data: seizing opportunities, preserving values. Executive Office of the President, Washington, DC

The White House (2019) Guidance for Regulation of Artificial Intelligence Applications. Memorandum for the Heads of Executive Department and Agencies. Washington, DC

Tourkochoriti I (2016) Speech, privacy and dignity in France and in the USA: a comparative analysis. Loyola Los Angeles Int Comp Law Rev 38(2):217–296

UN General Assembly (1990) Resolution 45/95 of 14 December 1990

UN Office of the High Commissioner for Human Rights (1988) General Comment No. 16: Article 17 (Right to privacy). The Right to Respect of Privacy, Family, Home and Correspondence, and Protection of Honour and Reputation. Adopted at the Thirty-Second Session of the Human Rights Committee, on 8 April 1988

United States International Trade Commission (2013) Digital Trade in the US and Global Economies. Part 1, Investigation No 332–531. USITC. Washington, DC

United States International Trade Commission (2014) Digital Trade in the US and Global Economies. Part 2, Investigation No 332–540. USITC. Washington, DC

Waters N (2009) The APEC Asia-Pacific Privacy initiative: a new route to effective data protection or a Trojan Horse for self-regulation. SCRIPTed: A J Law Technol Soc 6(1):75–89

Weber RH (2012) Regulatory autonomy and privacy standards under the GATS. Asian J WTO Int Health Law Policy 7(1):25–48

Weiss MA, Archick K (2016) U.S.-EU Data Privacy: From Safe Harbor to Privacy Shield. Congressional Research Service Report 7-5700. Washington, DC

Whitman JQ (2004) The two Western cultures of privacy: dignity versus liberty. Yale Law J 113 (6):1151–1221

Willemyns I (2020) Agreement forthcoming? A comparison of EU, US, and Chinese RTAs in times of plurilateral E-Commerce negotiations. J Int Econ Law 23(1):221–244

Wolfrum R, Stoll PT, Hestermeyer HP (eds) (2011) WTO – Trade in goods. Martinus Nijhoff Publishers, Leiden

WTO (2018) World Trade Report 2018: the future of world trade: how digital technologies are transforming global commerce. World Trade Organization, Geneva

WTO (2019) Joint Statement on Electronic Commerce, EU Proposal for WTO Disciplines and Commitments Relating to Electronic Commerce. Communication from the European Union. INF/ECOM/22. 26 April 2019

WTO Appellate Body (1996) WTO Appellate Body Report, United States – Standards for Reformulated and Conventional Gasoline, WT/DS2/AB/R, adopted 29 April 1996

WTO Appellate Body (1998) WTO Appellate Body Report, United States – Import Prohibition of Certain Shrimp and Shrimp Products, WT/DS58/AB/R, adopted 12 October 1998
WTO Appellate Body (2000) WTO Appellate Body Report, Korea – Measures Affecting Imports of Fresh, Chilled and Frozen Beef, WT/DS161/AB/R, WT/DS169/AB/R, adopted 11 December 2000
WTO Appellate Body (2001) WTO Appellate Body Report, US – Import Prohibitions of Certain Shrimp and Shrimp Products (Recourse to Article 21.5 DSU by Malaysia), WT/DS58/AB/RW, adopted 22 October 2001
WTO Appellate Body (2005) Appellate Body Report, United States – Measures Affecting the Cross-Border Supply of Gambling and Betting Services (US – Gambling), WT/DS285/AB/R, adopted 7 April 2005
WTO Appellate Body (2007) WTO Appellate Body Report, Brazil – Measures Affecting Imports of Retreaded Tyres, WT/DS332/AB/R, adopted 3 December 2007
WTO Appellate Body (2009) Appellate Body Report, China – Measures Affecting Trading Rights and Distribution Services for Certain Publications and Audiovisual Entertainment Products, WT/DS363/AB/R, adopted 21 December 2009
WTO Panel (2015) WTO Panel Report, Argentina – Financial Services, WT/DS453/R, adopted 30 September 2015
Wu M (2008) Free Trade and the protection of public morals: an analysis of the newly emerging public morals clause Doctrine. Yale J Int Law 33(1):215–252
Wunsch-Vincent S (2003) The Digital Trade Agenda of the US: parallel tracks of bilateral, regional and multilateral liberalization. Aussenwirtschaft 58(1):7–46
Yakovleva S (2020) privacy protection(ism): the latest wave of trade constraints on regulatory autonomy. Univ Miami Law Rev 74(2):416–519

**Mira Burri** Lucerne. Senior Lecturer and Managing Director Internationalization at the Faculty of Law, University of Lucerne, Principal Investigator NRP75 Project "The Governance of Big Data in Trade Agreements". CH-6002 Lucerne, Frohburgstrasse 3, P.O. Box 4466, Tel. + 41 (0)41 229 53 71. mira.burri@unilu.ch. Fields of interest: Internet Law, International Trade Law, Global Governance, Big Data and Digital Transformation.

# The Concept of Regulatory Arbitrage

**Thomas Coendet**

**Abstract** Scholars of different disciplines use the concept of regulatory arbitrage to describe situations in which economic agents structure their activities to navigate between different levels of regulation because the latter are associated with different levels of costs and benefits. At the roots, regulatory arbitrage therefore is a hybrid concept: arbitrage brings in the economic, regulation the legal perspective. Against a law and finance background, this chapter argues that realising the conceptual overlap of these two perspectives is highly productive not only for analysing regulatory arbitrage, but also to guide our thinking on how to manage and evaluate this phenomenon. So far, however, the concept of regulatory arbitrage has been more often used than analysed and conceptual analysis remains patchy. For communicating and researching this topic that is unhelpful. This chapter therefore works out a conceptual framework of regulatory arbitrage and shows how this connects and extends previous research.

## 1 Introduction

"Buy cheap, sell dear", it is the ground rule of any successful trade. In a short sale, also the reversed order of steps holds true: "sell dear, buy cheap". In any case, whoever acts on either of these maxims seeks to profit from prices moving in their favour. Whether more favourable prices are due to their own efforts or just due to the invisibly helping hand of the market, what lies in between buying and selling is *time*. Arbitrage works a little differently. To be sure, arbitrageurs still follow the maxim "buy cheap, sell dear", but they do so in making use of price differences that already exist in different market places for one and the same commodity, security or currency. What provides the opportunity for arbitrage on different markets thus is *space*, while arbitrageurs ideally seek to carry out their transactions simultaneously.

T. Coendet (✉)
KoGuan School of Law, Shanghai Jiao Tong University, Shanghai, China
e-mail: thomas.coendet@oxon.org

 
K. Mathis, A. Tor (eds.), *Law and Economics of Regulation*, Economic Analysis of Law in European Legal Scholarship 11,
https://doi.org/10.1007/978-3-030-70530-5_8

The concept of regulatory arbitrage transfers the idea of arbitrage into the law: one may not only look for different prices, but for different rules—rules that regulatory arbitrageurs consider more conducive to their business. The basis for this phenomenon is different jurisdictional spaces. If regulatory standards on banking, accounting, employment or environmental protection are less strict in country A, why not take one's business there? The phenomenon that businesses can exploit different regulatory levels in different jurisdictional spaces to gain a competitive advantage is hardly new. This is especially so, if one does not limit the phenomenon to public law rules and includes situations of private international law where parties subject their business structures and transactions to a particular private law that best fits their interests. Yet in today's technologically more advanced and globalised age, practices of regulatory arbitrage may still be more intense and difficult to cope with than ever. Indeed, an early use of the concept confirms both, its spatial character and its increase in recent time:

> Most regulatory systems are tied to particular geographical-political formations, most typically in the form of the nation-state. It is possible, therefore, for economic agents to move between different 'regulatory spaces' in order to obviate any perceived constraints associated with particular regulatory regimes. The instances of such 'regulatory arbitrage' have increased markedly in the post-war era as improvements in communications and technology have enabled economic institutions to successfully co-ordinate their activities over large expanses of international space. This form of regulatory dislocation has also loomed large in the recent history of the financial services industry, which is replete with examples of institutions organized to take advantage of geographical differences in regulation [. . .].[1]

A famous example for such regulatory arbitrage in the financial services industry is the development of the Eurodollar market in London in the 1960s. At the time, the United States (under Regulation Q) had limited the interest rate banks were allowed to pay on deposits and, moreover, required banks to hold reserves with the US central bank to secure these deposits. The restrictions could be avoided by placing dollars with European institutions, mostly situated in London. The London banks had two key advantages: they could offer higher interest rates on dollar deposits to attract American funds and the lack of any local regulation of the Eurodollar market allowed them to lend these dollar deposits on to other banks at cheaper rates than US banks. Thus, the competitive advantages of London banks reflected the regulatory restrictions of the American banks. The Bank of England was not keen to remove these competitive advantages by bringing banking and interest rate regulation up to American standards. It rather saw the development as a chance to re-establish London as the world's premier financial centre.[2]

The Eurodollar market provides an example where speaking of regulatory arbitrage seems fitting: different jurisdictional spaces result in different regulatory costs and opportunities that can be exploited. Economists and legal scholars use the concept of regulatory arbitrage, however, also to address situations within the

---

[1]Leyshon (1992), p. 251 (references omitted).

[2]Greenberg (1983), pp. 1493–1496; Leyshon (1992), p. 260; Windecker (1993), pp. 361–366.

same jurisdiction. An example of this are sale and repurchase agreements (repos) that replicate bank deposits. Instead of taking deposits and paying interest, a bank commits in a repo agreement to sell its "depositor" a security and to repurchase it at a higher price later, usually the following day. The difference between the sale and repurchase price will be the interest for the benefit of the "depositor". The regulatory arbitrage is seen in the fact that repo transactions can offer slightly better returns than ordinary deposits if the two instruments are treated differently under accounting and capital regulations.[3]

In the repo example the regulatory arbitrageur still considers different rules to structure the transaction. Going one step further, some also apply the concept of arbitrage when the transaction should simply avoid regulatory rules altogether. The situation is typically one in which financial derivatives replicate the cash flows of conventional financial instruments: if regulation imposes a cost on a non-derivative transaction there will be an economic incentive to use derivatives to work around this regulation.[4] An example is the use of put-call parity to synthesize a loan that would be subject to usury laws.[5] A more simple example to achieve the same result without a derivative is the payday loan: instead of charging a high interest rate on an unsecured loan with a typically very short time horizon, payday lenders charge an all-in fee for their services.[6] In both cases, the transaction yields an economic advantage (higher interest); yet it does not opt into another regulatory standard, it only avoids one.

Whether it makes sense to apply the concept of regulatory arbitrage in these three situations—exemplified in Eurodollars, repos, and payday loans—is not quite clear. Intuitively, the arbitrage concept seems most plausible for the first situation where different jurisdictional spaces result in different regulatory costs that provide the arbitrage opportunity. And even for that situation the author we quoted above deems it necessary to put the term in scare quotes.[7] The aim of this chapter lies not in fixing the "correct" understanding of regulatory arbitrage—although we may eventually venture a definition.[8] My starting point rather is Wittgenstein's suggestion that the meaning of a concept can be gleaned from its use.[9] The aim, therefore, will be to analyse the use of the arbitrage concept for regulatory matters along the three different situations sketched above. We will see that rationalising the concept in this way proves highly productive for understanding, managing, and evaluating regulatory arbitrage; it allows integrating previous research into a conceptual framework that for the first time links theoretical and practical, normative and empirical questions of the phenomenon. Comparison of arbitrage in finance and in law will, moreover,

---

[3] Kay (2016), p. 115.

[4] Partnoy (1997), p. 227.

[5] Knoll (2008), p. 96; Knoll (2002), pp. 75–76.

[6] Zingales (2015), p. 1353.

[7] Cf. supra quotation accompanying note 1 (speaking of "regulatory arbitrage").

[8] Cf. Willesson (2017), pp. 77–81 (providing an overview of different definitions).

[9] Wittgenstein (1984), sec. 43.

allow to posit several more specific theses. In particular, the comparison will reveal the conceptual element of legal risk and what I will call the paradox of regulatory arbitrage.

Our three examples already illustrate that situations and contexts of regulatory arbitrage tend to be normatively controversial. Is it right that payday loans provide a substitute for private credit that otherwise could not have been offered on these terms? Is it right that repo transactions aim to aggregate small private benefits for economic agents if this contributes to systemic risk in the financial sector? What should we make of regulatory competition between financial centres or of states that provide "financial casinos",[10] viz. financial havens that deliberately stay behind an international regulatory benchmark? These questions are important and not easy to answer. We hint at them here because our conceptual approach defers the evaluation of regulatory arbitrage to the end of the chapter. Not to start with normative issues seems advisable not only because cases of regulatory arbitrage can be very different, it is also more true to the question we want to ask. Our question is whether the concept of arbitrage has a meaningful analogy in the realm of law. And as it is with analogies, they only fit partially and so it must be worked out carefully in what way they make sense. The proposition that regulatory arbitrage is a meaningful analogy, in other words, does *not* imply that regulatory arbitrage shares all the characteristics of arbitrage in the economic realm. Most notably, while price arbitrage implies more efficient pricing and hence positive externalities, regulatory arbitrage may or may not be socially beneficial.

The chapter consists of three parts: the first part analyses the conceptual elements of regulatory arbitrage, the second part draws out some implications of this analysis, the third part concludes. As the examples tell, the argument develops against a law and finance background. Where clarity requires it, I will therefore speak of financial arbitrage and regulatory arbitrage to contrast arbitrage in the economic and legal realm.

## 2 Conceptual Elements

We introduced the concept of regulatory arbitrage with three typical situations. In the first two situations the regulatory arbitrageur selects between different sets of rules that he finds in the same (repo) or in different jurisdictions (Eurodollar). In the third situation (payday loan), he just avoids a regulatory rule. We can map these three situations of regulatory arbitrage therefore as either consisting in *regulatory avoidance* or *regulatory selection*, and the latter as occurring either within the same or between different jurisdictions. This section will develop the conceptual elements that unite these varieties of regulatory arbitrage: space, object, price, and risk.

[10] See Coffee (2013), p. 1260.

## 2.1 Space

Arbitrage is a spatial concept: arbitrageurs locate price differences in different markets for one and the same good and use them to their advantage. How does this spatial element transfer into regulatory arbitrage? The easy cases are those where we can start from distinct jurisdictional spaces—US and British jurisdiction, for instance. Here, the notion of regulatory arbitrage turns on the link between regulation and territorial-political institutions, most typically in the form of nation-states: if states vary in their regulatory standards, this naturally produces different regulatory spaces. It is therefore not surprising that economic geographers were among the first to mention instances of "regulatory arbitrage".[11]

If we shift into a single jurisdiction, like in the repo example, the spatial element of arbitrage seems lost at first. Nonetheless lawyers especially should not have difficulty to recognise different regulatory spaces. Within the same jurisdiction, each rule or set of rules to govern a particular activity can be conceptualised as a discrete space: you are either inside or outside the scope of the rule. The repo agreement works with the basic legal categories of loan and sales contracts, thus transactions that link to either category are connecting to different regulatory spaces. Unequal regulatory levels between a jurisdiction's financial sectors bring out the same issue: it is not uncommon that banking, capital markets, and insurance regulation provide for differing regulatory levels for the same transaction, hence creating opportunities for moving transactions between these regulatory spaces. "Shadow banking" is an example: transactions are moved out of the banking system into capital markets to avoid the costs associated with bank capital regulations.[12] The discourse on financial regulation captures this phenomenon as well in a spatial concept: it is the "boundary problem" of financial regulation.[13]

What about the situation in which economic agents are just avoiding a particular regulatory standard like in the payday loan example? It seems that in this situation there is only one regulatory space involved and therefore it would be misleading to speak of arbitrage. But, in fact, the difference with the other situations merely is how the regulatory spaces are constructed. When jurisdictions offer different levels of regulation, one selects between two regulatory spaces that are both *positively* defined (Eurodollar). It is the same if one faces two different rules or set of rules (repo). If one only avoids a rule, however, the different regulatory spaces are defined *negatively*: transactions within the scope of the rule are regulated, those outside remain in the unregulated space. One could say that this is the "boundary problem" writ large: the boundary of a rule naturally creates two spaces, in- and outside the rule. A more precise approach would be to grasp this as a moment of negative dialectics: any rule

---

[11] See supra text accompanying note 1.

[12] See Adrian and Ashcraft (2012), p. 13.

[13] See Goodhart (2008).

states some positive content, which is also defined negatively by what it is not. The unregulated space belongs to the rule just as much as the void to the glass.[14]

## 2.2 Object

The object of an arbitrage transaction can be any item of economic value for which there exist different prices; it may be a commodity, security or currency. How does this map onto the concept of regulatory arbitrage? The idea sometimes is that the regulatory arbitrageur would shop for suitable regulations on a (global) market for regulation;[15] a notion that also informs the discussion on regulatory competition, exemplified in the theses that there exists a market for corporate law.[16] The idea of law as product is not without analytical appeal for it brings into focus the high economic stakes connecting to regulatory rules and the fact that regulation, indeed, can be produced (or not produced) by competing territorial-political institutions.[17] The Eurodollar market offers a striking example of regulatory competition between Britain and the US; an issue that resurfaced in the global financial crisis of 2007–2009: in its battle for business with New York, London had been willing to offer the regulatory approach of "light touch" regulation.[18]

Nevertheless, the idea of shopping for rules strains the arbitrage concept. In financial arbitrage, the purpose of the exercise is to profit from price differences in the same or equivalent financial instruments. The instruments are the objects of the transaction. In regulatory arbitrage, one does only metaphorically buy and sell regulatory rules. The purpose of the exercise rather is to achieve a particular economic result at lower regulatory cost.[19] The difference between financial and regulatory arbitrage thus is that financial arbitrage can exhaust itself in trading one or equivalent objects, while regulatory arbitrage only makes sense as part of a business or transaction the regulatory arbitrageur wants to carry out anyway. The object of regulatory arbitrage, therefore, is not a particular regulation, but the economic substance of a business or transaction, which is wrapped in a different regulatory clothing, if any.[20]

---

[14] Cf. Stekeler (2014), pp. 174–176.

[15] Kane (1988), p. 330; Kane (1993), pp. 179–180; Nabilou (2017), p. 596.

[16] Bar-Gill (2006); Cary (1973).

[17] See Romano (1985); for a critical assessment Stark (2019).

[18] French et al. (2009), p. 290.

[19] Fleischer (2010), p. 230.

[20] In a similar vein, Barry (2010), p. 74.

## 2.3 Price

Financial arbitrage involves different prices for the same or an equivalent security. Regulations do not carry a price tag; as just explained, they are not bought and sold in the arbitrage process. The difference produces the question how to pin down the price element in regulatory arbitrage. In a law and economics perspective, it seems more accurate to start with the concept of regulatory cost rather than price: the price of a regulation is the reflex of the regulatory cost associated with it. The focus of the regulatory arbitrageur thus are costs, rather than prices. Edward Kane speaks of the net regulatory burden (or subsidy) that a regulator imposes on (or grants to) its regulatees, which results from a cost-benefit analysis of a particular regulation.[21] (Note that the perspective is the one of the *regulatory arbitrageur* and therefore of his cost-benefit analysis; we use this perspective as a starting point and come back to the problems this involves shortly.)

The cost approach works well for the situation where the regulatory arbitrageur can choose between any two or more given set of rules. What will be the returns if deposits are structured as ordinary deposits under one set of capital and accounting rules, or as repo agreements under another set of capital and accounting rules? The higher returns on one side will mean a higher cost on the other. But what if the regulatory arbitrageur only circumvents a rule? If the arbitrage analogy holds, there should be a different regulatory cost associated with the regulated space (inside the scope) and the unregulated space (outside the scope of the rule). Economic analysis of law has interpreted the cost of regulation as a tax. Interest rate ceilings for bank deposits or short term loans, for instance, are then a 100% tax levied on the income the bank or lender would have earned in absence of the regulation.[22] If the transaction merely avoids a particular regulatory rule, the arbitrage thus takes place in between an area with cost in the form of a regulatory tax and a tax-free zone, as it were.

Kane connected the idea that the regulator imposes a net regulatory burden on regulatees with the concept of a "law of one regulatory burden". Obviously, this suggests to apply "the Law of one Price" to regulatory arbitrage.[23] In conventional economics, this law posits that "all objects with the same observable characteristics should sell at the same price."[24] The reason behind this law is price arbitrage: if the same object sells at different prices, this provides a riskless profit opportunity. So, arbitrageurs will buy where the price is low and sell where the price is high, thereby evening out prices on different market places.[25] If all arbitrage opportunities have been taken, the object consequently will sell at one price. Financial markets are thought to embody the Law of one Price particularly well because simultaneously

---

[21]Kane (1988), p. 333.

[22]Posner (1971); Kane (1981), p. 357; further Story and Walter (1997), p. 129; Gerding (2016), p. 362.

[23]Kane (1988), p. 333; more explicitly, Kane (1981), pp. 357, 359.

[24]Stiglitz (2009), p. 313.

[25]Weber (1894), p. 77.

buying and selling the same security for two different prices seems straightforward. Empirical studies on the issue suggest a more mixed result.[26]

We have seen that in the equation of regulatory arbitrage "costs" take the position of "price" in financial arbitrage. So, if financial arbitrage leads to one price, regulatory arbitrage should lead to one burden. Kane argues the law of one regulatory burden as follows: "because inefficient patterns of regulation impose excessively burdensome costs [. . .] on regulatees [. . .], the burdened parties must be expected sooner or later to develop avoidance strategies by which to throw these burdens aside."[27] Regulatory arbitrage would thus cause inefficient regulatory burdens to dissipate if all regulatees avoid costly regulation. Partnoy has recently argued in a similar vein, though with different emphasis. He submits that the default position for regulatory arbitrage is the "law of *two* prices": so long as (a) the regulator does not close the gap between regulated and unregulated transactions *and* (b) there remain some regulated transactions, the price wedge between regulated and unregulated transactions will persist.[28] Kane's and Partnoy's analysis are hence comparable, yet with a different view on how regulatory arbitrage will unfold in practice: Kane implies that regulatees eventually will avoid all inefficient regulated transactions and thus establish a level playing field of one regulatory burden, while Partnoy considers this less likely in making the law of two prices the paradigm of regulatory arbitrage.

There are several conceptual problems in mapping the analogy between financial and regulatory arbitrage in this way. First, it can be questioned whether the price wedge between regulated and unregulated transactions disappears even if *no* regulated transactions remain. From the perspective of regulatory arbitrageurs that is of course true: they now all have the same regulatory burden (viz. none). Still, there exists a significant difference to the situation of price arbitrage. In price arbitrage, the lower and higher price will resolve into a single price. Regulatory arbitrage, on the other hand, cannot alter or dissolve regulations *de jure*. And so even if a certain regulation is altered *de facto* because no regulated transactions remain, the *fact* that the regulation remains in force marks a difference to price arbitrage. As a result, the costs associated with the regulation remain as a practical reason why businesses conduct their business in the way they do. In other words, even if there remain no regulated transactions and all players are subject to the same burden (viz. none), the regulation provides an ongoing reason not to move business back into the regulated area. In this sense, therefore, the "cost wedge" between regulated and unregulated transactions persists.

Second, if the regulator unites regulated and unregulated transactions under a common standard, this does not remove the "cost wedge" either. The conceptual reason for this is the logic of the "boundary problem" we have discussed earlier.[29] Whatever rule the regulator posits, it will inevitably produce *two* regulatory *spaces*:

---

[26]Akram et al. (2009); Lamont and Thaler (2003).

[27]Kane (1988), p. 333 (emphasis omitted).

[28]Partnoy (2019), p. 1036.

[29]See supra text accompanying note 14.

inside and outside the scope of the rule. If one, on top of that, accepts the argument of regulation as a tax levied on regulated transactions, the two regulatory spaces will also reflect in *two* regulatory *burdens*: transactions subject to the rule will carry a higher cost than the ones outside of it.[30] The importance of "the law of two regulatory burdens", so understood, consists in providing a theoretical explanation for one of the key lessons some observers have drawn after the global financial crisis: "Each law inheres already its circumvention; each rule can be understood as a 'premium for new rule arbitrage'".[31] Indeed, if regulation inevitably provides a premium for working around it via legal engineering, rule- and decision-makers would better take "the law of two regulatory burdens" to heart.

Third, there is a crucial ambiguity in Kane's proposition that regulatory arbitrage would cause *inefficient* regulation to dissipate. When he states the proposition as an argument for his "law of one regulatory burden", it suggests that regulation might be either efficient or inefficient and regulatory arbitrage would merely whittle away the latter. Regulation is efficient if its benefits outweigh the costs for establishing and enforcing it. A regulatory scheme for systemic risk in banking, for instance, is efficient if it effectively reduces systemic risk and provides this benefit at a cost that is lower than the cost following from a potential financial crisis.[32] However, Kane also adopts the proposition that regulation is a form of tax and therefore a cost and not a benefit. That suggests that from the perspective of the *individual* regulatory arbitrageur, there is no such thing like efficient regulation. If regulatees strive to avoid costly regulation and any regulation is costly, regulatory arbitrage would then erode *any* regulation, not just the inefficient one. I think we should resolve this tension as follows. On the one hand, it is good regulatory policy to assume that regulatory arbitrageurs may also target regulations that are a net gain to society, but a net regulatory burden to them. Such policy is precisely what "the law of two regulatory burdens" establishes and advises.[33] On the other hand, if one disposes of the category of efficient regulation, the analogy between financial and regulatory arbitrage becomes potentially misleading. While financial arbitrage makes prices more efficient and thereby provides a benefit to society at large, regulatory arbitrage will not have this effect if it targets efficient regulations. The upshot of this is that efficiency of regulatory arbitrage should not be reduced to the "cost-perspective" of the regulatory arbitrageur. One must also factor in the benefits regulation provides to individual regulatees *and* to society at large. We will come back to this issue in the evaluative part of the chapter.

---

[30]See supra text accompanying note 22.

[31]Zeitler (2012), p. 678.

[32]For such an analysis, see Independent Commission on Banking (2011), chap. 5.

[33]See supra text following note 30.

## 2.4 *Risk*

In theory, arbitrage provides a riskless profit opportunity. This distinguishes it from speculation where one seeks to profit from price differences that develop over time: "buy cheap, sell dear". In practice, however, arbitrage is anything but riskless: closing the gaps between market prices requires time and capital.[34] This has notably been emphasised for financial arbitrage. Even the simplest trade that, for instance, seeks to profit from a difference in futures prices between London and Frankfurt will require considerable sophistication and entail risk. The trade becomes risk arbitrage: "In risk arbitrage, an arbitrageur does not make money with probability one, and may need substantial amounts of capital to both execute his trades and cover his losses. Most real world arbitrage trades in bond and equity markets are examples of risk arbitrage in this sense. Unlike in the textbook model, such arbitrage is risky and requires capital."[35]

The fact that risk comes back into the arbitrage concept throws up the question who bears the risk when *regulatory* arbitrage fails. Against the background of financial arbitrage, the question almost seems trite: who else than the arbitrageur should bear the loss if, for instance, he misjudged the equivalence of the securities he was trading against one another? So why should the regulatory arbitrageur not shoulder the *legal* risks involved in his operation? Regrettably, the answer is not that simple. For one thing, institutions that practiced "shadow banking" to save the costs of regulated banking operations and that were bailed-out during the global financial crisis after these operations had failed did not bear the risk of regulatory arbitrage; as Kane put it elegantly, shadow banking meant "safety-net arbitrage".[36] Moreover, it is not a trivial issue how to allocate legal risk if the regulatory arbitrageur has the letter of the law on his side. We will come back to this problem in the following section when considering the legal strategies against regulatory arbitrage.[37]

The conceptual element of risk yet marks another significant difference between financial and regulatory arbitrage. In financial arbitrage the risk consists in financial loss, while the trade itself typically carries no legal risk in the sense that it might be considered illegal later. In regulatory arbitrage the particular risk consists in the possibility that the legal set-up might fail because courts or regulators deem it to conflict with the law. A court may decide that tax avoidance actually is tax evasion or that a payday loan actually is just as much subject to usury laws than an ordinary private credit. In contrast to financial arbitrage, *regulatory* arbitrage has its *raison d'être* in the tension to existing regulations and therefore typically carries legal risk. Hence it is misleading to conceptualise regulatory arbitrage as "perfectly legal". Characterising regulatory arbitrage in this way is, of course, standard rhetoric of

[34]Cf. Hardie and MacKenzie (2012).

[35]Shleifer and Vishny (1997), p. 36; see also Bodie (2019).

[36]Kane (2014), p. 775.

[37]See infra text following note 48.

legal experts devising a set-up that should avoid or opt into a particular regulatory standard. Whether a set-up is legal or not is, however, *not* for regulatory arbitrageurs to decide, but for courts and regulators.

# 3 Implications

This section works out the implications of the conceptual analysis in three steps. First, I will show how the elements of space and regulatory cost lead one to understand regulatory arbitrage as a dynamic concept that involves innovation. Second, I will map the basic legal strategies against regulatory arbitrage and discuss how they respond to its spatial and dynamic properties. Third, I will examine how the link of innovation and regulatory arbitrage structures how we evaluate the latter. The section therefore unfolds along the keywords: dynamics, strategies, and evaluation.

## *3.1 Dynamics*

Regulatory arbitrage involves a spatial element: the arbitrageur operates between different regulatory spaces; moving business from New York to London or avoiding an interest rate cap, for instance.[38] This suggests one should understand regulatory arbitrage as a one-off move to exploit a regulatory gap or geographical limitation of the regulation; a move that the rule-maker (legislator) or decision-maker (regulatory authority and courts) might then counter by extending the scope of the regulation. The lawyer might be tempted to see the episode end here: he has dealt with the case at hand, that's it. Such a view, however, fundamentally misunderstands both the phenomenon and its conceptual analysis. The basis for the arbitrage is a regulation that involves regulatory cost; it therefore starts from an economic incentive to reduce or avoid this cost. The reaction of the rule- or decision-maker to close down the arbitrage opportunity only removes the latter, but not the economic incentive that initiated the process. Because any new rule the regulator posits will recreate the difference between regulated and unregulated transactions ("the law of two regulatory burdens"), the basic conditions for regulatory arbitrage persist.[39] Regulatory arbitrage thus is fundamentally a dynamic concept: it puts the phenomenon of regulation and regulatory avoidance on a timeline.

The dynamic character of what this chapter calls regulatory arbitrage is sometimes staged as a race between hares (rule-makers) and hedgehogs (rule-breakers) suggesting that the courts tend to show sympathy with the hedgehogs: "They do not

[38]Cf. supra text following note 13.

[39]Cf. supra text accompanying note 30.

intervene [. . .] if smart players change the rules of the game with reference to private autonomy."[40] I do not think that this is a particularly helpful explication of the phenomenon—the literary connotations take the eyes off the hare, as it were.[41] A more suitable concept to explain the dynamics inherent in regulatory arbitrage is what Kane calls the "regulatory dialectic". Drawing on Hegel (as Kane likes to think),[42] he envisions the political processes of regulation and the economic processes of regulatory avoidance as opposing forces that result in an open-ended dialectical struggle. More specifically, regulation forms the *thesis* that burdens regulatees with costs; the latter will consequently react with regulatory avoidance (*anti-thesis*). If the regulator, then, answers avoidance with reregulation, the new regulation provides a *synthesis*, which at the same time marks a new regulatory *thesis* that starts the process anew.[43] Kane thus describes a *temporal* dialectic between regulators and regulatees, which matches with the *spatial* dialectic we have suggested for the regulatory rule.[44]

The dynamics of regulatory arbitrage should be understood to reflect an intrinsic quality of the capitalist system. In a capitalist system, businesses have an incentive to stay ahead of the market in order to reap first mover advantages. Such advantages fuel innovative processes in the economy to come up with new products that serve (or do not serve)[45] end users, yet also to have an edge over competitors in terms of information and trading strategies. Seen like this, product innovation and arbitrage trading stay on common ground. Once new products become market standard and arbitrage opportunities have been taken, first mover benefits vanish and markets equilibrate, as reflected in the Law of one Price. However, the incentives for businesses to keep an edge remain and push against market discipline and regulation. Fernand Braudel therefore saw capitalism as the system of the "counter market" (*contre-marché*) in which sophisticated players try to stay ahead of the market—this makes capitalism a fundamentally dynamic system.[46] Within this capitalist dynamic, regulatory arbitrage combines innovation *and* arbitrage: because avoiding regulatory cost can confer significant competitive advantages on market participants, it drives innovation that does not result in new products or arbitrage that makes prices efficient, but in smart business structures, financial instruments and strategies about how to sidestep regulation.[47] This overlap between innovation and arbitrage marks a key issue for the evaluative part.[48]

---

[40] Schanze (1995), p. 166.

[41] Cf. Schäfer (1995), p. 180.

[42] Cf. Mueller (1958).

[43] See Kane (1981), pp. 355–356; Kane (1983), pp. 96–97; Kane (1988), pp. 332–333; Kane (1993), pp. 182–184; for examples, see Finnerty (1985); Mosebach (2000).

[44] See supra text accompanying note 14.

[45] See Akerlof and Shiller (2015).

[46] See Braudel (1997); Wallerstein (1991); in a similar vein, Kay (2016), p. 66.

[47] Cf. Kane (1981), p. 358; Leyshon (1992), p. 251.

[48] See infra text accompanying note 69.

## 3.2 Strategies

The regulatory dialectic results in an obvious problem: as regulatees move on to avoid the latest reregulation, which is followed by the next reregulation, rule books grow in size and complexity. A prominent example are the Basel rules for the prudential regulation of banks that evolved from about 30 pages in 1988 to over 600 pages within the next twenty five years.[49] Needless to say, that this "Tower of Basel" (Haldane) will increase regulatory cost and is consequently unlikely to abate incentives to avoid these rules. Besides increasing complexity, a regulatory strategy that seeks to deal with regulatory arbitrage by catching up with regulatees runs into further problems. Catching up means solving problems of the past, whereas the economic incentive structure inherent in regulatory arbitrage ("the law of two burdens") suggests that rule- and decision-makers should focus on how to solve the problems lying ahead when dealing with the case at hand. Regulation of regulatory arbitrage must be forward looking. However, planning ahead cannot mean trying to anticipate all the moves regulatees may possibly make to avoid burdensome regulations. The knowledge, or rather omniscience, necessary for such a "regulatory calculus" will never be concentrated in a single regulatory mind.[50] Far from being effective, the attempt to close *all* the loopholes in one comprehensive set of regulations will result in an overly complex regulatory framework.

A strategy against regulatory arbitrage should thus be mindful about legal complexity, sensitive to the economic incentives it sets, forward looking, and account for the constraints on regulatory knowledge. The spatial element of regulatory arbitrage adds a further analytical layer. If different regulatory spaces result from differing regulatory levels among jurisdictions, the usual strategy calls for harmonisation.[51] Harmonised national standards, so the idea, establish a single regulatory space. The Basel Accords to harmonise capital requirements of banks on an international level again provide the paradigm. If different regulatory spaces open up within the same jurisdiction—between the financial sectors of banking, insurance, and capital markets, for instance—the standard strategy suggests a functional approach, ensuring that transactions equivalent in economic substance are treated in the same way.[52] Same economic substance, same regulatory space. Finally, in the situation where different regulatory spaces result *ex negativo* from the regulatory rule itself, the classic strategy suggests to implement the spirit rather than the letter of the law.[53] The spirit enlarges the regulatory space to include the

---

[49] See Gerding (2016), pp. 365–367; Haldane (2012), pp. 6–8.

[50] Cf. Hayek (1945), p. 530.

[51] E.g. Eichengreen (2010), p. 108; G-20 (2008), p. 2; Macey (2003), pp. 1353–1354.

[52] E.g. Merton (1995), p. 39; Möslein (2014), pp. 28–29; Kay (2016), pp. 117, 211.

[53] E.g. McBarnet (2010), p. 16; Tröger (2016), p. 199; Kay (2016), p. 211.

transaction that sought to avoid the regulatory rule. All these standard strategies are, however, not without their drawbacks.[54] We consider them each in turn.

Harmonisation obviously runs into political and practical limitations. Despite all the efforts after the global financial crisis, we are far from having a unified set of rules for international financial markets. To begin with, it is not possible to force or even motivate other countries to close down "financial casinos" when it benefits them and they are not incentivised to internalise the costs they impose on others by running such institutions.[55] Yet even if a common set of rules emerges, like in the Basel Accords, this is not equal to a harmonised regulatory practice. Embedding international agreements into a national regulatory practice will always result in differences because of diverging regulatory cultures, starting conditions and institutions.[56] Moreover, the conceptual argument that regulation inevitably results in "two regulatory burdens" suggests that a *single* regulatory space literally is a *utopia*.[57] So the *regulation* of shadow banking, for instance, will always cast a shadow that opens a new space for shadow banking.[58] Harmonisation thus not simply closes down, but also produces opportunities for regulatory arbitrage: "Paradoxically, regulations intended to remove artificial competitive advantage can also create opportunities to gain competitive advantage. A legally based level playing field opens up new sources of competitive advantage, with some more able than others to creatively escape even harmonised regulatory restrictions."[59]

The functional approach to emphasise the economic substance rather than the legal form indeed seems very sensible to cope with regulatory arbitrage. Still, it remains to be clarified what that substance should mean: lawyers, economists, accountants, compliance officers, regulators, and judges will all have their own idea and be in a different position to argue for it. In particular, professionals familiar with the finest details of financial regulations will have a considerable argumentative advantage.[60] What is more, in regulatory practice even the idea of substance runs through its own dialectic: the anti-formalist rule "substance over form" can itself be used in a formalistic way to create new regulatory boundaries and retain arbitrage opportunities.[61] Finally, a more substantive approach will not dispense to as well formulate specific regulatory rules as regards the economic context it should govern. This is notably because regulatees will push for more specific guidance—at times, to

---

[54]For the particular strategies against regulatory arbitrage in the field of private international law, see Junker (2019), pp. 97–99; Riles (2014).

[55]Coffee (2013), p. 1269.

[56]Riles (2014), pp. 77–83.

[57]Cf. supra text following note 29.

[58]Cf. Kessler and Wilhelm (2013), pp. 252–255.

[59]McBarnet and Whelan (1992), p. 140; in a similar vein, Riles (2014), p. 83.

[60]Cf. MacKenzie (2009), pp. 127–129, 134–35.

[61]McBarnet and Whelan (1991), pp. 865–868.

know better how to avoid the regulations.[62] Yet practice of financial regulation suggests that even regulators themselves may not be willing to switch to a more substantive approach because they do not trust how regulatees would use the discretion that comes with a more flexible approach. British experiences with principles-based regulation of wholesale financial markets indeed justify such scepticism.[63]

Finally, the spirit. The spirit of the law is a dynamic concept. As such it fits the conceptual analysis we have established for regulatory arbitrage: its dialectics of space and time.[64] This analysis suggests that a regulatory strategy must be able to: (a) flexibly adjust regulatory spaces in the case at hand by giving rules a broad (er) reading and (b) be able to do so continuously to cope with avoidance strategies that follow up on earlier regulatory decisions. Practical implementation will, however, require that regulators have the necessary discretion and confidence to embrace the uncertainty that necessarily comes with such a dynamic approach. John Kay points out the challenge: "this would require a dramatic and permanent shift in both the calibre of regulatory staff and the balance of political influence between regulators and regulated activities."[65] Moreover, arguments favouring a formal approach to the letter of the law can rely on a powerful legal guarantee: the rule of law. Regulatees can and, in fact, do argue that they have the right to know where they stand, that the law shall not have retroactive effect, and that there exist limits on discretion and safeguards against arbitrary state action.[66] And in contrast to implicit financial guarantees of governments for systemically important financial institutions, these rule of law guarantees are explicit legal categories. That the legal risks involved in regulatory arbitrage fall on the arbitrageur is therefore even less clear than for financial arbitrage.[67]

The optimal strategy to manage regulatory arbitrage is therefore likely to consist of a combined approach resting on the idea of dynamic regulation. This is not the place to work out this strategy in any detail. We only seek to create a basic frame of reference based on the conceptual analysis of regulatory arbitrage. To sum up our argument thus far, consider the reasons and direction of a dynamic approach to financial regulation presented in the Stiglitz Report:

> Regulation must be dynamic [. . .] financial institutions will try to circumvent regulations. Regulators have to be especially attentive to the ever-present attempts at regulatory arbitrage and circumvention, including through the creation of arms-length special purpose vehicles. By definition, regulations reduce profits because they restrict potentially profitable actions. [. . .] The fact that firms are always inventing ways of circumventing regulations means that

[62]McBarnet and Whelan (1991), p. 864; Kay (2016), p. 212; for an example, Casey and Lannoo (2009), pp. 125–126, 134.

[63]Black (1995), p. 109; Black (2011).

[64]See supra text accompanying note 14 and 44.

[65]Kay (2016), p. 117.

[66]McBarnet and Whelan (1991), p. 857.

[67]Cf. supra text accompanying note 36.

governments have to view regulation as a dynamic process and provides an argument for legal frameworks that give regulators wide latitude to respond to the public interest.[68]

## 3.3 Evaluation

In whose interest is regulatory arbitrage? The Stiglitz Report suggests a clear-cut dichotomy: regulatory arbitrage aims at private cost-benefits and collides with the public interest; thus, it only serves the private interests of the regulatory arbitrageur. That the answer is more ambivalent can be seen from the link between innovation and arbitrage in the concept of regulatory arbitrage.[69] Our evaluation of regulatory arbitrage therefore starts from these two elements.

For many the *innovation* link provides the inroad for a more positive view on regulatory arbitrage. Apparently, one does not need to be an economist to appreciate the nexus between innovation and welfare benefits of the real economy in order to arrive at a benign view on innovation also in other areas. The notion, then, that financial innovation allows reducing transaction costs and increasing efficiency, risk sharing, and stability in the financial system, readily carries over into the legal discussion.[70] However, it does not follow that innovation relating to regulatory arbitrage will imply the same welfare benefits that we like to associate with innovation in the real economy or other areas. On the contrary, many commentators rather start from the opposing view that engaging in regulatory arbitrage in finance wastes real resources because nothing is produced or created.[71] In addition, if regulatory arbitrage targets regulation that provides a net gain to society it will reduce social welfare.[72] To be sure, to take this more sceptical starting point does not preclude one from arguing that some regulations may indeed be inefficient. But the further step that regulatory arbitrage would contribute to social welfare because it allows inefficient regulation to be avoided is still speculative for there exists no "theory of how frequently regulation is inefficient and the magnitude of the inefficiency".[73] Finally, evaluating regulatory arbitrage only under the aspect of innovation overlooks that a different kind of cost-benefit analysis will be required when the arbitrage takes place between different jurisdictions or regulators.[74]

Taking the *arbitrage* element, then, to evaluate regulatory arbitrage is highly suggestive. To begin with, comparison with financial arbitrage reveals an important

[68] Stiglitz (2010), pp. 82–83.

[69] See supra text accompanying note 48.

[70] See Mullineux (2010), p. 246; Macey (1995), pp. 82, 84, 93; Fleischer (2010), p. 275; Möslein (2014), pp. 31–32; contra: Stout (1995), pp. 57, 67–68; Partnoy (2019), pp. 1041–1042.

[71] Merton (1995), p. 39; Partnoy (1997), p. 215; Shah (1997), p. 92; Kay (2016), p. 116.

[72] See Kay (2016), p. 117; cf. supra text accompanying note 32.

[73] Zingales (2015), p. 1350; Partnoy (1997), p. 241; cf. Kay (2016), p. 117.

[74] See Trachtman (2000), pp. 342–343; Tarko and Farrant (2019).

similarity: as a rule, both forms of arbitrage are, so to speak, not for everyone. Who seeks to profit from financial or regulatory arbitrage opportunities must combine considerable capital, time, and intelligence. Among these, capital is most important, as arbitrage services may still be bought from investment banks, hedge funds, accountants, law firms, consultants, etc. In any case, whether it takes place in finance or law, arbitrage is a business of professionals. At the same time, there exist notable differences between financial and regulatory arbitrage. Most importantly, financial arbitrage has the benefit of making prices more efficient—as the Law of one Price suggests. We have seen that regulatory arbitrage cannot have the same effect; it is limited by "the law of two regulatory burdens".[75] The key difference therefore is that financial arbitrage has a guaranteed direct benefit for the unsophisticated for efficient market prices protect any investor from overpaying. Regulatory arbitrage, on the other hand, does not necessarily have this consequence. Even if such arbitrage is construed to signal that regulatory costs are too high, this is no information the unsophisticated could act upon.[76]

Some therefore conclude that regulatory arbitrage is unfair: "the less wealthy and less sophisticated are often unable to avail themselves of the arbitrage and so only they pay the higher regulatory cost."[77] The qualification ("often") is important, otherwise it pushes the argument too far: regulatory arbitrage can result in institutional settings that are accessible to the less sophisticated. The emergence of a market for wealth management products ("WMPs") in China provides an example. WMPs belong to China's shadow banking system and have been analysed as an example of regulatory arbitrage in emerging markets.[78] These products sprung up mainly as a reaction to governmental interest rate ceilings on bank deposits—reminiscent of the situation in the US under Regulation Q.[79] Retail investors, in particular, profited from WMPs because they shielded them against having their capped returns from bank deposits eaten up by inflation. So regulatory arbitrage offered here possibilities for the less wealthy and sophisticated. (At the same time, the example illustrates how difficult it is to assess the welfare benefits of regulatory arbitrage. Besides benefits for retail investors and smaller borrowers, some commentators credited the WMP market for pushing the liberalisation of interest rates;[80] while others voiced concerns about systemic risk and consumer protection, and argued that—in addition to floating interest rates—well-designed regulation would enhance the efficiency of this market.[81])

Evaluating regulatory arbitrage along its innovation and arbitrage components, however, may also be limiting. The arbitrage analogy to what we usually call gaming

[75] See supra text accompanying note 23–29.

[76] In a similar vein, Partnoy (2019), p. 1035.

[77] Knoll (2002), p. 63.

[78] See Acharya et al. (2020).

[79] See supra text following note 1.

[80] Jiang (2015), p. 3.

[81] See Shen (2015).

or circumventing regulatory rules, explicitly frames this activity in economic terms. This is not per se a problem. The argument advanced so far was to show exactly how the arbitrage analogy is an analytically fruitful way to think about the issue. Nevertheless, the risk with this framing is to steer the discussion into a narrow consequentialist perspective. It might then be overlooked that regulatory arbitrage also has an important political and deontic perspective that differentiates it from financial arbitrage: adjusting *prices* is not the same as "adjusting" *rules* through arbitrage. More specifically, the political aspect is about the legitimacy of whom is to set and change the rules in a certain social context, while the deontic aspect captures the idea that there might be a value in following rules as such.[82] Indeed, those scholars with a more sociological approach to regulatory arbitrage touch upon these problems: they establish that there is not much respect for the spirit of the law in some business contexts and raise the concern that the link of regulatory arbitrage to capital may move powerful elites beyond legal control.[83]

Thus, there is little overall assurance that regulatory arbitrage is unproblematic in its economic, political and social consequences. The notion that such arbitrage is an elitist game that wastes intellectual talent and money to activities that potentially undermine the rule of law and impose significant costs on society at large is well founded.[84] It would be sociologically naïve if legal professionals would dispel these concerns in simply relying on the idea that regulatory arbitrage *will* increase efficiency for such an axiom has no sound basis.[85] On this point, economic research offers the legal professional nothing more than a *promise* that regulatory arbitrage may in some cases spur efficiency and increase social welfare. (Some have suggested that the tension between this promise and the issues with regulatory arbitrage could be resolved by introducing a presumption to the effect that the onus is on the regulatory arbitrageur to show that his innovation serves some useful purpose and not just seeks to avoid regulation.[86] However, if such a presumption comes into play ex ante, as a variant of the precautionary principle, it still turns on the doubtful assumption that we could validly separate "socially useful" from "bad" innovation in advance.[87])

[82]See generally Heath (2011).

[83]McBarnet and Whelan (1991), p. 873; Shah (1997), p. 101; McBarnet (2010), p. 16; further also Fleischer (2010), pp. 264–272; Pistor (2019), chap. 7.

[84]See references in notes 71 and 83.

[85]Zingales (2015), p. 1350; see also Ford (2017), p. 156.

[86]Schäfer (1995), p. 180; Zingales (2015), p. 1357; Partnoy (2019), p. 1039.

[87]Ford (2017), p. 141.

## 4 Conclusion: Regulatory Arbitrage and its Paradox

We started the conceptual analysis of regulatory arbitrage with three situations: in the first, the arbitrageur chooses between different jurisdictions; in the second, between different sets of regulations; and in the third, he avoids a particular regulation. More specifically, we categorised the first two as regulatory selection and the third as regulatory avoidance. Our argument was that all these situations can be meaningfully addressed as regulatory arbitrage and we may therefore use this concept confidently, without scare quotes. Regulatory arbitrage hence appears as an activity that seeks to exploit the cost differentials for the same or an essentially similar economic activity, which result from the fact that this activity is subject to regulation. In other words, the concept implies that any regulation creates arbitrage opportunities: a regulatory rule produces different regulatory spaces, each carrying a different regulatory cost. In economic parlance, this point can be expressed as "the law of two regulatory burdens". We thus conclude that the arbitrage analogy is a productive tool for analysing situations of regulatory selection and avoidance. However, there is still one more element to the analogy between financial and regulatory arbitrage, which we have not considered thus far and that we address now briefly to wrap up: the arbitrage paradox.

The Law of one Price throws up a problem that financial economics discusses as the so-called arbitrage paradox: if perfectly efficient markets continuously yield a single price, arbitrageurs would have no incentive to watch out for mispricings because all price-relevant information would always already be in the price. But if so, what incentive could there be to engage in the costly business to gather price-relevant information in the first place?[88] One solution to this paradox is that efficient financial markets only display very short-term mispricings that are sufficient to incentivise arbitrageurs to stay ahead of market development.[89] Does "the law of two regulatory burdens" also suggest a paradox? It does, but this paradox proves to be even more at odds with the facts of life: if regulation imposes a cost on economic activity and hence incentivises arbitrage driving economic activity out of regulated areas, why should there be regulation incentivising arbitrage in the first place? In real life, processes of regulatory arbitrage clearly do not have such a paradoxical effect. This invites us to embed the phenomenon of regulatory arbitrage into a wider socio-economic, political and cultural context. Whether regulatory arbitrage opportunities, in fact, will and can be exploited depends on a number of limiting factors: transaction costs to carry out the arbitrage are obviously limiting; so are the capacities of the arbitrageur (time, talent, capital). These factors are, however, not specific to *regulatory* arbitrage. Specific limiting factors are the *legal* risk that is involved in moving around and in between different regulatory settings, and the *deontic* constraints that come with having rules in place.[90]

---

[88]See Grossman and Stiglitz (1980), p. 393.

[89]Akram et al. (2009), p. 1742.

[90]See supra text accompanying note 36 and 82.

The regulatory arbitrage paradox thus leads us to understand this phenomenon as more than just a narrow cost-benefit analysis, and more than mere regulatory avoidance. Economists and sociologists have placed financial arbitrage into a richer and more realistic societal context than the one of standard financial models.[91] As this chapter suggests, normative debate and empirical research on regulatory arbitrage should move into the same direction.

**Acknowledgement** I am grateful to Hans-Bernd Schäfer and Tobias Tröger for their comments on a draft of this chapter. The support by the Programme for Professor of Special Appointment (Eastern Scholar) at Shanghai Institutions of Higher Learning is acknowledged.

## References

Acharya V, Qian J, Su Y, Yang Z (2020) In the shadow of banks: wealth management products and issuing banks' risk in China. Social Science Research Network, Rochester

Adrian T, Ashcraft AB (2012) 'Shadow Banking Regulation' (Federal Reserve Bank of New York) Staff Report. No. 559

Akerlof GA, Shiller RJ (2015) Phishing for phools: the economics of manipulation and deception. Princeton University Press, Princeton

Akram QF, Rime D, Sarno L (2009) Does the law of one price hold in international financial markets? Evidence from tick data. J Bank Finance 33:1741–1754

Bar-Gill O (2006) The market for corporate law. J Inst Theoret Econ (JITE) 162:134–160

Barry J (2010) On regulatory arbitrage. Texas Law Rev 89:69–78

Black J (1995) 'Which arrow?' Rule type and regulatory policy. Public Law:94–117

Black J (2011) The rise, fall and fate of principles based regulation. In: Alexander K, Moloney N (eds) Law reform and financial markets. Edward Elgar, Cheltenham, pp 3–34

Bodie Z (2019) Robert C. Merton and the science of finance. Ann Rev Finance Econ 11:1–20

Braudel F (1997) Die Dynamik des Kapitalismus, 3rd edn. Klett-Cotta, Stuttgart

Cary WL (1973) Federalism and corporate law: reflections upon Delaware. Yale Law J 83:663–705

Casey J-P, Lannoo K (2009) The Mifid revolution. Cambridge University Press, Cambridge

Coffee J (2013) Extraterritorial financial regulation: why E.T. can't come home. Cornell Law Rev 99:1259–1302

Eichengreen B (2010) International financial regulation after the crisis. Daedalus 139:107–114

Finnerty J (1985) Zero coupon bond arbitrage: an illustration of the regulatory dialectic at work. Finance Manage 14:13–17

Fleischer V (2010) Regulatory arbitrage. Texas Law Rev 89:227–289

Ford C (2017) Innovation and the state: finance, regulation, and justice. Cambridge University Press, New York

French S, Leyshon A, Thrift N (2009) A very geographical crisis: the making and breaking of the 2007–2008 financial crisis. Cambridge J Regions Econ Soc 2:287–302

G-20 (2008) Washington-Declaration of the Summit on Financial Markets and the World Economy. Washington

Gerding EF (2016) The dialectics of bank capital: regulation and regulatory capital arbitrage. Washburn Law J 55:357–384

Goodhart C (2008) The boundary problem in financial regulation. Natl Inst Econ Rev 206:48–55

[91] Shleifer and Vishny (1997); Hardie and MacKenzie (2012).

Greenberg RD (1983) The Eurodollar market: the case for disclosure. California Law Rev 71:1492–1515
Grossman SJ, Stiglitz JE (1980) On the impossibility of informationally efficient markets. Am Econ Rev 70:393–408
Haldane A (2012) The Dog and the Frisbee: Speech at the Federal Reserve Bank of Kansas City's 366th Economic Policy Symposium
Hardie I, MacKenzie D (2012) The material sociology of arbitrage. In: Knorr-Cetina K, Preda A (eds) The Oxford handbook of the sociology of finance. Oxford University Press, Oxford, pp 187–202
Hayek FA (1945) The use of knowledge in society. Am Econ Rev 35:519–530
Heath J (2011) Following the rules: practical reasoning and deontic constraint. Oxford University Press, Oxford
Independent Commission on Banking (Great Britain) (2011) Final report: recommendations, London
Jiang W (2015) The future of shadow banking in China. Social Science Research Network, Rochester
Junker A (2019) Internationales Privatrecht, 3rd edn. C.H. Beck, München
Kane E (1981) Accelerating inflation, technological innovation, and the decreasing effectiveness of banking regulation. J Finance 36:355–367
Kane E (1983) Policy implications of structural changes in financial markets. Am Econ Rev 73:96–100
Kane E (1988) Interaction of financial and regulatory innovation. Am Econ Rev 78:328–344
Kane E (1993) Reflexive adaptation of business to regulation and regulation to business. Law Policy 15:179–189
Kane E (2014) Shadowy banking: theft by safety net. Yale J Regul 31:773–807
Kay J (2016) Other people's money: masters of the universe or servants of the people? Profile Books, London
Kessler O, Wilhelm B (2013) Financialization and the three utopias of shadow banking. Compet Change 17:248–264
Knoll MS (2002) Put-call parity and the law. Cardozo Law Rev 24:61–91
Knoll MS (2008) The ancient roots of modern financial innovation: the early history of regulatory arbitrage. Oregon Law Rev 87:93–116
Lamont OA, Thaler RH (2003) Anomalies: the law of one price in financial markets. J Econ Perspect 17:191–202
Leyshon A (1992) The transformation of regulatory order: regulating the global economy and environment. Geoforum 23:249–267
Macey J (1995) Derivative instruments: lessons for the regulatory state. J Corp Law 21:69–93
Macey J (2003) Regulatory globalization as a response to regulatory competition. Emory Law J 52:1353–1379
MacKenzie D (2009) Material markets. Oxford University Press, Oxford
McBarnet D (2010) Financial engineering or legal engineering? Legal work, legal integrity and the banking crisis. University of Edinburgh, Edinburgh
McBarnet D, Whelan C (1991) The elusive spirit of the law: formalism and the struggle for legal control. Mod Law Rev 54:848–873
McBarnet D, Whelan C (1992) International corporate finance and the challenge of creative compliance. In: Fingleton J, Schoenmaker D (eds) The internationalisation of capital markets and the regulatory response. Graham & Trotman, London, pp 129–142
Merton RC (1995) A functional perspective of financial intermediation. Finance Manage 24:23–41
Mosebach M (2000) Regulation avoidance in the banking industry: the case of 364 day lines of credit. J Int Finance Manage Account 11:198–206
Möslein F (2014) Finanzinnovation und Rechtsordnung: Eine Einführung. In: Möslein F (ed) Finanzinnovation und Rechtsordnung: Gestaltung, unternehmerischer Einsatz und Marktregulierung. Schulthess, Zürich, pp 3–44

Mueller GE (1958) The Hegel legend of 'thesis-antithesis-synthesis. J Hist Ideas 19:411–414
Mullineux AW (2010) Financial innovation and social welfare. J Finance Regul Compliance 18:243–256
Nabilou H (2017) Regulatory arbitrage and hedge fund regulation: the need for a transnational response. Fordham J Corp Finance Law 22:557–604
Partnoy F (1997) Financial derivatives and the costs of regulatory arbitrage. J Corp Law 22:211–256
Partnoy F (2019) The law of two prices: regulatory arbitrage revisited. Georgetown Law Journal 107:1017–1044
Pistor K (2019) The code of capital: how the law creates wealth and inequality. Princeton University Press, Princeton
Posner RA (1971) Taxation by regulation. Bell J Econ Manage Sci 2:22–50
Riles A (2014) Managing regulatory arbitrage: a conflict of laws approach. Cornell Int Law J 47:63–119
Romano R (1985) Law as a product: some pieces of the incorporation puzzle. J Law Econ Organ 1:225–284
Schäfer HB (1995) Hare and hedgehog revisited: the regulation of markets that have escaped regulated markets: comment. J Inst Theor Econ (JITE) 151:177–181
Schanze E (1995) Hare and hedgehog revisited: the regulation of markets that have escaped regulated markets. J Inst Theor Econ (JITE) 151:162–176
Shah A (1997) Regulatory arbitrage through financial innovation. Account Audit Account J 10:85–104
Shen W (2015) Wealth management products in the context of China's shadow banking: systemic risks, consumer protection and regulatory instruments. Asia Pac Law Rev 23:91–123
Shleifer A, Vishny RW (1997) The limits of arbitrage. J Finance 52:35–55
Stark J (2019) Law for sale: a philosophical critique of regulatory competition. Oxford University Press, Oxford
Stekeler P (2014) Hegels Phänomenologie des Geistes: ein dialogischer Kommentar. Meiner, Hamburg
Stiglitz JE (2009) Selected works of Joseph E. Stiglitz. Oxford University Press, Oxford
Stiglitz JE (2010) The Stiglitz report: reforming the international monetary and financial systems in the wake of the global crisis. New Press, New York
Story J, Walter I (1997) Political economy of financial integration in Europe: the battle of the systems. MIT Press, Cambridge, MA
Stout LA (1995) Betting the bank: how derivatives trading under conditions of uncertainty can increase risks and erode returns in financial markets. J Corp Law 21:53–68
Tarko V, Farrant A (2019) The efficiency of regulatory arbitrage. Public Choice 181:141–166
Trachtman JP (2000) Regulatory competition and regulatory jurisdiction. J Int Econ Law 3:331–348
Tröger T (2016) How special are they? Targeting systemic risk by regulating shadow banking. In: Lomfeld B, Somma A, Zumbansen P (eds) Reshaping markets: economic governance, the global financial crisis and liberal utopia. Cambridge University Press, Cambridge, pp 185–207
Wallerstein I (1991) Braudel on capitalism, or everything upside down. J Mod Hist 63:354–361
Weber M (1894) Die Börse I. Vandenhoeck & Ruprecht, Göttingen
Willesson M (2017) What is and what is not regulatory arbitrage? A review and syntheses. In: Chesini G, Giaretta E, Paltrinieri A (eds) Financial markets, SME financing and emerging economies. Springer International Publishing, Cham, pp 71–94
Windecker GH (1993) The Eurodollar deposit market: strategies for regulation. Am Univ J Int Law Policy 9:357–384
Wittgenstein L (1984) Philosophische Untersuchungen. In: Tractatus logico-philosophicus, Tagebücher 1914–1916, Philosophische Untersuchungen. Suhrkamp, Frankfurt am Main, pp 225–580

Zeitler FC (2012) Vergessene Ursachen der Banken- und Finanzkrise. Wertpapier-Mitteilungen 66:673–678

Zingales L (2015) Presidential address: does finance benefit society? J Finance 70:1327–1363

**Thomas Coendet** Shanghai. Shanghai Distinguished Professor at Shanghai Jiao Tong University, KoGuan School of Law; Dr. iur., M.Jur. (Oxford), thomas.coendet@oxon.org. Fields of Interest: Private Law (Contract, Banking, Law and Finance), Financial Regulation, Comparative Law, Legal Theory.

# (Un)intended Consequences of Macroprudential Regulation

**Moran Ofir and Yevgeny Mugerman**

**Abstract** The chapter examines the effects of several macroprudential tools on household choices in the mortgage market. In recent years, following the global financial crisis, central banks have imposed macroprudential policy tools on mortgage loans in order to protect the banking system from systemic risk associated with highly leveraged homeowners. Using a unique and detailed dataset on mortgage loans taken in Israel in the last decade, we empirically estimate the impact of these regulations on household choices and the housing market. In particular, we examine borrowers' response to the following regulatory restrictions: Loan-to-Value (LTV) limits of 75% for first time buyers, 70% for home improvers, and 50% for investors; a payment-to-income (PTI) limit of 50%; a 2/3 limit on the adjustable rate component; and a 30-year maturity limit. We found that overall, the regulatory provisions tested in this project influenced the borrowers' responses. Interestingly, two of these provisions served as an anchor to the borrowers. We obtained an increase in mortgage loans maturity following the imposed maturity limit and an increase in PTI ratio following the imposed PTI limits. We argue that these unintended consequences of the tested macroprudential regulation are a result of the anchoring and adjustment heuristic.

## 1 Introduction

Housing is the largest asset owned in most households' portfolios. Therefore, a rapid change in the price of residential real estate has severe repercussions for household wellbeing, for the stability of the financial system, and for decisions made by

M. Ofir (✉)
Interdisciplinary Center (IDC) Herzliya, Herzliya, Israel
e-mail: mofir@idc.ac.il

Y. Mugerman
Bar-Ilan University, Ramat Gan, Israel
e-mail: yevgeny.mugerman@biu.ac.il

 
K. Mathis, A. Tor (eds.), *Law and Economics of Regulation*, Economic Analysis of Law in European Legal Scholarship 11,
https://doi.org/10.1007/978-3-030-70530-5_9

policymakers and regulators. Understanding the effectiveness of actions taken by regulators and policymakers in times of rapid price changes can shed light on their effectiveness in reducing the escalating aggregated financial risk for homeowners on the one hand and in shaping household behavior on the other.

The steep rise in residential real estate prices that occurred in Israel in the last decade created a complicated socioeconomic problem that engulfed many Israeli families, mostly young households and low-to mid-income earners. On the one hand, years of slow and inadequate housing-starts in the early 2000s, a steep drop in real interest rates following the 2008 global financial crisis, and the fact that the Israeli tax system gives investment in real estate an edge over financial assets, all combined to create a demand surge. On the other hand, due to rigid supply-side limitations, the reaction to the rising demand was slow, creating a bottleneck of new homes on which a rising number of investors competed with young households and subsequent buyers.

As in other countries across the world, rents and house prices in Israel have increased to unprecedented levels making many markets unaffordable, particularly for the lowest income households. But while affordable housing has often been difficult to find for many low-income households, in recent decade the problem has begun to encompass households that are not only low-income earners, but also young professional and mid-income households. The nature, causes, manifestations and extent of this new problem of housing affordability varies between households and, of course, it also differs between different localities, regions, and countries as well as the regulatory reactions to the problem and the aforementioned pricing trends.

In addition to the housing affordability problem, the rapid rise in prices created a potential systemic risk to the local financial system, which financed most mortgages. As a precautionary measure, and in order to strengthen the resilience of the financial system in the case of unexpected shocks in the real estate sector, the Central Bank of Israel, as other central banks worldwide, imposed a number of restrictions, regarded as macroprudential tools (MPTs).

MPTs are financial policies aimed at ensuring the stability of the financial system to prevent substantial disruptions in vital financial services necessary for stable economic growth. The stability of financial system is at greater risk when institutions and investors have high leverage and are overly reliant on long-term debt. High financial vulnerability increases the likelihood that a negative shock would cause a market distress as well as other negative externalities to the relevant industry and to other related industries. MPTs aim to reduce the financial system's sensitivity to shocks by limiting the buildup of financial vulnerabilities.

Since the global financial crisis of 2008, macroprudential housing-finance tools have been increasingly utilized to reduce financial system vulnerabilities related to housing market imbalances.[1] Applying a combination of several MPTs can have various consequences for the behavior of the average mortgage lender and borrower,

[1]Galati and Moessner (2012) and Claessens (2015).

and for the stability of the entire financial system. Macroprudential policy can directly affect household borrowing through wealth and income constraints by limiting or expanding access to the mortgage market.

The literature discussing MPTs focuses on their effects on the stability of the financial system, mostly from the point of view of regulators and financial institutions,[2] rather than on behavior of the individual mortgage borrower. As such, some of the studies find that during downturns in the residential real estate market, Loan-to-Value (LTV) limits lower bank losses.[3] Moreover, aggregate cross-country studies find that LTV limits are effective in moderating the increase in house prices, thereby reducing the risks and consequences of bubbles in real estate markets.[4] Thus, further research is needed on the effectiveness of such constraints from the borrowers' perspective.[5]

More specifically, the IMF[6] used microdata to analyze the real estate market and the housing prices in Israel.[7] The main MPTs tested in this report were LTV and payment-to-income (PTI) ratio limits. The main findings of the analysis were that both LTV and PTI limits had partial success in lowering the number of transactions, but there was little evidence that neither had any success in lowering the growth rate of housing prices.

Tzur-Ilan[8] estimated the effect of an LTV limit on loan terms in the Israeli mortgage market and found that this MPTs had affected mortgage contract terms by increasing the interest rate but had not affected credit rationing. The LTV limit induced borrowers to buy cheaper assets and to move farther from high demand locations to lower-graded neighborhoods.

Our chapter focuses on several macroprudential tools implemented in Israel during the years 2010–2014 and examines the affects they had on the average borrower. In particular, we concentrate on Loan-to-Value (LTV) limits (of 75% for first time buyers, 70% for home improvers, and 50% for investors), payment-to-income (PTI) limit of 50%, 2/3 limit on the adjustable rate component, and a 30-year maturity limit. For all MPTs tested, we found borrowers decisions to have been affected by the specific regulatory provision. Two regulatory provisions tested served as an anchor to the borrowers- PTI limits and maturity limits.

The remainder of this chapter proceeds as follows: Sect. 2 reviews the literature in behavioral analysis of mortgage decision-making, Sect. 3 focuses on the seminal

---

[2]Mugerman et al. (2018) propose a dynamic model of bank actions in the shadow of LTV ratio regulation.

[3]Krznar and Morsink (2014) and Lim et al. (2011).

[4]International Monetary Fund (2011).

[5]For another example of testing the borrowers' decision-making in a different loan market—peer-to-peer lending—see Ayal et al. (2018).

[6]International Monetary Fund (2014).

[7]The micro data included in the report are based on a survey of households' plans for housing tenure and expected housing prices.

[8]Tzur-Ilan (2017).

heuristic of anchoring and adjustment, Sect. 4 describes the Israeli housing market, while Sect. 5 describes the dataset. Then, Sects. 6 and 7 present the research design and results, respectively. Finally, Sect. 8 discusses the main findings and conclusions.

## 2 Behavioral Analysis of Mortgage Decision-Making

Despite the vast amount of literature dealing with housing finance, there are few papers which focus on the *behavioral* aspects of housing decisions. Campbell[9] uses the American Housing Survey to show evidence that mortgage borrowers make several mistakes that leads to important implications for equilibrium in the mortgage market. For example, he found that the decision to refinance fixed-rate mortgage (FRM) is challenging for many households, particularly poorer and less educated ones, and therefore they pay higher mortgage rates than necessary.

Brunnermeier and Julliard[10] found that households suffer from money illusion ("the inability to properly distinguish changes in nominal values due to changes in real fundamentals from changes due to inflation") when they decide whether to rent or buy a house. A reduction in inflation can generate a substantial increase in housing prices, and, therefore, can create inefficiency in the housing market. They identified an empirical proxy for mispricing in the housing market and show that it is largely explained by movements in inflation. However, their paper focused on the decision to buy a house and not on how to finance the transaction.

Paiella and Pozollo[11] examined whether households can accurately gauge their circumstances in terms of (non-mortgage related) risk exposure and make an appropriate choice of either fixed-rate mortgage (FRM) or adjusted-rate mortgage (ARM). They showed that most household characteristics proxying for exposure to other non-mortgage related risks and for individual risk aversion are irrelevant for the choice. The choice depends, to a great extent, on the relative price of the mortgages and on whether the household faces liquidity constraints. Liquidity constrained households find ARMs particularly attractive because their initial payments are generally the lowest; they tend to overlook the overall cost of the mortgage, and (as evidence suggests) ARM holders do not fully take into account the risk of a rise of the reference interest rates. On the other hand, lenders price this risk too high and borrowers end up paying a high price for the benefit of low initial payments.

Two more recent papers show that mortgage borrowers make few systematic mistakes. Agarwal, Rosen and Yao[12] found that over 40% of mortgage borrowers

---

[9]Campbell (2006).

[10]Brunnermeier and Jullliard (2008).

[11]Paiella and Pozzolo (2007).

[12]Agarwal et al. (2012).

sub-optimally refinance their mortgages. Agarwal, Ben-David and Yao[13] found evidence that borrowers exhibit the sunk cost fallacy: borrowers who paid an upfront cost in the past are 8.4% less likely to refinance their mortgage every month as compared to borrowers who do not pay the upfront cost. However, both papers found that financial sophistication helps to explain the suboptimal decision making by borrowers.

Lastly, Mugerman, Ofir and Wiener[14] examine the effect of changes in the short-term market interest rate on the decision of homeowners to choose between fixed rate mortgages (FRM) and adjustable rate mortgages (ARM). The results of the analysis demonstrate a significant association between FRM preference and short-term interest rate reduction. Moreover, the analysis shows that the change in the short-term interest rate is more salient to the borrowers in periods of a high interest rate environment. When faced with the difficult task of choosing between FRM and ARM, individuals employ a limited number of heuristics to simplify this decision. Decision makers are bounded by the availability of information the market provides through its general media and judging this information by its representativeness. From that perspective, the change in short term interest rates is available for mortgage borrowers and can be representative of the FRM-ARM decision.

## 3 Anchoring and Adjustment

The anchoring and adjustment effect is one of the most frequently tested behavioral heuristics. Highly robust, it also has a variety of implications on financial as well as on non-financial decision-making. The heuristics was first introduced in Tversky and Kahneman's[15] seminal paper. As they explain, decision makers conduct estimates by starting from an initial value that is adjusted to yield the final answer, but the adjustments are typically insufficient: "different starting points yield different estimates, which are biased toward the initial values".[16]

In their paper, Tversky and Kahneman asked the subjects of the experiment comparative and absolute questions regarding the percentage of African nations in the United Nations (UN). In the comparative question, subjects indicated whether the percentage of African nations is higher or lower than a numeric anchor. The numeric anchor was determined according to the spin of a roulette wheel. Then, the subjects were asked an absolute question regarding their personal estimate of the actual percentage of African nations in the UN. They found that the absolute judgements were assimilated to the provided numeric anchor value. The mean estimate of the percentage of African nations in the UN among subjects who

[13]Agarwal et al. (2014).

[14]Mugerman et al. (2016).

[15]Tversky and Kahneman (1974).

[16]Tversky and Kahneman (1974), p. 1128.

received the high numeric anchor was 45%, compared to 25% for subjects who received the low numeric anchor.

A significant number of studies demonstrate the prevalence of the anchoring heuristic described by Tversky and Kahneman[17]. Most of the existing research papers are experimental studies, conducted with university students in laboratory settings with a list of questions that the participants may not have used in natural situations. A small number of studies have had the participants face real-life settings and showed the heuristic to be robust.[18]

Regarding the magnitude of the anchoring heuristic, the literature shows that the higher the ambiguity, and the lower the familiarity, relevance, or personal involvement with the problem, the stronger the anchoring effect.[19] In addition, the literature shows that the informational relevance of values may affect decision makers' susceptibility to the anchoring effect.[20] More specifically, Strack and Mussweiler[21] show that anchor values which are similar or identical in judgmental dimensions to the estimates yield a significant effect on the magnitude of anchoring.

## 4 The Israeli Housing Market

The effects of the global financial crisis of 2008 on the Israeli economy and its financial system were significant, though less so than in most other developed countries.[22] Several factors mitigated these effects, including the timing of the crisis, which followed five years of rapid growth, and several structural features of the local financial system, such as tight banking regulation, conservative mortgage market and absence of complex assets as mortgage backed securities (MBS). The combination of these factors helped prevent the development of over-leveraging in the real estate market.

The Central Bank of Israel, however, acknowledging the fact that Israel is a rather open economy highly sensitive to fluctuations in exchange rates, lowered interest rates in tandem with other major central banks across the globe. The healthy condition of the local economy, combined with the low interest rate environment, contributed to a trend of rising asset prices in the real estate market, mainly

[17]See Plous (1989), Chapman and Johnson (1999), Epley and Gilovich (2001), Mussweiler and Englich (2005), McElroy and Dowd (2007); and more recently Hurwitz et al. (2018); see Furnham and Boo (2011).

[18]See Ariely et al. (2003), Englich et al. (2005), Critcher and Gilovich (2008); and more recently Mugerman et al. (2016).

[19]Van Exel et al. (2006).

[20]Hastie et al. (1999), Marti and Wissler (2000), Englich et al. (2005).

[21]Strack and Mussweiler (1997).

[22]Eckstein et al. (2011).

residential real estate prices. Thus, between the years 2008 and 2016, home prices in Israel increased in each year and the total increase was higher than 100%.

Concurrently, during these years the volume of housing loans increased by 95%. This phenomenon raised concerns among banking regulators and policymakers. As widely described in the literature, housing prices and mortgages tend to move together and influence each other in a two-way feedback loop.[23] These correlated trends impose high risks on borrowing individuals, financial institutions, and the financial system.

As concern grew, regulators and policymakers enacted a set of MPTs to curb the rapidly growing demands for housing and housing loans. These tools, which included restrictions and guidelines to Israel's commercial banks, were imposed by the supervisory division in the Central Bank of Israel, mainly to protect the banking system itself from risks associated with excessively leveraged borrowers.

The first MPT was introduced in May 2010 and included a set of new guidelines requiring banks to maintain an additional allowance of at least 75 basis points for outstanding housing loans with an LTV of over 60% (the LTV was measured on the date the loan was provided). The rationale was that by making the mortgage loans more expensive to the commercial banks themselves, they would be forced to roll over the added cost to borrowers with a higher LTV.

The second MPT was introduced in October 2010. The Israeli Banks Supervisor issued new directives concerning capital provision for loans with high LTV ratios. The exiting provision required banks to put forward capital provisions ranging from 35% to 75% (depending on the borrower's specific characteristics); the new guidelines required 100%, for loans with an LTV ratio of more than 60% (on the date of issue) and where the variable interest rate proportion of the loan was 25% and higher. The new guidelines did not apply to housing loans originally amounting to less than 800,000 NIS. Since the limits would force the banks to tie up more capital against these loans, borrowers wanting to take a loan with an LTV ratio higher than 60% faced higher interest rates, which made them choose loans with a lower LTV ratio. Following the second limitation imposed in this area, banks began repricing loans with LTV ratios higher than 60%.

An additional restriction was the imposition of a differential LTV limit on housing loans on November 2012. This restriction limited the LTV ratio as follows: first-time buyers would be restricted to an LTV ratio of 75%; subsequent buyers (who sell their property and buy a new one at the same time) would be restricted to an LTV of 70%; and investors (who own more than one property) would be restricted to 50%. The rationale behind the restrictions was that limiting the investors' leverage would also limit the demand for housing and the price increase trend would lose some steam.

The continuous rise in home prices, forced the regulator to impose new measures in February 2013. These focused on the banking system capital adequacy ratios. For the purpose of calculating capital adequacy ratios, housing loans with LTV ratios of

[23] Crowe et al. (2011).

up to 45% would be weighted at 35% (unchanged from previous weighting). Housing loans with an LTV ratio of between 45% and 60% would be weighted at 50%, and loans with an LTV ratio of 60–75% would be weighted at 75%.

The final restrictions were imposed on August 2013, targeting three different aspects of new mortgage loans. First, the payment to income (PTI) ratio was limited to 50% of the borrower's income. Second, the portion of the loan at an adjusted interest rate was limited to two thirds of the entire loan for all loan periods. Finally, loan maturity was limited to 30 years. Our paper focuses on these regulatory restrictions, examining the effectiveness of each separately.

## 5 The Dataset

Our main body of data is based on the Central Bank of Israel data on mortgage loans between July 2011 and December 2016. The data is highly detailed, including the specifications for all mortgage components related to the examined MPT. In addition, we use a long list of different control variables, mainly macroeconomics measures relating to the Israeli economy and the Israeli residential real estate market.

### *5.1 Data Construction: Loan-to-Value Ratio (LTV)*

The loan-to-value ratio subcategory is divided into six tranches all referring to new or renewed mortgages by the following LTV ratios: <30%, 30–45%, 45–60%, 60–75%, 75–90%, >90%.

First, we divided the six tranches into two main tranches as following—loans with LTV ratio up to 60% and loans with LTV ratio from (including) equals to 60%. This division is aimed to examine the effects of differential LTV limits requirements that were imposed on housing loans on November 2012 (Fig. 1).

In addition, we divided the six tranches into two different main tranches as following—loans with LTV ratio up to 45% and loans with LTV ratio from (including) equals to 45%. This division is aimed to examine the effects of new requirements brought forward by the regulator on November 2012, which forced the banking system to change the capital adequacy ratios for new mortgage loans (Fig. 2).

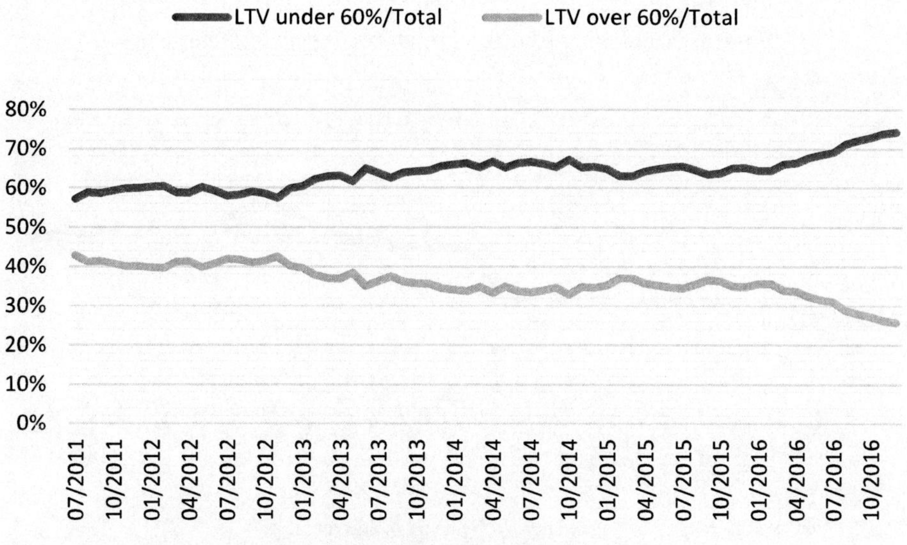


**Fig. 1** New & Renewed Mortgages Divided by 60% LTV Level

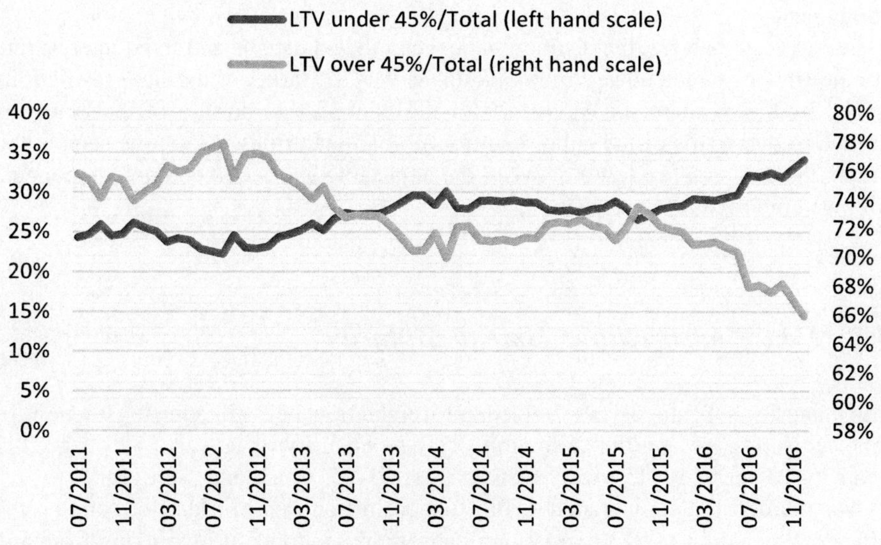


**Fig. 2** New & Renewed Mortgages Divided by 45% LTV Level

## 5.2 *Data Construction: Adjusted Rate Mortgages (ARM) and Fixed Rate Mortgages (FRM)*

The sum of mortgages granted (new and renewed) is divided into two main categories: the sum of components that carry an adjustable rate and the sum of components

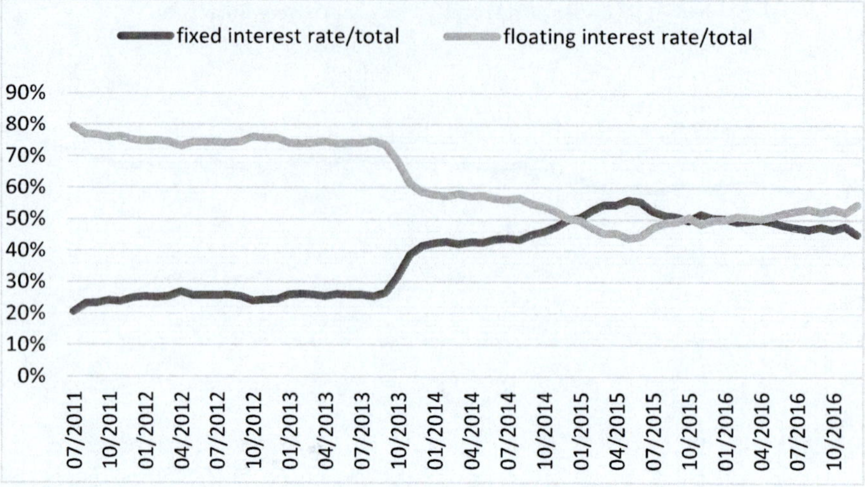


**Fig. 3** New & Renewed Mortgages Divided by Type of Interest Rate

that carry a fixed rate. Figure 3 shows the convergence over time of these two components.

As suggested above, the distinction between the adjustable and fixed interest rate components of new/renewed mortgage loans was the target of the final restrictions issued by the regulator in August 2013: the floating rate portion of the loan was limited to two thirds of the entire loan for all loan maturities. As can be seen in the graph, the convergence trend between the adjustable and the fixed rate components followed the regulatory restriction.

## 5.3 *Data Construction: Time to Maturity*

The maturity subcategory is divided into eight tranches, all referring to new or renewed mortgages by the following years to maturity: <1 year, 1–2 years, 2–5 years, 5–10 years, 10–15 years, 15–20 years, 20–25, years, and >25 years.

We divided the eight tranches into two main tranches in order to examine the effects of the August 2013 regulation: loans with time to maturity ranging from and including one year to 25 years and loans with maturity ranging from 25 years and above. Figure 4 depicts the sharp rise of the mean mortgage maturities following the regulation.

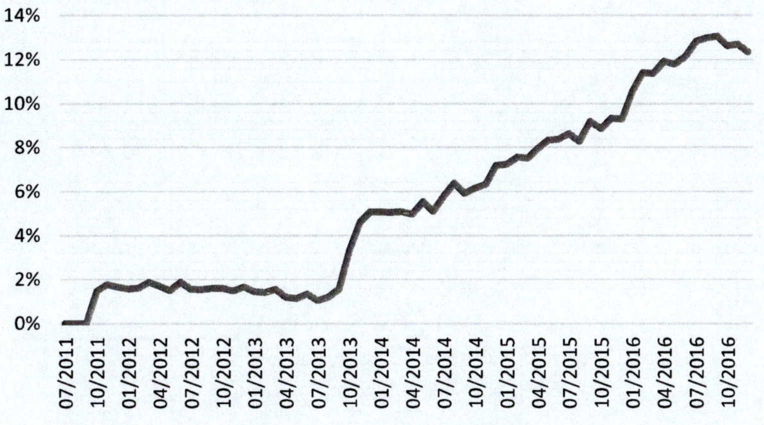


**Fig. 4** Mortgages with maturity of over 25 years as a percentage of total mortgages

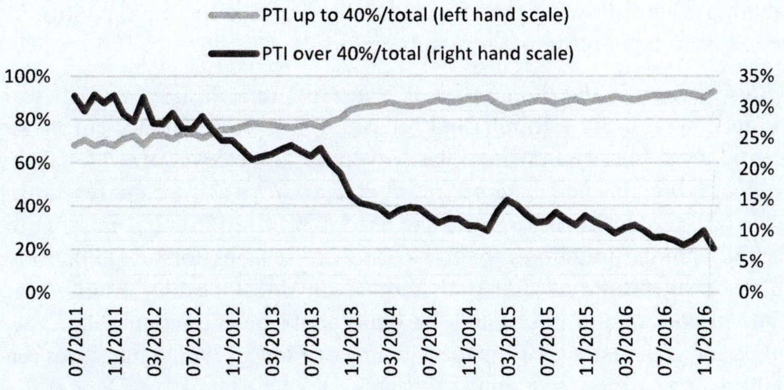


**Fig. 5** New/renewed mortgages divided by the 40% PTI level

## *5.4 Data Construction: Payment-to-Income Ratio (PTI)*

The PTI subcategory is divided into five tranches in order to examine the effects of the August 2013 regulation all referring to new or renewed mortgages: <20%, 20–30%, 30–40%, 40–60%, >60%.

We divided the five tranches into two main tranches – loans with PTI ratio up to 40% and loans with PTI ratio above 40% (Fig. 5).

## *5.5 Control Variables*

To estimate the effect of these regulatory provisions we control for several macroeconomics measures related to the Israeli market and to the local residential real

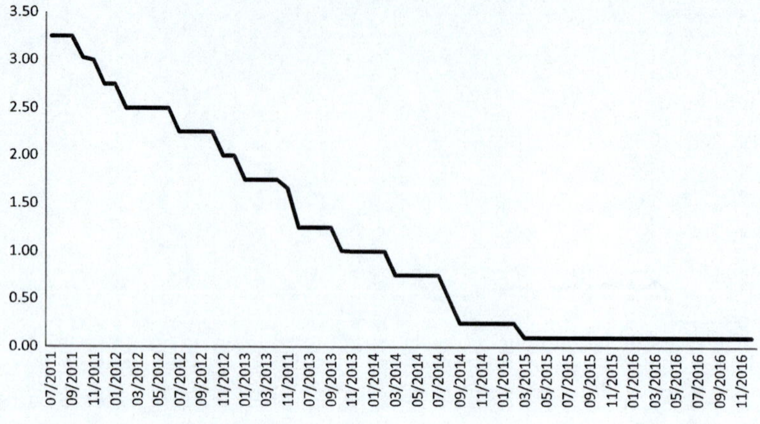


**Fig. 6** The central bank of Israel's interest rates

estate market. The following paragraphs briefly describe the main control variables and the major trends during the research period.

1. *Monthly change in the Bank of Israel's interest rate*. In line with the rest of the developed world, the Central Bank of Israel has progressively cut its key rates since the great financial crisis to the November 2016 level of 0.1% (Fig. 6).
2. *Monthly change in the consumer price index (CPI).* During the research period, Israel's CPI has declined for 3 years in a row (2014–2016), thus missing the Bank of Israel's annual inflation target (1–3%). The reasons for this deflation include regulatory interventions aimed to reduce the local cost of living, the global decline in commodity prices and the rapid adoption of e-commerce. The largest component of the Israeli CPI is the shelter price index, which measures real estate rental prices (24.3%, see Control Variable 3). Importantly, residential real estate prices are not part of the CPI (Fig. 7).
3. *Monthly change in the shelter component of the CPI,* which, as mentioned above, accounts for 24.3% of the entire index. As stated above, the change in shelter prices as represented by the change in rent prices differs from the change in residential real estate prices. The change in shelter prices was 14.7% over the period studied (Fig. 8).
4. *Monthly change in residential real estate prices.* During the period examined, residential real estate prices grew by 37.6%, outpacing the change in the CPI's shelter component by 255% (Fig. 9).
5. *Change in average* monthly *wage of all employees.* After a modest increase in unemployment rates following the global financial crisis, Israel's unemployment rate declined in the following years. A tight labor market combined with an increase in the minimum wage in the last decade were among the main contributors to the steady rise in the average monthly wage, as seen in Fig. 10.

6. *Monthly change in population*. The annual growth rate of Israel's population in the examined period is 1.8%; this includes Israeli citizens living in Israel and permanent residents as well (Fig. 11).
7. *Monthly change in the number of completed houses*. Figure 12 shows that despite the structural efforts made by different policymakers to increase the supply of finished houses, in order to moderate the price trends, their number has been erratic during the research period.
8. *Monthly change in number of housing starts*. As with the number of finished houses, the number of housing starts has failed to create a sizable momentum during the examined period, as shown in Fig. 13.

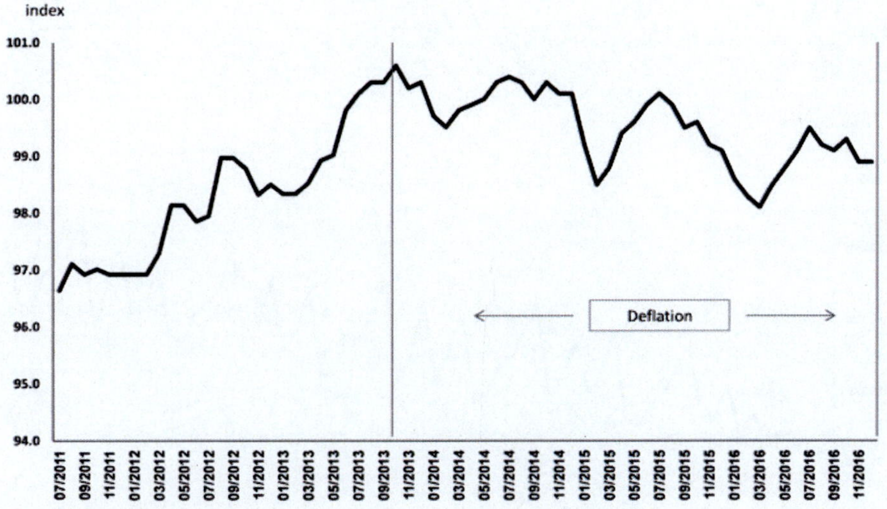


**Fig. 7** Consumer price index (CPI)

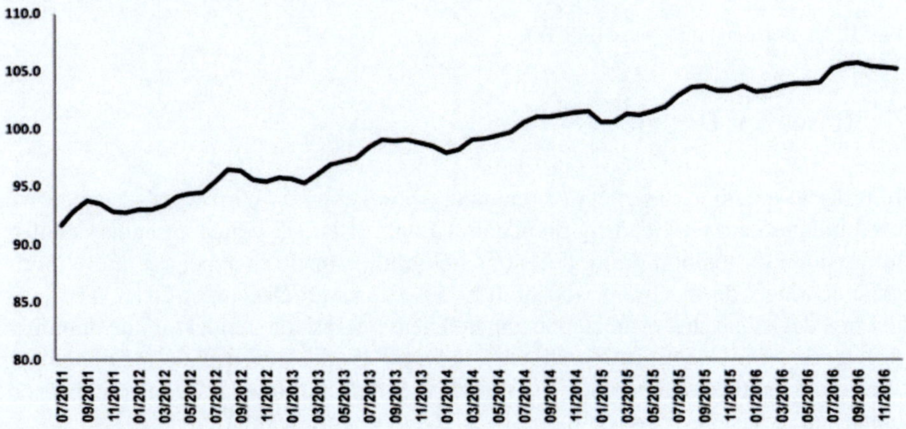


**Fig. 8** The shelter price index

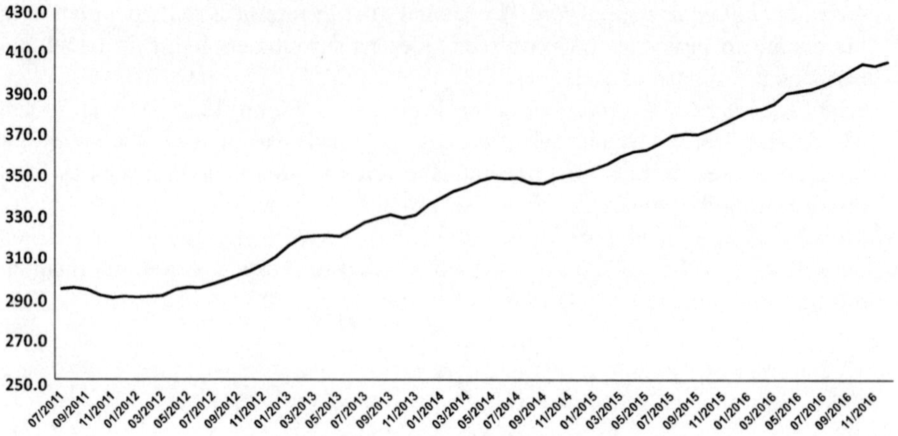


**Fig. 9** Residential real estate prices

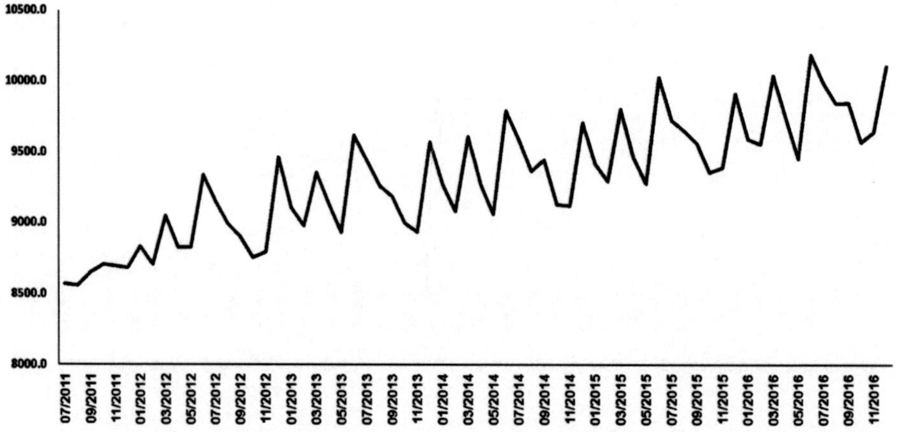


**Fig. 10** Average monthly wage (in NIS)

# 6 Research Design

In order to examine the effect of regulatory provisions on borrowers' decision we used unique data provided by the Central Bank of Israel, which contains detailed information on the borrowing decisions households made as appeared in the mortgage contracts during the period of July 2011 through December 2016. The borrowing decisions are estimated using a linear regression model of the monthly differences. Our identification strategy is based on the difference's methodology. We employed this methodology to estimate the impact of regulatory intervention on household decisions vis-à-vis these decisions in the pre-regulation period.

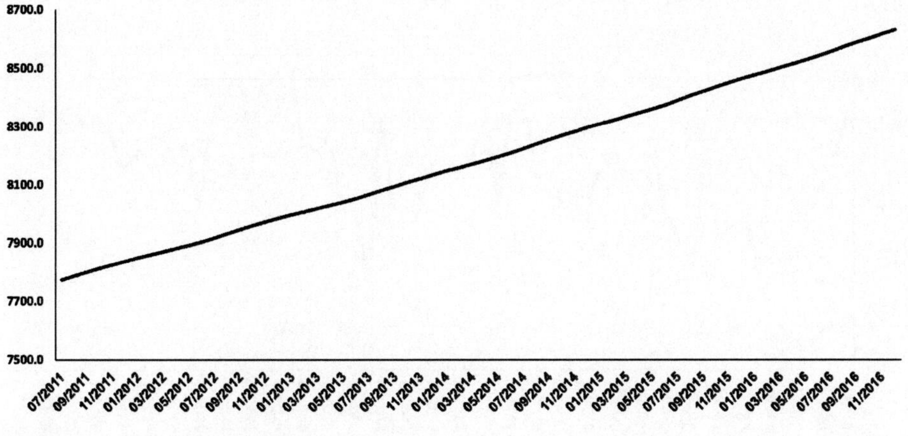


**Fig. 11** Population (thousands)

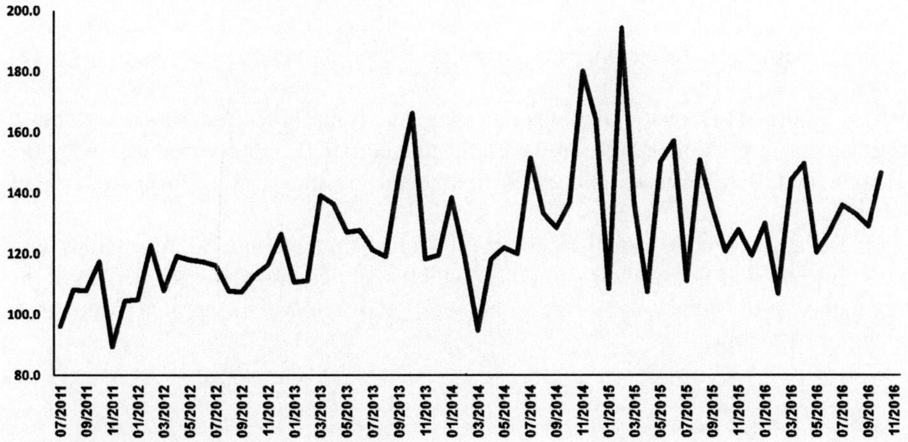


**Fig. 12** Finished houses index

As mentioned, we relied on detailed monthly data on mortgage loans (new and renewed) between July 2011 and December 2016. In addition, we collected data on the specific month in which the regulatory change was implemented. We then used this data to construct a regulatory provision dummy variable, which equals 1 for the period following the change, effective from the month of the respective regulatory intervention, and 0 otherwise. We regressed the following proportions (n) of the total mortgages: (1) LTV ration of over 60%; (2) LTV ratio of over 45%; (3) PTI ratio of over 40%; (4) proportion of adjusted interest rate mortgages; and (5) maturities of over 25 years—on the regulatory provision dummy variable as well as on various macroeconomic factors detailed below:

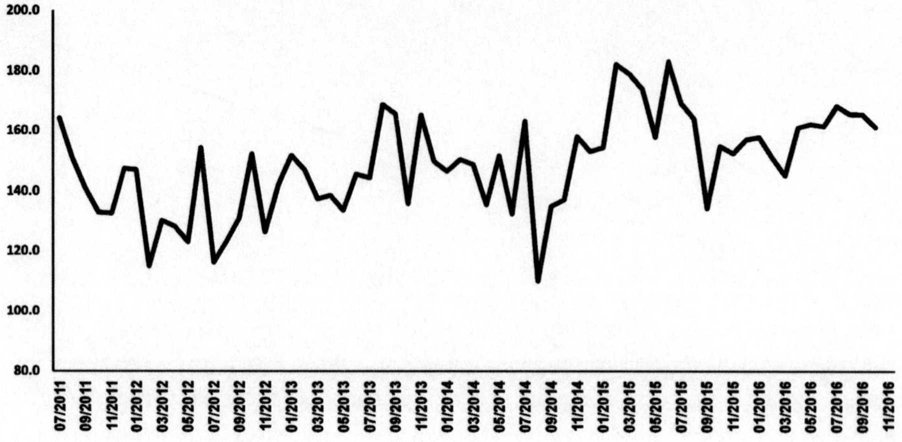


**Fig. 13** Housing starts index

$$\text{Houshold Decision}_t = \alpha + \beta * \text{regulatory\_provision}_t + \lambda_t + \mathcal{E}_t, \qquad (1)$$

where Houshold Decision$_t$ denotes the aggregate households' decision in month $t$; regulatory _ provision$_t$ is a dummy variable that equals 1 for the period following the change and 0 otherwise; and $\lambda_t$ is the vector of the control macroeconomics variables.

We examined robust standard errors (clustering on the temporal dimension). Our main interest was in the estimation of β, which captures the differences effect of the regulatory provisions on mortgage choices, *above and beyond* macroeconomic changes over time.

## 7 Results

Table 1 below presents Equation 1's estimation results of the five regulatory interventions. Each column represents a different OLS regression model. The dependent variables are: in Column 1—the proportion of LTV ratio of over 60%, defined as the new and renewed mortgages with LTV ratio of over 60% divided by the total of new and renewed mortgages; in Column 2—the proportion of LTV ratio of over 45%, defined as the new and renewed mortgages with LTV ratio of over 45% divided by the total of new and renewed mortgages; in Column 3—the proportion of PTI ratio of over 40%, defined as the new and renewed mortgages with PTI ratio of over 40% divided by the total of new and renewed mortgages; in Column 4—the proportion of adjusted interest rate mortgages, defined as the new and renewed mortgages with adjusted interest rate divided by the total of new and renewed mortgages; and, finally, in Column 5—the proportion of maturities over 25 years, defined as the new and renewed mortgages with maturity of over 25 years divided by the total of new and renewed mortgages.

The independent variables are: the indicator of the respective regulation, equals 1 if the regulation was passed and 0 otherwise; the monthly change in the primary interest rate of the Bank of Israel (ln); the monthly change in the Israeli headline CPI (ln); the monthly change in the shelter component of the CPI (ln); the monthly change in home prices index (ln); the monthly change in the average hourly wage in all sectors (ln); the monthly change in the housing finished index (ln); the monthly change in the housing starts index (ln); the monthly change in the nominal GDP (ln); the monthly change in population growth rate (ln)—not presented. Robust standard errors are reported in parentheses below the coefficient estimates. Finally, *, **, *** indicate statistical significance at the 10%, 5%, and 1% levels, respectively.

| | LTV ratio of over 60% (1) | LTV ratio of over 45% (2) | PTI ratio of over 40% (3) | adjusted interest rate (4) | maturity of over 25 years (5) |
|---|---|---|---|---|---|
| Indicator of respective regulation | **−0.0657875 *** (0.0093263)** | **−0.0437412*** (0.0050528)** | **0.1407682*** (0.007927)** | **−0.2199048*** (0.0136459)** | **0.0666015*** (0.0070019)** |
| Monthly change—Interest Rate Bank of Israel (ln) | −0.0520152 (0.0337655) | −0.172039 (0.0207561) | 0.0277565 (0.0331794) | −0.022126 (0.0571168) | 0.0573099** (0.0293072) |
| Monthly change—CPI (ln) | −1.034447 (1.285507) | 0.3897995 (0.7869801) | −1.747677 (1.265049) | 1.442525 (2.17772) | −0.3547887 (1.11741) |
| Monthly change—CPI Shelter (ln) | 1.235526 (0.9437811) | 0.5003228 (0.5839956) | 0.9465333 (0.9430258) | −2.008387 (1.623373) | 0.2364322 (0.832969) |
| Monthly change—Home prices index (ln) | 1.141702 (0.777853) | −0.1742839 (0.4527815) | 1.840387** (0.728544) | −1.542723 (1.254153) | 0.2331187 (0.6435185) |
| Monthly change—Average hourly wage (ln) | −0.1098233 (0.1190905) | −0.0144832 (0.0736183) | 0.181859 (0.1175657) | −0.0510427 (0.2023837) | 0.0890298 (0.1038451) |
| Monthly change—Housing finished index (ln) | −0.0023338 (0.198021) | −0.0036875 (0.012243) | −0.0171757 (0.0196252) | 0.0161128 (0.0337838) | −0.0119869 (0.0173348) |
| Monthly change—Housing starts index (ln) | 0.0152905 (0.0330585) | 0.0186037 (0.0203984) | 0.0197108 (0.0327009) | −0.0295401 (0.0562931) | −0.0091231 (0.0288845) |
| Monthly change—GDP Growth (ln) | −0.8151238 (0.9285238) | 0.0308411 (0.5767746) | 1.622726* (0.9166388) | 0.3057967 (1.577949) | 0.5845754 (0.8096615) |
| Other Controls | Yes | Yes | Yes | Yes | Yes |
| Observations | 65 | 65 | 65 | 65 | 65 |
| $R^2$ | 0.5448 | 0.6341 | 0.8847 | 0.8522 | 0.6834 |

The results show that the regulatory intervention is associated with a statistically significant change in the households' behavior. This possibly suggests that households' decisions may have been influenced by the regulator-induced anchor. The coefficients of the other control variables are mostly insignificant.

Nevertheless, borrowers did not always shift the borrowing decision due to the regulatory intervention in the indented direction. While the coefficients of the regulatory dummy variables are negative for regressions (1), (2) and (4) the same coefficients are positive for regressions (3) and (5). It means that by setting maximum limits to PTI and mortgage maturities, the regulator created anchors that were perceived by households as suggested figures in their specific cases and as a result we see an increase both in average PTI rations and in the mortgage maturities.

We suggest that the anchoring and adjustment heuristic may have influenced households' decisions in such manner that they perceived the maximum PTI and maturity limits as a relevant *average* maturity anchor and consequentially increased mortgage PTI ratio and maturity. These results can be treated as unintended consequences of the regulatory provisions by showing a gap between "law on the books" and "law in action". The main goal of MPTs is to reduce systemic risks but de facto, it achieved the opposite.

## 8 Conclusions

We studied the effects of several macroprudential policy tools on household choices in the mortgage market. Using a unique and detailed data on mortgage loans between the years 2011–2016 we empirically estimated the impact of these restrictions on household choice and as a result, on the housing market. We examined the borrowers' response to the following macroprudential policy tools:

1. Loan-to-Value (LTV) limits: LTV of 75% for first time buyers, LTV of 70% for home improvers, and LTV of 50% for investors.
2. Changes in the required capital adequacy of the banks: Housing loans with LTV ratio under 45% will be weighted as 35%, housing loans with an LTV ratio of between 45% and 60% will be weighted as 50%, and Housing loans with an LTV ratio of 60–75% will be weighted as 75%.
3. The third regulation includes three different provisions: Payment-to-Income (PTI) limit of 50%, limit of 2/3 on the adjustable rate component, and maturity limit of 30 years.

We found that the regulatory provisions tested did not always influence the borrowers' response as expected by the regulator. For two macroprudential tools tested, the regulatory limit served as an anchor for the borrowers and influenced their decisions. Specifically, we found an increase in mortgage loans maturity following the regulation that imposed maturity limits and an increase in PTI ratio following the regulation that imposed PTI limits.

Since housing is the most important asset in the portfolio of most households, the effect of behavioral biases can lead decision makers to systematic errors that, in turn, can cause a substantive loss of economic value. A better understanding of the effect of these heuristics on mortgage borrowers' decisions can improve the design of market reforms in this area to maximize market efficiency and minimize households' economic loss. Specifically, the anchoring heuristic has proven to be extremely powerful and influential on people decisions. Our research suggests that this heuristic should be carefully considered, before making regulatory interventions, to avoid possible unintended consequences.

By examining the influence of regulatory restrictions on decision makers' behavior, we believe that our paper can contribute to the understanding of market functioning beyond the theoretical predictions or in other words, to the understanding of one potential source for the gap existed between "law on the books" and "law in action". Our findings concerning this functioning should be further investigated, especially considering the implications of the MPTs on mortgage markets.

## References

Agarwal S, Rosen R, Yao V (2012) Why do borrowers make mortgage refinancing mistakes? Working Paper, Federal Reserve Bank of Chicago

Agarwal S, Ben-David I, Yao V (2014) Systematic mistakes of borrowers in the mortgage markets. Working Paper

Ariely D, Loewenstein G, Prelec D (2003) "Coherent Arbitrariness": stable demand curves without stable preferences. Q J Econ 118:73–105

Ayal S, Bar-Haim D, Ofir M (2018) Behavioral Biases in Peer-to-Peer (P2P) lending. In: Venezia I (ed) Behavioral finance: the coming of age. World Scientific Publishers (2019), Ch. 11, pp 367–400

Brunnermeier MK, Jullliard C (2008) Money illusion and housing Frenzies. Rev Financ Stud 21 (1):135–180

Campbell J (2006) Household finance. J Financ 61:1553–1604

Chapman GB, Johnson EJ (1999) Anchoring, activation, and the construction of values. Org Behav Human Decis Process 79:1–39

Claessens S (2015) An overview of macroprudential policy tools. Ann Rev Financ Econ 7:397–422

Critcher CR, Gilovich T (2008) Incidental environmental anchors. J Behav Decis Making 21:241–251

Crowe C, Dell'Ariccia G, Igan D, Rabanal P (2011) Policies for Macrofinancial Stability: Options to Deal with Real Estate Booms, IMF Staff Discussion Note 11/02

Eckstein Z, Fischer S, Flug K (2011) Israel and the Global Crisis 2007–2009. Bank of Israel. https://www.boi.org.il/deptdata/mehkar/crisis/crisis_2007_2009_eng.pdf

Englich B, Mussweiler T, Strack F (2005) The last word in court- A hidden disadvantage for the defense. Law Human Behav 29:705–722

Epley N, Gilovich T (2001) Putting adjustment back into the anchoring and adjustment heuristic: differential processing of self-generated and experimenter-provided anchors. Psychol Sci 12:391–396

Furnham A, Boo HC (2011) A literature review of the anchoring effect. J Socio-Econ 40:35–42

Galati G, Moessner R (2012) Macroprudential policy — a literature review. J Econ Surv 27:846–878

Hastie R, Schkade DA, Payne JW (1999) Juror Judgment in civil cases: effects of plaintiff's requests and plaintiff's identity on punitive damages awards. Law Human Behav 23:445–470

Hurwitz A, Sade O, Winter E (2018) Can mandatory minimum annuity laws have unintended consequences? An experimental study. Hebrew University Working Paper

International Monetary Fund (2011) Macro prudential Policy: An Organizing Framework, IMF Policy Paper SM/11/54
International Monetary Fund (2014) Israel: Selected Issues. IMF Country Report 14/48
Krznar I, Morsink J (2014) With Great Power Comes Great Responsibility: Macro prudential Tools at Work in Canada. IMF Working Paper WP/14/83
Lim CH, Columba F et al (2011) Macro prudential Policy: what instruments and how are they used? Lessons from Country Experiences. IMF Working Paper WP/11/238
Marti MW, Wissler RL (2000) Be careful what you ask for: the effect of anchors on personal injury damages awards. J Exp Psychol Appl 6:91–103
McElroy T, Dowd K (2007) Susceptibility to anchoring effects: how openness-to-experience influences responses to anchoring cues. Judgement Decis Making 2:48–53
Mugerman Y, Ofir M, Wiener Z (2016) How do homeowners choose between fixed and adjustable rate mortgages. Q J Financ 6(4):1–21
Mugerman Y, Tzur J, Jacobi A (2018) Mortgage loans and bank risk taking: finding the risk sweet spot. Q J Financ 8(4):1–30
Mussweiler T, Englich B (2005) Subliminal anchoring: judgmental consequences and underlying mechanisms. Organ Behav Human Decis Process 98:133–143
Paiella M, Pozzolo AF (2007) Choosing Between Fixed and Adjustable Rate Mortgage. Economics & Statistics Discussion Paper No. 33/07
Plous S (1989) Thinking the unthinkable: the effects of anchoring on likelihood estimates of nuclear war. J Appl Soc Psychol 19:67–91
Strack F, Mussweiler T (1997) Explaining the enigmatic anchoring effect: mechanisms of selective accessibility. J Personal Soc Psychol 73:437–446
Tversky A, Kahneman D (1974) Judgment under uncertainty: heuristics and biases. Science 185 (4157):1124–1131
Tzur-Ilan N (2017) The effect of credit constraints on housing choices: the case of LTV limit. Bank of Israel discussion paper 2017.03
Van Exel N, Brouwer W, van den Berg B, Koopmanschap M (2006) With little help from an anchor. Discussion and evidence of anchoring effects in contingent valuation. J Socio-Econ 35:836–853

**Moran Ofir** Herzliya. Assistant Professor of Law and Finance at the Interdisciplinary Center (IDC) Herzliya. 8 University Street, Herzliya 4610101, Israel. Tel. + 972 9 9602 856. mofir@idc.ac.il. Fields of Interest: Law and Finance, Corporate Law, Empirical Legal Studies, FinTech, Economic Analysis of Law, Financial Regulation, Behavioral Economics.

**Yevgeny Mugerman** Ramat-Gan. Assistant Professor of Finance at Bar-Ilan University and a visiting fellow at the Federmann Center for the Study of Rationality. 5290002 Ramat Gan, Bar-Ilan University, The Graduate School of Business Administration, Tel. + 972 (0)3 531 89 14. yevgeny.mugerman@biu.ac.il. Fields of Interest: Behavioral Finance and Corporate Governance.

# Precautionary Antitrust: A Precautionary Tale in European Competition Policy

**Aurelien Portuese**

**Abstract** European competition policy applied to digital markets is at a turning point: new regulatory tools are under consideration and traditional antitrust analysis is altered given the new business realities embodied by tech platforms. These envisaged new solutions together with novel antitrust enforcement is justified, on one side, as the appropriate mean to overcome the error of under-enforcement of competition policy in digital markets whereas, on the other side, some criticize this new approach as erring in over-enforcement. Both claims that the other side is erring in its antitrust analysis are unsatisfactory. Each stance does not err, but rather, epitomise preferences towards regulation. This chapter argues and evidences that the new approach advocated by the European Commission for competition enforcement towards digital markets illustrates a preference for precaution. In the vein of the precautionary principle, the Commission's perspective reveals a precautionary antitrust enforcement. It is neither a policy error nor a legal flaw—it is a regulatory preference for precaution over innovation and disruption. After having Introduced the Precautionary Principle (Sect. 1), this chapter defines Precautionary Antitrust and evidences it so that it becomes apparent that the European competition policy towards digital markets have adopted a regulatory preference leaning in favour of precaution over innovation (Sect. 2). We then conclude on our suggested explanatory framework as a guiding principle in the foreseeable trends in European and American antitrust enforcements (Sect. 3).

A. Portuese (✉)
Antitrust and Innovation Policy, Information Technology and Innovation Foundation, Washington, DC, USA



K. Mathis, A. Tor (eds.), *Law and Economics of Regulation*, Economic Analysis of Law in European Legal Scholarship 11,
https://doi.org/10.1007/978-3-030-70530-5_10

## 1 Introduction: The Precautionary Principle in a Nutshell

The European legal philosophy increasingly epitomises a precautionary approach towards life, human actions, and corporate conducts.[1] Considered to be "one of the most controversial principles in EU law"[2] Europeans have been keen to conceptualise the precautionary principle as a guiding principle for regulatory interventions in numerous sectors of societies[3] whenever there is a risk of irreversible damage.[4] This cautionary approach to regulations by Europeans distinguishes them from, say, their American counterparts.[5] Indeed, the EU environmental policy is enshrined as being "based on the precautionary principle" according to Article 174 of the 1992 Maastricht Treaty on the European Union [now Article 191 of the Treaty on the Functioning of the European Union].[6]

This precautionary approach towards (probable or hypothetical) risks originates with the precautionary principle,[7] and is informally even more ancient[8] It can be argued that the precautionary principle rests upon the epistemological condition which contends that in the absence of knowledge and/or of scientific certainties, one must not refrain from adopting regulatory measures.[9] It can further be induced that the precautionary principles are the legal embodiment of the culture where excuses for the damage caused by lack of knowledge are no longer acceptable. Even in the absence of information or proven probability of future harm, regulators can be held liable for regulatory reasons rather than on a traditional liability system where the causal link needs to be demonstrated and where the lack of information functions as an exemption liability rule. In that regard, the precautionary principles function as a rule aimed at tackling the 'unknown unknowns' such as "awareness-based heuristics".[10] Nevertheless, the precautionary principle participates in both the weakening of the causal link in engaging legal responsibility as well as the recognition of the absence of any excuse based on lack of knowledge potentially invoked by regulators and decision-makers for any harm caused by any activities in our

[1]Garnett and Parsons (2017), Persson (2016), Stefansson (2019), Lardeur (2003), Wiener and Rogers (2002), Vogel (2001a, b), Sand (2000), Slovic et al. (2000) and Shrader-Frechette (1991).

[2]Purnhagen (2014), p. 454.

[3]European Court of Justice such as C-157/96 & C-180/96 (1998) UK v Commission, I-2269, para. 99; Green Paper on the General Principles of Food Law in the European Union of 30 April 1997 (COM(97) 176 final); Bocchi (2016).

[4]Manson (2007) and Persson (2016).

[5]At the World Trade Organization (WTO), see Article 5(7) of the WTO Agreement on Sanitary and Phytosanitary Agreement defines precaution and the Codex Alimentarius, Appendix VIII, Working Principles for Risks Analysis for Food Safety for Application by Governments, CAC/GL 62-2007, para. 12. See Milieu et al. (2011), p. 14.

[6]Doyle and Carney (1999).

[7]Garnett and Parsons (2017), pp. 502–504; Boehmer-Christiansen (1994).

[8]Garnett and Parsons (2017), pp. 502–504; Boehmer-Christiansen (1994).

[9]Carter and Peterson (2015).

[10]Grant and Quiggin (2013).

societies. The precautionary principle first emerged in international environmental agreements and conventions.[11] Such precautionary principle encapsulates the essence of the sheer reluctance to generate uncontrolled (and potentially unintended) consequences from individual and corporate behaviours.[12] Stigmatised as being anti-innovation, disincentivizing investments and marginalising science,[13] the precautionary principle nevertheless enjoys both regulatory prestige and legal entrenchment despite its lack of operational context[14] in dealing with "theoretical risks".[15] The number of occurrences and the wide range of areas of law where the precautionary principle is invoked has never ceased to increase and expand.[16]

Interestingly for antitrust purposes, the precautionary principle experienced notable intakes into consumer-related activities as early as the 13 April 1999 when the Council adopted a Resolution urging the Commission "to be in the future even more determined to be guided by the precautionary principle in preparing proposals for legislation and in its other consumer-related activities and develop as a priority clear and effective guidelines for the application of this principle". The European Commission had immediately pulled the trigger for a wide-ranging application of the precautionary principle into European regulations with the Communication (2000) on the Precautionary Principle.[17] The Commission's approach to the precautionary principle was formally endorsed by the Council of Ministers' Nice Resolution where they stated that the precautionary principle is justified "*where scientific evidence is insufficient, inconclusive or uncertain and there are indications through preliminary objective scientific evaluation that there are 'reasonable grounds' for concern that the potentially dangerous effects on the environment, human, animal or plant health may be inconsistent with the chosen level of protection*". While its presence in EU secondary law can hardly be comprehensively accounted for given its wide application,[18] the EU precautionary principle suggests that there is a general duty to lean towards regulatory interventionism whenever there is uncertainty and threat of irreversible damage.[19] The EU precautionary principle permeates all spheres of

---

[11] See London Declaration of 1987; Hague Declaration of 1990; 1985 Vienna Convention; 1992 UN Framework Convention on Climate Change.

[12] On the distinction between the precautionary logic and the precautionary principle, see Trouwborst (2009b), pp. 113–114.

[13] Gray and Brewers (1996); Resnik (2003); Sunstein (2005); Portuese and Pillot (2018).

[14] Indeed, Allhoff and Henschke (2018), p. 56; Löfstedt (2014) p. 1090; Garnett and Parsons (2017); Todt and Lujan (2014); Origgi (2014); Milieu et al. (2011), pp. 36–37.

[15] The Lancet (2000).

[16] See Commission of the European Communities (2000), p. 8.

[17] See Commission of the European Communities (2000), p. 7.

[18] See, for instances, Directive 2001/18/EC (GMOs); Directive 2009/127/EC (Pesticide Machinery); Regulation (EC) No. 1946/2003 (GMOs); Directive 2011/65/EU (Restriction of Hazardous substances); Regulation (EC) No. 178/2002 (Food safety);Council Regulation (EC) No.708/2007 (Alien aquatic species); Directive 2013/30/EU (Offshore safety); Regulation (EC) No. 1334/2008 (Use of flavorings).

[19] Garnett and Parsons (2017), pp. 508–509.

regulations in Europe, sometimes implicitly so, such as illustrated with the case as early as 1983 of *Sandoz*[20] in the area of internal market law.[21] In *Sandoz*, Netherlands wished to enforce a restriction on the sale of vitamin-fortified foods for human health purposes. Excessive intakes of vitamins could potentially be harmful to human beings, but uncertainties prevailed as to the extent of this potential harmfulness. The Court of Justice sided with the Netherlands who wished to protect its citizens as long as the restriction was deemed to be proportionate.[22] This judgment has been perceived by many as applying the precautionary principle not explicitly but signalled the pervasiveness of this principle in the European legal thought subsumed with protectionism to some extent.[23] The precautionary principle is, however, said not to "*justify the adoption of arbitrary decisions*"[24] by the identification of (general) factors triggering recourse to the precautionary principle. These factors are:

1. Identification of potentially negative effects: the conduct or product envisaged must imply negative effects;
2. Scientific evaluation: the evaluation of the available scientific information makes up for incomplete risk assessment;
3. Scientific uncertainty: risk evaluators incorporate prudential aspects despite insufficient scientific data.[25]

Poised with uncertainties and fraught with probabilities,[26] the precautionary principle entails a cautionary approach to future consequences, however highly hypothetical. Are these regulatory trends inferring a status quo bias for good or for bad?[27] With the precautionary principle, regulatory inaction often appears costly, whilst regulatory action generates expected benefits[28] In a dramatic shift away from the error-cost framework, which emphasised the imperceptible Type I error costs (costs of acting) over Type II error costs (cost of "enacting"), the precautionary principle emphasises the imperceptible costs of "enacting" over the costs of acting[29] According to advocates of the precautionary principle, "*we should move our*

[20]C-174/82 (1983) Sandoz BV. ECR 2445.

[21]Purnaghen (2014).

[22]On the interactions between the precautionary principle and the proportionality principle in practice, see the cases C-343/09 Afton Chemical Limited v Secretary of State for Transport, ECLI:EU:C:2010:419, para. 53; Case 54/85 Ministère Public v Xavier Mirepoix, ECLI:EU: C:1986:123, para. 16; C-504/04, Agrarproduktion Staebelow, ECLI:EU:C:2006:30, para. 40.

[23]See also Case T-13/99, Pfizer, 2002 E.C.R. 11-03305; Case C-127/O2, Cockle Fishers, 2004 E.C.R. 1-07405. See MacMaolain (2003); The Lancet (2000); Majone (2002), p. 95; Stokes (2008), p. 496.

[24]See Commission of the European Communities (2000), p. 13.

[25]See Commission of the European Communities (2000), pp. 13–14; Trowborst 2002

[26]Gollier and Treich (2003); Milieu et al. (2011), pp. 40–43.

[27]See Commission of the European Communities (2000), where it is argued p. 20.

[28]Gollier and Treich (2003).

[29]Purnhagen (2014).

*priorities from being biased towards avoiding false positives in the direction of avoiding false negatives*" since "*we need a decision rule that can compensate for the difference in goals between science and practical decision making [. . .] The Precautionary Principle seems to be precisely cut out for that job*"[30]

One could hastily conclude had the error-cost framework is being applied to the precautionary principle. This principle does not presuppose a faulty application of the error-cost framework with an exaggeration of Type II error costs and a discounting of Type I error costs.[31] It disapplies the error-cost framework and associated cost-benefit analyses, in favour of a legal philosophy where caution about hypothetical endeavours trump assessment of probable alternatives.[32] The precautionary principle over-estimate the probabilities of negative effects and under-estimate the breadth of positive consequences to be reaped off the envisaged activities: the precautionary principles stifles innovation and creativity. Allhoff considers that "if the precautionary approach is meant to do something different than cost-benefit analysis, then it would be paralysing":[33] indeed, the precautionary principle discards the relevance of cost-benefit analyses and the error-cost framework and substitutes a new regulatory philosophy towards uncertainties and innovation: caution at (almost) all costs.

It is undoubtedly true that the European approach to regulations contributes to the European "*soft power*"[34]—the ability of the EU to export its norms abroad through a regulatory race on precaution where the "*Brussels effect*"[35] appears increasingly influential.[36] It remains true that the precautionary principle implies a deterrence effect on disruptive (and *a fortiori* risky) activities. This deterrence effect runs counter the logical dynamics of innovation.[37] Consequently, some have convincingly argued that the precautionary principle stifles innovation[38] provides excessive regulatory discretion,[39] thus harms economic welfare of our societies in times when precisely the knowledge economy and digital innovation are most needed and tremendously praised. Interestingly, the precautionary principle is inherently linked with the ecosystem approach[40]—this essential feature partakes to our extrapolation of the precautionary principle in antitrust enforcement concerning digital ecosystems.

---

[30]Persson (2016), pp. 138–139.

[31]Peterson (2017).

[32]Sunstein (2005) and Turvey and Mojduszka (2005).

[33]Allhoff (2009), p. 20; Sunstein (2005); Portuese and Pillot (2018).

[34]Laïdi (2019).

[35]See Bradford (2020).

[36]Wiener and Rogers (2002), p. 318.

[37]Orset (2014).

[38]Portuese and Pillot (2018) and Orset (2014).

[39]Purnaghen (2014), p. 455; Turvey and Mojduszka (2005).

[40]Trouwborst (2009a), p. 107; Trouwborst (2009b).

Departing from these introductory insights, we will weave the precautionary principle in the rationale of EU antitrust enforcement, especially with respect to digital markets. This chapter aims at developing a hypothesis for a better understanding of the EU competition policy applied to digital markets: the precautionary principle surreptitiously prevails in the enforcement of EU antitrust with respect to digital markets. This hypothesis offers a more convincing alternative than the prevailing error-cost framework within which one may err on excessive interventionism or may err on excessive restraint. The precautionary principle offers a coherent explanatory framework according to which the current policy outcomes and legal solutions adopted are explained along a philosophical leaning pervading the European legal scholarship—the precautionary principle. Applied to antitrust enforcement, this corrosive trend dubbed "precautionary antitrust" entails numerous implications and queries. This chapter discusses them and explores an alternative approach whereby the innovation principle echoes the precautionary principle in order to reach more balanced competition policy outcomes. The chapter concludes with an assessment of the merits of this balancing exercise in the context of highly innovative markets.

## 2 Precautionary Antitrust in Europe

Competition policy in Europe, especially applied to digital markets, have become prone to adhere to a precautionary approach characteristic of the precautionary principle. We aim at evidencing our claim by outlining essential elements of EU antitrust enforcement and reforms which portray the elements of the precautionary principle. In order to demonstrate that the fundamental features of the precautionary principle are already (or tend to be increasingly) present in the EU antitrust enforcement, we shall use two explicit illustrations to the precautionary principle in EU antitrust enforcement (a) as well as two implicit illustrations (b). We evidence that the EU has chosen precaution over innovation, favours the certainties of the present over uncertainties of future outcomes, incentivises the preservation of (digital) ecosystems and current ordering of markets whilst deterring the disruption of traditional markets via innovation dynamics. Moreover, EU antitrust enforcement has shown a strong reluctance to the bigness of firms, irrespectively of their innovativeness, and cherishes smaller firms as they are presumed to infer lower risk to society. Precautionary antitrust in Europe entails backwards-looking analysis while *ex-ante* regulatory tools are being designed whereas traditional antitrust would induce a forward-looking analysis with *ex-post* antitrust liability. Therefore, precautionary antitrust not only epitomises a conceptualised reluctance to perceive and usher innovation, but it also represents a paradigmatic change of the nature of antitrust enforcement from *ex post* liability regime to ex ante regulatory framework. This section develops and evidences this line of arguments.

## 2.1 *Two Explicit Illustrations of Precautionary Antitrust*

The essence of the precautionary principle lays on the need, despite the lack of scientific knowledge or relevant information, to intervene before the theoretical risks materialise and well ahead of the harm caused by the hypothetical detrimental consequences of an action. Thus, timing is essential and regulatory intervention before damage materialised represent the very logic of the precautionary principle: *ex-ante* regulatory tools become justified based on this principle. In the same vein, the precautionary principle infused into EU antitrust enforcement begets ex ante regulatory tools enabling intervention prior to any harm caused (Sect. 2.1.1).

On the other hand, another fundamental feature of the precautionary principle entails that, given the epistemological limitations regarding the consequences of an action, it is no longer the regulator who bear the burden of proving the possible harm which justifies intervention, and often, the prohibition of the envisaged course of actions. In a dramatic shift of the burden of proof under the precautionary principle, it becomes the innovator, the manufacturer, the individual who has to demonstrate to the absence of detrimental effect of the proposed action. It is they who bear the burden of proof—thus, everything becomes de facto prohibited or regulated unless proven harmlessness. This counter-intuitive norm, when applied to innovative sectors of our economy, nevertheless represents the essence of the precautionary principle. It now, and even more in the near future, represents the essence of precautionary antitrust (Sect. 2.1.2).

### 2.1.1 Ex Ante Antitrust Enforcement: Interim Measures Resurrected

On the 16th of October 2019, the European Commission ordered the US chipmaker Broadcom to stop applying certain provisions of its agreements with six of its main customers.[41] The interim measures decision is justified on the basis that this prohibition warrant "*serious and irreparable damage to competition*" on certain markets for systems-on-a-chip for TV. Competition Commissioner Margrethe Vestager justified the measure by arguing that:

> We have strong indications that Broadcom, the world's leading supplier of chipsets used for TV set-top boxes and modems, is engaging in anticompetitive practices. Broadcom's behaviour is likely, in the absence of intervention, to create serious and irreversible harm to competition. We cannot let this happen, or else European customers and consumers would face higher prices and less choice and innovation. We, therefore, ordered Broadcom to immediately stop its conduct[42]

Interestingly, these interim measures were intended to be decided at the start of the opening of the investigations on the 26th of June 2019. Indeed, in a statement at

---

[41]European Commission (2019a).

[42]European Commission (2019a).

the opening of the investigations against Broadcom, Commissioner Vestager argued that:

> TV set-top boxes and modems are part of our daily lives, for both work and for leisure. We suspect that Broadcom, a major supplier of component for these devices, has put in place contractual restrictions to exclude its competitors from the market. This would prevent Broadcom's customers and, ultimately, final consumers from reaping the benefits of choice and innovation. We also intend to order Broadcom to halt its behaviour while our investigation proceeds, to avoid any risk of serious and irreparable harm to competition[43]

The allegedly exclusionary practices, falling within the ambit of Article 102 TFEU, are (1) setting exclusive purchasing obligations; (2) granting rebates or other advantages conditioned on exclusivity or minimum purchase requirements; (3) product bundling; (4) abusive IP-related strategies and (5) deliberately degrading interoperability between Broadcom products and other products.[44] Broadcom's market dominance has been identified in the supply of systems-on-a-chip for TV set-top boxes and modems. These interim measures were deemed to be "*indispensable*" in the Statement of Objections in order to "*ensure the effectiveness of any final decision taken by the Commission at a later date*".[45] This early assessment was based on the need "*the suspected anti-competitive behaviour damages the market irreparably [. . .]*".[46] In other words, "*interim measures can only be granted if a company's behaviour constitutes, at first sight, an infringement of competition rules and if there is a risk of serious and irreparable harm to competition*".[47] In the present case of Broadcom, the Statement of Objections considered that the alleged competition concerns were "*serious*" and that there was a risk of "*elimination or marginalisation of competitors before the end of proceedings*".[48] It thus appears that the European Commission has an *a priori* clear view on the course of the investigations since interim measures were, in a rare fashion, envisaged at their opening. The justifications given for Broadcom interim measures decision echo the parlance associated with the precautionary principle. Indeed, interim measures were deemed "*indispensable*" in order to avoid "*irreversible damage*", "*serious and irreparable harm*" so that regulatory intervention is considered to be necessary. These criteria are exactly those pertaining to the precautionary principle when this principle is invoked in order to avoid, despite uncertainties, generating potentially serious and irreversible harm as provided by the definition of the European Environment Agency in the area of environmental protection:

> The precautionary principle provides justification for public policy and other actions in situations of scientific complexity, uncertainty and ignorance, where there may be a need to act in order to avoid, or reduce, potentially serious or irreversible threats to health and/or the

[43]European Commission (2019b).
[44]European Commission (2019b).
[45]European Commission (2019b).
[46]European Commission (2019b).
[47]European Commission (2019b).
[48]European Commission (2019b).

environment, using an appropriate strength of scientific evidence, and taking into account the pros and cons of action and inaction and their distribution.[49]

These interim measures are explicitly "*precautionary*" in their nature according to Commissioner Vestager as revealed in her answer given to a Member of the European Parliament (MEP) on the 5th of July 2017. Spanish MEP Ramon Luis Valcarcel Siso asked, in a question entitled "*Applying precautionary measures in antitrust cases*", whether, following the fine imposed in the 2017 Google Shopping decision, "*temporary measures*" could oblige companies to abide by remedies before the end of antitrust investigations. He asked:

> [C]ompanies affected by the unfair practices identified have reported that their business was severely damaged as a result of those practices during the years that DG Competition took to come to a verdict. In the fact of this situation, Commissioner Vestager has suggested that temporary measures may be introduced to oblige companies being investigated in antitrust cases to cease unfair practices even before those practices have been proven to exist. The aim of those measures would be to have DG Competition respond to any sign of unfair practices in such a way that those affected by the practices would not have to wait the several years that it usually takes to close investigations of that type [. . .] Could the Commissioner provide more detailed information on the proposal?[50]

Interim measures have been dormant instruments of EU competition policy for many years.[51] Article 8 of the Council Regulation (EC) No. 1/2003 of 16 December 2002 provides for interim measures and states that "*in cases of urgency due to the risk of serious and irreparable damage to competition, the Commission, acting on its own initiative may by decision, on the basis of a* prima facie *finding of infringement, order interim measures*" (Article 8(1)). The interim measures decision can be renewed if deemed necessary and appropriate (Article 8(2)). The Regulation also acknowledges the ability for competition authorities of the Member States to order interim measures when applying EU competition rules (Article 5). In reality, Article 8 of the Regulation codifies the seminal EU case *IMS Health Inc*[52] of 2001

[49]European Environment Agency (2013), p. 649; Principle 15 of the non-binding Rio Declaration on Environment and Development; WT/DS26/AB/R, EC—Measures Concerning Meat and Meat Products, para. 123.

[50]Valcarcel Siso (2017).

[51]Commission Decision of 18 August 1982 (IV/30.6969—Distribution system of Ford Werke AG—interim measures, OJ 1092 L256; Commission Decision of 29 July 1983 (IV/30.698—ECS/AKZO: interim measures), OJ 1983 L252; Commission Decision of 29 July 1987 (IV/32279—BBI/Boosey & Hawkes: interim measures) OJ 1987 L286; Commission Decision of 26 March 1990 adopting (IV/33.157 Ecosystem/Peugeot—Provisional measures); Commission Decision of 25 March 1992 (IV/34.072—Mars/Langnese and Schoeller—interim measures); Commission Decision of 11 June 1992 (IV/34.174—Sealink/B&J—Halyhead: interim measures); Commission Decision of 3 July 2001 (Case COMP D3/38.044—NDC Health/IMS Health: interim measures, OJ 2002 L59).)

[52]Case T-184/01 T, IMS Health Inc. V European Commission, II-2351. This case suspended the Commission Decision in COMP D3/38/044 NDC health/IMSHealth: Interim measures, July 3, 2001.

discussing an interim measures decision.[53] In *IMS Health Inc,* the Court referred to the general Article 105(2) of the Rules of Procedure which permits judges to apply interim measures when necessary to be able to "*have enough time to be sufficiently informed so as to be in a position to judge a complex factual and/or legal situation*" or "*where it is desirable in the interests of the proper administration of justice that the status quo be maintained pending a decision [...]*".[54] In short, the interim measures here referred to compulsory licensing of IP rights to competitors. Because the interim measures, in that case, would be the opposite to what they are deemed to pursue (namely, in French, *mesures conservatoires* which imply the preservation of the *status quo*). Instead they would alter the market structure and modify the firm's business model together with the competitive constraints at stake. The European judge has suspended the interim measures decision of the European Commission based on "*potentially very important economic consequences*" for the firm subject to the interim measures decision and based on the "*serious encroachment on its property rights*".[55]

Because of their long dormancy,[56] MEP Valcarcel Siso rightly referred to EU interim measures as a "*proposal*" formulated by Commissioner Vestager to which she replied on the 21st of September 2017, foretelling the *Broadcom* decision a few months later:

> The Commission already has the power to impose so-called interim measures. Such measures ensure that whilst an investigation is being carried out, no serious and irreparable damage is caused to competition that could not be remedied at the conclusion of the Commission procedure. The power of the Commission to impose interim measures is set out in Article 8 of Council Regulation (EC) No. 1/2003. This article codifies the two conditions outlined by the Court of Justice of the European Union in its case-law on interim measures. These two conditions are cumulative:
>
> A) there must be a prima facie finding of an infringement; and
>
> B) there must be an urgent need for protective measures due to the risk of serious and irreparable harm to competition.
>
> The Commission recognises that the speed and timely nature of an intervention, if necessary, may be crucial in antitrust cases. For this reason, the Commission carefully analyses in each case whether the imposition of interim measures is appropriate [...] The Commission will not hesitate to decide on interim measures in suitable cases.[57]

Within a matter of months, the Commissioner "resurrected" EU interim measures for the *Broadcom* case, and thus, has paved the way for paradigmatic changes in EU competition enforcement from *ex-post* antitrust liability to *ex-ante* regulatory tools immune from the theoretical claims of "*irreversible*" damages to competition. Big

[53] Case 792/79R (1980) Camera Care v. Commission, ECR 119; Lang (1981), p. 52; Morris (1985), p. 108; Mantzari (2020).

[54] Id. para. 20.

[55] Id. para. 27.

[56] Mantzari (2020).

[57] See Vestager (2017).

tech companies, and more generally digital players, may not have to end years of investigations before some regulatory obligations become enforceable: as early as the opening of investigations, interim measures can, and will, be imposed so that, irrespective of the alteration of the market structure *a contrario IMS Health Inc.*'s *res judicata*, the foreseen damages derived from the alleged exploitative and exclusionary abuses are minimised through *ex ante* regulatory tools.

This trend partakes to the more generally precautionary approach to EU competition enforcement illustrated with the recent "*new competition tools*"[58] to be devised under the new mandate of Commissioner Vestager: these "*new competition tools*" (NCT) are blatant departures from the existential feature of competition policy—*I.e. ex-post* antitrust liability as part of corrective justice regime—towards a more pre-emptive nature of competition policy—*I.e. ex-ante* precautionary antitrust as part of deontological justice regime. In short, (antitrust) liability when excuses are no longer acceptable for modern and accountable regulators: (antitrust) precaution becomes the norm and absence of harm (either to be evidenced or to be expected) becomes the rule.[59] The "*new competition tools*" imagined by Commissioner Vestager are necessitated by "*structural competition problems*" not currently addressed in a "*timely and effective manner*". She justified new tools in the following way:

> The world is changing fast, and it is important that the competition rules are fit for that change. Our rules have an inbuilt flexibility which allows us to deal with a broad range of anti-competitive conduct across markets. We see, however, that there are certain structural risks for competition, such as tipping markets, which are not addressed by the current rules. We are seeking the views of stakeholders to explore the need for a possible new competition tool that would allow addressing such structural competition problems, in a timely and effective manner ensuring fair and competitive markets across the economy.[60]

These tools are part of reform comprising a "*holistic and comprehensive approach*"[61] which includes: (1) vigorous enforcement of competition rules "*including the use of interim measures and restorative remedies, where appropriate*"; (2) ex-ante regulation of digital platforms, especially those designated as "*gatekeepers*"; (3) a "possible new competition tool" designed to address structural competition problems such as market tipping.[62] It appears that the interim measures

[58] See European Commission (2020a) and Euractiv (2020).

[59] Autorité de la Concurrence (2020) Décision No 20(MC-01) relative à des demandes de mesures conservatoires présentées par le Syndicat des éditeurs de la presse magazine, l'Alliance de la presse d'information générale e.a. et l'Agecne France-Presse, April 9, 2020.

[60] Autorité de la Concurrence (2020) Décision No 20(MC-01) relative à des demandes de mesures conservatoires présentées par le Syndicat des éditeurs de la presse magazine, l'Alliance de la presse d'information générale e.a. et l'Agecne France-Presse, April 9, 2020.

[61] Autorité de la Concurrence (2020) Décision No 20(MC-01) relative à des demandes de mesures conservatoires présentées par le Syndicat des éditeurs de la presse magazine, l'Alliance de la presse d'information générale e.a. et l'Agecne France-Presse, April 9, 2020 [hereinafter: Autorité de la Concurrence (2020) Décision No 20].

[62] Autorité de la Concurrence (2020) Décision No 20.

are part of a broader change of perspective inducing ex-ante, swift interventions either before the opening of investigations (ex-ante regulations) and/or at the very early stage of the investigations (interim measures as seminally illustrated in the Broadcom decision). Months and years of investigations, followed by years of court proceedings, seem no longer to please the European Commission who target a new kind of abuse which is, in fact, a theoretical risk of irreversible damage—"*market tipping*". This vague notion, together with one of "*gatekeepers*", refer to few tech giants who may potentially "*create a threat to competition*" by "*tipping*" the market—in other words, by monopolising the market by entrenched positions.[63] Also, Commissioner Vestager identified "structural lack of competition" as the second scenario of the structural competition problems. The structural lack of competition refers to what is deemed not to yield competitive outcomes even without firms engaging into anti-competitive conducts: markets reveal "*systemic failures*" due, for instance, to technological obstacles or risk of tacit collusion for algorithm-driven companies in oligopolistic market structures.[64] These threats and risks to competition are serious, irreversible, and may damage competition as a whole so that urgent interventions, ex-ante tools and vigorous enforcement are needed, according to the new thinking of the European Commission. Additionally, the European Commission launched in June 2020 an "*Inception Impact Assessment*", as part of the proposed "*Digital Services Act package*", aimed at assessing the need for "*ex-ante regulatory instrument for large online platforms with significant network effects acting as gatekeepers in the European Union's internal market.*[65]" Because precaution is better than cure according to common-sense old *adagio*, Commissioner Vestager prefers to intervene on digital markets which "*fail*" structurally by regulating them at the expense the industry dynamics with respect to innovativeness and without having evidenced potential consumer harm. This increasingly regulatory trend in antitrust enforcement, especially regarding big digital platforms, pertains to the shift away from a liability regime towards a no-fault regulatory regime.[66] Market failures are addressed pre-emptively without much emphasis on potential regulatory failures. In that regard, Type I error costs are discarded while Type II error costs are exaggerated in coherence with the logic underpinning the precautionary principle.

With respect to the ex-ante NCT, the European Consumer Organisation (the Bureau of European Union Consumers—"BEUC") posits that "*the European Commission (DG Competition) should have additional powers in its toolbox to carry-out market investigations, even in the absence of dominance by a single player. BEUC, therefore, favours option 3: A market structure-based competition tool with a horizontal scope, which would allow the Commission to impose behavioural and, where appropriate, structural remedies to improve the functioning of markets*

[63] Autorité de la Concurrence (2020) Décision No 20.

[64] Autorité de la Concurrence (2020) Décision No 20.

[65] European Commission (2020b).

[66] German Ministry of Economic Affairs and Energy (2017), p. 106.

*independently of the finding of an infringement of Article 101 or 102 TFEU*'.[67] Such outrightly support of the *ex-ante* competition tools as structural remedies to competition concerns may be both surprising and puzzling given the unconditioned return to an overdue structuralist approach to competition such an approach suggests. How can we impose, "*independently of the finding of an infringement of Article 101 or 102 TFEU*", behavioural (namely, fines and orders) or even structural (namely, divestitures and ownership unbundling) without concerns for the rule of law and the due process? How can we establish the need to regulate and intervene irrespectively of the need to demonstrate any harm to competition—let alone to consumers? Such hasty conclusion foretells the inevitable difficulties to demonstrate harm as well as the lengthy investigations launched against digital players which both may generate unpleasant consumers and voters regarding the alleged inefficacy of the European administration to address their popular concerns. Be that as it may, Commissioner Vestager has made clear that the Broadcom interim measures decision "*is a sign of things to come*"[68] In the same vein, the use of interim measures especially for digital platforms is commanded by several reports on digital competition.[69] Consequently, ex-ante intervention (regulation and/or interim measures) shall undoubtedly gain prominence in the near future[70] as evidence of the precautionary approach to antitrust enforcement.

### 2.1.2 Shifted Burden of Proof: Antitrust Enforcement Without Evidence

If the ability to intervene ahead of the damage via *ex-ante* regulations, such as interim measures constitute, an essential component of the precautionary principle, another essential component deserves scrutiny: the shift in the burden of proof inherent to the precautionary principle. As we shall now demonstrate, this shift of the burden of proof both pertains to the precautionary principle and appears in recent antitrust reforms suggested by, or advised to, Commissioner Vestager.

First, let us delve into the extent to which the precautionary principle implies a shift of the burden of proof. In order to prevent the regulator from intervening on the basis of theoretical risks of irreversible damage, the individual has to demonstrate under the precautionary principle the absence of harm or damage to be caused with the envisaged course of actions.[71] This means that the burden of proof has been reversed with the precautionary principle as compared to traditional liability regimes: uncertainties no longer prevent the regulator from intervening, but only certainties of innocuousness demonstrated by the individual can wave off regulatory

[67]BEUC (2020).

[68]Vestager (2019).

[69]See, for instances, the Furman Report (2019), BRICS Report (2019) and Cremer Report (2019).

[70]See also ECN+ Directive on the 11 December 2018.

[71]Trouwborst (2009a), p. 110.

intervention.[72] Indeed, the European Commission observed that, in applying the precautionary principle for prior approval of products before they are marketed, "*the legislator, by way of precaution, has clearly reversed the burden of proof by requiring that the substances be deemed hazardous until proven otherwise. Hence it is up to the business community to carry out the scientific work needed to evaluate the risk*".[73] The European Commission further considers that "*action taken under the head of the precautionary principle must in certain cases include a clause reversing the burden of proof and placing it on the producer, manufacturer or importer, but such an obligation cannot be systematically entertained as a general principle*".[74] The seminal text defining the precautionary principle, the 1998 Wingspread Declaration, encapsulates explicitly such reversed burden on proof: "*When an activity raises threats of harm to human health or the environment, precautionary measures should be taken even if some cause and effect relationships are not established scientifically [. . .] In this context, the proponent of the activity, rather than the public, should be the burden of proof*".[75]

Second, let us scrutinise the recent calls for reforms of antitrust enforcement in Europe with respect to digital markets: the shift of the burden of proof appears as conditional to the new line of thinking. On the one hand, Commissioner Vestager has clearly stated that, given the difficulty to demonstrate consumer harm in the allegedly anti-competitive conducts of big digital platforms, she reflects on proposals for shifting the burden of proof onto big digital platforms: it would be for digital platforms to demonstrate the absence of harm to competition/consumer/innovation caused by their behaviours.[76] To exemplify Commissioner Vestager's thoughts, one of her advisers used the example of the Uber company:

> Say for instance, Uber started offering higher rates for those drivers who used its platform more often", said this person. "This would put competitors at a disadvantage because drivers would start favouring Uber to carry out their trips over competing apps. Under the proposed change it would be Uber who would need to show its behaviour is causing no harm to competition rather than the Commission having to prove it.[77]

Consequently, without doubt, it can be argued that the suggested (and probably soon materialised) shifts in the burdens of proof reveal the pervasiveness of the precautionary principle into EU antitrust enforcement towards digital platforms. The shift of the burden of proof, limited to big tech companies with no specific, convincing reason, bears a number of detrimental effects in the enforcement of a modern antitrust policy. First, it introduces structural presumptions according to which big digital platforms' conducts are deemed anti-competitive unless proven otherwise. Such structural presumptions preclude a same-level playing field of

[72] Wiener and Rogers (2002), p. 321.

[73] See Commission of the European Communities (2000), p. 20.

[74] See Commission of the European Communities (2000), pp. 20–21.

[75] Wingspread Conference on the Precautionary Principle (1998).

[76] See Craig (2019).

[77] See Espinoza and Fleming (2019).

enforcement to all players and prejudges on any consumer/innovation harm in order to prevent an arbitrarily selected range of conducts by a handful of companies to, for instance, enter new markets and disrupt incumbents for the benefits of consumers and of the competitive process. Structural presumptions derail the rule of law and introduces an unfair two-level playing field in antitrust enforcement. Second, while in digital sectors, the introduction of new products or services yields high risks (thus generate expectations of high returns), the chilling effect of the reversed burden of proof—which can never be met given the inability to demonstrate any innocuousness—will be disastrous on the innovation and competitiveness of our economies. Premiums are *de facto* granted to established products and services (e.g. firms' expansions through external growth/mergers), and price tags are put on new products and services (e.g. firms' expansion through innovation). Third, Europe would become the place where not to introduce new products and services in digital markets as compared to other places in the world which would, correspondingly, gain from this self-inflicted cost on innovation. For these reasons, and potentially many others, the reversed burden of proof applied specifically to a few platforms in the digital markets is both incoherent and unconvincing from both a legal and an economic perspective.

Nevertheless, such reversed burden of proof has been suggested quite influentially in high-level reports. Primarily, the so-called "Cremer Report" commissioned by the European Commission and delivered on early 2019, make the following proposals:

> We propose that competition law should not try to work with the error cost framework on a case by case basis. Rather, competition law should try to translate general insights about error costs into legal tests. The specific characteristics of many digital markets have arguably changed the balance of error costs and implementation costs, such that some modifications of the established tests, including allocation of the burden of proof and definition of the standard of proof, may be called for. In particular, in the context of highly concentrated markets characterised by strong network effects and high barriers to entry (I.e. not easily corrected by markets themselves), one may want to err on the side of disallowing potentially anti-competitive conducts, and impose on the incumbent the burden of proof for showing the pro-competitiveness of its conduct.[78]

Another influential illustration of this can be seen in the so-called "Furman Report" for the UK Competition & Markets Authority where it is stated that "*the principal alternative considered by the Panel has been the introduction of a legal presumption against acquisitions by large digital companies, with the burden placed on parties involved to provide proof that the merger will not be anti-competitive*".[79] In a similar vein, the French competition authority (Autorité de la Concurrence) embraces such shift of the burden of proof for mergers because the reversal would *enable "timely intervention for addressing anticompetitive conduct whenever they arise*".[80] Therefore, the reversed burden of proof carries the dual advantage to

[78]Cremer Report (2019), p. 4.

[79]Furman Report (2019), p. 101.

[80]Autorité de la Concurrence (2020), p. 9.

out-source the duty to evidence from the regulator to the private actor as well as to enable, together with interim measures, speedy intervention given the probable inability of this private actor to demonstrate the absence of harm.

## 2.2 *Two Implicit Illustrations of Precautionary Antitrust*

As we have seen above, the logic of the precautionary principle has been (or is soon to be) adopted in European antitrust enforcement towards digital platforms—especially those big tech companies referred to as gatekeepers. The demonstration of the pervasive entrance of the precautionary principle into such enforcement nevertheless proves to be even more apparent when the implicit logic of recent antitrust decisions is deciphered.

Indeed, by way of two implicit illustrations, we shall demonstrate in this section that the precautionary logic has taken roots in the EU antitrust enforcement. These two illustrations are: (1) the abandonment of the requirement to evidence harm: no longer is consumer harm required to be demonstrated, only reduction in the consumer choice suffices; (2) the preference of deterrence and destruction of innovation over disruption and destructive creation. We shall delve into these illustrations successively, before concluding on the fate of the rise of this European precautionary antitrust enforcement.

### 2.2.1 Choice over Welfare: The Precautionary Theory of No Harm

The traditional antitrust enforcement improved over the years in order to depart from formalistic criterion and presumptions in order to ensure that antitrust sanctions conducts by firms which harm consumers, and thus, decrease economic welfare. Consequently, modern antitrust enforcement has developed around a theory of harm: antitrust interventions are justified if and only if consumer harm can be demonstrated.[81] Absent evidence of consumer harm, competition authorities are illegitimate to intervene. Thus, the consumer welfare standard determines the appropriateness of antitrust interventions, irrespectively of the (reduction of the) number of firms. Indeed, the superior efficiency of dominant firms may drive out less efficient competitors but not only are consumers not harmed by such superior efficiency in products and services, but instead, they derive consumer gains from it.

However, the so-called theory of harm inherent to antitrust enforcement has suffered over the last few years, major criticisms both in the academic literature and in the decisional practice of the European Commission.[82] Indeed, even though in

[81]C(209/10 (2012) Post Danmark A/S v Konkurrenceradet, ECLI:EU:C:2012:172, para. 20.

[82]Akman (2015), Deutscher and Makris (2016), Wright and Ginsburg (2013), Crane (2009), Lande (2001) and Behrens (2015).

antitrust enforcement welfare trumps choice[83] as a standard of enforcement, it appears that absent consumer harm, dominant firms may be found to infringe competition rules due to their superior efficiency which drives competitors out of the markets. The legal and economic test which has, for long, prevented equally efficient competitors from being excluded by dominant firms was the "as-efficient-competitor" test.[84] However, this test seems to have lost its relevance when it comes to the assessment of the anti-competitiveness of conducts by big tech companies. It thus appears that less efficient competitors may successfully claim that some conducts are deemed anti-competitive absent consumer harm but on the sole basis that choice for consumers of digital products and services are being reduced.[85] Consequently, while a precautionary theory of "no harm" emerges, consumer choice nowadays trump consumer welfare as the standard of European antitrust enforcement in digital markets. Two recent decisions illustrate this trend: the *Google Shopping* decision,[86] and the *Google Android* decision.[87]

In the *Google Shopping* decision, Commissioner Vestager fined Google for having "*abused its market dominance as a search engine by promoting its own comparison shopping service in its search results, and demoting those of competitors [. . .] therefore denying other companies the chance to compete on the merits and to innovate. And most importantly, it denied European consumers a genuine choice of services and the full benefits of innovation*".[88] Google is said to have manipulated its complex algorithms to both promote its platform, Google Shopping, at the expense of competitors and have thus demoted competitors' placements in search results. Google used its market dominance in the search engine market in order to leverage it into the market for comparison shopping services. Consequently, Google is accused of having violated Article 102 TFEU.[89] According to the Commission, Google should not have self-preferred Google Shopping via leveraging its market dominance because competitors were unable to compete, and consumers were given fewer choices of comparison shopping services in Google search results. Google responded that changes to its algorithm mostly followed consumer preferences and end-consumers are those who benefit from Google's algorithm improvements and alterations.[90] Google argued that competitors experienced a reduction in their web traffic only because of inferior efficiency and consumer preferences, not because of exclusionary practices[91] Nevertheless, the European Commission imposed a quasi-essential facility remedy whereby Google search must not

[83] See Wright and Ginsburg (2013), pp. 2046–2047.

[84] See European Commission (2005), pp. 19–20; Akman (2015), pp. 274–280.

[85] Wright and Ginsburg (2013), p. 2422.

[86] Case AT/39740 (2017) Google Search (Shopping), June 27, 2017.

[87] Case AT.40099 (2018) Google Android, July 18, 2018.

[88] European Commission (2017).

[89] Portuese (2017), Portuese (2018) and Nazzini (2015).

[90] Manne and Wright (2016), Kokkoris (2017) and Renda (2015).

[91] Kokkoris (2017).

discriminate between Google Shopping and its competitors so that no self-preferencing and no demotion can be alleged. Absent such *de facto* "*search neutrality*" towards downstream rivals,[92] Google would face subsequent behavioural and/or structural remedies. Google appealed the decision on September 11, 2017, notably by asserting that the alleged abusive conduct is not anti-competitive and are quality improvements that constitute competition on the merits.[93] Demoting rivals through superior efficiency or leveraging is pro-competitive as long as consumer preferences are better satisfied with those changes.[94] The harm caused, and evidenced in the Google Shopping decision, is only the harm caused to competitors for which no "as-efficient-competitor test" can be applied given the unparalleled situation of Google in terms of costs and profits[95] Thus, in the lack of as-efficient competitor as Google, the European Commission has been bound to speculate on the merits of less efficient rivals in light of algorithmic changes decided by Google.[96] Where is the theory of harm in the Google Shopping decision? Discussions about the potential harm caused by Google's algorithm appear only at the end of the decision—i.e. para. 593 *et subs*. The European Commission does not find evidence of harm but only "*potential*" foreclosure of competitors which "*may lead to higher fees for merchants, higher prices for consumers, and less innovation [. . .]*".[97] According to the Commission, consumers may suffer from Google's conduct as such conduct "is likely to reduce the ability of consumers to access the most relevant comparison shopping service" given Google's dominance on general search results and because the label "*Sponsored*" for Google Shopping products "*is likely to be understandable only by the most knowledgeable users*".[98] Even more interestingly, the Commission concludes that the conduct "risks undermining the competitive structure of the national markets for comparison shopping services", thus hacking back to a structure-conduct-performance approach where consumer choice rather than consumer harm is the essential standard for assessing the competitiveness of a given conduct. Be that as it may, the theory of harm in the Google Shopping decision is absent:[99] either harm demonstrated refers to (less efficient) competitors, or harm refers to potential risks of damage caused onto consumers without evidence yet[100] As Bergkamp notes, "*does Google's favourable positioning and display of Google Shopping, an ad service, result in harm to consumers? Note that these ads keep Google's services free to users*" *before concluding that* "*in short, to find harm, the Commission provided data to show a diversion in user traffic. To be able to do so, it*

[92]Portuese (2017), Portuese (2018) and Hoppner (2017).

[93]T-612/17 Google and Alphabet v Commission, 2017/C 369/51.

[94]Renda (2015).

[95]Portuese (2018) and Nazzini (2015).

[96]Kucharczyk (2017).

[97]Case AT/39740 (2017) Google Search (Shopping), June 27, 2017, para. 593 et seq.

[98]Id. at paras. 597–598; Reyna and Martin (2017) and Iacobucci and Ducci (2019).

[99]Manne and Rinehart (2013), p. 2.

[100]Portuese (2017), Portuese (2018) and Daly (2017).

*made assumptions regarding user behaviour. Where the Commission provided evidence to back up these assumptions, the evidence was weak and constituted at best a suggestion of an issue*".[101] Consequently, it appears that the *Google Shopping* decision portrays a precautionary approach where only theoretical risks of damage to consumers are envisaged and where the preservation of the competitive structure in the markets for consumer choice appears to the objective sought by the regulator.

In the *Google Android* decision, Commissioner Vestager considered that Google had imposed three types of restrictions "on Android device manufacturers and network operators to ensure that traffic on Android devices goes to Google search engine"—in other words, Google leveraged its market dominance in the search engine market in order to deny Android's "*rivals the chance to innovate and compete on the merits*".[102] The impugned restrictions are constituted by illegal tying of two sorts: (1) trying of the Google Search app as pre-installed on Android devices; (2) tying of the Google Chrome browser as pre-installed on Android devices. These tying practices cemented Google search engine market dominance due to the alleged status quo bias of consumers.[103] Because Android has been produced and supplied for free to device manufacturers,[104] Google argued that these contractual restrictions were necessary in order to compensate for major investments and on-going improvements of the Android operating systems.[105] Furthermore, thanks to these contractual restrictions, Google has been able to foster competition rather than to deplete it in a market originally dominated by Apple's IoS.[106] The Commission considered that Android OS and Apple IoS are not competitors (I.e. do not exert sufficient "competitive constraints" to one another) and were on different narrowly defined product markets. Namely, the open-sourced operating systems market for Android OS, and the closed operating systems market for IoS.[107] Thus since Apple IoS and Android OS are deemed not to compete against each other according to the European Commission, Android OS enjoys a strong market dominance on the narrow market of open-sourced OS.[108] This market dominance was made possible, the Commission explains, only by the cementing of the market dominance of Google search.[109] Therefore, irrespectively of the ad-financed business model of Google which consist here in supplying for free Android OS to manufacturers in exchange of digital products (Google Search app and Google Chrome) which generate ad-related income,[110] the European

[101] Bergkamp (2019), pp. 537–539.

[102] European Commission (2018).

[103] Akman (2018) and Holzweber (2018).

[104] Hyrynsalmi et al. (2014).

[105] Sidak (2015) and Akman (2018).

[106] Todd (2017).

[107] Reinhardt (2016).

[108] Case AT.40099 (2018) Google Android, July 18, 2018, paras. 155–190.

[109] See, in the same vein, Etro and Caffara (2017) and Vezzoso (2018).

[110] Sidak (2015) and Hyrynsalmi et al. (2014).

Commission focuses on the leveraging power of the contractual restrictions imposed by dominant players. It thus discounts the effective competitor Android OS has become in the face of Apple IoS for the benefit of competition and innovation.[111] Of course, Google restricted the use of its proprietary apps in order to protect Android digital ecosystem,[112] an objective found to be unconvincing by the European Commission.[113] In the Google Android decision, the articulated theory of harm proves to be quite vague again, with a potentially indirect consumer harm speculated through the cementing of Google search market dominance through pre-installed apps.[114] Nevertheless, the inability of consumers to switch (or even uninstall) these apps for better, more innovative apps has not been demonstrated—thus, inducing any observer to conclude that consumer harm is not evidenced (let alone sought to be evidenced) as long as Google apps may prove to be of superior efficiency from a consumer perspective.[115] Indeed, the Google Android decision speculates that the potentially indirect consumer harm can be inferred:

> The Commission concludes that the tying of the Google Search app with the Play Store is capable of restricting competition because it:
>
> 1) provides Google with a significant competitive advantage that competing general search services providers cannot offset [. . .]; and
>
> 2) helps Google to maintain and strengthen its dominant position in each national market for general search services, increases barriers to entry, deters innovation and tends to harm, directly or indirectly consumers [. . . .][116]

As a matter of principle, the theory of harm in the Google Android decision is absent: it is more a theory of reduced choice imposed by Google through contractual restriction, irrespectively of the economic rationale for imposing such restrictions, with speculation that these restrictions might have deterred innovation.[117] Hence, the theory of (consumer) harm becomes a theory of probable fewer choice and lower innovation. It remains unsubstantiated that the introduction of Android OS has harmed consumers as a credible competitor to Apple IoS[118] However, the precautionary decision in Google Android disregards the underpinned logic of these contractual restrictions (I.e. obligations in exchange of Android OS supplied for free) and jettisons the overall novel business model of Google Android.[119] Consequently, following the Google Android decision which jeopardises Google's

[111]Walker (2016), Hyrynsalmi et al. (2014) and Sherr (2011).

[112]Hyrynsalmi et al. (2014).

[113]Kadar (2019), p. 447.

[114]Portuese and Wright (2020), pp. 173–179.

[115]Todd (2017) and Portuese (2019a).

[116]Case AT.40099 (2018) Google Android, July 18, 2018, para. 773.

[117]Portuese (2019a, b).

[118]Portuese and Wright (2020), pp. 175–179.

[119]Akman (2018) and Todd (2017).

business model of ad-financed free digital products,[120] Google Android envisaged switching towards a more closed, chargeable OS (thus charging end-consumers eventually) which would thus create a real tangible consumer harm.[121] In conclusion, in the Google Android decision, it can be argued that there is a theory of "no harm" where contractual restrictions are narrowly perceived as lowering choice and innovation for business partners without a proper understanding of the benefits these business partners have been able to reap off in exchange of these restrictions.[122] With respect to innovative business models of highly innovative companies which invest massively in research and developments, the European Commission appears to favour a precautionary approach with traditional business models easily grasped by the regulator.

### 2.2.2 Regulation Over Disruption: The Precautionary Approach to Digital Ecosystems

In accordance with the logic of the precautionary principle,[123] it is recommended to ban or regulate activities which are novel and thus for which the associated consequences are, from an antitrust perspective, uncertain and unsettled. As illustrated above, the ad-financed business model of Google departs from the traditional price-based analysis of competition enforcement.[124] It is thus no surprise that Google has been fined three times for more than €8 billion over a couple of years only.[125] Beyond the mere instance of Google, this illustrates a precautionary approach towards the essence of the emergence of digital ecosystems—namely, leveraging adjacent markets through interoperability in order to offer consumers multiple services within a digital ecosystem.[126]

Currently, big tech companies are said to operate on different spaces with approximately well-delineated spheres of actions.[127] Thus, if Facebook dominates social media, Google dominates search, whereas Amazon dominates online retail and Apple dominates media services.[128] This simplistic portrayal of the digital world errs in understanding the industry dynamics and the thrive for innovation each and every big tech company, as well as small digital platforms, seek. Indeed, Facebook enters online retailing, Google has successfully competed on Apple's operating systems and digital services, while Amazon dominates comparison shopping

[120] Sidak (2015) and Hyrynsalmi et al. (2014).

[121] Kastrenakes and Patel (2018) and Portuese (2019a, b).

[122] Todd (2017).

[123] See Sect. 2 of this chapter.

[124] Sidak (2015) and Hyrynsalmi et al. (2014).

[125] Portuese (2019b).

[126] Akman (2018) and Holzweber (2018).

[127] Galloway (2017).

[128] See, for instance, the US Congress Hearing on July 2020, France 24 (2020).

services instead of Google Shopping. These big tech companies are not delivering one (or even a range of) product or service—they aim at creating interoperabilities so that they can ever rip off network externalities inherent to the digital revolution. It is also because consumers expect ancillary products and services to be offered by the major platform that these platforms either enter a new niche market or tend to buy out downstream players. In the winner-take-all paradigm of the digital revolution,[129] network effects are key to success, and a lack of ability to reap them off may constitute the beginning of the end for companies such as Blackberry, Nokia, Yahoo!, Napster, and others who have been unable to build such digital ecosystem.[130]

However, the precautionary principle dislikes uncertainties—so precautionary antitrust shuns leveraging which may mean, rather than a step forward the erection of a digital ecosystem following consumer preferences, the cementing of market dominance in another market through unfair and anti-competitive practices. These super digital platforms are perceived not so much with their abilities to make flourishing millions of start-ups and digital entrepreneurs who want to create the next app or service,[131] but rather as tantalising attempts to monopolise the market.[132] But, they do not monopolise the market, they ferociously compete against one another. Granted, the size of their platforms and their cash-flows are unparalleled so that they may very well form a distinct category—be they nicknamed gatekeepers or super-platforms. Nevertheless, they compete against one another in a digital fight which, despite oligopolistic, remains real. Prof. Petit comes with an elegant depicting of this situation: they are "moligopolies"—they may enjoy great market dominance in some segments of the digital world, but they ferociously compete against one another in an oligopolistic environment.[133] Oligopoly may not infer lack of competition, quite the contrary: the massive capital required for these digital platforms as well as the inherent network effects all participate in the reduction of the number of firms on the markets given the need for firms' consolidation.[134] Nevertheless, such consolidation is being used for investing a massive amount of money into innovation in order to out-compete competitors: the money invested in R&D demonstrate that none of these companies may allegedly be said to enjoy the "quiet life" often referred to when one tries to identified monopolies.[135] They are not quietly enjoying their market power with old-fashioned products and services. Instead, they constantly innovate and make intakes into markets where they are

[129]Irwin (2019).

[130]Manne and Stapp (2019).

[131]Stengel (2019).

[132]Marty and Warin (2020), Subramaniam et al. (2019), Vezzoso and Nicholls (2019) and Kitsing (2020).

[133]Petit (2020).

[134]Petit (2020).

[135]Bourreau and de Streel (2020), Motta and Peitz (2020), Gautier and Lamesch (2020) and Bryan and Hovenkamp (2020).

not dominant in order to offer the most attractive digital ecosystem consumers may want to switch to.[136] They compete over attention markets: advertisers are their customers over which they compete. They out-compete their competitors by way of disruption which, itself, can only be made possible via innovation. Innovation demonstrates the strength of the competitive constraints exerted against one another, and more generally, in the digital world.

Against this background, to what extent can it be said that precautionary antitrust illuminate EU competition enforcement towards digital markets? At least three instances provide for an answer. First, the relevant market is defined very narrowly in the digital markets, whereas digital companies disrupt markets in order to have a viable chance to prosper in them.[137] Also, such narrow market definition precludes an accurate understanding of the economic rationale underpinning the digital ecosystem: some products and services are created at a loss only because they may funnel consumers and advertisers towards more lucrative sectors of the digital ecosystem. Precautionary antitrust favours narrow market definitions so that unrestrained market dominance can more easily be demonstrated as the initial stage towards prohibition and early regulatory intervention. Second, whereas digital platforms enter new markets by way of disruption through either leveraging or merging, both conducts are increasingly perceived with suspicion, representing threats of irreversible damage by competition authorities. Digital players can challenge traditional incumbents only with alternative ways of entering and prospering in the given market. Whereas the essence of competition means that new entrants (albeit powerful one in their original markets) are perceived as beneficial in order to challenge incumbents, the suspicion surrounding leveraging by digital platforms preclude them from having a safe antitrust harbour in their endeavour to challenge traditional incumbents. Also, the inability of the digital platform to enter the market via disruption may lead to prospects of mergers with nascent companies in order to effectively challenge traditional incumbents. Again, with the emerging concern of "killer acquisitions", digital platforms are suspiciously seen as killing competition, whereas the main objective remains to tackle powerful incumbents. Again, precautionary antitrust may preclude, without harm evidenced, the ability of digital platforms to build up digital ecosystems with full-fledged disruptions in a number of sectors of our economy for the benefit of innovation and end-consumers. Third, precautionary antitrust, less akin to embrace an economic approach to competition enforcement, favours the introduction of socio-political objectives into antitrust enforcement in order to prevent irreversible damage to any sort of legitimate concern. For instance, the digital disruption ushered from innovation may bring about consumer benefits in terms of low prices, increased quality products, new services, etc. However, it may also bring about disruption for other stakeholders, such as cost for customers, retailers, employees, etc. An illustration of this can be seen in the disruption created by Amazon in the supermarkets' sectors where shop

[136] Ringel et al. (2020).

[137] See market definitions in Google Shopping and Google Android decisions discussed above.

closures, employees redundancies, emptied centre-towns, left behind rural area are visible harms irreversibly caused by Amazon' s superior efficiency and by Amazon's consumers' preferences for online shopping with greater choice and lower price.

Traditional antitrust enforcement would remain blind on social issues since other areas of law and policies are better suited to address these legitimate popular concerns. However, precautionary antitrust embrace these concerns with the introduction of socio-political goals into the objectives of the competition policy so that these damage caused by "*competition overdose*"[138] are being minimised through *ex-ante* regulation, fines and, if necessary, bans. Precautionary antitrust portrays goodwill in the minimisation of social harm but may end up creating other social costs since social welfare and innovation cannot be maximised as they could be. Indeed, the necessary creative destruction inherent to any innovation dynamics, especially for digital innovation where shocks can be profound, remains intolerable for precautionary antitrust every time some threats, risks, potential harm can be identified which would damage human lives and the cherished ways of life. Here, there is a stark dichotomy between, on the one hand, the pursuit of digital innovation (and disruption) for the benefits of consumers even if it necessarily comes with the associated destruction of out-competed elements of ways of living, and on the other hand, the laudable objective not to harm anyone or not to damage anything when some corporate conducts can identify risks and threats of such damage. The inherent creative destruction of market capitalism appears multiplied with the digital innovation. In contrast, the citizens' expectations for safety, certainty, preservation of the ways of living with the precautionary principle remains appealing and called for. How to round up this new antitrust paradox? It appears that precautionary antitrust applied to digital markets, rather than solving this paradox, sides with excessive care and safety legitimately expected by citizens while shunning away the digital innovation benefits expected by consumers.

## 3 Conclusion

This chapter has conceptualised the rise of precautionary antitrust in the EU competition enforcement towards digital markets. Based upon the precautionary principle, precautionary antitrust constitutes a new area of application of this well-known principle: antitrust regulation. The essential elements of the precautionary principle have been, and are increasingly so, witnessed in the way the European Commission enforces competition policy in digital markets: ex ante regulatory tools, shifted burden of proof, action before any harm materialise, scientific and information uncertainties, and a reluctance to praise novel conducts and innovative endeavours in favour of safety and preservation of the current equilibria.

[138]Stucke and Ezrachi (2020).

Precautionary antitrust emerged in Europe but may very well transplant itself in the United States with the rising Neo-Brandeisians who, quite ironically when compared with the initial transplantation of US antitrust laws and doctrine in Europe, perceive the European stance towards digital markets as an example.

In the global race towards digital innovation, the emergence of the knowledge economy, and disruptive business practices, with precautionary antitrust, it appears that Europe has chosen its side: precaution over innovation; safety and certainties over efficiency and uncertainties.

## References


Akman P (2015) The concept of abuse in EU competition law. Hart Publishing, Bloomsbury

Akman P (2018) A preliminary assessment of the European Commission's Google Android decision. CPI Antitrust Chronicle, December 2018, pp 2–7

Allhoff F (2009) Risk, precaution, and emerging technologies. Stud Ethics Law Technol 3(2):1–27

Allhoff F, Henschke A (2018) The Internet of Things: foundational ethical issues. Internet of Things 1–2:55–66

Autorité de la Concurrence (2020) Contribution de l'Autorité de la Concurrence au débat sur la politique de la concurrence et les enjeux numériques. 19 février 2020. https://www.autoritedelaconcurrence.fr/sites/default/files/2020-02/2020.02.19_contribution_adlc_enjeux_numeriques_vf.pdf

Behrens P (2015) The ordoliberal concept of 'Abuse' of a dominant position and its impact on article 102 TFEU. In: Nihoul P, Takahashi I (eds) Abuse regulation in competition law, proceedings of the 10th ASCOLA Conference, Tokyo

Bergkamp PA (2019) The European Commission's Google Shopping decision: could bias have anything to do with it? Maastricht J Eur Comp Law 26(4):524–539

BEUC (2020) Digital Services Act (Ex-ante rules) and new competition tool, BEUC Contribution to Roadmaps. BEUC-X-2020-059, June 30, 2020. http://www.beuc.eu/publications/beuc-x-2020-059_beuc_response_to_roadmaps_dsa_ex-ante_and_nct.pdf

Bocchi M (2016) Is the EU really more precautionary than the US? Some thoughts in relation to TTIP negotiations. EJIL: Talk! August 9, 2016. https://www.ejiltalk.org/is-the-eu-really-more-precautionary-than-the-us-some-thoughts-in-relation-to-ttip-negotiations/

Boehmer-Christiansen S (1994) The precautionary principle in Germany - enabling government. In: O'Riordan T, Cameron J (eds) Interpreting the Precautionary Principle. Cameron May, London, pp 31–60

Bourreau M, de Streel A (2020) Big tech acquisitions - competition & innovation effects and EU merger control. CERRE Issue Paper, February 2020. https://www.cerre.eu/sites/cerre/files/cerre_big_tech_acquisitions_2020.pdf

Bradford A (2020) The Brussels effect: how the European Union rules the world. Cambridge University Press, Cambridge

BRICS Report (2019) Digital era competition: A BRICS view. http://bricscompetition.org/upload/iblock/6a1/brics%20book%20full.pdf

Bryan KA, Hovenkamp HE (2020) Antitrust limits on start-up acquisitions. Rev Ind Organ 26:1–22

Carter JA, Peterson M (2015) On the epistemology of the precautionary principle. Erkenntis 80 (1):1–13

Commission of the European Communities (2000) Communication from the Commission on the precautionary principle. 1 final, 2.2.2000, pp 7 et seqq

Craig E (2019) Vestager considers shifting burden of proof for big tech. Global Competition Review. October 31, 2019

Crane D (2009) Technocracy and antitrust. Texas Law Rev 86:1159
Cremer Report (2019) Competition policy for the digital era. Final Report. European Commission. https://ec.europa.eu/competition/publications/reports/kd0419345enn.pdf
Daly A (2017) Beyond 'Hipster Antitrust': a critical perspective on the European Commission's Google decision. Symposium on Google Shopping. Eur Competition Regul Law Rev 3:188–192
Deutscher E, Makris S (2016) Exploring the ordoliberal paradigm: the competition-democracy nexus. Competition Law Rev 11(2):181
Doyle A, Carney T (1999) Precaution and prevention: giving effect to article 130r without direct effect. Eur Energy Environ Rev 8(2):44–47
Espinoza J, Fleming S (2019) Margrethe Vestager eyes toughening 'burden of proof' for Big Tech. Financial Times. October 30, 2019
Etro F, Caffara C (2017) On the economics of the Android case. Eur Competition J 13 (2-3):282–313
Euractiv (2020) Commission charts new competition tool 'fit for the digital age'. Euractiv, June 12, 2020. https://www.euractiv.com/section/digital/news/commission-charts-new-competition-tool-fit-for-the-digital-age/
European Commission (2005) Discussion paper on the application of article 82 of the treaty to exclusionary abuses. December 2005
European Commission (2017) Antitrust: Commission fines Google €2.42 billion for abusing dominance as search engine by giving illegal advantage to own comparison shopping service. Press Release, June 27, 2017
European Commission (2018) Antitrust: Commission fines Google €4.34 billion for illegal practices regarding Android mobile devices to strengthen dominance of Google's search engine. Press Release, IP/18/4581
European Commission (2019a) Antitrust: Commission imposes interim measures on Broadcom in TV and modem chipset markets. Press Release, 16 October 2019
European Commission (2019b) Antitrust: Commission opens investigation into Broadcom and sends statement of objections seeking to impose interim measures in TV and modem chipsets markets. Press Release, 26 June 2019
European Commission (2020a) Antitrust: Commission consults stakeholders on a possible new competition tool. Press Release IP/20/977
European Commission (2020b) Inception Impact Assessment - Digital Services Act package: Ex ante regulatory instrument for large online platforms with significant network effects acting as gatekeepers in the European Union's internal market. Ares(2020)2877647, June 2, 2020
European Environment Agency (2013) Late lessons from early warnings II: science, precaution and innovation. EEA Report 1/2013
France 24 (2020) Congress panel concludes GAFA companies have monopoly power, July 30, 2020. https://www.france24.com/en/video/20200730-congress-panel-concludes-gafa-companies-have-monopoly-power
Furman Report (2019) Unlocking digital competition - report of the digital competition expert panel. https://assets.publishing.service.gov.uk/government/uploads/system/uploads/attachment_data/file/785547/unlocking_digital_competition_furman_review_web.pdf
Galloway S (2017) The four: the hidden DNA of Amazon, Apple, Facebook, and Google. Random House Large Print, New York
Garnett K, Parsons DJ (2017) Multi-case review of the application of the precautionary principle in European Union Law and Case. Risk Anal 37(3):502–516
Gautier A, Lamesch J (2020) Mergers in the digital economy. CESifo Working Paper, No. 8056. https://www.econstor.eu/bitstream/10419/215058/1/cesifo1_wp8056.pdf
German Ministry of Economic Affairs and Energy (2017) White paper - digital platforms. digital regulatory policy for growth, innovation, competition and participation. https://www.bmwi.de/Redaktion/EN/Publikationen/white-paper.pdf?__blob=publicationFile&v=2

Gollier C, Treich N (2003) Decision-making under scientific uncertainty - the economics of the precautionary principle. J Risk Uncertainties 27:77–103

Grant S, Quiggin J (2013) Inductive reasoning about unawareness. Econ Theory 54(3):717–755

Gray JS, Brewers JM (1996) Towards a scientific definition of the precautionary principle. Mar Pollut Bull 32(11):768

Holzweber S (2018) Tying and bundling in the digital era. Eur Competition J 14(2-3):342–366

Hoppner T (2017) Duty to treat downstream rivals equally: (merely a natural remedy to Google's monopoly leveraging abuse). Eur Competition Regul Law Rev 3:208–222

Hyrynsalmi S, Suominen A, Mäkilä T, Knuutila T (2014) The emerging application ecosystems: an introductory analysis of Android ecosystem. Int J E-Bus Res 10(2):61–81

Iacobucci E, Ducci F (2019) The Google search case in Europe: tying and the single monopoly profit theorem in two-sided markets. Eur J Law Econ 47:15–42

Irwin N (2019) It's a winner-take-all world, whether you like it or not. The Atlantic, June 17, 2019

Kadar M (2019) Article 102 and exclusivity rebates in a post-intel world: lessons from the Qualcomm and Google Android cases. J Eur Competition Law Pract 10(7):439–447

Kastrenakes J, Patel N (2018) Google will start charging Android device manufacturers fee for using its apps in Europe. The Verge, October 16, 2018

Kitsing M (2020) Scenarios for digital platform ecosystems. In: 5th international conference on computer and communication systems (ICCCS), IEEE, pp 453–457

Kokkoris I (2017) The Google case in the EU: is there a case? Antitrust Bull 62(2):313

Kucharczyk J (2017) When product innovation becomes a competition law infringement: preliminary thoughts on the Google Shopping Decision, symposium on Google Shopping Decision. Eur Competition Regul Law Rev 3:193–197

Laïdi Z (2019) The hardening of soft power. Project Syndicate, November 4, 2019. https://www.project-syndicate.org/commentary/hardening-of-soft-power-by-zaki-laidi-2019-11?barrier=accesspaylog

Lande RH (2001) Consumer choice as the ultimate goal of antitrust. Univ Pittsburgh Law Rev 62 (3):503

Lang JT (1981) The powers of the commission to order interim measures in competition cases. Common Mark Law Rev 18:49–61

Lardeur KH (2003) The introduction of the precautionary principle into EU law: a pyrrhic victory for environmental and public health law? Decision-making under conditions of complexity in multi-level political systems. Common Mark Law Rev 40:1455

Löfstedt RE (2014) A possible way forward for evidence-based and risk-informed policy-making in Europe: a personal view. J Risk Res 17(9):1089–1108

MacMaolain C (2003) Using the precautionary principle to protect human health: Pfizer v Council. Eur Law Rev 28:723

Majone G (2002) What price safety? The precautionary principle and its policy implications. Common Mark Stud 40:89

Manne G, Rinehart W (2013) The market realities that undermined the FTC's antitrust case against Google. Harvard Journal of Law & Technology. Occasional Paper Series - July 2013

Manne G, Stapp A (2019) This too shall pass: unassailable monopolies that were, in hindsight, eminently assailable. Truth on the Market Blog, April 1, 2019. https://truthonthemarket.com/2019/04/01/this-too-shall-pass-unassailable-monopolies-that-were-in-hindsight-eminently-assailable/

Manne G, Wright J (2016) Google and the limits of antitrust: the case against the case against Google. Harv J Law Public Policy 34:171–244

Manson NA (2007) The concept of irreversibility: its use in the sustainable development and precautionary principle literatures. Electron J Sustain Dev 1:3–15

Mantzari D (2020) Interim measures in EU competition cases: origins, evolution and implications for digital markets. CLES Research Paper Series 1/2020

Marty F, Warin T (2020) Innovation in digital ecosystems: challenges and questions for competition policy. No 2020s-10, CIRANO

Milieu, TMC Asser Instituut, Pace (2011) Consideration on the application of the precautionary principle in the chemicals sector. Final Report. August 2011
Morris V (1985) Interim measures in EEC competition cases. Int Tax Bus Lawyer 3:102–118
Motta M, Peitz M (2020) Big tech mergers. Information Economics and Policy. 100868
Nazzini R (2015) Google and the (ever-stretching) boundaries of Article 102. J Eur Competition Law Pract 6:301
Origgi G (2014) Fear or principles? A cautious definition of the precautionary principle. Mind Soc 13(2):1–11
Orset C (2014) Innovation and the precautionary principle. Econ Innov New Technol 23 (8):780–801
Persson E (2016) What are the core ideas behind the precautionary principle? Sci Total Environ 557–558:134–141
Peterson M (2017) Yes, the precautionary principle is incoherent. Risk Anal 37(1):2035–2038
Petit N (2020) Big tech and the digital economy: the moligopoly scenario. Oxford University Press, Oxford
Portuese A (2017) Fine is only one click away - symposium on the Google Shopping Decision. Eur Competition Regul Law Rev 3(2017):1–6
Portuese A (2018) When demotion is competition: algorithmic antitrust illustrated. The Google Shopping Decision. Concurrences. No-2018: 26–29
Portuese A (2019a) The rise of precautionary antitrust: an illustration with the EU Google Android decision. CPI EU Column, November, 17, 2019
Portuese A (2019b) Google AdSense for search: fines always come in threes. CPI EU Column, 29, April 2019
Portuese A, Pillot J (2018) The case for an innovation principle: a comparative law & economics analysis. Manchester J Int Econ Law 15:214–237
Portuese A, Wright J (2020) Antitrust populism: towards a taxonomy. Stanf J Law Bus Financ 25:131–181
Purnhagen K (2014) The behavioural law and economics of the precautionary principle in the EU and its impact on internal market regulation. J Consumer Policy 37:453–464
Reinhardt K (2016) Google cites Apple competition in EU Android dispute. Investor's Business Daily, November 10, 2016
Renda A (2015) Searching for harm or harming search ? A look at the European Commission's antitrust investigations against Google. CEPS Report No 118, September 2015
Resnik D (2003) Is the precautionary principle unscientific? Stud Hist Philos Sci, Part C: Stud Hist Philos Biol Biomed Sci 34:329–344
Reyna A, Martin D (2017) Online gatekeeping and the Google Shopping Antitrust Decision: the beginning of the end or the end of the beginning? Symp Google Shopping Eur Competition Regul Law Rev 3:204–207
Ringel M, Baeza R, Panandiker R, Harnoss JD (2020) In innovation, big is back. Boston Consulting Group, June 2020. https://image-src.bcg.com/Images/BCG-Most-Innovative-Companies-2020-Jun-2020-R-4_tcm9-251007.pdf
Sand PH (2000) The precautionary principle: a European perspective. Hum Ecol Risk Assess 6:455–458
Sherr I. (2011) Google's Android updates increase competition with Apple. Dow Jones Institutional News. May 10, 2011
Shrader-Frechette KS (1991) Risk and rationality: philosophical foundations for populist reforms. University of California Press, Berkeley
Sidak JG (2015) Do free mobile apps harm consumers? San Diego Law Rev 52:619–694
Slovic P, Flynn J, Mertz CK et al (2000) Nuclear power and the public: a comparative study of risk perception in France and the United States. In: Renn O, Rohrmann O (eds) Cross-cultural risks perception: a survey of empirical studies. Kluwer Academic Press, Dordrecht, pp 55–102

Stengel J (2019) Apple, Google and other titans are snatching up start-ups to fuel innovation. The secret behind their successful corporate coupling. CNBC, September 23, 2019. https://www.cnbc.com/2019/09/23/why-apple-google-are-snatching-up-start-ups-to-fuel-innovation.html

Stefansson O (2019) On the limits of the precautionary principle. Risk Anal 39(6):1204–1222

Stokes E (2008) The EC Court's contribution to refining the parameters of precaution. J Risk Res 11:491

Stucke ME, Ezrachi A (2020) Competition overdose: how free market mythology transformed us from citizen kings to markets servants. Harper Business, New York

Subramaniam M, Yyer B, Venkatraman V (2019) Competing in digital ecosystems. Bus Horizons 62(1):83–94

Sunstein C (2005) The law of fear. Beyond the precautionary principle. Cambridge University Press, Cambridge

The Lancet (2000) Caution required with the precautionary principle. Editorial 356(9226):256

Todd PF (2017) Out of the box: illegal tying and Google's suite of apps for the Android OS. Eur Competition J 13:62

Todt O, Lujan JL (2014) Analysing precautionary regulation: do precaution, science, and innovation go together? Analysing precautionary regulation. Risk Anal 34(12):2163–2173

Trouwborst A (2002) Evolution and status of the precautionary principle in international law. Cambridge University Press, Cambridge

Trouwborst A (2009a) Prevention, precaution, logic and law. The relationship between the precautionary principle and the preventative principle in international law and associated questions. Erasmus Law Rev 2(2):105–127

Trouwborst A (2009b) The precautionary principle and the ecosystem approach in international law: differences, similarities and linkages. Rev Eur Commun Int Environ Law 18:26

Turvey CG, Mojduszka EM (2005) The precautionary principle and the law of unintended consequences. Food Policy 30:145–161

Valcarcel Siso RL (2017) Applying precautionary measures in antitrust cases. Question for written answer E-004559/2017. European Parliament. Rule 130, PE 607.713

Vestager M (2017) Answer on behalf of the Commission. E-004559/2017, European Parliament, September 21, 2017

Vestager M (2019) Digital power at the service of humanity. Conference on competition and digitisation, Copenhagen, November 29, 2019

Vezzoso S (2018) Android and forking restrictions: on the hidden closedness of 'Open'. Mark Competition Law Rev 11(2):17–45

Vezzoso S, Nicholls R (2019) Decentralised digital ecosystems and competition law: a conceptual framework. SSRN 3484479

Vogel D (2001a) Risk regulation in contemporary Europe: an American perspective. Presentation at the Center for Analysis of Risk and Regulation. London School of Economics, 29 January 2001

Vogel D (2001b) Ships passing in the night: the changing politics of risk regulation in European and the United States. Robert Schuman Centre for Advanced Studies. European University Institute, Working Paper 2001/16

Walker K (2016) Android's model of open innovation. Google Europe Blog, April 20, 2016

Wiener J, Rogers M (2002) Comparing precaution in the United States and Europe. J Risk Res 5 (4):317–349

Wingspread Conference on the Precautionary Principle (1998) Consensus statement on the January 26, 1998. https://www.sehn.org/sehn/wingspread-conference-on-the-precautionary-principle

Wright J, Ginsburg D (2013) The goals of antitrust: welfare Trumps choice. Fordham Law Rev 81:2405–2423

**Aurelien Portuese** Adjunct Professor of Law, Brussels School of Governance, Vrije Universiteit Brussels, Pleinlaan 5, 1050 Brussels; Director of Antitrust & Innovation Policy, Information Technology and Innovation Foundation, 700 K Street NW, Suite 600 Washington, DC 20001, Tel + 202 449-1351, aurelien.portuese@gmail.com Fields of Interest: Antitrust Law & Economics, Economic Analysis of Law, Innovation Policy.

# Regulation and Deregulation of Financial Markets from the Perspective of Law and Economics

**Mariusz J. Golecki**

**Abstract** Three different models of regulation are discernible as a regulatory and evolutionary response to the potential risks related to financial innovation, namely: transaction-oriented, institution-oriented, and market-oriented model. It seems that the market-oriented model of regulation has not accidentally been adopted by many jurisdictions. Taking the unusual and diversified evolution of derivatives market into account, two lessons should possibly be remembered. Firstly, the financial crisis proved that regulation is necessary and good regulation requires a sound normative theory of both derivatives and investors' behaviour. Additionally, it seems that the judicial regulatory capacity could still play an important, albeit limited, role among the regulatory instruments and institutional arrangements. Thus, the judicial governance remains a significant alternative to market and political processes, whereas in majority of cases the regulatory framework seems to depend primarily on the quality of regulators, especially public agencies.

## 1 Introduction

This chapter concentrates on three competitive regulatory theories of financial law, namely: the "origin of law" hypothesis, the "incompleteness of law" theory and the "normative uncertainty" hypothesis. According to the 'legal origin' theory legal institutions developed within the common law legal systems create better conditions for the protection of shareholder's interests in comparison with the civil law systems. Concurringly, companies in the common law systems could have developed much faster, having better access to financial resources. Sometimes the legal origin hypothesis is being elaborated further, to contain two substantial claims: the "law matters" claim and the "legal origins" claim. According to the "law matters" claim, legal rules create the institutional framework for market economy, establishing property rights and enforcing contracts. Legal rules and their enforcement by the

M. J. Golecki (✉)
University of Lodz, Łódź, Poland

 
K. Mathis, A. Tor (eds.), *Law and Economics of Regulation*, Economic Analysis of Law in European Legal Scholarship 11,
https://doi.org/10.1007/978-3-030-70530-5_11

state could thus indirectly influence the economic output attracting investors by safeguarding their potential returns. Therefore, the quality of regulation plays an important economic role, even if transaction costs are relatively low. Additionally, the "legal origins" claim states that the quality of laws varies depending on the fact that legal system belongs either of common law or to civil law legal family. The major weakness of the origin of law theory such as its institutional asymmetry and its strong dependence upon the overstated differences between civil law and common law could possibly be overcome.

The incomplete law theory does not build on the strict distinction between the legal families concentrating rather on the type of institutional arrangements and therefore it seems to be a much more promising candidate for the positive theory of the regulation of derivatives. The fundamental assumption purported by K. Pistor and Ch. Xu is that firstly, law is in general inherently incomplete and secondly, that the incomplete system cannot be effectively enforced. It seems that even if the incompleteness of law theory applies to the financial regulations concerning market for shares and shareholder capital, for various reasons it is not necessarily an adequate instrument to be used within the development of derivatives. Firstly, it does not capture the fundamental difference between the stock exchange traded derivatives and the Over the Counter (OTC) derivatives. Secondly, the smooth evolution from judge-made or statutory rules to the sophisticated regulatory frameworks administered by specialized regulatory agencies is questionable.

The question remains how to combine innovation with security under the conditions of uncertainty. This fundamental regulatory consideration could be called the normative uncertainty theory. Therefore, the normative theory of regulation would favour the capability to adopt the regulation to changing circumstances rather than fixed regulatory approach, concentrated on one particular purpose. Such an approach is very often called reflexive regulation. Not intending to define reflexive regulation or a wider concept of reflexive governance, it is still important that it is oriented on the maximization of the dynamic efficiency as juxtaposed with the mere static allocative efficiency. The reflexive regulation could also be associated with the I. Ayres' and J. Braithwaite's theory of responsive regulation and the so-called Australian theory of regulation. The main point is that the reflexive or responsive regulation should be based on a flexible regulatory framework, which means *inter alia* that it should be based on principles rather than on rules.

The difference between rules and principles could be expressed in various ways. Within the context of the theory of regulation perhaps the most significant difference concerns much higher degree of flexibility and openness of principles in comparison with the relatively well entrenched and precise rules. Thus the major features of reflexive regulation contain the predominance of the purpose-oriented rules and principles, a vast scope of discretional powers, the hierarchy of legal remedies in a form of the so-called pyramid of sanctions and the dialogical-discursive approach as the regulator collects data and transforms private information revealed within the process of regulation into the public one.

The last feature of the responsive regulation, namely the discursive process of adaptation and dialogical character of the regulator-agent interactions, is sometimes described in terms of a bargain taking place between the regulatory agency and the operating business enterprise. This contractual aspect of the relation plays an important role in regulatory endeavour, since the regulator, due to the constant monitoring and dialogue with the regulated subjects, could obtain the relevant private information possessed by the business entities.

It examines the adequacy of these regulatory approaches and their relative merits within the light of the asymmetry of financial crisis. The asymmetry claim will be based on the comparison of two different applications of derivative instruments under various regulatory regimes. The paramount role played by the credit default swaps (CDS) in the US financial crisis will thus be contrasted with the so-called "Polish toxic currency options crisis". In both cases the rapid expansion of financial instruments (CDS in the US and vanilla currency put options in Poland) had been anticipated by regulatory failures. Nevertheless, both the causes and the effects of the regulatory failures were extremely different. These facts beg the question whether or under which circumstances the internationally (G 20, Basle Committee) or regionally (EU) coordinated regulatory response could be both applicable and successful in terms of its influence upon still diversified and fragmentized financial markets. The second part of the chapter will concentrate on the notion of evolution of law as a process induced by the change of the economic theory within the light of policy recommendations concerning derivatives and in a broader sense the speculation as a kind of market activity. The brief look at the deregulatory reform (Commodities Futures Modernization Act 2000) in the United States justifies some scepticism towards any theory of linear legal evolution, especially in a form of the "incomplete law theory". Additionally, the dynamic growth of financial innovation does not facilitate the regulatory task. The question remains how to combine innovation with security under the conditions of uncertainty (the normative uncertainty hypothesis). In this respect the recent financial law legislation in the UK (2000), UE (2006), Germany (2007), Poland (2008) and France (2009) will finally be contrasted with the alleged purposes of the future US regulation of the OTC derivatives.

It seems that under the "normative uncertainty" any valuable theory of derivatives' regulation should promote "dynamic efficiency" and flexibility rather than fixed regulatory approach, concentrated on one particular purpose.

It seems that the recent economic crisis requires a differentiated response. Different markets have been affected by various types of market failure. In the US a deregulatory policy on Over-the-Counter (OTC) derivatives has resulted with overexposure towards risk and created very good conditions for excessive speculation on credit derivatives, especially credit default swaps (CDS), leading to liquidity problems and gradually infecting the whole system of banking and financial markets. Additionally, the crisis had an immense impact on other markets, where the toxic financial instruments such as the CDS-styled derivatives and collateralized debt obligations (CDOs) have not even been offered. The problem of the Polish toxic currency options will be analysed against that background. Thus, the paper will concentrate on a typical market failure having a huge impact on economic performance. Some feasible institutional alternatives to market transactions such as direct government action linked to the proposals of legislative intervention and judicial process will be investigated. The multilevel legal and institutional structure creates some biases and paradoxes. The question arises whether and how they can effectively be managed by the multilevel judicial structure, on both national and international levels. The purpose of this chapter is thus to explore and normatively evaluate the institutional capacity of the so-called 'judicial governance' understood as a system of governance alternative to both: market mechanism and political process.

## 2 The Rise and Fall of the Regulatory State on Financial Markets

The problem with any coherent derivatives' regulation is that such a theory is always dependent on economic theory. Since there is no coherent normative economic theory of derivatives, it is very difficult to expect lawyers to provide with any coherent legal theory as well.[1] Is then the whole effort doomed to failure? It seems that the economic function of derivatives is somehow paradoxical. Neoclassical economics regards derivatives as the necessary instrument providing not only liquidity or risk spreading, but enabling the existence of the perfectly competitive market, since without derivatives there is no possibility to meet one of the core requirements of the General Equilibrium Theorem—the complete or contingent contract claim, according to which there should be the market for any possible state of affairs.[2]

The paradox lies however, in the fact that derivatives work efficiently within a perfect competitive market structure, whose existence is conditioned upon the effective work of derivatives.[3] As R. Coase observed many years ago, economists very often behave as if we lived in an ideal world of zero transaction costs, or to put it differently, within a world of perfect competitive market economy.[4] Unfortunately, not all derivative markets are perfectly competitive and arguably there are not always zero transaction cost worlds.[5] The sheer fact is that derivative markets are diversified, since it is very difficult to analyze derivatives as such. Certainly, an optimal regulation concerns well institutionalized stock-exchange. This is not to say that

---

[1]Huang (2000), p. 482.

[2]Walras (1874), Arrow and Debreu (1954) and Arrow (1983); As Hermalin et al. (2007), pp. 7–8 explain, those conditions are extremely unrealistic from the regulatory perspective, because: "In a neoclassical exchange economy of the sort analyzed by Walras or Arrow-Debreu, there is little need for either contracts or contract law, since buyers and sellers can exploit all gains from trade through spot transactions."

[3]Cf. Hu (1993), pp. 1457 and 1464–1467; Huang (2000), pp. 472 and 491–498.

[4]Coase (1990), pp. 15–16.

[5]One can even claim that the present recent framework and the functional characteristic of the OTC market reflected the typical market failure or that the OTC market was at east to some extend based on the aggregated market failures such as information asymmetry, hold-up, network effect and the unequal bargaining power. Kyle (1989), p. 317; Mahoney (1997), p. 1453.

there is no place for the OTC derivatives—the question should be raised however how to minimize the possible market failures on the OTC derivatives markets. Additionally, the dynamic growth of financial innovation does not facilitate the regulatory task.

Thus, the question remains how to combine innovation with security under the conditions of uncertainty. This fundamental regulatory consideration could be called the normative uncertainty theory. The theory is based on two assumptions. Firstly, the regulators cognitive capacity is limited and the access to information remains costly. Secondly, it is generally not clear what kind of financial innovations and under which conditions could be desirable from the perspective of basic policies and principles such as efficiency maximization? This second assumption could be regarded as an extended version of the so-called generic normative indeterminacy of derivative innovation suggested by Ronel Elul and exhaustively explained by Peter H. Huang.[6] Such regulatory strategy would be based on the assumption that some decisions of regulatory bodies are at least partially taken up under the veil of ignorance.

Therefore, the normative theory of regulation would favour the capability to adopt the regulation to changing circumstances rather than fixed regulatory approach, concentrated on one particular purpose. Such an approach is very often called reflexive regulation.[7] Not intending to define reflexive regulation or a wider concept of reflexive governance, it is still important that it is oriented on the maximization of the dynamic efficiency as juxtaposed with the mere static allocative efficiency, so often associated with the law and economics scholarship.[8] Reflexive regulation could also be associated with the I. Ayres' and J. Braithwaite's theory of responsive regulation and the so-called Australian theory of regulation.[9] The main point is that the reflexive or responsive regulation should be based on a flexible regulatory framework, founded on principles rather than on rules.[10]

The difference between rules and principles could be expressed in various ways.[11] Within the context of the theory of regulation perhaps the most significant difference concerns much higher degree of flexibility and openness of principles in

---

[6]Cf. Elul (1995), p. 73; Huang (2000), pp. 498–500 and 503–505.

[7]Cf. Nonet and Selznick (1995), ch. 4; Black (2000), pp. 297–299.

[8]The concept of the reflexive regulation is however notoriously vague; cf. Deakin and Hughes (1999), pp. 169 and 173–175; Lenoble and Maesschalck (2003), p. 244, Armour et al. (2008).

[9]Ayres and Braithwaite (1992), Gunningham and Grabovsky (1998) and Braithwaite (2002).

[10]Within the context of the financial crisis cf. K. Alexander, Supplemental written evidence to the oral evidence submitted on 23 June 2009 by Dr. Kern Alexander to Treasury Select Committee, point 3 Rules versus discretion in capital regulation at p. 12 Macro-prudential regulation and principles-based regulation, [in:] 'House of Commons, Treasury-Fourteenth Report, Banking Crisis: regulation and supervision', Session 2008-09, Treasury Committee Publications, available at: http://www.publications.parliament.uk/pa/cm200809/cmselect/cmtreasy/767/767we03.htm, ed. 31.08.2009, p. 2.

[11]Cf. Schauer (1991), pp. 47–52; Kaplow (1992), pp. 557–629.

comparison with the relatively well entrenched and precise rules.[12] Thus the major features of reflexive regulation includes the predominance of the purpose-oriented rules and principles, a vast scope of discretional powers, the hierarchy of legal remedies in a form of the so-called pyramid of sanctions and the dialogical-discursive approach as the regulator collects data and transforms private information revealed within the process of regulation into the public one.[13]

The last feature of the responsive regulation, namely the discursive process of adaptation and dialogical character of the regulator-agent interactions, is sometimes described in terms of a bargain taking place between the regulatory agency and the operating business enterprise. This contractual aspect of the relation plays an important role in regulatory endeavour, since the regulator, due to the constant monitoring and dialogue with the regulated subjects, could obtain the relevant private information possessed by the business entities. The information centred strategy reflects the fact that the access to the relevant private information on derivative strategies, techniques, methods and relevant practices is otherwise difficult to collect and prohibitively expensive. The communication between the regulator and entrepreneurs plays an important if not crucial role, according to the contemporary network-oriented theories of regulation.[14]

Nevertheless, the acceptance of the responsive regulation in a style proposed by I. Ayres and J. Braithwaite raises some well-known problems. One of the most serious issues consist in the fact that it is not clear how the regulator could sustain the cooperation with the agents whose activities are being regulated, thus being the subject of constrains.[15] The economically sound proposition for a more relational approach and cooperation based strategy on behalf of regulators could potentially suffer from the lack of clear limits of both the inevitable uncertainty of regulation and of legal position. Furthermore, the indeterminacy concerning the scope of regulator's power could be a further hinderance, given the fact that this strategy should be based on wide discretion.

Certainly, the principle based regulation is always affected by the limited scope of accountability of regulatory bodies. Sometimes it is even suggested that the responsive regulation contradicts basic constitutional principles, such as the proportionality principle, leading to the illegitimate interference of public bodies with the potential economic actions of private agents, who are unable to predict the potential strategy, purposes and actions of regulators.[16] These observations even if valuable, seem to be

[12]Julia Black distinguishes four forms of principles-based regulation: formal, substantive, full and polycentric; cf. Black (2008), pp. 425–430.

[13]The same dialogue based mechanism could be applied to the global coordination of regulatory activity. The example of such a dialogue based communication between two regulators: the US Exchange Commission and the EU Commission, has been analyzed by Alexander et al. (2006), pp. 647–673.

[14]For the characteristics of the institutional theories of regulation, in both, information based and network oriented forms cf. Morgan and Yeung (2007), pp. 53–79.

[15]Yeung (2004), pp. 37–51.

[16]Yeung (2004), pp. 167–170.

far-fetched, given the fact that the actions of regulators are not deprived of substantial control of legality. The judicial control of administrative actions seems to be the best way of combining the regulatory efficiency with the requirement of the rule of law and constitutional accountability. Additionally, the division of power and tasks between the regulators and the courts seem to be a constant point of reference for any feasible and realistic theory of regulation.[17]

The future regulatory frameworks will have to be responsive and multi-purposive. This is especially important given the fact that the regulators lack a solid normative economic theory, thus are regulating under uncertainty. If the regulation should be multi-purposive, reflexive and adequate in a sense that it maintains the balance between restrictive and liberal attitudes, then three different kinds of regulatory frameworks could possibly be distinguished:

1. transaction-oriented regulation (e.g. contract for differences—both statutory and judge-made law, as in the UK: statutory consequences of *the Gamming Act 1845* set out in judicial decisions; common law on contracts for differences);
2. institution-oriented regulation (the institutional regulation as in *FSA 1986*—stock exchange regulator (might be private), commodities, OTC, securities, banking system, etc.);
3. market-oriented regulation (the need for integrated supervision in form of the *FSMA 2000*, *MiFID 2006*, probably the future US regulation).

It seems that the evolution of the regulatory regimes could usefully be analyzed against the above distinction between transactions-oriented, institution-oriented, and market-oriented regulations. Thus, the transaction-oriented regulatory designs could be named the regulation of the first generation, whereas the institutional-oriented model might be termed the regulation of the second generation. Consecutively, the market-oriented regulatory frameworks should be called the regulation of third generation. The evolution of law on derivatives could satisfactorily be explained in terms of the combination of the gradual change of economic rationale and the abrupt, even revolutionary alteration of legal regulation. Two turning points could be indicated. The first one marks the departure from the transaction-oriented approach towards the institutional-oriented regulation. The second one could be associated with the recent shift from the institution-oriented to the market-oriented regulation. This process is discernible within the vast majority of analyzed jurisdictions. In the United States of America the original common law-based doctrine against differences, as established by courts, was obviously the transaction-oriented one, since it clearly concentrated on the substantial distinction between the contract with the physical delivery and the contract performed by set-off. This doctrine had been elaborated by courts on a case by case basis. It obviously takes some time to establish precise and thorough judge made law. In case of the doctrine of contemplated delivery it took just 9 years between the initial judgment of the Supreme Court of Illinois in *Pickering v. Cease* and the ultimate establishment of the doctrine by the

[17] Black (1997), p. 33.

US Supreme Court in *Irwin v. Williar.*[18] With regards to the first-generation derivative regulation both elements were present. The initial differences in the application of the doctrine against speculation finally led to the harmonizing activity brought about by the US Supreme Court. Later on, the drawbacks of that regulatory approach became so obvious that it did not take even 20 years when the Supreme Court demolished the doctrine of contemplated delivery and destroyed the whole transaction-oriented regulation in *Board of Trade of Chicago v. Christie.*[19] At the same time Justice O.W. Holmes was probably quite aware of the fact that the judgment in *Christi* would create a thoroughly new type of regulatory arrangement. Its novelty laid not so much in the fact that it considerably liberalized the previous anti speculative approach, but rather in the paradigm shift from the transaction to the institutional-oriented model of regulation. Additionally, the anti-speculative approach had been changed only in respect of the organized stock exchanges. The difference between the physical and contemplated delivery has been replaced with the distinction between the stock exchange based derivatives and the over-the-counter or bucket shop based illegal speculation.

The later statutory unfolding of the same regulatory approach has been abruptly changed only in the year 2000, when the remnants of the *Christi* based regulatory framework has been ultimately rejected and substituted with its opposite, the deregulation.[20] But even though the result of the *Commodities Futures Modernization Act 2000 (CFMA)* has finally been somehow opposite to other third generation regulations such as *British Financial Services and Markets Act 2000*, the logic of the regulatory paradigm shift from the institution-oriented to the market-oriented regulation has not been shattered. This logic initiated the market-oriented deregulation of the over-the-counter derivatives. Moreover, one of the major rationales for the reform was the need for the more coherent regulatory vehicle that would have substituted the patchwork of the *ad hoc* issued exemptions with the broader deregulatory framework. In other words, the enactment of the *CFMA* 2000 was a market-oriented regulation *a rebours*. Needless to say, the forthcoming American regulation will have to become a market-oriented one if it is expected to recover the major weakness of the CFMA deregulatory reform. Meanwhile, the US Secretary of the Treasury, Timothy F. Geithner characterized the awaited American regulation of derivative as: "(1) preventing activities in those markets from posing risk to the financial system; (2) promoting the efficiency and transparency of those markets; (3) preventing market manipulation, fraud, and other market abuses; and (4) ensuring that OTC derivatives are not marketed inappropriately to unsophisticated parties.".[21]

[18]The Supreme Court of Illinois Pickering v. Cease, 79 Ill. 328 (1875), 329 and The US Supreme Court Irwin v. Williar 110 U.S. 499 (1884).

[19]Board of Trade of Chicago v. Christie Grain & Stock Co., 198 U.S. 236 (1905).

[20]That statutory development of Christi based second generation regulation would include: Future Trading Act 1921, Grain Futures Act 1922, Securities Exchange Act 1934, Commodities Exchange Act 1936, The Commodity Futures Trading Commission Act 1974.

[21]The letter from the Secretary of the Treasury Timothy F. Geithner to Senator Harry Reid, May 13 2009.

The same path-dependence could be detected in European jurisdictions. n France the 1885 reform of the futures market (*"sur les marchés à terme*") introduced the distinction between the contract for differences and the stock exchange futures. A very similar regulatory framework had been introduced by the German *Stock Exchange Law 1896* (*Börsengesetz 1896*) *(RGLB 157)* The classification of these regulations are however, much more complex than in case of the US law. It seems that the European regulations worked as a peculiar combination of statutory law and judge made doctrine of contracts for differences. All the above mentioned statutory regulations were institution-oriented and thus constituted an equivalent of the American *Christi* case in terms of the type of regulation. These regulations were second generation ones even if they were gradually amended and liberalized. The drive towards liberalisation of the financial markets in general and the markets for derivatives in particular did not change the character of the liberalizing regulatory interventions, which thus could be described as the institution oriented deregulatory devices.[22] This does not constitute the whole story about the European regulatory framework. In terms of its function every regulation whether the British *Gaming Act 1845*, French *Law nr 1885-03-28 of 28.03.1885* on the markets of futures or German *Stock Exchange Law 1896* created an institutional-oriented model supplemented with the transaction-oriented judge made law. The statutory component introduced the distinction between the regulated stock exchange based derivatives as valid and recognized financial instrument. Additionally, the jurisprudence of the courts established the limits of speculation outside this institutional framework.[23]

Accordingly, courts were free to evaluate on the case by case basis whether the given transaction was to be regarded as mere wager which was void or a valid contract. The statutory or common law regulation was broad enough to provide with necessary degree of flexibility, since it was based on some open-ended rules or vague definitions of the contracts of differences.[24] Strikingly all three European jurisdictions applied the concept of unenforceability of gaming contracts whereas the American common law treated them as void and even illegal. This combination of the statutory based regulation of second generation and the judicial supplementary regulation of the first generation continued to operate till the enactment of the post *MiFID 2006*, third generation regulatory devices with one exception, namely the

---

[22]This would certainly refer to the British Financial Services Act 1986. the French Law on Modernization of Financial Activities(de modernisation des activités financier), Law nr 96-597 of 02.06.1996, German Law on Amendment of the Stock Exchange Act (Gesetz zur anderung des Börsengesätzes) of 11.07.1989. For the UK cf. Black (1997), pp. 83 and 116; for France cf. Medjaoui (1996), for Germany cf. Schwark (1990), p. 473.

[23]For France cf. e.g. Cour de cassation, Chambre commerciale, 08.07 2003, Vantrou vs. Banca Commerciale Italiana France, n 45–46, 06/11/2003, 1818–1820, for Germany: BGH 172/1980, Neue Juristische Wochenschrift 1981, p. 1898, BGH 172/1980, Neue Juristische Wochenschrift 1981, p. 1898, BGH 136/1995 Neue Juristische Wochenschrift 1996, p. 1167.

[24]Cf. Universal Stock Exchange Ltd v. Stracham [1896] AC 166 in English law, §§ 763 and 764 of the German Civil Code, art 1965 of the French Civil Code, and recently the sec. 5 of Gambling Act 2005, which in fact confers the considerable amount of discretion to the FSA.

British FSMA 2000 which in fact anticipated the *MiFID 2006* and strongly influenced the EU regulation.[25] The case of the British regulation is remarkable, since the statutory regulation obviously belonged to the third generation, but the practice of the regulatory agency and the main financial supervisor remained institution-oriented. In other words, the FSA operated in an institution-oriented way within the market-oriented regulatory framework.[26]

The enactment of the *FSMA 2000* could thus be described as a move from institution (stock exchange oriented *FSA 1986*) to a new, more market-oriented regulatory framework.[27] That framework does not concentrate on a particular institution, embracing the whole spectrum of agents, transactions, markets and institutions.[28] The exhaustive scope of regulation has been combined with the creation of the integrated supervisor (FSA), but the existence of such a single supervision does not necessarily belong to the essential characteristics of the market-oriented regulations. At the same time the enactment of the *Commodity Futures Modernization Act 2000* could be perceived as a step back from the institution-oriented CEA regulation to the transaction-oriented one, with the definition of the derivative transaction becoming a crucial element of the regulatory regime and virtually establishing the boundaries and scope of the potential regulation. Alternatively, the same fact, namely the passage of the *Commodity Futures Modernization Act*, could be perceived as a market-oriented deregulation, since in fact it created the whole complex of the unregulated OTC derivative market exempted from any supervision. Thus, the British and American approaches can be usefully contrasted. The *FSMA 2000* adopted the liberal approach toward OTC derivatives, accompanied by extensive supervision. The regulation could therefore be responsive and complete. On the other hand, the American regulation created a heavily regulated patchwork leaving large unregulated sectors of the market. Hence, it could be stated that the *CFMA 2000* generally focuses on the regulation of products and markets, whereas under the British *FSMA 2000* the market-oriented nature of regulation concentrates on information standards and customer protection. As a result, all potential derivative transactions are organized and supervised; there is, for example, no restriction for a natural person as an unsophisticated and unauthorized party to enter highly sophisticated derivative transaction, provided that the product is offered by an authorized person, complying with all consumer protection requirements. The *FSMA 2000,* as a market-oriented regulation, contains the principle of segmentation, which is based on the assumption that the access to the financial market should be open and at the same time the participants should be covered by different levels and intensity of

[25]These would include: French Code monétaire et financier, Version consolidée au 1 avril 2009 as amended by the Ordonnance nr 2009-15 of 08.01.2009 (CMF), German new Stock Exchange Act (Börsengesetz) of 16.07.2007, (BGBl. I S. 1330, 1351).

[26]The Financial Services Authority (2009), pp. 86–88.

[27]Cf. The Financial Services Authority (2009), pp. 86–88.

[28]For the characteristic of the FSA 1986 development of the regulatory structure cf. Black (1997), p. 48.

regulatory instruments, beginning with the authorization requirements for the business institutions and ending with the consumer and credit protection rules in case of physical, unauthorized persons.[29] As such, the regulation essentially aims at the creation of the biggest possible market characterized by the highest prudential standards. It seems then that the market-oriented model of regulation has not been adopted accidentally by the European Commission (*MiFID 2006*) and many other jurisdictions including the UK, Germany and France.

## 3 Judicial Governance in Case of Market Failure, Radical Change and Uncertainty

The comparative institutional analysis suggests three potential types of remedies being deployed in the case of the so-called market failure. A market failure takes place when parties are not acting in a rational way or the exchange is not voluntary due to ignorance or information asymmetries, or alternatively there is no relevant market solution whatsoever. According to the classical definition proposed by Francis M. Bator, the market failure is 'the failure of a more or less idealized system of price-market institutions to sustain "desirable" activities or to estop "undesirable" activities'.[30] The failure usually results from high transaction costs or lack of access to competitive market leading to one-sided bargains.[31] Typically such a situation might take place within the context of the Over-The-Counter derivative transactions. Those "tailored", individually negotiated and highly sophisticated if not opaque contracts seem at least in many cases to be strikingly one-sided. Moreover, such *ex post* unbalanced transactions result from information asymmetry. The question arises, whether and possibly how should the regulator intervene in the event of such market failures.

According to the first feasible alas allegedly paradoxical option, the institutional response to a market failure might be provided by the market itself.[32] This institutional alternative is a realistic one under the assumption that parties may effectively insure against unpredictable events on the market. The strategy is strictly connected with the general equilibrium theorem and the concept of the complete contract (contingent contract claim), i.e. the contract whose terms capture all possible states of affair, all possible contingences. The economic theory of complete contingency contract is however, significantly weakened by the assumption of the existence of transaction costs. If transaction costs are high enough then it is not profitable for a party to spend resources on filling the gaps within a contract. The problem of *ex post* gap filling is not a matter of market governance since in majority of cases it is

[29]Black (1997), pp. 88–91.
[30]See Bator (1958), p. 351.
[31]Coase (1990), p. 95.
[32]Coase (1990), pp. 97–102.

dependent rather on the preferences of the legislator or the court. Hence the market solution under the assumption of positive transaction costs is effectively being superseded by state regulation and regulatory policy, the governmental intervention thus becoming the only institutional alternative.[33] Given the fact that the existence of transaction costs leads to gaps in contracts, the state could effectively prevent *ex post* construction of contracts. The typical instrument which may be deployed in those circumstances is a set of default rules which operate unless bargained out by the parties. The stronger regulatory instrument is the set of mandatory rules set out in case of a typical market failure, e.g. information asymmetry. Finally, it is commonly believed that courts should supplement the market in case of high transaction costs. According to Ronald Coase: "when the market transactions are so costly as to make it difficult to change the arrangement of rights established by the law [. . .] the courts directly influence economic activity. It would therefore seem desirable that the courts should understand the economic consequence of their decisions and should [. . .] take these consequences into account when making their decisions.".[34] Courts typically also intervene in case of market failures, such as fraud, or duress of deceit. This intervention, though legitimate and even necessary, should not, however, be too intrusive consequently, even gross inequalities between parties resulting from the differences in bargaining skills are justified.[35]

The question arises whether judges are prepared to solve the problem of allocation and distribution of resources under the assumption of uncertainty, risk and bounded rationality. Within this context three economic models of judicial governance could be distinguished. The Posnerian model is based on the assumption that courts should adopt the solution that would have been generated by markets, since the market transaction is being regarded as the optimal institutional design, the first best choice. Courts should thus adopt the "market mimicking" strategy, aligning their judgments with potential (virtual) market solution. Therefore, judicial governance becomes a perfect substitute for market. This doctrine is supported by the economic analysis of contract law. The economic analysis of contracts requires that the Pareto-efficient contract is prepared and concluded freely and is at least *ex ante* improving the position of at least one party. The other party cannot be *ex ante* worse off. If such a relationship happens the contract is not Pareto-efficient. The proponents of that concept very often refer to such a model contract as the hypothetical bargain or hypothetical contract[36] The hypothetical bargain may be perceived as an ideal generalized normative standard, a pattern of efficient exchange. Such a hypothetical bargain is to be implemented both as a standard against which potential benefit taken out of the contract is measured and as a normative model according to which the contract may be constructed or adapted. In both cases the concept of hypothetical bargain is crucial. According to this model the contract made by parties should

[33]Coase (1990), pp. 15–16.

[34]Coase (1990), p. 119.

[35]Posner (2003), p. 115.

[36]Posner (2003), pp. 12–15.

specify some physical characteristics such as date, place of performance or the price of a commodity for every possible future state of nature. Only such a contract, namely "the complete contingent claims contract" leads to efficient outcomes.

The fact that it is virtually impossible to make a "complete contingent claims contract" because of high transaction costs or other factors, is not relevant if the hypothetical contract is treated as a normative model. According to the Coasian theory of institutional alternatives, judicial governance is perceived as a residual allocative framework within the high transaction costs environment. This approach toward courts as institutions could be derived from the normative interpretation of the Coase theorem, which endorses that judges successfully apply distributive schemes enhancing, at least in the common law, the overall efficiency of law, accordingly with the so-called efficiency of the common law hypothesis.[37]

The certainty of a legal position, however, sets out the limits of the efficiency enhancing strategy. In other words: courts under some assumptions could be an institutional alternative to markets and yet they are not ideal substitutes. Moreover, the costs of judicial governance should also be taken into account.[38] This approach seems to be typical for the recent development of judicial governance. Such a model of active courts is based on the assumption that judges could directly influence both allocative and distributive consequences, due to the process of proportionality analysis based on the so-called weighing and balancing of the conflicting rights and principles. These ideas coincide at least to some extent with the Calabresian model, which is based on the assumption that different values should be preserved by the judiciary.

Hence the axiological pluralism becomes the background of judicial activity. Judicial governance differs from markets in a significant way. The issues which courts must deliberate on are left for the courts precisely due to the fact that courts have to take different values into account. The market solution is not adequate in many cases, because of the fact that the market is not perfect (market failure model). Fairness, justice (distributional effects) and efficiency should be equally taken into account.[39]

The typical example of sub-optimal contracts is a contract made in case of a serious threat (duress), fraud, or sometimes by mistake. The enforcement of such a contract would minimize the aggregate social welfare because it would be transferred to those using threats and to potential means to protect against them. Thus, in the presence of a contract failure resulting from high transaction costs the court should interpret the contract according to the hypothetical result of a bargaining process in a zero transaction-cost environment. This proposition was first presented by Guido Calabresi and Douglas Malamed.[40]

---

[37]Coase (1990), pp. 123–128.

[38]Coase (1990), pp. 114–117.

[39]Calabresi (1982).

[40]Calabresi and Melamed (1972), pp. 1089–1128.

The problem of judicial governance might certainly be scrutinized on a much broader basis. In the fourteenth century, courts in the US had started to establish and implement the common law doctrine against speculation.[41] The development of this judicial doctrine eventually led to the declaration of the invalidity of all speculative contracts for differences as expressly stated by the US Supreme Court (see *Irwin v. Willar* 110 U.S. 508-509 (1884). Courts thus became the forerunners of the anti-speculative policy adopted later on by statutory law, including *Future Trading Act (1921)* and *Grain Futures Act (1922)*, *Commodities Exchange Act (1936)*, regulating commodity futures and *Securities Exchange Act (1934)* being a core of anti-speculative financial law (Stout 1999; Huang 2000).

On the other hand, in *Board of Trade of Chicago v. Christie* Justice O. W. Holmes exploited the opportunity for the reform to the greatest possible extend. He legalized all previously invalid openly speculative transactions such as contracts for differences, provided they were concluded at the regulated stock exchange. The US Supreme Court decided to liberalize anti-speculative laws, since as Justice Holmes had put it: "in a modern market, contracts are not confined to sales for immediate delivery. People will endeavor to forecast the future, and to make agreements according to their prophecy. Speculation of this kind by competent men is the self-adjustment of society to the probable".[42] More recently judicial decisions set out the legal status of many derivative transactions; in *Procter & Gamble Co. v. Bankers Trust Co.*, 925 F. Supp. 1270 (S.D. Ohio 1996) the legal nature of certain interest rate swaps has been defined as contracts, not securities. Moreover, the judgment in *Caiola v. Citibank*, 137 F. Supp. 2d 362, 364–65 (S.D.N.Y. Apr. 2, 2001) had impact on the evaluation of the legal status of the so-called soft law regulations issued by International Swap and Derivatives Association (ISDA) for the OTC derivative transactions. The court held that certain provisions of the ISDA Master Agreement could have prevailed over the statutory provisions of the Securities Exchange Act. Against this background it seems that courts are residual lawmakers: in case of market failure and state (legislation/administration) failure. The question arises whether judges are able to be responsive in highly complex derivative cases, since even recently judicial interventions play an important role in the regulatory framework.

---

[41]See Pickering v. Cease, 79 Ill. 328 (1875), 329, Harris v. Tubbrige, 83 N.Y. 92,95 (1880), Bigelow v. Benedict, 70 N.Y. 202 (1877), Pixley v. Boynton, 79 Ill. 351 (1875), Kirkpatrick & Lyons v. Bonsall, 72 Pa. 155 (1872), Wolcott v. Heath, 78 Ill. 433 (1875); Sandborn v. Benedict, 78 Ill. 309 (1875); Lyon v. Culbertson, 83 Ill. 33 (1876); Williams v. Tidemann, 6 Mo. App. 269 (Mo. Ct. App., 1878); Rudolf v. Winters, 7 Neb. 125 (1878), Gregory v. Wendell, 40 Mich. 432 (1879); Kingsbury v. Kirwan, 77 N.Y. 612 (N.Y. Ct. App., 1879); Wallace v. Taggart, 14 Bush 727 (Ken. Ct. App., 1879); Tenney v. Foote, 4 Ill. App. 594 (Ill. Ct. App., 1879); Beveridge v. Hewitt, 8 Ill. App. 467 (Ill. Ct. App., 1881); Hawley v. Bibb, 69 Ala. 52 (1881); Melchert v. American Union Telegraph Co., 11 F. 193 (Cr. Ct., 1882); Cobb v. Prell, 15 F. 774 (Cr. Ct., 1883).

[42]Board of Trade of Chicago v. Christie Grain & Stock Co., 198 U.S. 236 (1905), p. 247.

In the UK, where the statutory provisions seem to play an important role in regulating derivatives, the ultimate application of statutory provisions rested also upon courts. In the UK the legal definition of a wagering had been proposed by Hawkins J. in *Carlill v. Carbolic Smoke Ball Co*. [1892] 2 Q.B. 484, 490–491 in the following way:

> a wagering contract is one by which two persons, professing to hold opposite views touching the issue of a future uncertain event, mutually agree that, dependent upon the determination of that event, one shall win from the other, and the other shall pay or hand over to him, a sum of money or other stake.

In this way the famous English case *Universal Stock Exchange Ltd v. Strachan* [1896] AC 166 set out the English doctrine of gamming transactions, thus substituting sec. 18 of the Gaming Act 1845, which stated:

> All contracts or agreements, whether by parole or in writing, by way of gaming or wagering, shall be null and void; and no suit shall be brought or maintained in any court of law or equity for recovering any sum of money or valuable thing alleged to be won upon any wager.

The same could be said about some peculiar aspects of derivatives treated on the stock exchange, such as the binding force of broker's commercial custom and its force for the principal.[43] The nature of the unenforceable wagering contract has been endorsed in *Earl of Ellesmere v. Wallace* [1929] 2 Ch. 1. Additionally, the function of derivative transaction has been analysed in some cases such as *Metelmann v. N.B. R* (1984), where it was stated that derivatives may also serve as an efficient tool to mitigate loss due to the change of price.[44] Likewise, in more recent cases under the *Financial Services Act 1986* the courts tried to identify the legal nature of derivative transactions or to analyse the problems of legal capacity to enter the sophisticated derivative transaction. This was necessary due to the vagueness of some provisions of the FSA (*City Index v. Leslie* [1991] AC 98).

## 4 Judicial Governance and the Polish Toxic Options Case

The above question could be addressed in reference to the case of the Polish currency toxic options. Since 2008 over 10,000 Polish companies engaged in contracts designed to protect them from a stronger Polish currency złoty. The main economic reason for this strategy was the fact that the value of the Euros they earned from selling goods and services in Europe had continuously been decreasing for last consecutive 5 years. However, the unexpected collapse of the Polish currency since October 2008 has had very serious financial and economic consequences leading to many prospective bankruptcies. The Polish Financial Supervision

[43]Nickalls v. Merry, L.R. 7 H.L. 530, Robinson v. Mollett, L.R. 7 H.L. 802.

[44]Ch. Lloyd's Report 1/1984, p. 614.

Authority (PFSA) estimated that at least 99 Warsaw Stock Exchange-listed companies concluded the option deals in 2008.[45]

Both macro and micro effects were discernible. On the macro level, the rise of unemployment and bankruptcy of so many enterprises, massive loss of the bigger, including the biggest stock exchange listed companies, will have a considerable impact on the whole national economy. On the micro level the prospects of relationship between banks and investors are not clear since many banks had allegedly acted as financial advisors breaching their fiduciary duties and inciting small firms to conclude such toxic derivative transactions, especially toxic currency options, where the banks in fact hedged against the decrease of the Polish currency.[46] The information on risk exposure had not been properly disclosed. Moreover, many contracts notoriously contained some hidden provisions or suffered other serious formal defects. Dissatisfied firms claimed not only misrepresentation, but also more serious defects such as deceit and fraud accompanied by breach of fiduciaries duties by banks' representatives.

Under these conditions two issues should be addressed. Firstly, the question arises whether the case of Polish toxic currency options is a market or government failure. Secondly, under the assumption that there was a real market failure, how should the government and the judiciary respond to the potentially disastrous economic consequences of those contracts for a group of business entities? As to the first question, there seems to be no unanimously accepted answer. Thus, each contract should be scrutinized on an individual basis. This requires control performed by the courts. In fact, the majority of loss-suffering disappointed companies have brought claims against banks, submitting for resolution or invalidation of those option contracts. One of the possible solutions is to adopt the position, that those contracts as bets or contracts for differences were valid but not enforceable. There is no sensible straightforward solution on the level of national contract law, regulated by the Polish Civil Code.[47]

The other option under consideration is the issuing of general legislation rendering the majority if not all option contracts void or voidable, depending on the version of the bill. Three bill proposals have been prepared so far but there is no political consensus as to which one of them should be implemented.

This is not however, the complete *milieu* of the case as the European Union's normative influence should also be taken into account. Poland is a member of the EU since May 2004. In 2006 the European Council adopted the EU's *Markets in Financial Instruments Directive* (MiFID), stipulating minimum requirements of the protection of individual unsophisticated investors. The implementation of the directive would have solved the problem of toxic options provided the contracts

[45]Komunikat KNF z dnia 17 grudnia 2008 r. w sprawie wpływu walutowych instrumentów pochodnych na banki i spółki publiczne, (Announcement of 17.12.2008 on the impact of derivatives on banks and public limited companies, Warsaw 2009), pp. 1–4.

[46]Karkowski (2009), p. 231.

[47]Karkowski (2009), p. 198.

where fraudulent or unbalanced. In other words, if the options contracts had constituted a typical case of market failure, the problem would have been solved by the implementation of the directive. The Polish Government failed to adopt the directive however, thus acting in breach of the EC law. Still the national courts could apply the non-implemented directive while resolving the disputes between banks and investors, according to the constitutional principle of the EU friendly interpretation of the European law, which has been adopted by the Polish Constitutional Tribunal in 2005.[48]

However, the extent of such interpretation would be seriously diminished by the limitations of the principle of horizontal effect, which was adopted by the European Court of Justice, in *Marshall v Southampton and South West Hampshire*, Case 152/84 [1986] ECR 723. In this case the ECJ stated that: "the binding nature of a directive, which constitutes the basis for the possibility of relying on the directive before a national court, exists only in relation to 'each Member State to which it is addressed'. It follows that a directive may not of itself impose obligations on an individual and that a provision of a directive may not be relied upon as such against such a person." How should courts operate under those circumstances? Which model of judicial governance would be the optimal one, which fits best the contemporary complex structure of multilevel legal system? It seems that the model of multilevel international judicial governance could provide with a feasible solution under the assumption that the political process cannot result with an adequate remedy to the market failure.

## 5 The Court as an Impartial Spectator: Towards a Normative Model of Judicial Governance

Those findings could be proven within a light of Sen's concept of normative evaluation and legal analogues in a multilevel global system.[49] In one of his papers A. Sen has correctly observed that social sciences are predominantly based on the legal contractual paradigm. Additionally, he proposed to concentrate on the competitive idea derived from the Smithian "Impartial Spectator" paradigm, when he observed:

> The basic idea is pithily put by Smith in *The Theory of Moral Sentiments*, in the context of judging one's own conduct, as the requirement to 'reexamine it as we imagine an impartial spectator would examine it,' or as he elaborated in a later edition of the same book: 'to examine our own conduct as we imagine any other fair and impartial spectator would examine it.' [...] However, the impartial spectator as a judgmental device has some important differences from the framework that emerges from the analogy with a legal contract. While the contractarian approach attempts to eliminate the influence of vested interests by imagining a contract - in the original position - in which people are unaware of

[48] See Judgment of 11 May 2005, K 18/04.

[49] Sen (2006), pp. 247–266.

> their own exact identities and thus of their own special interests, the Smithian approach of the impartial spectator tries to do this through examining how things would look to a "fair and impartial spectator [. . .]."[50]

Thus, the competitive paradigm is marked by the triadic relationship, which characterizes arbitration and adjudication. The idea is based on the concept of impartiality, objectivity and fairness. Those ideals are not attainable within the world shaped by normative frameworks based on the contractarian paradigm. However, it does not necessarily mean that they are not attainable at all and that the whole idea of impartiality is too idealistic to be useful in real life. It seems that impartiality, objectivity, and fairness are still basic normative presuppositions of any adjudicative process. The legal process should be at least to some extend imbued with those values, corresponding with the idea of the Smithian impartial spectator. The question remains whether such a model of the judicial governance and judicial regulative framework does fit the complex regulatory environment such as financial market and derivative regulation.

The problem of two parties' bargain has been explored by game theory which provides satisfactory models and hypothetical optimum solutions to this problem. If two parties are negotiating in case of monopoly or monopsony, it is regarded as a typical bargaining problem. Is there any satisfactory solution to the problem? It seems that more sophisticated concepts deployed by the game theory doctrines should be analyzed from the perspective of potential solution to the bargaining problem and potential search for the criterion of fair, just exchange in those circumstances. Additionally, the adjudicator cannot rely on the hypothetical bargain in competitive equilibrium because the whole "hold up" problem results from the lack of relevant market. Thus the "hypothetical bargain" successfully implemented in "contract failure" cases is obsolete.

On the other hand, it is necessary to refer to some impartial ideal model of just, fair and efficient bargain in order to check whether the party "in urgent need" is injured by the other party extracting some "excessive benefit or unfair advantage". Whether the benefit is excessive or not, it should be somehow compared to the hypothetical division of surplus from the exchange stemming from the face-to face ideal bargaining process. In order to reconstruct a sound criterion for a fair division of surplus in monopoly, the following solution provided by the game theory may be contemplated. Hence, the problem of a "market failure" could be analyzed from the perspective of potential solution to bargaining problem. The problem of the choice of the terms of contract may be presented as another non-cooperative game, namely Rubinstein's bargaining game.[51]

In this game both players are making proposals (offers and counteroffers) until one of the offers is accepted. The factor of time in which the agreement is reached is taken into account, so that $\delta$ represents the amount of decrease for a party for each period of time. If A offers x, he retains the share $1 - x$. Additionally, the discount of

[50] Sen (2006), pp. 262–263.

[51] Rubinstein (1982), pp. 97–109.

time should be taken into account. In these circumstances the counteroffer from B is more attractive for A than his next offer if it gives $(1 - x)\,\delta$. The game illustrates the thesis that the outcome of the bargaining process is diminishing in time ("the cake is shrinking"), so that the sooner one offer is accepted, the better. This game has a unique subgame-perfect equilibrium:

A offers B: $\delta/(1 + \delta)$ and does not accept any counteroffer from B. B accepts any offer equal or greater than $\delta/(1 + \delta)$ or makes a counteroffer of $(1 - x)\delta$. A receives $1 - x$ or $1/(1 + \delta)$.

The strategy of A is never to accept a counteroffer, taking into account that the B's counteroffer is not larger than $(1 - x)\delta$. The best strategy of B is to take the initial offer. Thus, A makes the offer large enough so that B is not able to make a counteroffer preventing repetition of the same offer. The question arises whether such a game may have a unique efficient solution. If a unique solution was attainable then it would correspond with terms of the hypothetical bargain. The problem of the division of the surplus would thus be solved and the efficient outcome would be assured as R. Coase admitted in *Notes on the Problem of Social Cost*: "It is certainly true that we cannot rule out such an outcome if the parties are unable to agree on the terms of exchange, and it is therefore impossible to argue that two individuals negotiating an exchange *must* end up on the contract curve, even in a world of zero transaction costs in which the parties have, in effect, an eternity in which to bargain".[52]

It is important to note that if the players in Rubinstein's bargaining game had eternity in which to bargain then the game would have had a very appealing characteristic. The model assumes that in special case ($\tau \to 0$) where there is no time interval between the rejection of proposal and a new proposal there is virtually the advantage of the party who makes the offer first. There are no incentives to cheat in this game and no mechanism for sustaining commitments is required. Within time the game converges to Nash bargaining solution. Additionally, the possible asymmetries between the parties result from the different attitudes to the passage of time. In fact, the interpretation of Rubinstein's bargaining game stresses that the more patient party has more bargaining power. The difference does not lie in the bargaining skill because both parties are rational optimizers.

Still, all those characteristics of the Rubinstein game are feasible under the assumption that bargaining is costless. If transaction costs are zero, the lapse of time between offer and counteroffer does not matter. As Coase has rightly observed, the peculiar feature of the zero transaction cost world is that: "when there are no costs of making transactions, it costs nothing to speed them up, so that eternity can be experienced in a split second".[53] This means that the Coasian zero transaction cost world corresponds to the Rubinstein's bargaining game with no time interval between the rejection of proposal and a new proposal. This observation does not

[52]Coase (1990), p. 161.

[53]Coase (1990), p. 15.

exhaust the advantages of modelling a hypothetical bargain in lines of the Rubinstein bargaining game.

There is an additional advantage of this approach being adopted as a part of judicial governance strategy. The result of the game corresponds to the Nash solution to the bargaining problem.[54] The Nash bargaining solution indicates the unique outcome of bargaining process which is efficient and predictable. This means that the parties bargaining in the zero transaction cost world will certainly agree at terms indicated by the Nash bargaining solution. Moreover, the Nash bargaining solution provides the mechanism of distribution of the surplus from cooperation and thus its implementation vindicates the robustness of the Coase theorem. Additionally, the efficiency of such a contract might be taken for granted since the Nash bargaining solution could be characterized as consisting in judicial determination of a unique split of revenue out of infinite number of possible efficient (in the sense of Pareto efficiency) outcomes.

This solution refers to the existence of the single rule *f* selecting a unique point denoted $x =$ where *P* denotes payoff space, *c* denotes conflict point, which corresponds with the position of the party if no contract is agreed. The unique bargaining solution that satisfied those axioms is a function, where *P* is payoff space, *c*—conflict point. The bargaining outcome is represented in utilities $(u_1, u_2)$ The Nash bargaining solution is a function $f(P,c)$ such as:

$$(P, c) \rightarrow f(P, c) = \arg\ \max\ (u_1 - c_1)(u_2 - c_2) \qquad (1)$$
$$x \in P, x \geq c$$

Bargaining solution satisfies four axioms:

- Independence of equivalent utility representation:

If a different von Neumann-Morgenstern representation of players' preferences over bargaining outcomes is chosen, this does not affect the bargaining outcomes in real terms but only its utility representation. In other words, standardization (e.g. multiplying) the outcome has no influence upon result:

$$F_i(P, c) = u_i* \Rightarrow a_i f_i(P, c) + b_i = a_i u_i^* + b_i a_i > 0 \qquad (2)$$

- Symmetry:

If the bargaining problem (P,c) is symmetric, than the solution must assign equal payoffs to both players:

$$\{(u_1, u_2)\ P\ (u_2, u_1)\ P\}\ c_1 = c_2\ f_1(P, c) = f_2(P, c) \qquad (3)$$

- Independence of irrelevant alternatives:

[54]Nash (1950), pp. 155–162.

If $f$(P,c) is the solution to bargaining problem (P,c) and a reduced set of feasible payoff combinations Q, in which $f$(P,c) is still a feasible payoff combination, then it also has to be the solution to (Q,c). This is possible because of the fact that only some irrelevant alternatives are missing:

$$Q\,P\,f(P,c)\;Q\,f(Q,c) = f(P,c) \tag{4}$$

- Weak efficiency (Pareto-optimality):

  Players fully exploit payoff opportunities:

$$x^{'} > f(P,c)\;x^{'}\;X \tag{5}$$

Those axioms characterizing the Nash bargaining solution could be interpreted as the conditions of the fair division or an axiomatic expression of the Smithian idea of impartiality. Within the context of OTC derivative transactions, the idea of regulating or re-drafting contractual terms by the Smithian impartial spectator seems to correspond with the axiomatic assumptions based on the Nash bargaining solution and with the solution itself. The requirements of good faith and fair dealing refer to the universalized conditions of symmetry and independence of both irrelevant alternatives and equivalent utility representation. It has been proved that the Nash bargaining solution provides an exclusive possibility to determine the output of the bargaining process.

Within the normative context the Nash bargaining solution could serve as a criterion of fair exchange against which the court may measure the contract made by parties.

The question however remains whether the normative model of judicial governance has already been deployed within a broader regulatory framework. The case for the court-based regulation seems to be promising on basis of at least two positive theories of regulation, namely the legal origin theory and the incompleteness of law theory. Both models extensively rely on the potential capacities of judge-made-law and judicial regulatory initiative. However, the robustness of those theories has not been examined within a specific context of derivatives and legal attitude towards speculation.

## 6 Conclusion

The normative Coase theorem suggests that the regulation and judicial decision should pursuit efficiency and diminish transactional costs.[55] Derivatives may serve this purpose in two distinctive ways. Derivative transactions might be used as the

[55]Coase (1960), p. 115.

alternative to the efficient breach of contract. As an effect the price volatility does not affect the contract if the contractors are hedged. Thus, the function of the efficient breach is substituted by derivatives, but the outcome of the transaction is probably more efficient because in the absence of litigation some additional transaction costs are avoided. The derivative OTC markets are regulated by soft law enforced in non-jurisdictional way. Under the assumption that two factors shifted derivatives from disregarded set of gambling practices to highly regarded set of financial transactions, both legal and economic aspects are mutually entangled and indispensable. Accordingly, three different scopes of regulation are discernible as a regulatory and evolutionary response to the potential risks related to financial innovation, namely the transaction oriented, the institution oriented, and the market-oriented regulations. It seems that the market-oriented model of regulation has not accidentally been adopted by many jurisdictions recently. Taking the unusual and diversified evolution of derivatives market into account, two lessons should possibly be remembered. Firstly, the financial crisis proved that regulation is necessary and good regulation requires a sound normative theory of both: derivatives and investors' behaviour. Additionally, it seems that the regulatory potential of courts could still play an important, albeit limited, role. Meanwhile the normative theory of regulation seems to favour judicial activism in financial law. On the other hand, the positive theories of regulation do not prove the superiority of judicial institution, albeit they seem to emphasize their important role in acting as interstitial legislators and executors. Thus, the judicial governance remains significant alternative to market and political processes. Its significance should not be overstated however, especially when taking the limits of judicial resources into account. In other words, judges are and perhaps should remain the lawmakers of last resort. In the majority of cases the regulatory framework seems to depend primarily on the quality of regulators, especially public agencies. At the same time the output of the flexible regulatory process should remain under the control of judges so that the principle of rule of law is to be safeguarded. Thus, the quality of regulation will in the future depend on the division of labour between courts and regulators.

## References


Alexander K, Ferran E, Jackson H, Moloney N (2006) Transatlantic financial services regulatory dialogue. Eur Bus Organ Law Rev 7:647–673

Armour J, Deakin S, Sarkar P et al (2008) Shareholder protection and stock market development: an empirical test of the legal origins hypothesis. ECGI Working Paper Series in Law, Working Paper N.108/2008. http://ssrn.com/abstract=1094355

Arrow KJ (1983) Collected papers of K. Arrow. General equilibrium, vol 2. Cambridge

Arrow KJ, Debreu G (1954) Existence of an equilibrium for a competitive economy. Econometrica 22:265–290

Ayres I, Braithwaite J (1992) Responsive regulation: transcending deregulatory debate. Oxford University Press, Oxford

Bator F (1958) The anatomy of market failure. Q J Econ 72:351

Black J (1997) Rules and regulators. Clarendon Press, Oxford, p 33

Black J (2000) Proceduralising regulation. Oxf J Leg Stud 20:297–299
Black J (2008) Forms and paradoxes of principles-based regulation. Capital Mark Law J 3:425–430
Braithwaite J (2002) Restorative justice and responsive regulation. Oxford University Press, New York
Calabresi G (1982) A common law for the age of statutes. Cambridge
Calabresi G, Melamed AD (1972) Property rules, liability rules and inalienability: one view of the Cathedral. Harv Law Rev 85:1089–1128
Coase RH (1960) The problem of social cost. J Law Econ 3:1–44
Coase RH (1990) The firm, the market and the law. University of Chicago Press, Chicago
Deakin S, Hughes A (1999) Economic efficiency and the proceduralisation of company law. Company Financ Insolvency Law Rev 3:169
Elul R (1995) Welfare effects of financial innovation in incomplete markets with several consumption goods. J Econ Theory 11:73
Gunningham N, Grabovsky P (1998) Smart regulation. Clarendon Press, Oxford
Hermalin BE, Katz AW, Craswell R (2007) Contract law. In: Polinsky AM, Shavell S (eds) Handbook of law and economics, vol 1. Amsterdam, pp 7–8
Hu HTC (1993) Misunderstood derivatives: the causes of informational failure and the promise of regulatory incrementalism. Yale Law J 102(1457):1464–1467
Huang PH (2000) A normative analysis of new financially engineered derivatives. South Calif Law Rev 75:491–503
Kaplow L (1992) Rules versus standards: an economic analysis. Duke Law J 42:557–629
Karkowski P (2009) Toksyczne opcje - od zaufania do bankructwa (Toxic options- from trust to bankruptcy). GreenCapital.pl, Warsaw, p 231
Kyle AS (1989) Informed speculation with imperfect competition. Rev Econ Stud 56:317
Lenoble J, Maesschalck M (2003) Toward a theory of governance: the action of norms. Kluwer Law International, The Hague, p 244
Mahoney PG (1997) The allocation of government authority: the exchange as regulator. Va Law Rev 83:1453
Medjaoui K (1996) Les marchés à terme dérivés et organisés d'instruments financiers. Etude juridique, Mimeo, Thêse, Paris
Morgan B, Yeung K (2007) An introduction to law and regulation. Cambridge University Press, Cambridge
Nash JF (1950) The bargaining problem. Econometrica 18:155–162
Nonet P, Selznick A (1995) Law and society in transition. University of California Press, Berkeley, Ch. 4
Posner RA (2003) Economic analysis of law. Aspen Publishers, New York
Rubinstein A (1982) Perfect equilibrium in a bargaining model. Econometrica 50(1):97–109
Schauer F (1991) Playing by the rules. Clarendon Press, Oxford, pp 47–52
Schwark E (1990) Spekulation–Markt-Recht. Zur Neuregelung der Börsentermingeschäfte. In: Baur F, Hopt KJ, Steindorff E, Mailändered KP (eds) Festschrift für Ernst Steindorff zum 70. Geburstag am 13. März 1990. Walter de Grutyter, Berlin, p 473
Sen A (2006) Normative evaluation and legal analogues. In: Drobak JN (ed) Norms and the law. Cambridge University Press, Cambridge, pp 247–266
Stout LA (1999) Why the law hates speculators: regulation and private ordering in the market for OTC derivatives. Duke Law J 49:765–770
The Financial Services Authority (2009) The turner review. A regulatory response to the global banking crisis. March, pp 86–88
Walras L (1874) Elements d'economie politique pure. L. Corbaz, Lausanne
Yeung K (2004) Securing compliance. Hart Publishing, Oxford

**Mariusz J. Golecki** Lodz and Warsaw. Professor at the University of Lodz, Department of Legal Theory and Philosophy of Law, Director of the Institute of Comparative and Interdisciplinary Research in Law, University of Lodz, Faculty of Law and Administration, ul. Kopcinskiego 8/12, 90-232 Łódź, Poland, mjgolecki76@gmail.com. Fields of Interest: Economic Analysis of Law, Behavioural Law and Economics, Legal Philosophy and Legal Theory, Theory of the EU law, Comparative Law.

# Privatizing Income Security for Disabled Workers: Unintended Consequences and Labour Market Imbalances

**Ann-Sophie Vandenberghe**

**Abstract** The need to address the overuse of public schemes for sickness benefits and disability insurance, to reduce labour distortions caused by such programs, and the desire to shift the schemes' emphases away from mere maintenance of the benefits towards rehabilitation of the disabled, have motivated the Dutch Government to privatize income security for disabled workers. In the Netherlands, private employers are currently forced to continue to pay wages in case of worker sickness or disability for a period of 2 years. The purpose of this chapter is to consider the question whether the benefits of such policies outweigh the costs. Nowhere in Europe has the rate of growth of self-employed, temporary and flexible work relationships increased as it has in the Netherlands since the privatization movement. While it appears that the situation of many workers has improved (i.e. public disability enrolment numbers have decreased), the situation of many other workers has deteriorated (i.e. the group of employees who have no permanent employment has increased).

## 1 Introduction

A typical feature of modern Dutch labour law is that private employers are obliged to continue to pay the wages of workers who are unable to perform their work due to sickness or disability for a period of 2 years.[1] Such wage guarantee exists also in other European labour laws, but nowhere in Europe does the wage guarantee in case

[1]Article 7:629 Civil Code Inability to work due to sickness, pregnancy or the delivery of a child
- 1. Where the employee is unable to perform the contracted work due to sickness, pregnancy or the delivery of a child, he remains entitled to 70 % of his wages fixed in money terms for a period of 104 weeks [. . .].

A.-S. Vandenberghe (✉)
Rotterdam Institute of Law and Economics (RILE), Erasmus School of Law, Rotterdam, The Netherlands
e-mail: vandenberghe@law.eur.nl



K. Mathis, A. Tor (eds.), *Law and Economics of Regulation*, Economic Analysis of Law in European Legal Scholarship 11,
https://doi.org/10.1007/978-3-030-70530-5_12

of sickness or disability last as long as in the Netherlands. This feature—the 2-year wage guarantee in case of sickness or disability—has not always been part of Dutch labour law. It is the result of a structural reform program of the public scheme of sickness benefits and disability insurance, which started in the Netherlands at the end of the twentieth century. This reform is considered to be the 'privatization' of income security for disabled workers, although it should be noted that it is only a partial privatization. The private employer must continue to pay wages but 'only' for 2 years. If it turns out that the worker is still unable to perform work after these 2 years, the employer is entitled to dismiss the worker who then becomes eligible for public insurance disability benefits.[2] Moreover, it should be noted that the Dutch privatization of 'sick pay' went hand in hand with the privatization of worker re-integration. Private employers are also forced by law to provide services to reintegrate disabled workers into the workforce. In the context of this contribution, income security for disabled workers means an entitlement to continued wage payments as well as an entitlement to workplace accommodations and work adaptations to enable disabled workers to stay in paid working relationships.

The purpose of this chapter is to consider the question whether the benefits of the privatization policy outweigh the costs. A law & economics approach to public policy analysis using the Kaldor-Hicks efficiency framework will be applied, according to which *all* possible advantages and disadvantages of a legal rule should be taken into account.[3]

The chapter proceeds as follows. In Sect. 2, the meaning of privatization in the context of income security for disabled workers from a law & economics perspective will be explained. In law & economics terms, privatization in this context means a shift from a public system of forced transfers towards a private system of forced transfers to provide income security. Within a law & economics frame of thinking it is important to distinguish a voluntary transfer from a forced one, irrespective of whether the latter takes places place within a public or private scheme. Section 3 considers the benefits and shortcomings of a forced *public* scheme of income security in general. The origins and measures of the *privatization* operation, which took place in the Netherlands starting at the end of the twentieth century, will be outlined in Sect. 4. An overview of the advantages and disadvantages of the Dutch privatization operation will be given in Sect. 5. Of particular concern is the large increase in self-employed, flexible and temporary work relationships in the Netherlands since the privatization operation. This flexibilization (or de-integration) trend is remarkable because for a long time, starting with Ronald Coase's article "The Nature of the Firm" of 1937, the idea has been that permanent employment (firm integration) is used to save on the transaction costs of using the external, flexible

---

[2]Article 7:670 Civil Code Termination ban

- 1. An employer may not terminate the employment agreement during the time that the employee is unable to perform his work due to sickness, unless this inability:

a. has lasted for at least 2 years.

[3]De Geest (2015).

labour market. Current policy discussions, legislative proposals and initiatives in the Netherlands all purport to restore the balance on the labour market. Different strategies are possible to tilt the balance towards permanent employment, and this chapter envisions the strategy of making permanent employment inherently attractive again as a way to organize and coordinate work. To that end we draw in Sect. 6 on the wisdom of the first Dutch Law on the Employment Contract of 1907 which has a scheme for the allocation of risks in case of non-performance of the work contracted for, which strikingly corresponds to what we would expect under an efficient legal system, and which provides for the application of 'no work, no pay' as the main rule and 'no work, yet pay' as the exception.

## 2 Privatizing Income Security: Classification and Meaning from a Law & Economics Perspective

The inability to perform work due to disability or illness is problematic for risk-averse workers who depend on their income from work to provide for themselves (and their families). A social security system deals with this problem by providing income security to disabled workers usually through a public scheme of sickness benefits and disability insurance. From a law & economics perspective, social security can be classified as a 'forced' transfer system as opposed to a 'voluntary' transfer system. The distinction between a voluntary transfer of private property rights (through contract, and with consent of both parties) and a forced transfer (whereby one party, the initiative-taker, consents, and the other party, the forced one, has not given his prior consent) is a pillar of the law & economics literature.[4] Why can social security be classified as forced transfer system? Because the government takes the initiative to generate a positive externality for workers in the form of income security (without their prior individual consent), but forces the workers (and their employers) in return to pay social security contributions. This 'forced transfer' system is similar to that which applies to public roads, the military defense system and the judicial system. The government takes the initiative to provide these benefits to its citizens but forces them in return to pay a compensation for it, in the form of taxes. How then is a legal obligation of private employers to continue to pay wages to their workers who are unable to perform work due to sickness or disability to be classified? It is also a forced transfer, a private obligatory service. The law forces private employers to provide income security to their own workers. This type of forced transfer system is similar to the military draft: the government forces the draftee to provide services and in return it offers military protection to the draftee and their family for life. Hence, social security (public sickness benefits and disability insurance) as well as the legal obligation of private employer to continue to pay wages to disabled workers have in common that they are both forced transfer

[4]Calabresi and Melamed (1972).

systems of income security: one is a public system of forced transfers, the other is private system of forced transfers. Shifting from a public to a private system of forced transfers is what is meant by 'privatization' of income security for disabled workers. The real alternative to 'forced' transfers are 'voluntary' transfers. In the latter case, the provision of income security is based on the consent of the party who provides it (the initiative-taker) and on that of the party who receives it. Examples are private charity, voluntary family support (provided that the support is not based on a legal obligation to support family members) and of course, market insurance contracts providing income support in case of disability.

## 3 The Public Scheme of Income Security: Benefits and Shortcomings in General

All peoples throughout all of human history have faced the uncertainties brought on by unemployment, illness, disability, death and old age. In the realm of economics, these inevitable facets of life are said to be threats to one's economic security. Traditional sources of economic security are: assets, labor, family and charity. After World War II, welfare states adopted a public system of social insurance to provide economic security to workers. Workers are insured against the risk of income loss due to unemployment, disability, and old age. Compared to the traditional sources of economic security, social security provides huge benefits to workers. The system does not make a distinction between deserving and undeserving recipients. It establishes a routine that applies to all cases in which people lack an income through paid labor, regardless of the reason. An entitlement is created which does not have to be justified on a case-by-case basis. However, social security policy may not always be as benign as originally thought: social insurance programs may distort work incentives and harm the economy.[5] Elderly persons who receive social security benefits have those benefits taxed if they continue to work. They are given incentives to withdraw from the labour force. A reduced number of workers reduces the output of the economy. Unemployment compensation subsidizes the marginal allocation of time from work to leisure. Economic output is smaller. The search for work is prolonged. Disability compensation generates false claims and false medical certification of disability. Reasonably healthy people withdraw from work. Again, economic output is smaller and the material situation of individuals declines. Existing social insurance programs could start to change eligibility criteria and benefits levels in such a way as to preserve their insurance function with minimal harm to the economy. But, social insurance programs have an inherent feature which makes it inherently difficult to solve all problems: they are collectively funded and bureaucratically administered. According to Jennifer

[5]Rottenberg (1986).

Roback Morse, this makes it difficult to address problems of (a) moral hazard and rent-seeking, (b) common pool problems and (c) the entitlement mentality.[6]

***Moral Hazard and Rent-Seeking*** The governmentally operated program must have well-defined eligibility criteria, benefit formulae and the like. The program must be administered by a bureaucracy with a minimum of discretion in the application of these rules. In an ideal system, all people who are rightfully entitled to the benefit, would receive the benefit. Furthermore, all who are not rightfully entitled would not receive the benefit. In other words, there would be no type I or type II errors. However, it is not possible to create a set of rules that will fully cover every case. Some discretion is necessary in practice. Moral hazard is a substantial problem in income support programs. For a person can make himself eligible for the insurance benefit by reducing his work effort. Moreover, the transfer payment, is a higher than normal return, created through political means. Economists define 'rent' as an economic return in excess of the normal market rate. The existence of these rents create the incentive of rent-seeking. The potential recipient expends some resources, perhaps simply in the form of foregoing earning power, in order to qualify for the transfer. Persons make themselves eligible for the transfer without meeting the implicit eligibility criteria, namely, being without funds through no fault of their own. When they present themselves to the social insurance system, the person they encounter may know perfectly well that they do not meet the implicit contractual standard of the program. But because they meet the explicit, readily measurable eligibility criteria the bureaucrat has little choice but to approve the transfer. The bureaucrat might feel quite confident that an applicant for aid is a shirker, but they could not prove it. They might not be able to quantify or even articulate their reasons. In a bureaucratically administered program, all of the tacit information about whether a person is simply shirking, or really is in need, is lost; all the tacit knowledge about a person's specific situation and character is lost to the system.

***Common Pool Problem*** A common pool resource is one which belongs to a group. The tragedy of the commons is a particular problem for common pool resources. Everyone in the group has a right to use the resource freely, with little or no accountability to the rest of the group. Similarly, tax funded social insurance programs have a common pool resource quality to them, and so are susceptible to the tragedy of the commons. The person who spends the money is not the person who earned it, or who raised it. The money flows to the social insurance bureaucracy, independently of the actions of any particular bureaucrat. Bureaucrats do not have, and cannot have, a personal stake in how the money is spent. The programs are bureaucratically administered, by people who are accountable neither to the recipients of the transfers nor to the contributors (donors). The agency is accountable only to the procedures that have been created for it by the legislature.

---

[6]Roback Morse (1997).

***The Entitlement Mentality*** There is one further problem to the creation of an entitlement that depends on only a few, readily measureable criteria. Roback Morse calls this problem "the entitlement mentality".[7] People come to take seriously the claim that all that matters is whether they meet the legally stated, explicit criteria of the program. If they are entitled to the benefit, why no claim it? Indeed as more and more people take part in the program, the person on the margin of participating might argue to himself: "Everyone else is doing it. If I do not take the opportunity to use this program, I will feel like a sucker." In the entitlement mentality, the Prisoner's problem emerges dramatically. Why should I restrain myself from opportunistic behaviour, when I know that other people are not restraining themselves?

## 4 Privatizing Income Security for Disabled Workers: The Case of the Netherlands

This section provides a short overview of the origins and the measures of the Dutch policy reform program towards privatization of income security. By the end of the twentieth century, the high level of public disability insurance enrolment was considered to be one of the major social and economic problems of the Netherlands; indeed, the Netherlands was characterized as the country with the most out-of-control disability program of OECD countries.[8] The Netherlands had one of the highest disability enrolment numbers in Europe and failed to re-integrate a sufficient number of disabled workers into the labour market. In 1996, the Dutch government decided to structurally reform its public disability insurance system. Under the then prevailing public scheme of sickness benefits and disability insurance, employees who were unable to perform work, were entitled to public sickness benefits from the first day of sick leave onwards, and for a period of 52 weeks. After this period they were entitled to public disability benefits (maximum 80% of last wages) until retirement. At the time of introduction of the system (1967), the expectation was that about 200,000 persons would make use of it.[9] However, in 1991, more than 900,000 people received public disability benefits. The public system was heavily overused. The Netherlands has a relatively healthy population and has a well-developed health care system. How then is it possible that so many people are unable to perform work due to sickness or disability? It has been said that the very high enrolment level into the Dutch public disability program in the second half of the twentieth century was the result of the system being used to smoothen the transfer from an industrial economy to a service economy. Indeed, inability to perform work may be due to sickness and disability (physical and mental impairments) but it may also be due to the depreciation of labour market skills in

[7]Roback Morse (1997), p. 541.

[8]Burkhauser et al. (2008).

[9]Westerhout (1995), p. 1.

combination with the absence of a system that helps workers to retrain or re-school to attain the skills necessary for the new economy.

In 1996, the Dutch Government decided to reform its public scheme of social security system by creating an environment in which individual employers and employee would take more responsibility in dealing with the problem of disability. To that end, a legal duty for private employers to continue to pay wages in case of employee sickness for a period of 52 weeks was introduced.[10] Only after this initial period of 52 weeks (during which the employer had to continue wage payment), were disabled employees entitled to enroll in the public disability insurance program. However, this measure did not seem to lead to a reduction in the enrolment into the public disability insurance program. In a new round of program restructuring (2002), the Dutch Government required employers to rehabilitate and accommodate their sick workers.[11]

At the beginning of 2003, 993,000 people received public disability benefits, the highest number ever, both in absolute terms as well as in relative terms: 13 out of every 100 persons of the labor population. This led to a call for further regulation. In 2004, the duty to continue to pay wages was extended to 104 weeks.[12] Obligations to rehabilitate employees have become stricter. The employer is obliged to take efforts to rehabilitate (reintegrate) disabled workers either within the company or outside. A failure to provide sufficient effort to re-integrate worker is sanctioned by a duty to continue to pay wages during a third year of disability.

From this background it becomes clear that the Dutch privatization of 'sick pay' went hand in hand with the privatization of worker re-integration. Private employers are forced by law to provide services to reintegrate disabled workers into the workforce, either within the firm or outside the firm. Prior to the reform operation, a public administrative agency was responsible for providing services to help worker to rehabilitate. It is safe to say that the public agency was not very well able to help workers to reintegrate.

## 5 The Privatization Policy in the Netherlands: Advantages and Disadvantages

At first sight, the measures taken seem to have been effective without causing too many negative effects.[13] The number of people who receive public disability benefits has indeed decreased both in absolute as well as in relative terms.[14] In June 2016, 810,000 persons received public disability benefits: 10 out of every 100 persons of

[10]Law on the Extension of the Obligation to Continue Sick Pay (Wulbz, 1996).

[11]Law on the Improvement of Gatekeeper or Gatekeeper Protocol (WVP, 2002).

[12]Law on the Lengthening of the Obligation to Continue Sick pay (Wulbz, 2004).

[13]Friperson and de Jong (2013).

[14]Central bureau of statistics Netherlands (cbs).

the labour population.[15] Of course, an evaluation of the new policy solely in terms of disability enrolment numbers would be too narrow. According to a Kaldor-Hicks framework for normative policy analysis *all* advantages and disadvantages must be taken into account.

A reduction of public disability enrolment numbers may indeed be a sign that the group of disabled workers benefits from this privatization operation. Where previously, they would have been 'written off', being paid in order not to work (by receiving permanent disability benefits), they are now enabled to continue to stay in a paid work relationships. In that case, the Dutch economy as a whole benefits because more people are available and motivated to perform work.

It can however be argued that the actual presence of work-limiting impairments, such as mental disorders, cancers and heart diseases, cannot be influenced by employers. Why then impose upon private employers the obligation to provide income security? Because there are reasons to believe that private employers have the opportunity to reduce the consequences of these impairments.[16] Diseases which may have completely impaired workers from performing work in former times, no longer present a complete hindrance. Private employers are able to implement work adaptations, such as flexible working hours, assistive technologies, or facilitate vocational rehabilitation.[17] Yet, the costs of complying with these tasks differ between private employers. In general, large companies are better able to perform these tasks than small and medium-sized companies. After all, large companies benefit from possibilities to pool risks and from economies of scale. The problem for small and medium-sized companies is to some extent solved through the possibility to insure the risk of sick pay by private insurance contracts. Such market insurance is available in the Netherlands.

A further and probably more important concern with private sick pay is that it may decrease employment, particularly of workers with poor health. Similar to employment protection legislation, the protection benefits workers who have a job but may deteriorate the position of those workers who are looking for a job. Employers may try to avoid costs and financial risks by not hiring statistically 'risky' employees, the most vulnerable group of workers. To some extent, non-discrimination laws may address this problem.

Another criticism of the system is that it does little to incentivize workers to resume work in case of sickness or disability. It should be noted, that while the law merely entitles workers to 70% of their wages when they are unable to perform the work contracted for, most collective labour agreements have provisions, which entitle the workers to 100% of their wages during the first year of absence.

The most worrisome effect is that since the privatization operation, the rate of self-employed and flexible work relationships has nowhere grown in Europe as

[15]Total labour population in 2016: 8.9 million.

[16]Koning (2016).

[17]Autor (2011), pp. 4–5.

much as in the Netherlands.[18] It may be argued, that employers in the Netherlands have responded to private sick pay by an increased use of self-employed, temporary or flexible contracts. Flexible forms of work are on the rise in the Netherlands. The group of workers without permanent employment has increased. In 2016, more than 1.8 million people—i.e. over one-fifth of the Dutch labour force—were in flexible employment, up from merely 1.1 million in 2003. Between 2003 and 2016 the number of on-call (standby) and replacement workers more than doubled, while the number of permanent workers declined from nearly 5.7 million (2003) to just over 5.2 million (2016).[19] In June 2015, TNO Innovation for Life and Statistics Netherlands published an overview report on the dynamics of the Dutch labour market, with a focus on flexibilisation of labour. According to the report, in 2014, the proportion of Dutch employees with flexible work relationship increased again, to 22% (2004:15%). The proportion of the self-employed without personnel also increased in the same period (from 8 to 12%), with the combined result that the proportion of permanent jobs dropped to 62% (73% in 2004).

**Imbalance in the Dutch Labour Market**

Compared to permanent workers, workers who are in a temporary or flexible work relationship have lower levels of work security and are often not adequately compensated for this lower security by means of higher wages. They get employment contracts of fixed duration, usually for one year; temporary employment contracts can be renewed but according to Dutch law employees are entitled to a permanent contract after two renewals.[20] Employers are free to renew temporary contract and what we see is that they rather replace the temporary worker by another temporary worker after two renewals, than to give a permanent contract. The result is an unbearable imbalance on the Dutch labour market. On the one hand, we see employers going through great effort to maintain disabled workers employed by accommodating workplaces to their needs; on the other hand, the very same employer easily dismisses a temporary worker who is very willing and able to perform the work contracted for. A real tragedy is when temporary workers work very hard for their employers thinking that it will increase their changes to obtain a contract renewal or a permanent contract, but that in reality the extra efforts provided do not increase their chances. For certain types of jobs, it has become standard practice of firms to have them only performed by flexible, temporary or self-employed workers. It is a remarkable trend. For a long time, the idea has been that by making use of long-term, permanent employment contracts, firms can reduce costs relative to the use of external markets to contract for labour.[21] In Coase's analysis firms vertically integrate as long as the costs of internal organisation are lower than the transaction costs of using markets. De-integration occurs when the

---

[18]Blanchflower (2015).

[19]Central bureau of statistics Netherlands (cbs).

[20]The Work and Security Act (Wet Werk en Zekerheid, 2015).

[21]Coase (1937).

costs of internal organisation are higher than the costs of using the market. There are no reasons to believe that the costs of using the external, temporary labour market have decreased substantially during the past decades in the Netherlands. Hence the flexibilisation (or 'de-integration') trend is probably due to an increase in the costs of using internal organization (i.e. permanent employment contracts) to organize and coordinate work.

Current labour policy discussions and legislative proposals and initiatives in the Netherlands all concern the question of how to restore the balance in the labour market.[22] Some of these proposals purport to make flexible employment forms more expensive hoping that it will tilt the balance back towards permanent employment. This is however a risky strategy. It makes the use of flexible forms of employment less attractive but does not make the use of permanent employment inherently more attractive as a form to coordinate and organize work. In the remainder of this chapter, an alternative strategy is envisioned. It asks how the use of permanent employment contracts can be made attractive again. To that end, we will draw on the wisdom of the first and original Dutch Law of the Employment Contract (1907) which provides for a economically sensible allocation of the risk of non-performing, whereby the regime of 'no work, no pay' is considered as the main rule, and 'no work, yet pay' as the exception.

## 6 Who Should Bear the Risk That the Work Contracted for Is Not Performed? 'No Work, No Pay' or 'No Work, Yet Pay'?

### *6.1 Risk Allocation for Work Not Performed: An Economic Analysis*

Employment contracts are part of the way in which the production of goods and services is organized. Goods and services do not fall out of the sky but require the cooperation between numerous inputs, including capital, entrepreneurship and labour. An employment contract is a special kind of contract, but it is a contract, a consensual relation between two parties involving an exchange: work in return for pay. It is a way to mobilize labour. The benefit for the employer is the work that is performed; the benefit for the employee is the wage that is being paid. Just as in the case of other contracts, events may prevent the promisor (employee) to perform the work contracted for or may render performance more costly for them. The law of employment contracts has to solve the question: Who should bear the risk that the work contracted for cannot be performed?

Three different regimes are possible:

[22] E.g. The Law on the labour market in balance (Wab, 2020).

1. The risk can be absorbed entirely by the employee: this is the case when the employer can claim damage compensation for non-performance;
2. The risk can be split between the parties: this is the case when the employer cannot claim damage compensation whereas the employee cannot claim the counter-performance (i.e. the payment of the wage); a shorthand notification for this arrangement is 'no work, no pay': the employer does not receive the benefit from the work being performed whereas the employee does not receive the benefit of being paid;
3. The risk can be transferred entirely to the employer: this is the case when the employer cannot claim damage compensation whereas the employee can claim the counterperformance (i.e. the payment of the wage); a shorthand notification for this arrangement is 'no work, yet pay': the employer does not receive the benefit of the work being performed, whereas the employee does receive the benefit of being paid.

Each one of these arrangements allocates the risk of contractual non-performance in a different way. Under regime 1, the risk is allocated to the employee; under regime 2 ('no work, no pay'), the risk is shared between the parties; under regime 3 ('no work, yet pay'), the risk is allocated to the employer. Efficiency requires the risk to be absorbed by whichever party can prevent it or bear it more cheaply.[23]

The employment contract is a contract with specific economic features: *ex ante* contract drafting cost are high (uncertainty about the future), *ex post* contract drafting costs are high (bilateral monopoly problems), monitoring costs are high (problem of non-observability), and enforcement costs are high (problem of non-verifiability).[24] Given these features, it has been argued in the law & economics literature that arrangement 1 ('the risk is entirely allocated to the employee') is not an efficient regime. Why is that employees should not pay damage compensation to the employer when work is not performed? From an incentive point of view, it would be problematic to impose a legal sanction (i.e. damage compensation) on employees for not performing their work. Employees are usually paid a fixed wage, independent of their productivity. Because monitoring costs are high, employees decide to a large extent themselves how hard they will work. What motivates an employee to do more than what is minimally required? Many employees are intrinsically motivated. They work hard, because they like working hard or because they want to do good for their employer. The application of expectation damages in case work has not been performed, would compensate the employer for their lost profits. Under this damage measure, a hard working employee (who produces more on any given day) would have to pay more than a low productivity worker. Paradoxically, an employee could mitigate the expected sanction, *ex ante*, by lowering his work effort. In other words, expectation damages would destroy the intrinsic motivation to work hard.[25] The

[23]Posner and Rosenfield (1977) and White (1988).

[24]Williamson et al. (1975) and Epstein (1984).

[25]De Geest et al. (2001).

need to preserve intrinsic motivation in employment contracts provides an argument for the application of the rule of 'no work, no pay' in case of contractual non-performance rather than to make the employee liable for not performing the work contracted for. In other words, the efficient rule is regime 2, which is to split the risk in case work is not performed: the employer does not obtain the benefit of the work and the employee does not obtain a wage. A system of 'no work, no pay' gives employees incentives to perform the work contracted for without destroying intrinsic motivation to work hard.

In which cases would regime 3 ('no work, yet pay') be efficient? Such regime is efficient in cases in which the employer is able to exercise control over the situation so as to allow an employee who is willing to perform to perform. For example, a late delivery or a machine breakdown are situations the consequences of which are under the control of the employer. The employer is better able to prevent such events from occurring or to deal with the consequences of such events occurring. To give employers incentives to take measures to avoid that employees cannot work, a rule of 'no work, yet pay' should apply. In addition, such a rule would be efficient in cases in which the employer is in a better position to insure the employee against income losses when he cannot perform due to reasons which are outside his control.

## *6.2 Risk Allocation Under the First Dutch Law of the Employment Contract (1907)*

The first Dutch Law of the Employment Contract dates back to 1907. The law deals with the allocation of risk in case of non-performance of work in three articles (articles 1638b, 1638c and 1638d of the Civil Code). The then adopted scheme appears to follow an efficiency pattern.

Article 1638b (old) Dutch Civil Code specified: "No wages are due for the period during which the employee has not performed the work contracted for".[26] The main rule is that when no work has been performed there is no entitlement to wages, i.e. 'no work, no pay'. Hence, the main rule is *not* that employees have to pay damage compensation to their employers when work is not performed. This corresponds to what is economically optimal because when employees would have to pay damage compensation, it would destroy intrinsic motivations for employees to work hard.

The next two articles were exceptions to the main rule and constitute a 'no work, yet pay' regime as they entitled workers to their wage in cases in which work has not been performed.

Article 1638c (old) Dutch Civil Code specified: "The employee remains entitled to his wages for a relatively short period of time if he has not been able to perform the

[26]Meijers (1924), p. 113.

work contracted for due to sickness or an accident."[27] Also, when the employee is legally obligated to fulfill a legal duty, like voting or a marriage, which cannot be done in their free time, they would be entitled to their wages. It is important to note that the employee was entitled to his wage, but only for a relatively short period of time (some days or weeks at most).

Article 1638d (old) Dutch Civil Code specified: "The employee remains entitled to their wages if they were prepared to perform the work, but the employer has not made use of it due to their fault or due to another cause which, reasonably, should be for account of the employer."[28] Examples are a late delivery of goods or a machine breakdown.

## *6.3 An Expansion of the Scope of 'No Work, Yet Pay' and the Attractiveness of Permanent Employment*

'No work, no pay' featured as the main rule under the original Dutch Law of the Employment Contract (1907). It is an economically sensible rule because it gives employees incentives to perform the work contracted for without destroying intrinsic motivation to work hard. The rule is the best guarantee to maximize the value of the employment contract. It makes from employment an attractive way to organize work in the firm because for employers it enhances the expectation that the work contracted for will actually be performed and will be performed well. The 1907 law provided for some exceptions to the main rule, but the exceptions in which 'no work, yet pay' applied were very limited in scope.

During the past decades, the scope of the rule of 'no work, yet pay' has been expanded in the Netherlands. The current rule laid down in art 7:629 of the Civil Code entitles employees who are unable to perform work due to sickness and disability to continued wages, not for relatively limited time period, but for a period of 2 years. To the employer, an expansion of the 'no work, yet pay' regime implies a loss of control over his work organisation; it decreases his expectation that the work contracted for will actually be performed. The very long period during which the worker is entitled to their wages (without performing), does little to incentivize the worker to prevent inability to perform work due to sickness or accident (when possible) or to incentivize employees to resume work quickly (when possible). Of course, the employer can hire replacement workers when a worker is absent, but hiring replacements may be costly, especially in a small labour market. Moreover, a worker for whom the performance of work is costly for other reasons than sickness (e.g. they find their work unpleasant or there is an alternative activity which they value more than the work contracted for) may strategically claim to be unable to work due to sickness to avoid the application of the rule of 'no work, no pay'. This

[27]Meijers (1924), p. 114.
[28]Meijers (1924), p. 122.

worker may think 'if my colleague who is unable to work due to sickness can stay at home for two years while being paid, why can't I stay home for a couple of days while being paid?' Control of the stated reasons for absence by the employer is possible, but is costly and may undermine employer and employee trust. All in all, it may make the use of permanent employment less attractive as a way to organize and coordinate work because it decreases employer expectations that the work contracted for will actually be performed. This may be an explanation for the current flexibilisation ('de-integration') trend. Restoring the value of 'no work, no pay' as the main rule in employment contracts may be a fruitful way of thinking about how to make the use of permanent employment attractive again.

## 7 Conclusions

With the privatization of income security for disabled workers, the Dutch government had particular goals in mind. In particular, it wanted to redress the overuse of the public scheme of sickness benefits and disability insurance, the labour market distortions caused by it, and to shift the emphasis in the public scheme away from mere maintenance of the benefits towards rehabilitation of disabled workers. Private employers are obliged to continue to pay the wages of disabled workers for a period of 2 years and are obliged to provide services to re-integrate disabled workers back in the workforce. The group of disabled workers and the Dutch economy may have benefited from this privatization policy. Where previously, disabled workers would have been 'written off', being paid not to work (by receiving permanent disability benefits), more workers with impairments are now able to stay in paid work relationships and contribute to the output of the Dutch economy. There is however a big downside. Nowhere in Europe has the rate of self-employed, flexible and temporary work relationships grown as much as in the Netherlands after the privatization operation. Current Dutch policy, legislative initiatives and proposals are all oriented at tilting the balance towards permanent employment. We drew on the wisdom of the first and original Dutch law on the employment contract (1907) for thinking about a strategy of how to make permanent employment attractive again. The 1907 law provided for a regime of 'no work, no pay' as the main rule for the allocation of risk in case the work contracted for is not performed. From an economic point of view, it is an efficient rule because it incentivizes worker to perform the work contracted for without destroying intrinsic motivations to work hard. By expanding the scope of the regime of 'no work, yet pay' during the last decades, private employers may have lost control over the organization of work. In particular, the expectation that the work contracted for in the employment contract will actually be performed has decreased. It is a possible explanation for the current flexibilisation ('de-integration) trend. Restoring the value of the rule of 'no work, no pay' may be a fruitful way of thinking about how to make the use of permanent employment attractive again.

## References

Autor D (2011) The unsustainable rise of the disability rolls in the United States: causes, consequences, and policy options. NBER working paper no. 17697

Blanchflower D (2015) Flexibility@work 2015 self-employment across countries in the Great Recession of 2008-2014, Randstad yearly report on flexible labor and employment. http://www.dartmouth.edu/~blnchflr/papers/flexibilitywork_2015.pdf

Burkhauser R, Daly M, de Jong P (2008) Curing the Dutch Disease: Lessons for United States Disability Policy. Michigan Retirement Research Center working paper 2008-188, Ann Arbor, Michigan

Calabresi G, Melamed A (1972) Property rules, liability rules and inalienability: one view of the Cathedral. Harv Law Rev 85:1089–1128

Coase R (1937) The nature of the firm. Economica 4:386–405

De Geest G (2015) Any normative policy analysis not based on Kaldor-Hicks efficiency violates scholarly transparency norms. In: Hatzis A, Mercuro N (eds) Law and economics: philosophical issues and fundamental questions. Routledge, New York, pp 183–202

De Geest G, Siegers J, Vandenberghe AS (2001) The expectation measure, labor contracts, and the incentive to work hard. Int Rev Law Econ 21:1–21

Epstein R (1984) In defense of the contract at-will. Univ Chic Law Rev 51:947

Friperson R, de Jong P (2013) Effecten van loondoorbetaling bij ziekte: een internationale verkenning [Effects of wage continuation in case of sickness: an international exploration]. TPEdigitaal 7:35–48

Koning P (2016) Privatizing sick pay: does it work? IZA World of Labor

Meijers E (1924) De arbeidsovereenkomst (Wet van den 13den Juli 1907 STBL. 193). Tjeenk Willink, Haarlem

Posner R, Rosenfield A (1977) Impossibility and related doctrines in contract law: an economic analysis. J Leg Stud 6:83–118

Roback Morse J (1997) The modern state as an occasion of sin: a public choice analysis of the welfare state. Notre Dame J Law Ethics Pub Policy 11:531

Rottenberg S (1986) The enemy of society. Society 23:19–22

Westerhout E (1995) Arbeidsongeschikt of Werkloos? [Work disability or unemployed?]. Research memorandum no 120. CPB Netherlands Bureau for Economic Policy Analysis, The Hague

White M (1988) Contract breach and contract discharge due to impossibility: a unified theory. J Leg Stud 17:353–376

Williamson O, Wachter M, Harris J (1975) Understanding the employment relation: the analysis of idiosyncratic exchange. Bell J Econ Manag Sci 6:250

**Ann-Sophie Vandenberghe** Rotterdam. Associate Professor at the Rotterdam Institute of Law and Economics (RILE), Erasmus School of Law. Burgemeester Oudlaan 50, Sanders Building (L) area 7.21, P.O. Box 1738, 3000 DR Rotterdam, The Netherlands, Tel + 31 (0)10 4082186. vandenberghe@law.eur.nl. Fields of Interest: Comparative Law and Economics, Contract Law and Economics, Employment and Consumer Contracts in particular.

# Regulating Innovation

**Markus Schreiber**

**Abstract** Innovation is one of the main drivers of economic growth. It is therefore no surprise that governments are increasingly trying to promote innovation through legal instruments. For this reason, the contribution analyses the interplay of law and economics in the regulation of innovation. The author examines the economic rationale behind such regulation. He assesses in which cases governments have legitimate reasons to interfere in the market economy in order to promote innovation. Furthermore, the legal possibilities and limits of influencing innovation are examined. In addition, the discussion includes the problems and economic consequences of legislators' attempts to promote innovation. Finally, the contribution attempts to identify "best practices" for the furtherance of innovation through regulatory means.

## 1 Introduction

Innovation[1] is one of the main drivers of economic growth.[2] This holds especially true for Switzerland, a country without natural resources that relies on a highly developed, specialised economy.[3] It is therefore no surprise that governments, including the Swiss Government,[4] are increasingly trying to promote innovation

[1]Many attempts have been made in a variety of academic fields to properly define the term "innovation". See Swann (2009), p. 25: "a bewildering variety of definitions". A proper discussion is beyond the scope of this contribution. See Schreiber (2019), pp. 12 et seq.

[2]Furman et al. (2002), p. 900; Swann (2009), pp. 234 et seq.; Verspagen (2011), p. 487; OECD (2015), p. 17.

[3]Porter (1990b), pp. 318, 321 et seq.

[4]Which has established, inter alia, the State Secretariat for Education, Research and Innovation.

M. Schreiber (✉)
Faculty of Law, University of Lucerne, Lucerne, Switzerland
e-mail: markus.schreiber@unilu.ch

 
K. Mathis, A. Tor (eds.), *Law and Economics of Regulation*, Economic Analysis of Law in European Legal Scholarship 11,
https://doi.org/10.1007/978-3-030-70530-5_13

through legal instruments. However, the exact interplay of regulation and innovation is not yet fully understood.[5]

To this end, the contribution will examine the economic rationale behind the regulation of innovation. It will assess in which cases governments have legitimate reasons to interfere in the market economy in order to promote innovation. It will also discuss to which extent the arguments in favour of regulating innovation differ from the traditional rationale of market regulation.

Subsequently, the legal possibilities and limits of promoting innovation will be examined. Which boundaries are set by constitutional law, e.g. the principle of equality or the principle of market neutrality? Which legal instruments are commonly used in an attempt to promote innovation?

In addition, the analysis will discuss the problems and economic consequences of legislators' attempts to promote innovation. Which factors contribute to a flawed regulatory framework for innovation or wrong incentives for market actors?

Finally, the contribution will attempt to identify "best practices" for the promotion of innovation through regulation. It will highlight examples of both well-functioning as well as misguided attempts to regulate innovation. It will also address how the legislator's approach towards innovation has changed over the decades.

## 2 The Rationale Behind the Regulation of Innovation

### *2.1 Overview*

The role of governments in promoting innovation can hardly be overstated.[6] From aviation to the Internet, examples of technologies whose development was largely shaped by governments' involvement are not hard to find. Despite this, from a legal perspective, market participants are *a priori* free in the degree to which they pursue innovation. In a liberal market economy, innovation is—at least in theory—primarily a task for private market actors, not the government. For this reason, any government interference in the market to promote innovation requires some form of legitimation. Before taking a look at the legal requirements for valid measures in Sect. 3, this section outlines the economic rationale behind such interventions.

---

[5]For early English-language research on the subject matter, see OTA (1979), p. 45; Stewart (1981); Ashford et al. (1985).

[6]Also cf. the general importance of government action and legal frameworks for economic activity described by Drezner (2008), pp. 33 et seq.

## 2.2 *Market Failure*

### 2.2.1 Introduction

Any type of regulation will, at least to some degree, be based on real or perceived market failures.[7] Thus, it is not surprising that market failures also constitute the main economic rationale to justify innovation policies.[8] Market failure is the inability of the market to deliver the optimal result,[9] with the "optimum" typically defined by either the Pareto-[10] or the Kaldor-Hicks-[11] efficiency. This section discusses those market failures that are most relevant for innovation policy.[12]

### 2.2.2 Externalities

Externalities (also called "spillover effects") occur when one market participant's actions positively or negatively affect other market participants, without any payment of remuneration or damages, respectively.[13] Positive externalities benefit others without the originator receiving any compensation. For this reason, there is not enough of an incentive to generate these positive externalities.[14] Negative externalities hurt others without the damaging party having to pay any compensation. For this reason, there is not enough of an incentive to avoid these negative externalities.[15] Externalities may be very far-reaching through space[16] and even time.[17]

---

[7]Cf. Stewart (1981), p. 1263; Veljanovski (2010), p. 20.

[8]OECD (2015), p. 27. Also cf. Swann (2009), pp. 257 et seq.; Edler and Georghiou (2007), pp. 956 et seq.; Lundvall and Borrás (2011), p. 613; Schreiber (2019), p. 111.

[9]Encyclopædia Britannica, "Market Failure", available at www.britannica.com/topic/market-failure.

[10]A market is Pareto-efficient when the resources and goods could not be redistributed without deteriorating at least one market participant's position, Swann (2009), p. 257.

[11]A market is Kaldor-Hicks-efficient when no redistribution is possible in which the market participants that gain an advantage from the redistribution could (at least in theory) compensate those that suffer from it, and the redistribution would still be (net) advantageous. See Hicks (1939), p. 706.

[12]Also cf. Schreiber (2019), pp. 111 et seq.

[13]Cf. Swann (2009), p. 260; Veljanovski (2010), p. 21.

[14]De Mesquita (2016), p. 100.

[15]De Mesquita (2016), p. 100.

[16]For example, when carbon emissions from a German energy utility may have effects on villages in Peru due to their climate change impact, see the ongoing case of Saúl Lliuya v. RWE, Superior Court (Oberlandesgericht) Hamm, case no. 5 U 15/17.

[17]This is also called a "temporal spillover", see Huber (2017). Also cf. the discussion of the rights of future generations at Gruber (2011) and Mathis (2011).

Negative externalities may become an important source of legitimation for innovation policy when innovation is seen as a potential remedy for the negative effect. For example, subsidies for renewable energy or other resource-efficient technologies may be legitimized by the diminishing effect on the negative externalities of greenhouse gas emissions.

Positive externalities with an impact on innovation are often created through research, especially basic research.[18] Since basic research is hard to monetize, there may be insufficient such research in the absence of government funding.

### 2.2.3 Monopolies

Due to the absence of competition, monopolies negatively affect the functioning of markets. However, the exact role monopolies play with regards to innovation are subject to debate. On the one hand, monopolies may have an insufficient incentive to produce innovations, since they do not face competition and can therefore expect monopoly rents without being innovative. On the other hand, companies may need sufficient size and funds to develop certain innovations.[19] Still, many times, the regulation of monopolized economic sectors (or the break-up of monopolies) has also been expected to promote innovation.[20]

### 2.2.4 Information Deficits

Information deficits may hinder the diffusion of innovations when the consumers are not sufficiently informed about the benefits of the innovative product. Governments may then seek to improve consumer's decision-making through information-based regulation. For example, the law may require producers of certain products to highlight their energy efficiency using standardized labels.[21] This allows consumers to recognise the most innovative products.

Public information campaigns may also be targeted at the negative effects of less innovative products, such as the EU's and many member states' information campaigns on the energy inefficiency of traditional light bulbs, which preceded their eventual ban.

---

[18] Ewers (1990), p. 150.

[19] Cf. Fritsch (2018), p. 164, however, also cf. the differentiated analysis; Fritsch (2018), pp. 195 et seq.; Wieddekind (2002), pp. 155 et seq.; Veljanovski (2010), p. 21.

[20] For example, this has been one of the stated goals of the European Union's harmonization policy towards a liberalized, regulated electricity market, cf. Directive (EU) 2019/944 recital 9, OJ 2019 L 158/125.

[21] These often include an easy-to-read colour scheme and a grade system, e.g. from G (worst efficiency) through A (best efficiency). See, for example, the European Union's labelling system as implemented under Regulation (EU) 2017/1369, OJ 2017 L 198/1.

### 2.2.5 Other Rationales

In addition to these neo-classical categories of market failures, supplementary rationales may justify innovation policy measures. In recent years, certain market characteristics have been identified which may hinder innovation, while not falling into any of the traditional market failure categories.[22] For example, in certain market sectors, there may not be enough pressure to adapt to new circumstances, thus stifling innovation.[23] Furthermore, path dependency may occur where certain technologies or processes have become so deeply entrenched as to leave little room for different approaches.[24]

Even in the absence of any "market imperfections",[25] governments and legislators may still find it justified to pursue innovation policies. In recent decades, general public interests have been used as a rationale for market interventions despite the lack of any neo-classical market failure.[26] Under this reasoning, innovation policy may support the development of new processes and technologies to improve, *inter alia*, public health (e.g. through research funding for new pharmaceutical products[27]), the environment (e.g. through favourable legal framework conditions for renewable energy producers[28]) or even traffic in cities (e.g. through incentives for electric vehicles including access to free parking spaces and bus lanes[29]).

Such public interests become especially relevant when the regulations' goal is not to promote innovation, but to curtail it. This has, for example, been the case for certain genome-related research and its applications. In Switzerland, the Gene Technology Act[30] stipulates various rules and criteria to prevent possibly harmful consequences resulting from genome editing. Such regulation that specifically prohibits certain applications of innovative technology constitutes a serious impediment

---

[22]Cf. OECD (2015), pp. 26 et seq.

[23]OECD (2015), p. 26, describes this as "inertia".

[24]Stack and Gartland (2003), A well-known, albeit controversial, example is the QWERTY computer keyboard layout, cf. David (1985) and the criticism at Liebowitz and Margolis (1990). While there is now considerable evidence that the QWERTY layout is actually a poor example of path dependencies, it may still serve as a simple way to illustrate the problem, as readers will immediately think of the many adjustments in keyboard production, software adaptation, user training etc. necessary to switch to a new standard.

[25]This is the term used at OECD (2015), p. 26, to denote those market circumstances that do not constitute neo-classical "market failures".

[26]Cf. Feintuck (2010); Schreiber (2019), p. 122.

[27]See the Swiss Federal Government's masterplan to strengthen biomedical research and technology, BAG (2013), pp. 76 et seq. Also cf. the discussion of innovation BAG (2013), pp. 31 et seq.

[28]Such as in Switzerland under Articles 15 et seq. Energy Act (Energiegesetz, SR 730.0).

[29]For a discussion of different monetary and non-monetary incentives for electric vehicles, see Gong et al. (2020). However, one may argue that the lack of a charging infrastructure and the fact the existing infrastructure has been optimised for internal combustion engines constitute a path dependency and thus a "market imperfection" in the sense described above.

[30]Gentechnikgesetz, SR 814.91.

to the economic freedom[31] of the relevant market actors.[32] It will therefore require high-ranking public interests such as the protection of life and health to justify the intervention.[33]

## 2.3 *Legitimacy*

### 2.3.1 Introduction

An economic or public interest-based rationale for the innovation-related government intervention is an important step towards a valid regulatory design. However, any government intervention will prove disadvantageous to certain market actors (e.g. those who want to use the innovation that has been curtailed, or those who do not offer the innovative technology that has been favoured by certain legislation). For this reason, beyond simple legal validity, additional sources of legitimisation may be necessary to ensure public acceptance of the measures.

### 2.3.2 Democratic Legitimacy

One of the most important sources of legitimacy is the democratic process, which traces the legislator's and executive's power directly back to the constituents.[34] However, many innovative sectors also pose very technically challenging regulatory questions that are often not addressed by the democratically elected legislators themselves. Instead, technical rules are often implemented in regulations or ordinances by the executive branch. While, depending on the applicable national laws, these typically require a basis in a parliamentary act,[35] the executive often has significant leeway as to the final regulatory design.

Another common practice is to have private regulatory bodies issue technical regulations. This may be beneficial when the government lacks sufficient knowledge on the topic to be regulated, which may often be the case with very innovative technologies or processes. The legislator may directly reference the private ruleset, thereby incorporating it into law. However, private rules may also simply be a response to legislative inactivity. In certain sectors, the law even prescribes that the legislator should only act when private rulemaking bodies cannot sufficiently

---

[31]Such as under Art. 27 of the Swiss Federal Constitution (Bundesverfassung, SR 101).

[32]See the discussion in Sect. 3.4 below.

[33]For the example of genome editing, Swiss constitutional law specifically demands that humans and the environment are to be protected from abuses of genome editing, Art. 120 Swiss Federal Constitution. Also cf. Schreiber (2019), pp. 120 et seq.

[34]Cf. Luhmann (2005), pp. 151 et seq. and 155 et seq.

[35]For the Swiss Federal Council, see Art. 182 para. 1 Swiss Federal Constitution.

regulate the issue at hand.[36] This is even more difficult when the public-private rulemaking takes place outside of the traditional national setting, as is the case with certain transnational rulemaking bodies.[37]

The question of democratic legitimacy is also more problematic when regulatory agencies have significant discretionary powers and can act independently from the democratically elected parliament.[38] This is especially relevant for innovation policy since many business sectors that are expected to be very innovative are also regulated by such independent regulatory agencies (e.g. the pharmaceutical[39] and energy[40] sectors).

### 2.3.3 Legitimacy Through Standardized Processes

Whenever the executive branch has a margin of appreciation in implementing innovation policy measures, market actors that do not benefit from these measures may feel disadvantaged. This may be the case when funding schemes do not have sufficient resources to support all eligible projects, or when regulatory benefits such as exemptions from certain provisions are granted only to selected projects.

In these cases, acceptance of the decision by all parties involved will depend to a large degree on whether they find the decision-making process to be fair and transparent.[41] When those that have not benefited from the support measures (or that have been affected by innovation-curtailing measures) believe that all of their arguments have been heard and that they stood a fair chance in a non-partisan process, they will be less likely to feel discriminated against. These procedural standards are often guaranteed in constitutional and human rights provisions.[42] However, well-designed innovation policy provisions will exceed the minimum standard of such procedural guarantees.

Transparent procedures are particularly relevant for innovation policy measures, since any decision to support one particular innovation will inevitably put other technologies or processes at a disadvantage, the same way that any curtailment of an innovation will benefit the existing, less innovative market actors. When private rulemaking bodies introduce technical norms, these will have a higher legitimacy

[36]For the Swiss electricity sector, see Art. 3 para. 2 Electricity Supply Act (Stromversorgungsgesetz, SR 734.7).

[37]Cf. Dingwerth (2005), pp. 71 et seq.

[38]Cf. Jones (1989), pp. 413 et seq.; Maggetti (2010), pp. 2 et seq.

[39]In Switzerland, by the Swiss Agency for Therapeutic Products swissmedic.

[40]In Switzerland, by the Federal Electricity Commission ElCom.

[41]For an exhaustive treatment of the subject, see Luhmann (2005); Also cf. Hirschi (2018), pp. 229 et seq.

[42]E.g., Art. 29 Swiss Federal Constitution, Art. 6 European Convention on Human Rights, SR 0.101.

when the private bodies represent a larger part of the market, and when different types of market participants are represented.[43]

# 3 Legal Options and Limits

## *3.1 Introduction*

Any innovation-related regulation will ultimately have to be implemented in the form of some legal instrument. Even direct monetary instruments such as subsidies will need to have a basis in law. At the same time, the law also sets limits as to how innovations may be regulated: Administrative decisions have to be made in accordance with the law, and the legislator itself is at least bound by constitutional and sometimes international law.

This section discusses both the legal options as well as the legal limits of innovation policy. However, to understand which legal instruments are available, it is first necessary to understand the different functions that the law may serve with regards to innovation.

## *3.2 Functions of the Law*

### 3.2.1 Overview

In German legal literature there is a dedicated area of research focusing on the law's functions with regard to innovation—legal innovation sciences (*rechtswissenschaftliche Innovationsforschung*).[44] The following overview largely follows the categorization proposed by these scholars but includes two additional categories (see Sects. 3.2.4 and 3.2.6).[45] Any innovation-related measure may serve several of these functions at the same time. Also, the same innovation will most often be subject to a variety of legal provisions, some of which may serve conflicting functions.[46]

---

[43]This is a problem with norms introduced by certain industry associations that, for example, do not include the consumers' perspective. Cf. Schreiber (2019), pp. 273 et seq.

[44]Hoffmann-Riem and Schneider (1998), pp. 396 et seq.; For an overview of this research area, see the volumes of the series Schriften zur rechtswissenschaftlichen Innovationsforschung. Nomos, Baden-Baden.

[45]This amended categorization has been published in Schreiber (2019), pp. 89 et seq.

[46]For example, any provision that serves an enabling or stimulating function will conflict with any provisions that serve a limiting function, Schreiber (2002), p. 235; Schreiber (2019), p. 90.

### 3.2.2 Enabling Function

The enabling function of the law serves to create space for innovative technologies or processes. It concerns the possibility to legally implement the innovation in the first place. For example, the Swiss Federal Act of 23 December 1959 on the Peaceful Use of Atomic Energy (which has now been replaced[47]) made the use of nuclear fission to create electricity legally possible for the first time. Before the introduction of this new law, international law would have prevented Swiss energy utilities from producing nuclear energy without the Swiss Government's involvement, since nuclear fuel could not be freely traded and Switzerland did not have uranium resources of its own.[48]

The enabling function may become relevant whenever prohibitory regulation[49] would otherwise prevent the innovation's implementation. Some authors even argue that the guarantees of economic freedom generally demand that the legal framework allows for innovative products and processes.[50]

### 3.2.3 Stimulating Function

The stimulating function exceeds the enabling function as it not only provides room for the innovation to be legally implemented, but even promotes its implementation over other, less innovative options.[51] It therefore presents larger challenges with regards to the economic freedoms, since other market participants with—at least from the legislator's perspective—less innovative products are not supported. This potentially creates a disturbance in the market.

Measures to stimulate innovation may either be aimed at specific technologies or processes, or they may pursue the goal of raising the general "innovation output" of a national economy or a specific market sector. In many cases, more specific measures will cause greater market disturbances, due to their discriminatory nature.

### 3.2.4 Enforcement Function

The existing legal research on innovation assumes that innovation can only be incentivized, but not "prescribed" by law.[52] However, recent legislative trends are

[47]By the Nuclear Energy Act, SR 732.1.

[48]Schreiber (2019), p. 91.

[49]See Hofstetter et al. (2014), p. 42.

[50]Hoffmann-Riem and Schneider (1998), pp. 396 et seq.; Schreiber (2002), p. 235; Cf. Schreiber (2019), p. 91.

[51]Cf. Schreiber (2002), p. 242; Hoffmann-Riem and Schneider (1998), p. 396; Also cf. Ashford and Hall (2011), p. 272.

[52]Cf. Hoffmann-Riem and Schneider (1998), p. 396; Schreiber (2002), p. 242.

starting to put this assumption into question. For example, energy efficiency regulations often prescribe a maximum energy consumption for specific products.[53] In this case, a certain level of innovation in terms of energy efficiency is prescribed by law. However, the exact means to reach this energy efficiency level are left to the market participants. Other energy efficiency regulation is even stricter and prescribes a certain amount of, e.g., insulation, renewable production etc.[54]

Under such regulation, there is no longer simply a legal incentive to be more innovative. Instead, a certain level of innovation is directly prescribed by binding law.[55] For this reason, it seems more appropriate to no longer include these examples in the stimulating function, but instead to speak of an "enforcement function".[56]

### 3.2.5 Limiting Function

The legal functions introduced so far aim to promote innovation. At the same time, the law also serves an important limiting function with regards to innovation. The law must ensure that innovative technologies, processes or business models do not have an overly negative impact on public health, the safety and economic well-being of workers, or other important public interests. This may be especially obvious in connection with potentially dangerous technologies such as nuclear energy or genome editing.

It may, however, also be important to curtail the negative impact of, for example, new business models such as Uber and Airbnb. These innovative businesses compete in market sectors that are typically subject to regulation. It must therefore be ensured that existing regulations are not circumvented. Also, some innovative businesses may use unusual employment models that replace employees with supposedly self-employed contractors. In these cases, legal scrutiny as to the actual employer-employee relationship seems necessary, even if it interferes with the innovative business model.[57]

---

[53] See Annex II of Regulation (EG) Nr. 1275/2008, OJ 2008 L 339/45, as amended by Regulation (EU) Nr. 801/2013, OJ 2013 L 225/1.

[54] In Switzerland, the Cantonal model laws on energy (Mustervorschriften der Kantone im Energiebereich, MuKEn) include such provisions. See, for example, Art. 1.17 para. 2, Art. 1.29 MuKEn 2014 (available at www.endk.ch/de/energiepolitik-der-kantone/muken). However, the model laws are not directly applicable laws, but only valid to the extent that a Canton incorporates them into its respective law.

[55] Schreiber (2019), pp. 92 et seq.

[56] See Schreiber (2019), pp. 93 et seq.

[57] For a discussion of such new businesses, see Katz (2015) and Tremblay-Huet (2018).

### 3.2.6 Blocking Function

The limiting function discussed above strives to minimise the negative impact of innovations. This means that the innovation can still be introduced to the market, but may become subject to certain regulations and may not be fully implemented to the degree that the innovator originally envisioned.

However, sometimes the law may prohibit the innovation altogether. This is currently the case in many countries with regards to human genome editing.[58] Historically, the ban of biological and chemical weapons through international law can serve as another example.[59]

In these cases, the law's function is no longer to limit the negative side effects, but to ban the innovation altogether. It therefore seems justified to no longer include these examples in the limiting function, but to instead speak of a blocking function of the law.[60]

### 3.2.7 Conflict Resolution Function

The final legal function to be discussed here is also the most basic function of the law: to resolve conflict. In the context of innovation, this means that the law resolves conflicts between the innovative technology, process or business model and the existing options.

As a historic example, the installation of electric power lines in Switzerland in the late nineteenth century led to conflicts with the existing telephone and telegraph lines. To protect these established technologies, the Swiss Federal Telegraph Directorate and later the Federal Act on the Installation of Telegraph and Telephone Lines[61] decided the conflict in favour of the telegraph and telephone lines.[62] In such instances, the conflict resolution function is closely related to the limiting function.[63]

However, when the conflict is resolved in favour of the innovative technology, the conflict resolution function may also serve to stimulate innovation.[64] For example, innovators may be exempt from liability or the options to bring legal claims against the innovators may be limited by law.[65]

[58] In Switzerland, this is prohibited by constitutional law, Art. 119 para. 2 lit. a Swiss Federal Constitution.

[59] The Protocol for the Prohibition of the Use in War of Asphyxiating, Poisonous or other Gases, and of Bacteriological Methods of Warfare (Geneva Protocol), SR 0.515.105, was signed on 17 June 1925.

[60] Schreiber (2019), pp. 96 et seq.

[61] Bundesgesetz betreffend die Erstellung von Telegraphen- und Telephonlinien, AS 11 251.

[62] Wyssling (1946), pp. 120 and 276.

[63] Schreiber (2019), p. 99.

[64] Schreiber (2019), p. 99.

[65] Hoffmann-Riem and Schneider (1998), p. 397.

When serving to resolve conflict, the law may also simply afford certain conflict resolution mechanisms, without any prior bias towards either the established or the innovative technology, process or business model.[66] Even in these cases, the conflict resolution function may also stimulate innovation when it increases the social acceptance[67] of innovations and helps to shorten approval procedures or other legal disputes.[68]

## 3.3 *Legal Instruments*

### 3.3.1 Introduction

Any number of different instruments may be used to pursue the goals laid out in the section above. It must also be noted that these instruments may be used in combination with one another and that they may serve more than one of the functions described above. Still, this section will name some of the most frequently used instruments for each of the functions.

### 3.3.2 Enabling Instruments

As the enabling function's implementation is directly related to the prohibitory regulation existing in each specific case, there are few legal instruments that could be named as classical examples for this function. One exception are legal standards, which are often used in an enabling function.[69] For example, the laws on electronic signatures have created the possibility to offer innovative digital signatures for documents for the first time.[70] In the absence of such laws, any innovative digital signature would have little value if it were not acknowledged under procedural law.[71]

---

[66] For example, the German legislator has introduced a conflict resolution entity for conflicts resulting from the legislation on renewable energy, the Clearingstelle EEG/KWKG, www.clearingstelle-eeg-kwkg.de/.

[67] See Wüstenhagen et al. (2007).

[68] Schreiber (2019), p. 99.

[69] Schreiber (2019), pp. 126 et seq.

[70] In Switzerland, this is implemented inter alia in the Federal Act on certification services in the area of the electronic signature and other digital certificate applications (Bundesgesetz über die elektronische Signatur, SR 943.03).

[71] For a thorough discussion of the innovation-related effects of digital signature regulation (in German), see Schreiber (2002). In Switzerland, the use of digital signatures is governed by the different procedural laws, see AS 2016 4651, pp. 4661 et seq.

### 3.3.3 Stimulating Instruments

The stimulating function has triggered the development of the most diverse range of legal instruments that are specific to innovation. Starting with the least intrusive measures, they may simply consist of normative ideas that are communicated in order to spark innovation. In this context, a specific idea may be communicated to the wider public in the hope that market participants will strive to implement it.[72] In German-speaking countries, the word "*Leitbild*" is used for these ideas, a word that may be roughly translated as "mission statement" or "paradigm", depending on the context, but that literally means "guiding image".[73] Such an innovation-related *Leitbild* is the "paperless office".[74] This term alone inspires market participants to imagine which steps would have to be taken to reduce the amount of paper used in an office. Thus, without any further explanation, ideas such as remote access to documents, digital signatures and open source online publications are invoked. Such *Leitbilder* may be introduced in legislation. For example, the Swiss cities of Zurich and Lucerne have implemented the *Leitbild* of a "2000 Watt Society"[75] in their municipal laws.[76]

Governments may also try to build up innovation clusters, i.e. areas that combine research and education institutions, innovative companies and the necessary infrastructure. Examples are the Boston Area and Silicon Valley in the United States[77] and the "Swiss Innovation Park" Switzerland Innovation.[78]

Beyond mere information and the build-up of infrastructure, the government may also gently "nudge" the market participants towards more innovative choices. The concept of nudging has been widely discussed[79] and is also used to promote innovation. An example of this can be seen in the colour-coding schemes used in energy efficiency labels.[80]

---

[72] Schreiber (2019), pp. 127 et seq.

[73] The word has also been discussed in English-language innovation research, see Kuusi and Meyer (2002).

[74] This term itself has been in academic use since at least the early 1980s, and the underlying ideas may date back to at least the 1960s, see Herschler and Slany (1982).

[75] A society in which the average annual per capita energy consumption is 2000 Watt or less. This Leitbild has first been formulated at the Swiss Federal Technical Institute (Eidgenössische Technische Hochschule) Zurich in the late 1990s, see www.local-energy.swiss/ueber-uns/geschichte.html#/.

[76] Art. 2ter para. 2 Gemeindeordnung der Stadt Zürich, AS 101.100; Art. 2 para. 2, Art. 3 Energiereglement Stadt Luzern, sRSL 7.3.1.1.1.

[77] For a discussion of US innovation clusters, see Baily and Montalbano (2018).

[78] www.switzerland-innovation.com/start .

[79] The seminal publication on this is Thaler and Sunstein (2008). For a discussion in this Springer series, see Mathis and Tor (2016).

[80] See note 104 supra.

Financial support for research and innovators is another commonly used instrument to promote innovation.[81] While this is not a legal instrument itself, financial support schemes must have a basis in law.[82]

The legislator may also set technological or process standards.[83] This is especially relevant for innovations whose diffusion depends on a prior build-up of infrastructure or a sufficient number of market participants offering certain services.[84] For example, the legislator may stipulate that all electric vehicle charging stations must include certain types of charging technology. This will allow consumers with different electric vehicle models to charge at any charging station, thereby dramatically increasing the number of charging stations available to any electric vehicle user.[85] This may help convince consumers to overcome "range anxiety"[86] when deciding whether to purchase an electric vehicle.

Intellectual property law may serve as an important tool to promote innovation.[87] In particular, patent law is an area of law primarily designed to stimulate (technological) innovation.[88] The idea behind patent protection is that if the innovator did not have the exclusive right to use their idea at least for a certain period of time, there would not be enough of an incentive to innovate. Any other market participant could immediately copy the innovation at a lower price, not having incurred the costs of research and development.[89] While significant criticism has been targeted at this idea,[90] intellectual property rights still provide a major financial incentive to innovate.[91] The innovation-stimulating effect of patent law is mostly confined to the initial invention,[92] but expectations of future (patent-protected) profits may also drive efforts to ensure actual diffusion in the market. At the same time, the reduced number of competitors that may implement the innovation due to the patent protection may also slow down diffusion.[93] Patent law offers the advantage of potentially

---

[81] Cf. Stewart (1981), pp. 1322 et seq.; OECD (2015), pp. 122 et seq.; Schreiber (2019), p. 137.

[82] See, for example, the Swiss Federal Act on the Promotion of Research and Innovation, SR 420.1.

[83] Scott (2010).

[84] Cf. Swann (2009), pp. 82 et seq.

[85] Schreiber (2019), p. 138.

[86] See Noel et al. (2019) and Xu et al. (2020).

[87] Cf. Mandel (2005).

[88] However, also see the highly relevant discussion of an alternative, morality-based justification for intellectual property at Merges (2019), pp. 84 et seq.

[89] Cf. Swann (2009), pp. 104 and 107 et seq.

[90] For an overview of the discussion, see Merges (2019) as well as the other contributions in the same volume.

[91] See, despite the criticism they voice with regard to patent protection, Shavell and van Ypersele (2001), p. 527; Also cf. Horowitz and Lai (1996); for innovation to combat climate change, Kim (2011).

[92] Hoffmann-Riem (2016), p. 434; Schreiber (2019), p. 140.

[93] Oppenländer (1977), pp. 369 et seq.; Also cf. Swann (2009), pp. 109 et seq.; Schreiber (2019), p. 140.

benefiting any invention, thereby being technologically neutral and open for any new developments.[94]

It has been mentioned before that markets that are less competitive may not offer the most innovation-friendly environment.[95] For this reason, competition law may serve an innovation-stimulating function. However, it may be difficult to distinguish between competition-damaging, illicit behaviour on the one hand and spectacular market success due to a disruptive innovation on the other hand.[96] Successful innovators will inevitably have a monopoly position on the innovation, at least initially.[97] For this reason, the legislator and regulatory agencies must ensure not to involuntarily stifle innovation.

A much more direct approach to promote innovation might involve a preferential treatment under the regulatory regime. This is also known as an "innovation waiver".[98] In Switzerland, energy law allows for such waivers.[99] Under Art. 1 para. 4 of the Low-Voltage Installations Ordinance,[100] the Federal Department of the Environment, Transport, Energy and Communications or, in lesser cases, the Federal Inspectorate for Heavy Current Installations may grant exemptions from certain provisions of the ordinance if "they prove to be obstructive for technical development".[101] For innovative digital financial enterprises (so-called "fintechs"), Art. 6 para. 2, Banking Ordinance[102] provides for a "regulatory sandbox".[103] Under this provision, such companies are exempt from the banking regulation. However, the provision does not define what a fintech is, but instead sets a threshold for the overall sum of public deposits, below which the financial institution is not said to run a "commercial activity" that would fall under the ordinance. Thus, the "sandbox" is technologically neutral and may extend to companies that are not actually fintechs.

Since government agencies buy large amounts of goods, public procurements may offer an opportunity to promote innovation.[104] This is especially true where public procurement law allows for the procurement decision to be (partially) based on the innovative character of the good. In Switzerland, the revised Public

[94]Schreiber (2019), p. 140.

[95]Sections 2.2.3 and 2.2.5 supra.

[96]Cf. the critical analysis by Teece and Coleman (1998).

[97]Wieddekind (2002), p. 162.

[98]Ashford et al. (1985), pp. 443 et seq.; also cf. Stewart (1981), pp. 1307 et seq. In the United States, a less traditional example are the State Innovation Waivers under section 1332 of the Affordable Care Act.

[99]Further examples can be found at Schreiber (2019), p. 142.

[100]Niederspannungs-Installationsverordnung, SR 734.27.

[101]"[. . .] erweisen sie sich für die technische Entwicklung als hinderlich [. . .]".

[102]Bankenverordnung, SR 952.02.

[103]Regarding the former version of the provision (that included a para. 3), see Schreiber (2019), p. 143, with further references.

[104]Cf. Schreiber (2019), pp. 143 et seq. As an early historical example; Lundvall and Borrás (2011), p. 600, mention the investments by King Henry VIII in iron cannons.

Procurement Act,[105] which entered into force on 1 January 2021, explicitly allows for the criterion of "innovativeness"[106] to be considered in the decision-making process (Art. 29 para. 1 revised Public Procurement Act).

Taxes and other financial burdens placed on undesired market behaviour may stimulate innovation in order to avoid them.[107] For example, the Swiss $CO_2$ levy on fossil thermal fuels under Art. 29 et seq. $CO_2$ Act[108] creates incentives to implement innovative technologies and processes to reduce fuel consumption. Governments may also follow an inverse approach and grant exemptions or reductions for certain levies. For example, some Swiss Cantons exempt electric or other low emission vehicles from the motor vehicle tax.[109]

The legislator may also create new markets by establishing tradeable permits or certificates that encourage innovation.[110] For example, certificates for renewable electricity create a monetary reward for the producers, while tradeable carbon permits encourage the use of innovative low-carbon technologies so that permits that are not needed can be sold on the market.

While it is often assumed that regulation will drive up costs and thus stifle innovation,[111] traditional regulative law that prohibits or prescribes certain behaviour may also have a stimulating effect on innovation. This is also referred to as "Porter's Hypothesis".[112] For example, environmental regulation will likely stimulate innovative technologies that reduce pollution, in order for companies to comply with the stricter regulations.

---

[105]Bundesgesetz über die öffentliche Beschaffung, AS 2020 641. The current version can be found under SR 172.056.1.

[106]"Innovationsgehalt".

[107]Veljanovski (2010), p. 32; also cf. Stewart (1981), p. 1310; Schreiber (2019), p. 147.

[108]$CO_2$-Gesetz, SR 641.71. Under the $CO_2$ Act, the term "Brennstoff" (thermal fuel) includes fossil fuels used for the generation of heat, the production of light, the production of electricity in thermal facilities or the operation of combined heat and power plants, but not motor fuels, Art. 2 para. 1, para. 2 $CO_2$-Act. However, producers and importers of motor vehicles may be subject to the sanction payments under Art. 10 et seq., Art. 13 $CO_2$ Act.

[109]E.g. § 19ter Ordinance on Taxes and Fees for Motor Vehicles, Bicycles and Ships (Verordnung über Steuern und Gebühren für Motorfahrzeuge, Fahrräder und Schiffe) of the Canton of Solothurn, BGS 614.62, which exempts "electric vehicles and solar vehicles" from the tax.

[110]Cf. Veljanovski (2010), p. 31; Stewart (1981), pp. 1373 et seq.; Schreiber (2019), p. 148.

[111]Cf. with regards to the debate in the USA Jaffe et al. (1995), pp. 153 et seq.

[112]After Porter (1990a), p. 88; for Switzerland in particular, see Porter (1990b), p. 323; also cf. Ashford and Hall (2011), pp. 276 et seq.; OECD (2011), pp. 54 and 60; Schreiber (2019), pp. 150 et seq.

### 3.3.4 Enforcement Instruments

One popular instrument to enforce a certain level of innovation is known as "technology forcing".[113] Under this approach, the law sets requirements, e.g. for a category of products, that cannot be fulfilled without the use of more innovative technology.[114] Often, the legislator will gradually increase the requirements to slowly push less innovative technologies out of the market over time.[115]

Instead of merely prescribing a certain level of innovation, the legislator may also enforce the use of specific innovations. For example, under Swiss energy law, certain high voltage power lines must be constructed as cables[116] instead of overhead lines, unless that would exceed a maximum cost increase value specified by law.[117]

### 3.3.5 Limiting and Blocking Instruments

The legal instruments used to limit negative side effects of innovation often correspond with traditional administrative regulation. They may range from *ex ante* regulation such as approval procedures and license requirements to *ex post* regulation such as liability provisions.[118]

However, the regulation of innovation may rely to a larger extent on self-governance by the industry, as the legislator may not possess enough knowledge of the innovation to effectively regulate it.[119] Some forms of "regulated self-regulation"[120] or other hybrids between traditional and self-regulation may also be used.[121] Other technology-specific instruments include funds established by law that market participants have to finance in order to safeguard against potential damages resulting from the technology.[122]

---

[113] Schreiber (2019), p. 154; also cf. Hettich (2015).

[114] Cf. Stewart (1981), pp. 1267 et seq. A similar approach forcing the use of existing, but not yet widely used technology, is sometimes called "action forcing", see Miller (1995), p. 65.

[115] Stewart (1981), pp. 1267 et seq.

[116] While the use of cables is commonplace in low-voltage applications, their use in high-voltage distribution lines is still innovative.

[117] Art. 15c Electricity Act (Elektrizitätsgesetz, SR 734.0).

[118] Cf. Schreiber (2019), pp. 158 et seq.; Stewart (1981), pp. 1264 et seq., 1269.

[119] Also see Sect. 4.1.

[120] This has been extensively described by German-speaking legal scholars as "regulierte Selbstregulierung", see Hettich (2014), pp. 269 et seq.; Hoffmann-Riem (2006).

[121] Cf. the "negotiated standard setting" described by Stewart (1981), pp. 1341 et seq.

[122] As established in Switzerland, for example, by Art. 15 Nuclear Energy Liability Act (Kernenergiehaftpflichtgesetz, SR 732.44).

A legislative exit from certain technologies will either be contained in an express prohibition of the technology itself[123] or exemptions from legal protections that are otherwise granted.[124]

### 3.3.6 Conflict Resolution Instruments

Since conflict resolution is the main function of the law, few specific instruments are needed. However, innovation policy may bring about specific provisions to resolve certain conflicts. The implementation of conflict resolution bodies has already been mentioned.[125] Laws may also grant certain innovations priority with regards to conflicting interests.

For example, the Swiss legislator has stipulated that the energy production from renewable sources is of national interest.[126] This allows authorities to consider renewable energy projects even in certain protected landscapes.[127]

## 3.4 *Legal Constraints*

Whether legal interventions are designed to promote or limit innovation, the legislator is bound by superior law.[128] This may be international law such as Art. XVI of the General Agreement on Tariffs and Trade (GATT), or supranational law such as European Union law. Most importantly, however, national constitutional law limits the options available to the legislator.

For example, most jurisdictions abide by the principle of legality, meaning that government actions must have a legal basis.[129] Depending on the national legal system, the principle of legality also sets forth certain requirements as to the legal provision that serves as this basis. Most jurisdictions require legal provisions to be clear enough for the addressees to understand what their rights and duties are.[130] This may be problematic when regulating innovation, since many provisions will

---

[123]For example, Art. 3 para. 1 lit. a of the Swiss Stem Cell Research Act (Stammzellenforschungsgesetz, SR 810.31) prohibits the production of embryos for the purpose of stem cell research.

[124]For example, no patent protection is granted for processes regarding the cloning of humans under Art. 2 para. 1 lit. a of the Swiss Patents Act (Patentgesetz, SR 232.14).

[125]See note 149 supra.

[126]Art. 12 Energy Act.

[127]For a discussion of this new provision, see Gerber (2019).

[128]Schreiber (2019), pp. 99 et seq. with further references.

[129]In Switzerland, for example, this is stipulated in Art. 5 para. 1 Federal Constitution.

[130]For the principle of clarity in the United States, see Re (2019). For the Swiss equivalent, see Schindler (2014), n. 33 et seq.

inevitably have to be of a very technical nature.[131] The legislator may also draft innovation-related provisions using an intentionally open wording, to avoid excluding technological developments that are hard to predict.[132] This may further reduce clarity.

The principle of legality may also prescribe that the basic provisions must be included in a parliamentary act (as opposed to a mere executive ordinance), especially when the provision interferes with fundamental rights.[133] This is problematic in the context of innovation policy, since ordinances are much more flexible and will thus often be the preferred tool to regulate innovations that may develop in an unforeseen manner and hence require timely adjustments to the legal framework.[134]

Innovation policy instruments may also interfere with the economic freedoms of market participants.[135] In Switzerland, the economic freedom is not only a subjective fundamental right,[136] but also a general constitutional principle.[137] Both provisions limit the legislator as well as regulatory agencies in the extent to which they can interfere in the market. While interventions in the market do not violate the principle of economic freedom *per se*, as long as they are not aimed specifically at eliminating competition,[138] the intervention must serve a public interest[139] and be proportional.[140] Thus, any innovation policy measure must be as competitively neutral as possible.[141] The economic freedom may also restrict governments' options to introduce innovations through state-owned enterprises.[142]

# 4 Common Problems

## *4.1 Lack of Knowledge*

Innovation processes are very hard to predict, and the ever-changing technological and business environment prevents governments from accurately assessing how to

[131]Schreiber (2019), p. 102.

[132]Schreiber (2019), p. 102.

[133]For Swiss law, see Schindler (2014), n. 36 et seq.

[134]For Swiss law, cf. Tschannen et al. (2014), p. 142; Schreiber (2019), p. 103.

[135]Schreiber (2019), pp. 107 et seq.

[136]As provided for by Art. 27 Federal Constitution.

[137]Art. 94 Federal Constitution.

[138]BGE 136 I 1 E. 5.5.2; BGE 125 I 182 E. 5c.

[139]See the regulatory rationales in Sect. 2 supra.

[140]Art. 36 Federal Constitution.

[141]For the concept of competitive neutrality, see Lanneau (2017).

[142]In Switzerland, state-owned enterprises may not substantially affect the economic freedom of private enterprises, and they must be exposed to the same competitive conditions as private enterprises, BGE 138 I 378 E. 6.3.2; Hangartner (2002), p. 55.

properly regulate innovation. For this reason, a lack of knowledge with regard to the specific innovation and its impact on the market is one of the major problems that governments face when trying to regulate innovation.[143] Since it is very difficult for governments to predict the emergence of innovations, the legislator will typically respond with a delay after the innovation has already been in use for some time. This is known as the "legal lag".[144]

The lack of knowledge may not only concern innovation itself, but also the consequences of regulation on innovation. This may lead to unforeseen incentives.[145] A lack of knowledge may similarly affect the legislator, regulatory agencies and courts.[146] It is the underlying reason for many of the following problems.

## 4.2 Unintended Consequences

The aforementioned lack of predictive capabilities as to the market's response to regulation often leads to unintended consequences. The primary example are perverse incentives for market participants who exploit innovation-specific regulation. This is often the case with subsidy schemes. In Germany, for example, high financial incentives for biomass energy have led farmers to abandon food production and instead focus on high-yield "energy corn".[147] This is referred to as the "food vs. fuel" problem.[148] Changes to the legal framework may also simply reduce incentives to innovate even for market participants acting in good faith.[149]

## 4.3 Inefficiency

Transactional costs not only exist with private negotiations. Government interventions carry their own transactional costs,[150] which may also be referred to as interventional costs.[151] These include direct interventional costs such as the higher

143 Schreiber (2019), p. 75 with further references; also cf. Stewart (1981), p. 1275; Hettich (2014), pp. 213 et seq.

144 Cf. Rustad and Koenig (2003), even though the study contained therein pertains to case law.

145 This will be discussed further below in Sect. 4.2.

146 Stewart (1981), pp. 1354 et seq.

147 Bayerischer Landtag (2013), p. 23.

148 Cf. Hartman (2013).

149 The complexity of trying to assess innovation incentives is exemplified by Mungan (2013).

150 Coase (1960), p. 18: "[...] [T]he governmental administrative machine is not itself costless. It can, in fact, on occasion be extremely costly".

151 This term is not yet widely used in the English language. For the German equivalent (*Interventionskosten*), see Eidenmüller (2015), pp. 106 et seq., who also notes the absence of a

administrative costs for the Government as well as indirect interventional costs, such as when a market intervention disturbs the markets' allocative function and thereby increases costs.[152] Thus, innovation policy measures may be considered to be inefficient when interventional costs exceed the transactional costs of a similar result based on private negotiation.[153]

It is also difficult to predict which results certain innovation policy measures will achieve and which support schemes will prove to be efficient. For example, both German and Swiss renewable energy support schemes have proven to be less efficient for photovoltaics than for wind energy.[154] However, when taking other considerations into account (such as the lower impact photovoltaics have on the landscape and animals when compared to wind energy), the efficiency analysis may change.[155]

## 4.4 *Legal Uncertainty*

Uncertainty as to the applicable laws has a negative impact on the willingness of market participants to invest in an innovation.[156] This uncertainty may result from two different situations. First, in the absence of legal provisions that specifically address an innovation, it is often unclear which existing provisions apply to the new technology or process. Due to the legal lag,[157] this situation is typical for the early market introduction of an innovation and creates considerable legal uncertainty until either amendments to the law are made, or court cases are decided.

Second, the lack of knowledge on innovation processes and how market participants will respond to any regulation[158] often leads to an "intervention spiral":[159] The first regulatory attempts lead to unintended consequences or inefficiencies, so further inventions take place to remedy the situation, thereby creating new unintended consequences or inefficiencies. This not only leads to frequent changes

corresponding discussion in the (primarily American) literature; also cf. Schreiber (2019), pp. 80 et seq.

[152]Eidenmüller (2015), pp. 109 et seq.

[153]Sacksofsky (2012), pp. 1635 et seq.; Schreiber (2019), p. 81.

[154]When measured in MWh of electricity produced per Euro/Swiss Franc invested in support schemes, see the numbers at Schreiber (2019), pp. 81 et seq.

[155]Schreiber (2019), p. 82.

[156]Cf. the call for a "predictable, legally secure system" for pharmaceutical innovations at Kraus (2014), p. 380; Regarding Kraus' example of the TRIPS agreement, also cf. Drezner (2008), pp. 176 et seq.

[157]See Sect. 4.1 above.

[158]See Sect. 4.1 above.

[159]This term seems to be used mostly in the German-speaking literature. For a use in English (albeit by native German speakers), see Bergmann et al. (1998), p. 168.

to the legal framework, but also tends to increase the amount of regulation over time.[160] Both increase the legal uncertainty for market participants.

### 4.5 Regulatory Lock-In

Lock-in effects occur when prior developments limit the options available at a later stage.[161] They are thus an example of path dependencies. Innovation may be obstructed when market participants have aligned themselves with existing technology and processes to a degree that would render switching to a new technology or process very difficult.[162] Lock-in effects are especially prevalent where industry standards exist.[163] This is exacerbated when the standard is not only a de-facto one, but prescribed or at least heavily encouraged by regulation. This may be referred to as regulatory lock-in.[164]

One possible example from Switzerland are the cantonal laws on the energy efficiency of buildings.[165] These often contain a legal presumption that the respective energy efficiency requirements have been satisfied when the building is certified according to the Swiss Minergie[166] standard.[167] This creates major incentives to construct buildings according to this standard, even if other standards or technologies may be more innovative.

## 5 Best Practices: An Attempt

### 5.1 Introduction

Every innovation process is different. Market sectors may differ considerably from each other. Some innovations may help to spur economic growth, others may also

[160] Schreiber (2019), p. 84. For example, the former Swiss Energy Ordinance grew from 22 pages in 1998 to 186 pages in 2015 (Hettich 2015, p. 575), and 206 pages in 2017 (Schreiber 2019, p. 84 n. 545).

[161] Cf. the—controversial—example of the QWERTY computer keyboard layout, note 107 supra.

[162] Markusson (2012), p. 389.

[163] Kline (2001), p. 103.

[164] See Stack and Gartland (2010), p. 117; van Calster (2008), p. 91.

[165] Schreiber (2019), p. 85.

[166] www.minergie.ch/.

[167] See, for example, Art. 1.30 para. 2 lit. b, Art. 1.51 para. 2, Art. 1.52 para. 1 of the Cantonal Model Laws in the Energy Sector (Mustervorschriften der Kantone im Energiebereich, MuKEn) 2014, available at www.endk.ch/de/energiepolitik-der-kantone/muken. These Model Laws are not directly applicable law, but only valid to the extent that the respective Canton actually implements them into its own law.

increase public health, help protect the environment or improve education. With such different innovation processes, it may come as no surprise that abstract findings, which may be applied to any new innovation process, are hard to come by. Indeed, there is hardly a "toolbox" that the legislator may utilize to steer innovation.

Nonetheless, some findings are of a more universal nature and should be considered whenever governments attempt to influence innovation. However, as the academic discussion on the interplay of law and innovation is still ongoing (and, in some jurisdictions, only in its infancy), these findings are only of a preliminary nature and almost certainly subject to further refinement in the future.

## 5.2 *Proper Focus on the Innovation Process*

The legal instruments that are available to govern innovation differ considerably depending on which part of the innovation process the legislator aims to influence. In the simple, linear model of innovation, which has resonated the most with legal scholars,[168] the innovation process consists of three steps:[169] The beginning of each innovation process is an invention, i.e. an idea that has proven to be functional, but that may not yet be entirely ready for market introduction. In a second step, this invention is transformed into a product or service that can be offered on the market. This is referred to as innovation in the narrow sense. Finally, the product or service has to find acceptance in the market by market participants willing to adopt it. This is referred to as diffusion.[170]

A well-designed innovation policy should clearly distinguish between these phases, in order to apply the proper legal instruments.[171] For example, invention may be stimulated by funding basic research. Innovation in the narrow sense may be supported through regulatory sandboxes which help to gauge the market potential of an innovation, or through the introduction of regulatory standards. Finally, the diffusion of an existing innovation may either be incentivized, e.g. with tax exemptions or other preferred treatment under regulatory law, or be enforced through, for example, technology forcing.

[168]Schreiber (2019), p. 40.

[169]This distinction can be traced back to Schumpeter (1947), p. 152, who seems to distinguish between the invention and the innovation process. The exact terminology and number of steps in the process varies. For an overview, see Godin (2006). Also cf. Stewart (1981), p. 1282.

[170]The most detailed treatment of the diffusion process is Rogers (2003).

[171]Cf. the legal instruments described in Sect. 3.3 supra.

## 5.3 *Analysis of the Existing Legal Framework*

The legislator should also avoid treating the law as a blank canvas that the proper innovation-specific instruments may simply be painted onto. In the twenty-first century, almost all areas of life are subject to a variety of legal provisions. The same holds true for most innovations. Rarely will an innovative product or process not encounter existing laws that may or may not be suited to govern that innovation.[172] The mere fact that there is no law that has been implemented specifically to address the innovation does not necessarily mean that there are no (general) laws that apply to the innovation. Even the Internet, which has often been referred to as an unregulated space,[173] has actually been the subject of legal scholarship from an early point on.[174]

For this reason, the first step with regard to a specific innovation should be a thorough analysis of the existing legal framework and how it applies to the innovation. Sometimes, the most important legal obstacles to an innovation may be provisions that were never designed to apply to that innovation.[175] In these cases, subtle changes to the legal framework may be more effective than the implementation of innovation-specific legal support schemes. For the same reason, traditional methods of statutory or (depending on the jurisdiction) case law interpretation are highly relevant for the legal analysis of innovation, in order to establish which of the existing laws apply.[176]

## 5.4 *Technological Openness*

Any attempt to regulate innovation must ensure not to exclude future developments. This is especially relevant for technological innovations. It will, inter alia, require legal definitions that are broad enough to also apply to future products or services that are not yet known. At the same time, this may lead to legal provisions that are ambiguous, which creates tensions with regard to the principle of clarity.[177] It is nonetheless crucial in order to avoid having the legislator essentially "picking winners and losers".

---

[172]Schreiber (2019), pp. 441 et seq.

[173]Cf. Kernighan (2017), p. 142, who describes the Internet as "[. . .] a free-for-all compared to the controlled environments of traditional phone companies [. . .]" but who also mentions that in recent years, it "[. . .] is becoming less free-wheeling and more constrained".

[174]See, for example, Dunne (1994).

[175]For example, my analysis in Schreiber (2019) has shown that the definition of a "final consumer" in the electricity market is currently the legal provision that most severely hinders the implementation of innovative energy storage technology.

[176]Schreiber (2019), pp. 441 et seq.

[177]See Sect. 3.4 supra.

For example, when a government agency attempts to promote innovation through its public procurement,[178] the tendering process must be carefully designed. If the requirements on the good or service to be procured are too detailed (e.g. by mentioning specific technologies), they may exclude potentially more innovative competitors from the bidding process. It is therefore preferable to merely define a desired outcome instead of prescribing how that outcome must be achieved.[179] For example, instead of prescribing a certain energy-efficient technology, the requirements should simply contain a maximum allowed energy consumption. It would then be up to the competing bidders to find the best way to stay below that threshold.

## 5.5 *Technological Neutrality*

The legislator must also ensure not to discriminate against certain technologies. This is closely related to the concept of technological openness, but has different legal implications:[180] The idea of technological openness concerns future developments that cannot be predicted yet. In order not to stifle innovation, it is important to maintain technological openness. The idea of technological neutrality instead focuses on competing technologies that are already on the market.

This is important as it implies that these competitors may immediately attack the law based on the principle of equal treatment[181] or, depending on the jurisdiction, the concept of competitive neutrality and economic freedom.[182] From a pure policy perspective, it is also significant because the government should not "pick winners and losers", but instead leave it to the market to find the most innovative solution. Thus, any supportive or restrictive regulation should be drafted in a way that does not unfairly distinguish between competing products or processes. In this context, it is notable that the Austrian legislator chose to introduce energy storage-specific legislation in support of the established pumped hydropower storage as well as the very innovative Power-to-Gas-technology, while not including any other type of energy storage (such as batteries or compressed air storage[183]).[184]

---

[178]See Sect. 3.3.3 supra.

[179]For Switzerland, see Steiner (2014), p. 162; Schreiber (2019), p. 145; also cf. Edler and Georghiou (2007), pp. 959 et seq.

[180]Schreiber (2019), p. 391.

[181]In Switzerland, Art. 8 para. 1 Federal Constitution.

[182]In Switzerland, Art. 27 and Art. 94 Federal Constitution.

[183]For an overview of energy storage technologies, see EASAC (2017), pp. 11 et seq.

[184]See § 111 para. 3 of the Austrian Electricity Act 2010 (Elektrizitätswirtschafts- und Organisationsgesetz 2010, Federal Law Gazette I No. 110/2010, as amended by Federal Law Gazette I No. 174/2013), which temporarily exempted these two technologies from the duty to pay electricity grid usage fees. For a discussion of energy storage regulation in the German-speaking countries, see Schreiber (2020).

## 5.6 Flexibility

As the discussion above has shown, the unpredictability of innovation processes and the market's reaction to regulation will often lead to undesired results. Thus, any innovation-specific legal framework has to be flexible enough to quickly adjust to unforeseen developments.[185] This flexibility may be achieved by only including the most basic provisions in a parliamentary act, while stipulating the details in an executive ordinance that can be quickly amended in the future.

Another option is for the law to refer to technical norms such as those commonly adopted by industry associations.[186] However, depending on the respective national interpretation of the principle of legality, the legislator may be limited to "static" references to an existing version of the norm, and barred from "dynamic" references that would include future amendments to the industry norm.[187] Thus, changes to the industry norm will typically require corresponding changes to the legal provision.

The legislator may even introduce "experimental" law, i.e. legal provisions that are only valid for a certain amount of time.[188] Shortly before the date of validity expires, the legislator then has the chance to evaluate the experiences made with the experimental provision and to decide on whether to perpetuate it. Again, the principle of legality may limit the legislator's options to introduce temporary law to cases which otherwise could not be effectively addressed.[189]

The idea of experimental law has been taken a step further with Germany introducing a legal framework specifically tailored to one particular research and demonstration project: the SINTEG-ordinance[190] provides a framework for a project on intelligent electricity grids using digital technology. Among other things, the project participants can claim reimbursements for certain regulation-induced costs that result from their participation in the project.[191] Such project-specific legal frameworks should only be introduced when they do not have an adverse effect on competition.

---

[185] Schreiber (2019), p. 448.

[186] In Switzerland, an important example are the SIA norms of the Swiss Society of Engineers and Architects (Schweizerischer Ingenieur- und Architektenverein). The norms are available at www.sia.ch/en/services/sia-norm.

[187] The latter is problematic since this essentially passes legislative power to the industry association.

[188] Regarding experimental law, see Müller and Uhlmann (2013), pp. 177 et seq.; for a more general treatment of temporary law, see Fagan (2013).

[189] Cf. Müller and Uhlmann (2013), p. 181.

[190] SINTEG-Verordnung, BGBl. 2017 I 1653, as amended by BGBl. 2019 I 706.

[191] §§ 6–9 SINTEG-ordinance. See Schreiber (2019), p. 449.

## 5.7 *Deregulation Versus Regulation*

Often, the idea of an innovation-friendly legal framework and the idea of deregulation are thought of as nearly interchangeable.[192] Contrary to this idea it should be mentioned that regulation may also lead to innovation. For example, the raised energy efficiency standards for lamps in the European Union (that effectively outlawed traditional, incandescent lightbulbs) initially led to consumer resentment because efficient lamps available at the time (compact fluorescent lamps, CFL) could flicker and emitted an unpleasantly "cold" white light. However, innovation quickly progressed and within a few years, highly efficient light emitting diodes (LED) became available, some of which even give off the warm, yellow-reddish light preferred by consumers for their households and many of which are now also dimmable.[193] This finding is consistent with Porter's hypothesis.[194] In other words: if necessity is the mother of invention, regulation can create the necessity.

Of course, this is going to function best when viable alternatives are indeed available or can be developed within a reasonable time. It may thus work most efficiently where innovative options are already available, but have not been widely adopted yet. Still, it seems worthwhile to further investigate the potentially innovation-inducing effect regulation can have.

In addition, clear rules increase legal certainty and can thus stimulate innovation.[195] This is especially important in sectors where large-scale, long-term investments have to be made, such as in the electricity grid or public transport infrastructure. Here, clear legal guidelines can aid the decision-making process. For example, the current efforts to prohibit the sale of new vehicles with internal (fossil) combustion engines in several countries may aid the producers of such vehicles in focussing their investments and efforts and thus be preferable to the ongoing uncertainty as to the technology's future.[196]

Still, any measure as intrusive as a technology ban must be revisited from time to time to ensure that the original justification is still valid. For example, the Swiss exit

---

[192] For an empirical study on how regulation and deregulation affect innovation, see Polemis and Tselekounis (2019).

[193] Also cf. Schreiber (2019), p. 463.

[194] See note 195 supra.

[195] Schreiber (2019), pp. 449 et seq.

[196] However, many industry associations are still critical of such a move. See, for example, the statement by the UK's Society of motor manufacturers and traders cited in a report by the BBC from 4 February 2020, "Petrol and diesel car sales ban brought forward to 2035", available at www.bbc.com/news/science-environment-51366123.

from new nuclear power plants[197] may have to be re-evaluated if more secure "generation IV"[198] technologies become available.

## 5.8 *Protection of Existing Interests*

Finally, despite the understandable enthusiasm for innovation, governments must also ensure that they continue to adequately protect existing interests. These may necessitate new regulation or at least limit the extent to which existing provisions may be altered to support the innovation.[199] Due to competing (private or public) interests in many sectors, the existing legal framework often represents an attempt to balance these interests that may have been refined over decades.[200]

For example, innovative renewable energy sources help to decrease the climate impact of energy production. However, they may interfere with interests such as landscape, bird and bat protection (in the case of wind energy), aesthetic considerations in old town centres (in the case of photovoltaics[201]) or they may lead to the aforementioned "fuel vs. food" problem (in the case of biomass). Thus, measures such as the national interest assigned to renewable energy by the Swiss legislator must be applied in a way that does not completely marginalise these existing interests.

# 6 Conclusion

As this contribution has attempted to show, the law may not only inhibit innovation, but also promote it. Key to an innovation-friendly legal framework is to understand how the existing provisions apply to new technologies and, where necessary, how amendments can be implemented. Any instrument of innovation policy must be carefully drafted so as to not exclude existing or future alternatives. Finally, despite the obvious interest in promoting innovation, law also serves to protect existing interests, which may be endangered by innovation. Thus, the legal framework may have to serve and balance a multitude of competing functions.

---

[197] Under Art. 12a Nuclear Energy Act (Kernenergiegesetz, SR 732.1), no new general licenses for the construction of nuclear power plants may be granted. Plants already in operation may continue to run as long as the safety requirements under the law are observed (which, under Swiss law, includes the operators' duty to follow technological developments and, if necessary, upgrade their plants, see Art. 22 para. 2 lit. g and h Nuclear Energy Act).

[198] Cf. Locatelli et al. (2013).

[199] Schreiber (2019), p. 450.

[200] Schreiber (2019), p. 450.

[201] It must be noted, however, that the most innovative solar modules are available in a variety of colors, prints and shapes, which helps to blend them into the environment.

While innovation processes may differ vastly across multiple sectors, it nonetheless seems worthwhile for legal scholars to try and better understand the interplay between law and innovation. This legal viewpoint will hopefully continue to be complemented by empirical studies from other disciplines. Thus, innovation law also serves as a good example of the importance of interdisciplinary research.

**Acknowledgement** This publication draws from the author's Ph.D. thesis (Schreiber 2019, in German). The author thanks Prof. Dr. Sebastian Heselhaus and Prof. Dr. Roland Norer at the University of Lucerne, Switzerland, for supervising the dissertation, and Mara Joss for comments on an earlier draft. The author was part of the energy research project SCCER CREST (www.sccer-crest.ch), which was funded by the Swiss Innovation Agency Innosuisse.

## References

Ashford NA, Hall RP (2011) The importance of regulation-induced innovation for sustainable development. Sustainability 3:270–292

Ashford NA, Ayers C, Stone RF (1985) Using regulation to change the market for innovation. Harv Environ Law Rev 9:419–466

Baily MN, Montalbano N (2018) Clusters and innovation districts: lessons from the United States experience. The Brookings Institution, Washington, D.C.

Bayerischer Landtag (2013) Abschlussbericht der Kommission zur parlamentarischen Begleitung der Energiewende in Bayern. Drucksache 16/17500, Munich

Bergmann H, Brockmann KL, Rennings K (1998) An economic approach to environmental agreements. Experiences from Germany. In co-operative environmental governance. In: Glasbergen P (ed) Public-private agreements as a policy strategy. Springer, Dordrecht, pp 157–178

Bundesamt für Gesundheit (BAG) (2013) Massnahmen des Bundes zur Stärkung der biomedizinischen Forschung und Technologie. Bern

Coase RH (1960) The problem of social cost. J Law Econ 3:1–44

David PA (1985) Clio and the economics of QWERTY. Am Econ Rev 75:332–337

De Mesquita EB (2016) Political economy for public policy. Princeton University Press, Princeton

Dingwerth K (2005) The democratic legitimacy of public-private rule making: what can we learn from the world commission on dams? Glob Gov 11:65–83

Drezner DW (2008) All politics is global. Explaining international regulatory regimes. Princeton University Press, Princeton

Dunne RL (1994) Deterring unauthorized access to computers: controlling behavior in cyberspace through a contract law paradigm. Jurimetrics 35:1–15

Edler J, Georghiou L (2007) Public procurement and innovation – resurrecting the demand side. Res Policy 36:949–963

Eidenmüller H (2015) Effizienz als Rechtsprinzip. Möglichkeiten und Grenzen der ökonomischen Analyse des Rechts, 4th edn. Mohr Siebeck, Tuebingen

European Academies Science Advisory Council (EASAC) (2017) Valuing dedicated storage in electricity grids. EASAC policy report 33. Halle and Brussels

Ewers H-J (1990) Marktversagen und Politikversagen als Legitimation staatlicher Forschungs- und Technologiepolitik. In: Krupp H (ed) Technikpolitik angesichts der Umweltkatastrophe. Physica-Verlag, Heidelberg, pp 147–160

Fagan F (2013) Law and the limits of government. Temporary versus permanent legislation. Edward Elgar, Cheltenham

Feintuck M (2010) Regulatory rationales beyond the economic: in search of the public interest. In: Baldwin R, Cave M, Lodge M (eds) The Oxford handbook of regulation. Oxford University Press, Oxford, pp 39–63
Fritsch M (2018) Marktversagen und Wirtschaftspolitik – Mikroökonomische Grundlagen staatlichen Handelns, 10th edn. Vahlen, München
Furman JL, Porter ME, Stern S (2002) The determinants of national innovative capacity. Res Policy 31:899–933
Gerber A (2019) Art. 12 Energiegesetz: Was ändert sich bei der Interessenabwägung (erneuerbare Energie vs. Natur-, Landschafts- und Umweltschutz)? In: Heselhaus S, Hänni J, Schreiber M (eds) Rechtsfragen der Energiewirtschaft. Dike Zurich, St. Gallen, pp 77–106
Godin B (2006) The linear model of innovation. The historical construction of an analytical framework. Sci Technol Hum Values 31:639–667
Gong S, Ardeshiri A, Rashidi TH (2020) Impact of government incentives on the market penetration of electric vehicles in Australia. Transp Res Part D Transp Environ 83:102353
Gruber M-C (2011) What is it like to be unborn? Our common fate with future generations. In: Klaus M (ed) Efficiency, sustainability, and justice to future generations. Springer, Dordrecht, pp 113–137
Hangartner Y (2002) Das Grundrecht der Wirtschaftsfreiheit. Recht – Zeitschrift für juristische Weiterbildung und Praxis 2002:53–62
Hartman BJ (2013) The renewable fuel standard: food versus fuel? Maine Law Rev 65:525–548
Herschler DH, Slany WZ (1982) The "Paperless Office": a case study of the state department's foreign affairs information system. Am Arch 45:142–154
Hettich P (2014) Kooperative Risikovorsorge. Regulierte Selbstregulierung im Recht der operationellen und technischen Risiken. Schulthess, Zurich
Hettich P (2015) Die Glühbirne – Lucifer neuer Zeiten. Schweizerisches Zentralblatt für Staats- und Verwaltungsrecht 116:567–588
Hicks JR (1939) The foundations of welfare economics. Econ J 49:696–712
Hirschi C (2018) Regulation and transparency as rituals of distrust: reading Niklas Luhmann against the grain. In: Alloa E, Thomä D (eds) Transparency, society and subjectivity. Palgrave Macmillan and Springer, Cham
Hoffmann-Riem W (2006) Gewährleistungsrecht und Gewährleistungsrechtsprechung am Beispiel regulierter Selbstregulierung. In: Bauer H, Schmidt R (eds) Wirtschaft im offenen Verfassungsstaat. Festschrift für Reiner Schmidt zum 70. Geburtstag. C.H. Beck, Munich, pp 447–466
Hoffmann-Riem W (2016) Innovation und Recht – Recht und Innovation. Recht im Ensemble seiner Kontexte. Mohr Siebeck, Tuebingen
Hoffmann-Riem W, Schneider J-P (1998) Zur Eigenständigkeit rechtswissenschaftlicher Innovationsforschung. In: Hoffmann-Riem W, Schneider J-S (eds) Rechtswissenschaftliche Innovationsforschung. Grundlagen, Forschungsansätze, Gegenstandsbereiche. Nomos, Baden-Baden, pp 389–412
Hofstetter D, Battke B, Cox B, Hughes J (2014) Power-to-gas in Switzerland – demand, regulation, economics, technical potential. Electrochaea, Zürich
Horowitz AW, Lai EL-C (1996) Patent length and the rate of innovation. Int Econ Rev 37:785–801
Huber BR (2017) Temporal spillovers. In: Mathis K, Huber BR (eds) Environmental law and economics. Springer, Cham, pp 43–57
Jaffe AB, Peterson SR, Portney PR (1995) Environmental regulation and the competitiveness of U.S. manufacturing: what does the evidence tell us? J Econ Lit 33:132–163
Jones TH (1989) Administrative law, regulation, and legitimacy. J Law Soc 16:410–425
Katz V (2015) Regulating the sharing economy. Berkeley Technol Law J 30:1067–1126
Kernighan BW (2017) Understanding the digital world. What you need to know about computers, the internet, privacy, and security. Princeton University Press, Princeton
Kim H-E (2011) The role of the patent system in stimulating innovation and technology transfer for climate change. Including aspects of licensing and competition law. Nomos, Baden-Baden

Kline D (2001) Positive feedback, lock-in, and environmental policy. Policy Sci 34:95–107
Kraus D (2014) Is TRIPS innovative enough? How to reconcile IP, innovation and health. In: Cremona M, Hilpold P, Lavranos N et al (eds) Reflections on the constitutionalization of international economic law, Liber amicorum for Ernst-Ulrich Petersmann. Martinus Nijhoff, Leiden
Kuusi O, Meyer M (2002) Technological generalizations and leitbilder – the anticipation of technological opportunities. Technol Forecasting Soc Change 69:625–639
Lanneau R (2017) Competitive neutrality. In: Marciano A, Ramello GB (eds) Encyclopedia of law and economics, living edition. Springer, New York. https://link.springer.com/referencework/10.1007/978-1-4614-7883-6
Liebowitz SJ, Margolis SE (1990) The fable of the keys. J Law Econ 33:1–25
Locatelli G, Mancini M, Todeschini N (2013) Generation IV nuclear reactors: current status and future prospects. Energy Policy 61:1503–1520
Luhmann N (2005) Legitimation durch Verfahren, 6th edn. Suhrkamp, Frankfurt am Main
Lundvall B-Å, Borrás S (2011) Science, technology, and innovation policy. In: Fagerberg J, Mowery DC, Nelson RR (eds) The Oxford handbook of innovation. Oxford University Press, Oxford, pp 599–631
Maggetti M (2010) Legitimacy and accountability of independent regulatory agencies: a critical review. Living Rev Democr 2010:1–9
Mandel GN (2005) Promoting environmental innovation with intellectual property innovation: a new basis for patent rewards. Temple J Sci Technol Environ Law 24:51–70
Markusson N (2012) Born again: the debate on lock-in and CCS. Energy Environ 23:389–394
Mathis K (2011) Discounting the future? Cost-benefit analysis and sustainability. In: Mathis K (ed) Efficiency, sustainability, and justice to future generations. Springer, Dordrecht, pp 165–180
Mathis K, Tor A (eds) (2016) Nudging – possibilities, limitations and applications in European law and economics. Springer, Cham
Merges RP (2019) Philosophical foundations of IP law: the law and economics paradigm. In: Depoorter B, Menell PS (eds) Research handbook on the economics of intellectual property law, vol 1. Edward Elgar, Cheltenham, pp 72–97
Miller AS (1995) Environmental regulation, technological innovation, and technology-forcing. Nat Resour Environ 10:64–69
Müller G, Uhlmann F (2013) Elemente einer Rechtssetzungslehre, 3rd edn. Schulthess, Zurich
Mungan MC (2013) Reverse payments, perverse incentives. Harv J Law Technol 27:1–48
Noel L, de Rubens GZ, Sovacool BK, Kester J (2019) Fear and loathing of electric vehicles: the reactionary rhetoric of range anxiety. Energy Res Soc Sci 48:96–107
Office of Technology Assessment (OTA) (1979) OTA priorities 1979. Washington, DC
Oppenländer KH (1977) Die Wirkungen des Patentwesens im Innovationsprozess. Gewerblicher Rechtsschutz und Urheberrecht 79:362–370
Organisation for Economic Co-operation and Development (OECD) (2011) Towards green growth. Paris
Organisation for Economic Co-operation and Development (OECD) (2015) The innovation imperative. Contributing to productivity, growth and well-being. Paris
Polemis M, Tselekounis M (2019) Does deregulation drive innovation intensity? Lessons learned from the OECD telecommunications sector. MPRA Paper No. 92770. https://mpra.ub.uni-muenchen.de/92770/
Porter ME (1990a) The competitive advantage of nations. Harv Bus Rev 90:73–91
Porter ME (1990b) The competitive advantage of nations. Free Press, New York
Re RM (2019) Clarity doctrines. Univ Chic Law Rev 86:1497–1562
Rogers EM (2003) Diffusion of innovations, 5th edn. Free Press, New York
Rustad ML, Koenig TH (2003) Cybertorts and legal lag: an empirical analysis. South Calif Interdiscip Law J 13:77–140

Sacksofsky U (2012) Anreize. In: Hoffmann-Riem W, Schmidt-Assmann E (eds) Grundlagen des Verwaltungsrechts. C.H. Beck, Munich

Schindler B (2014) Art. 5. In: Ehrenzeller B, Schindler B, Schweizer RJ, Vallender KA (eds) Die Schweizerische Bundesverfassung, St. Galler Kommentar, 3rd edn. Schulthess, Zurich

Schreiber L (2002) Innovationsgeeignetheit von Technikrecht am Beispiel der Signaturregulierung. In: Eifert M, Hoffmann-Riem W (eds) Innovation und rechtliche Regulierung. Schlüsselbegriffe und Anwendungsbeispiele rechtswissenschaftlicher Innovationsforschung. Nomos, Baden-Baden, pp 216–263

Schreiber M (2019) Rechtliche Innovationssteuerung am Beispiel der Power-to-Gas-Stromspeichertechnologie. Schulthess, Zurich

Schreiber M (2020) Regulation of energy storage systems in the DACH countries. Eur Energy Environ Law Rev 29:168–176

Schumpeter JA (1947) The creative response in economic history. J Econ Hist 7:149–159

Scott C (2010) Standard-setting in regulatory regimes. In: Baldwin R, Cave M, Lodge M (eds) The Oxford handbook of regulation. Oxford University Press, Oxford, pp 104–119

Shavell S, van Ypersele T (2001) Rewards versus intellectual property rights. J Law Econ 44:525–547

Stack M, Gartland MP (2003) Path creation, path dependency, and alternative theories of the firm. J Econ Issues 37:487–494

Stack M, Gartland MP (2010) Path dependence, modularity and the offshoring of (some) physician services. In: Sydow J, Schreyögg G (eds) The hidden dynamics of path dependence. Institutions and Organizations. Palgrave Macmillan, London, pp 113–128

Steiner M (2014) Nachhaltige öffentliche Beschaffung. Ein Blick auf das Vergaberecht des Bundes und die Perspektiven. In: Stöckli H, Zufferey J-B (eds) Aktuelles Vergaberecht 2014. Schulthess, Zurich, pp 149–176

Stewart RB (1981) Regulation, innovation, and administrative law: a conceptual framework. Calif Law Rev 69:1256–1377

Swann PGM (2009) The economics of innovation. An introduction. Edward Elgar, Cheltenham

Teece DJ, Coleman M (1998) The meaning of monopoly: antitrust analysis in high-technology industries. Antitrust Bull 43:801–857

Thaler RH, Sunstein CR (2008) Nudge – improving decisions about health, wealth, and happiness. Yale University Press, New Haven

Tremblay-Huet S (2018) Making sense of the public discourse on Airbnb and labour: what about labour rights? In: McKee D, Makela F, Scassa T (eds) Law and the "Sharing Economy"; regulating online market platforms. University of Ottawa Press, Ottawa, pp 393–420

Tschannen P, Zimmerli U, Müller M (2014) Allgemeines Verwaltungsrecht, 4th edn. Stämpfli, Bern

Van Calster G (2008) Against harmonization. regulatory competition in climate change law. Carbon Clim Law Rev 2:89–94

Veljanovski C (2010) Economic approaches to regulation. In: Baldwin R, Cave M, Lodge M (eds) The Oxford handbook of regulation. Oxford University Press, Oxford, pp 17–38

Verspagen B (2011) Innovation and economic growth. In: Fagerberg J, Mowery DC, Nelson RR (eds) The Oxford handbook of innovation. Oxford University Press, Oxford, pp 487–513

Wieddekind D (2002) Innovationsforschung, Wettbewerbstheorie und Kartellrecht. In: Eifert M, Hoffmann-Riem W (eds) Innovation und rechtliche Regulierung. Schlüsselbegriffe und Anwendungsbeispiele rechtswissenschaftlicher Innovationsforschung. Nomos, Baden-Baden, pp 134–170

Wüstenhagen R, Wolsink M, Bürer MJ (2007) Social acceptance of renewable energy innovation. An introduction to the concept. Energy Policy 35:2683–2691

Wyssling W (1946) Die Entwicklung der schweizerischen Elektrizitätswerke und ihrer Bestandteile in den ersten 50 Jahren. Schweizerischer Elektrotechnischer Verein, Zurich

Xu M, Yang H, Wang S (2020) Mitigate the range anxiety: siting battery charging stations for electric vehicle drivers. Transp Res Part C: Emerging Technol 114:164–188

**Markus Schreiber** Lucerne. Lecturer and Research Associate, Center for Law and Sustainability at the University of Lucerne. CH-6002 Lucerne, Frohburgstrasse 3, P.O. Box 4466, Tel. + 41 (0)41 229 59 47. markus.schreiber@unilu.ch. Fields of Interest: Energy and Climate Law, Law and Innovation, Public Law (Constitutional Law, Administrative Law), Legal Theory.

# Matching Commitments: A New Approach to Regulation of the Commons

**James W. Coleman**

**Abstract** No country can capture the full benefit of its efforts to provide global public goods such as protecting the climate or providing new medicines or technologies to a growing world. As a result, there is persistent under-investment in combating climate change and promoting innovation. This Article proposes a new solution to this well-studied social dilemma: matching commitments. It explains how matching commitments could be used in countries that adopt climate regulation to encourage action by other countries around the world. And it shows why this solution is better than other commonly-proposed solutions for encouraging action in recalcitrant countries.

## 1 Introduction

This Article proposes that unilateral climate regulators should divide their climate regulation between unconditional and conditional regulation and that the majority of their regulation should be conditional. That is, countries should unconditionally impose a modest carbon price on their emitters but also commit to a conditional matching commitment: a promise raise their carbon price as other countries increase their unconditional carbon price. As more countries adopted such matching commitments, it would have three major benefits. First, countries would be encouraged to raise their unconditional commitment to earn matching commitments from other countries. Second, total carbon prices would rise to levels that are more near optimal. Third, as linked prices rose in tandem, they would limit regulatory arbitrage by industries that might otherwise be pushed to countries with lax regulation.

---

J. W. Coleman (✉)
Southern Methodist University Dedman School of Law, Dallas, TX, USA
e-mail: jwcoleman@smu.edu

 
K. Mathis, A. Tor (eds.), *Law and Economics of Regulation*, Economic Analysis of Law in European Legal Scholarship 11,
https://doi.org/10.1007/978-3-030-70530-5_14

Domestic climate regulation presents a classic social dilemma.[1] Climate change depends on the total amount of greenhouse gases emitted by all countries, so no country has an incentive to adopt a globally optimal level of climate regulation because each country bears the full burden of its own greenhouse gas regulations and only captures a fraction of their benefit. And there is little hope of a truly binding and global treaty that could solve this dilemma by prescribing what each country should do.

As a result national climate regulation is politically challenging. Worse yet, unilateral climate regulations may cause industries and greenhouse gas emissions to move to countries without climate regulations, undercutting the environmental benefit that the regulation was supposed to provide. This problem, known as "carbon leakage" is uniquely acute for climate regulations because the harm from global warming does not depend on where emissions are located, so when emissions shift overseas, it is just as bad as if they were still emitted domestically. So every nation hopes that other nations will regulate, and no nation wants to be the only one to regulate.

Facing this dilemma, countries that want to cut global greenhouse gas emissions have generally taken a taken a three-pronged approach: (1) prescribe unilateral reductions in greenhouse gas emissions, (2) cajole (or occasionally threaten) other nations to reduce their greenhouse gas emissions, (3) hold out hope for an international treaty that will require reductions of all countries. This may be called the traditional climate strategy because it forms the basis for nearly all academic discussions of climate regulation, and nearly all government justifications for climate regulation.

This Article proposes a new strategy: climate matching commitments. Rather than relying on the unconditional abatements that characterize the traditional climate strategy, it relies on climate regulations that automatically ratchet up in response to regulations in other countries. For example, the European Union plans to cut its emissions by 40% by the year 2030, following the traditional strategy of unconditional commitments.[2] Instead, it could have agreed to unconditionally cut its emissions by 5%, but promise to add to that cut by matching a specified percentage of cuts in other key economies, such as the United States and China. Like traditional unconditional climate regulations these matching commitments would be unilateral. The EU would not negotiate with the U.S. or China—it would simply promise to match a portion of their emission abatements.[3] The EU could calibrate these matching rates to make it likely that its matching commitments added to its unconditional commitment would result in the same 40% cut overall. The actual

[1]Brewster (2010), pp. 245, 268, 304 ("The planet's atmosphere is a public good, and climate change constitutes a public bad.").

[2]European Commission (2014).

[3]Relying on unilateral mechanisms is important because persistent distributional disagreements have deadlocked climate negotiations. Coleman (2014), pp. 88, 105.

percentage could be more or less depending on the cuts adopted by the other target countries, but would have an expected value of 40%.

Such a system of climate matching commitments would encourage other countries to adopt their own climate regulations. When the United States, China, and other matching targets considered climate regulation they would know that if they adopted more stringent climate regulations, they would be rewarded with an additional benefit: more stringent European Union climate regulations. Stricter EU regulations would mean lower global greenhouse gas emissions, granting matching targets with an additional climate benefit. And stricter EU regulations would also mitigate the problem of carbon leakage: climate regulation would ratchet up in tandem, limiting industry's incentive to move to the country with less regulation. So when the EU adopted matching commitments, it would change the incentives of matching target countries—increasing the benefit they received from climate regulation and decreasing the economic cost of that regulation.

The benefits of matching commitments would increase if they were adopted by multiple countries. Just as the EU could adopt matching commitments that rewarded climate regulation in the U.S. and China, those countries could adopt their own reciprocal commitments rewarding regulations in other countries. For instance, under strong assumptions of transparency, credibility, and rationality game theory has shown that, if each country in the world set, first, a rate at which it would match unconditional emission reductions from other countries, and then, second, its own unconditional reduction, the resulting regulations would optimally control climate change even if countries chose rates entirely from selfish motives.[4] Thus, a worldwide move to matching commitments would radically transform the incentives for unilateral climate regulation: though each country could not directly capture the full benefit of its own increased regulation, it would receive that full benefit indirectly from the resulting regulation by other countries.[5]

It might seem strange to rely on other nations' matching commitments when choosing the stringency of domestic climate regulation, but the traditional model of climate regulation relies on the same trust. The conventional wisdom that supports the traditional model is that if countries that emit the most carbon adopt unilateral climate regulations, other countries will follow suit.[6] Thus, even though other countries have not formally committed to act in response to unilateral climate actions by the United States, the case for U.S. regulation usually includes the argument that other countries will respond. That is, the traditional model assumes that other countries will "match" our commitments to some degree—the matching model aids the case for regulation by making those matches explicit.

[4]Boadway et al. (2009).

[5]See also Wood (2011), (surveying other game theoretic solutions to climate change).

[6]Brewster (2010), pp. 245, 268, 278, ("The conventional wisdom among interest groups, policymakers, popular commentators, and academics is that national climate change legislation is useful not because of its direct environmental effects but because it puts the nation on a path to achieving a comprehensive climate change solution.").

This Article argues that matching commitments should be used to supplement and ultimately replace the traditional model of climate regulation. It lays out how matching commitments could push selfish nations toward optimal climate regulation. It also explains why there is a place for unconditional abatements in a matching system, but why the bulk of unilateral climate regulation should be done through matching commitments.

## 2 Why the Current Approach Is Not Working

The 2009 meeting of the United Nations Framework Convention on Climate Change was supposed to hammer out a global, enforceable treaty to succeed the 1997 Kyoto Protocol, and comprehensively address climate change.[7] But the negotiations failed. Instead, 114 countries signed an "Accord" stating that "deep cuts in global emissions are required according to science [...] so as to hold the increase in global temperature below 2 degrees Celsius."[8] Ten years later, that goal appears unachievable: emissions have risen, not fallen.[9] Nor is there any reason for confidence that the world can set and meet a new target using the traditional tools of treaty negotiations and unilateral actions. The Copenhagen Accord's failure demonstrated the political divide between developed and developing nations.[10]

Consequently, the 2015 Paris Agreement took a different approach. It abandoned the multilateral agreement model, and instead adopted an agreement to draw support through non-substantive voluntary agreements to mitigate climate change.[11] Namely, the Agreement does not state binding emission caps, nor does it vest any financial commitments in any of the participating countries.[12] In fact, the portions of the Paris Agreement that are legally binding are very similar to the existing U.S. obligations under the United Nations Framework Convention on Climate Change, and could thus be easily implemented based on existing U.S. law.[13]

In the absence of international action, individual jurisdictions have adopted myriad climate regulations that are slowing the growth in global carbon emissions, but these regulations do not show any signs of reversing that growth, much less of accomplishing the "deep cuts" prescribed by the Copenhagen Accord.

---

[7]Hunter (2010), pp. 4, 5, (outlining the Bali Action Plan created to provide a framework for the UNFCCC's Copenhagen Summit).

[8]United Nations Framework Convention on Climate Change (2009).

[9]Harvey and Gronewold (2019) and International Energy Agency (2020).

[10]Harvey and Gronewold (2019) and International Energy Agency (2020).

[11]Harvey and Gronewold (2019) and International Energy Agency (2020).

[12]Hongju Koh (2017), pp. 338, 352.

[13]Hongju Koh (2017), pp. 338, 352.

The European Union, along with other jurisdictions,[14] uses a cap-and-trade system, in which polluters are required to hold a permit to emit greenhouse gases.[15] Several other countries have adopted carbon taxes, in which polluters pay a fixed fee to the government for each ton of greenhouse gas emissions.[16] The United States has employed a third option: greenhouse gas performance standards for new automobiles[17] and for industrial sources of emissions.[18] The world's largest emitter, China, has adopted regulations that encourage energy efficiency and renewable power, which will reduce greenhouse gas emissions.[19]

---

[14]New Zealand uses such a system, Government of New Zealand, Ministry for the Environment (2011), p. 6, [hereinafter Emissions Trading Scheme], as do several U.S. states, Martella, supra note, at 19:30. New Zealand, however, currently allows covered entities to purchase unlimited allowances at a price of $12.50 NZ, Emissions Trading Scheme, supra at 29, which means that it does not absolutely cap emissions—indeed if there were widespread purchase of allowances at this price, the scheme would be closer to a carbon tax. See also Stavins (2008), pp. 367–371, (describing cap-and-trade systems of EU and U.S. states).

[15]European Commission (2008), p. 9, A cap-and-trade system limits emissions by capping the number of available permits, and keeps cost low by allowing emitters to purchase more permits from other polluters that can reduce their emissions cheaply. See, e.g., Stavins (1997), supra note [__] at pp. 305–307. The administrator of such a regime may distribute allowances to emitters based on their past emissions, simply auction them to the highest bidder, or adopt a more complex distribution system. Stavins (1997), pp. 305–307 (describing each system and noting that auctioning these permits makes a cap-and-trade system more like a carbon tax).

[16]Carbon taxes have been adopted in Costa Rica, Switzerland, and the Canadian province of British Columbia. Meyer (2010), p. 6; Schürch (2011), pp. 15–20; Bauman and Hsu (2012), (describing British Columbia's tax). Although Australia adopted a carbon tax in 2011, Clean Energy Act 2011, Act No. 131, available at http://www.comlaw.gov.au/Details/C2011A00131, it is likely to be repealed by the incoming Liberal/National government, Taylor (2013).

[17]Light-Duty Vehicle Greenhouse Gas Emission Standards and Corporate Average Fuel Economy Standards, 75 Fed. Reg. 25,324, 25,330 (May 7, 2010).

[18]Prevention of Significant Deterioration and Title V Greenhouse Gas Tailoring Rule, 75 Fed. Reg. 31514 (June 3, 2010) (requiring new sources to keep greenhouse gas emissions below a level set by local permitting authorities). The Environmental Protection Agency ("EPA") also proposed new standards for greenhouse gas emissions from fossil-fired utilities. Standards of Performance for Greenhouse Gas Emissions from New Stationary Sources: Electric Utility Generating Units, 79 Fed. Reg. 1430 (Jan. 8, 2014). Finally, EPA is due to release greenhouse gas standards for existing fossil fuel plants, Presidential Memorandum, Power Sector Carbon Pollution Standards (Jun. 25, 2013), http://www.whitehouse.gov/the-press-office/2013/06/25/presidential-memorandum-power-sector-carbon-pollution-standards, and new and modified refineries in the near future, Proposed Settlement Agreement, 75 Fed. Reg. 82,390 (Dec. 30, 2010) (announcing proposed settlement agreement, addressing greenhouse gas emissions standards for certain refineries).

[19]These regulations commit China to increase its energy efficiency by 20% between 2005 and 2010, and mandate that 16% of its energy come from renewable sources like wind, biomass, solar, and hydropower by the year 2020. Leggett et al. (2008), pp. 19–21; China has also committed to improving the efficiency of the power sector by shutting down old, inefficient coal plants and building efficient new plants. Leggett et al. (2008), p. 21; Most recently, China has announced plans to launch pilot greenhouse gas emissions trading programs in six provinces before 2013, with a possible national scheme by 2015. Reuters (2011); Finally, China is also pursuing miscellaneous measures such as promoting nuclear power. Leggett et al. (2008), supra at p. 21.

These myriad regulations, however, are not nearly stringent enough to meet the Copenhagen Agreement's two degree goal. The Copenhagen Agreement and the Paris Agreement created a process for countries to submit their plans for addressing climate change to the UN, and countries issue annual reports on their emissions and proposed climate policies.[20] But even if countries implemented all the climate regulations that they are planning over the coming years, greenhouse gas emissions will continue to rise.[21] Given the fundamental disagreement over how much each country should cut its emissions, this is not surprising: if each country emits the volume of greenhouse gases to which it believes itself entitled, the world will not meet its goals.

## 3 How Environmental Matching Commitments May Address Social Dilemma of Climate Change

Environmental matching commitments present an alternative to the traditional mode of climate regulation. There are several possible modes of climate matching commitment but this Article focuses on one: in this proposal each country uses climate matching commitments to set its total climate regulation level in two stages each year. In the first stage, it promises each other country a rate at which it will match their unconditional commitments. Imagine a four-country world of China, Eurasia, the Mideast, and Oceania. China would start each year by promising to match a certain percentage of commitments in Eurasia, the Mideast, and Oceania. For example: it could promise to match 50% of whatever unconditional commitment Eurasia adopted, 120% of whatever unconditional commitment the Mideast adopted, and 75% of whatever unconditional commitment Oceania adopted. Each country would adopt a matching rate for each other country in this fashion.

In the second stage, each country sets its own unconditional commitment. China would set its unconditional commitment considering the matching commitments that were made by Eurasia, the Mideast, and Oceania. Those matching commitments would encourage China to adopt more unconditional regulation because the bigger its commitment, the bigger the match provided by those countries.

In the end, each country's total level of regulation would be the result of its unconditional commitment plus its matching commitments. For China that would be its own unconditional abatement + 0.5 × Eurasia's unconditional abatement + 1.2 × the Mideast's unconditional abatement + 0.75 × Oceania's unconditional abatement. So if every country for some reason agreed to a 2% unconditional

[20]Hunter (2010), p. 4, (describing pledge and review process); Congressional Research Service (2019).

[21]Intergovernmental Panel on Climate Change (2014); See also Plumer (2014).

cut, China's total cut would be 6.9%.[22] Note that each country's matching commitments only targets the other countries' unconditional abatement—not the total of unconditional cuts plus matching cuts. Countries cannot commit to match each other's total abatements, because that would create a circularity problem—a country considering its own level of reduction cannot know its counterpart's total abatement because its total abatement depends, in part, on the country's own decision.

Game theorists have analyzed how countries would act if, rather than just using unconditional commitments, they used a mix of unconditional and matching commitments as described above. It turns out that, if all countries used matching commitments, selfish countries would adopt stricter controls because that would earn them bigger matching commitments from other countries.[23] In fact, if all countries played this "matching game" with full knowledge that other countries would be perfectly selfish and rational, climate regulation would be globally optimal by some measures.[24]

## 4 Conclusion

Many countries have proven willing to take unilateral steps to reduce greenhouse gas emissions. But the current model of international negotiations is not doing enough to encourage more cooperation, and it is putting cooperative countries at an economic disadvantage vis-à-vis their uncooperative competitors. Matching commitments are a better solution to the problem of harnessing unilateral action to encourage cooperation to provide a global public good. Climate matching commitments are an exciting tool to improve global regulation of carbon emissions.

## References

Bauman Y, Hsu S-L (2012) The most sensible tax of all. The New York Times, July 5, 2012, at A19

Boadway R, Song Z, Tremblay J-F (2009) The efficiency of voluntary pollution abatement when countries can commit. Queen's University, Department of Economics, Working Paper No. 1205. http://ideas.repec.org/p/qed/wpaper/1205.html. Accessed 08 Oct 2020

Brewster R (2010) Stepping stone or stumbling block: incrementalism and national climate change legislation. Yale Law Policy Rev 28:245–312

---

[22] That is, $0.02 + 0.5 \times 0.02 + 1.2 \times 0.02 + 0.75 \times 0.02 = 0.020 + 0.010 + 0.024 + 0.015 = 0.069$.

[23] Boadway et al. (2009) and Wood (2011), (surveying other game theoretic solutions to climate change).

[24] Specifically, each country would act as though it was covered in a bubble that trapped all greenhouse gas emissions, limiting their warming effect to the emitting country. As a result, countries like Russia that may have less to fear from climate change, might still emit more than is globally optimal, but they would at least act as though they were harmed by their own emissions. Boadway et al. (2009) and Wood (2011).

Coleman JW (2014) Unilateral climate regulation. Harv Environ Law Rev 38:87–126

Congressional Research Service (2019) Potential implications of U.S. withdrawal from the Paris Agreement on Climate Change. Apr. 5, 2019. https://crsreports.congress.gov/product/pdf/IF/IF10668. Accessed 08 Oct 2020

European Commission (2008) EU action against climate change: the EU emissions trading scheme 9, 2008. http://ec.europa.eu/clima/publications/docs/ets_en.pdf. Accessed 08 Oct 2020

European Commission (2014) 2030 Climate & Energy Framework, June 26, 2014. http://ec.europa.eu/clima/policies/2030/index_en.htm. Accessed 08 Oct 2020

Government of New Zealand, Ministry for the Environment (2011) Emissions trading scheme review panel, doing New Zealand's fair share: emissions trading scheme review 2011: final report. Wellington, June 30, 2011, http://www.climatechange.govt.nz/emissions-trading-scheme/ets-review-2011/review-report.pdf. Accessed 08 Oct 2020

Harvey C, Gronewold N (2019) CO2 emissions will break another record in 2019. E&E News, Dec. 4, 2019, https://www.scientificamerican.com/article/co2-emissions-will-break-another-record-in-2019/. Accessed 08 Oct 2020

Hongju Koh H (2017) Triptych's end: a better framework to evaluate 21st century international lawmaking. Yale Law J Forum 126:338–368

Hunter D (2010) Implications of the Copenhagen accord for global climate governance. Sustain Dev Law Policy 10(4–15):56–57

Intergovernmental Panel on Climate Change (2014) Summary for Policymakers. https://www.ipcc.ch/site/assets/uploads/2018/02/ipcc_wg3_ar5_summary-for-policymakers.pdf. Accessed 08 Oct 2020

International Energy Agency (2020) Global CO2 emissions in 2019. Feb. 11, 2020, https://www.iea.org/articles/global-co2-emissions-in-2019. Accessed 08 Oct 2020

Leggett J et al (2008) Congressional Research Service, RL34659. China's Greenhouse Gas Emissions and Mitigation Policies

Meyer PJ (2010) Congressional Research Service, R40593. Costa Rica: Background and U.S. Relations 6. http://assets.opencrs.com/rpts/R40593_20100222.pdf. Accessed 08 Oct 2020

Plumer B (2014) Two degrees: the world set a simple goal for climate change. We're likely to miss it., Vox, Apr. 22, 2014, http://www.vox.com/2014/4/22/5551004/two-degrees. Accessed 08 Oct 2020

Reuters (2011) China planning emissions trading in 6 regions. Apr. 11, 2011. http://www.reuters.com/article/2011/04/11/us-china-carbon-trading-idUSTRE73A1UY20110411. Accessed 08 Oct 2020

Schürch R (2011) CO2 taxation versus emissions trading – an analytical representation for Switzerland 15–20. https://occrdata.unibe.ch/students/theses/msc/39.pdf. Accessed 08 Oct 2020

Stavins RN (1997) Policy instruments for climate change: how can national governments address a global problem? Univ Chic Leg Forum 10:293–329

Stavins RN (2008) A meaningful U.S. cap-and-trade system to address climate change. Harv Environ Law Rev 32:293–371

Taylor L (2013) The Guardian, Australia could be left with no policy on climate change, Sept. 25, 2013, http://www.theguardian.com/world/2013/sep/25/australia-climate-change-policy-vacuum. Accessed 08 Oct 2020

United Nations Framework Convention on Climate Change (2009) Report of the Conference of the Parties on its Fifteenth Session, held in Copenhagen from 7 to 19 December 2009. http://unfccc.int/resource/docs/2009/cop15/eng/11a01.pdf. Accessed 08 Oct 2020

Wood PJ (2011) Climate change and game theory: a mathematical survey. Australian National University, Crawford School of Economics & Government, Working Paper No. 2.10, http://papers.ssrn.com/sol3/papers.cfm?abstract_id=1883944. Accessed 08 Oct 2020

**James W. Coleman** Dallas. Associate Professor of Law at Southern Methodist University Dedman School of Law. 3315 Daniel Ave., Dallas, TX 75205, U.S.A. Tel. + 1 214-768-4037. jwcoleman@smu.edu. http://www.EnergyLawProf.com/ @energylawprof Fields of Interest: Energy Law, Oil & Gas Law, Environmental Law, Empirical Legal Studies, International Trade & Corporate Law, Administrative Law, Regulatory Theory, Economic Analysis of Law.

# Index





K. Mathis, A. Tor (eds.), *Law and Economics of Regulation*, Economic Analysis of Law in European Legal Scholarship 11,
https://doi.org/10.1007/978-3-030-70530-5